Your Towns and Cities

Newark
IN THE GREAT WAR

Dedication

To every man, woman and child who contributed to
Newark-upon-Trent 1914-19

The image on the front cover is a painting by Michael Lees commissioned in 1959 by his brother, Lieutenant Colonel Richard Lees OBE, MC when he commanded the 3rd Battalion the Worcestershire and Sherwood Foresters. The painting of the 8th Battalion Sherwood Foresters marching off to the Great War symbolised not only the departure of the Regiment from Newark on 10 August 1914 but recognised the service of the Territorial soldier over generations. Photographs from Newark Library were used to ensure that uniforms and accoutrements were accurate, as well as shop names, business titles and even street lights. The painting is reproduced here by kind permission of Richard Lees.

Your Towns and Cities in the Great War

Newark
IN THE GREAT WAR

Trevor Frecknall

Pen & Sword
MILITARY

First published in Great Britain in 2014 by
PEN & SWORD MILITARY
an imprint of
Pen & Sword Books Ltd,
47 Church Street, Barnsley,
South Yorkshire.
S70 2AS

Copyright © Trevor Frecknall 2014

ISBN 9781783831678

The right of Trevor Frecknall to be identified as Author of this Work
has been asserted by him in accordance with the
Copyright, Designs and Patents Act 1988.

A CIP catalogue record for this book is available
from the British Library

*All rights reserved. No part of this book may be reproduced or transmitted
in any form or by any means, electronic or mechanical including photocopying,
recording or by any information storage and retrieval system,
without permission from the Publisher in writing.*

Designed by Factionpress

Printed and bound in Great Britain by CPI UK

Pen & Sword Books Ltd incorporates the imprints of
Pen & Sword Aviation, Pen & Sword Maritime,
Pen & Sword Military, Pen & Sword Select, Pen & Sword Military Classics,
Leo Cooper, Wharncliffe Local History

For a complete list of Pen & Sword titles please contact:
PEN & SWORD BOOKS LIMITED
47 Church Street, Barnsley, South Yorkshire, S70 2AS, England.
E-mail: enquiries@pen-and-sword.co.uk
Website: www.pen-and-sword.co.uk

Contents

Preface - 6
Acknowledgements - 7

Chapter One
The Circus Moves Out - and the Venue is Hell! - 9

Chapter Two
Crazy Horsemen - and Two Much Bravery - 27

Chapter Three
From Slapstick to the Somme - 73

Chapter Four
Tarnished Gold of Hard-Won Victory - 111

Chapter Five
And the Last Trick - to Achieve the Impossible! - 161

Postscript
The Daredevil Heroes Return - but the Crowd's Gone Home - 215

Where the bombshells fell on Newark - 219

Index - 238

Preface

Newark in the Great War explains how a typically patriotic, productive, proud, English market town (population circa 17,500) lost almost 500 brave souls – nobody will ever know exactly how many, such was the chaos – and discovered three or four times as many living heroes in the 1914-18 'war to end all wars'.

It is written basically by the folk involved ... by the soldiers who mostly marched from rat-infested hovels to live, fight, die or somehow survive in even unhealthier trenches up to their knees in mud and gore, 'fighting for King and country' though, if they had battled only for their bit, they would have been home by dinner time on day one ... by the ruling class who manned the multitude of committees established for the Defence of the Realm ... by the humble womenfolk who took the men's places in the factories while running their rag-tag homes and being forced to feed their children ever-decreasing meals ... by the blokes branded 'shirkers' irrespective of whether they had a good reason to stay out of the firing lines ... by the daintier females who knitted and sewed clothes to keep the Armed Forces warm, raised money for countless good causes, and provided life-saving food parcels for prisoners of war in Germany ... by the children who were able to attend schools for only half-days – because trainee soldiers were

billeted in their classrooms – and who were courted as cheap labour by employers shorn of man-power ... and by the refugees whose presence was a persistent reminder of the terrors waiting if the enemy invaded.

Contemporary letters, notes and reports – all written while the unprecedented horror was unfolding – have been pieced together by journalist Trevor Frecknall. He respected it as by far the most important reporting assignment of his 52-year career. If his account is chaotic and disjointed, there's a very good reason: the reality of life was completely chaotic, disjointed and, of course, dangerous.

The purposes of *Newark in the Great War* are to pay tribute to everyone who contributed to this unique epic – and to remind current and future generations why We Will Remember.

Acknowledgements

Among the many who gave invaluable assistance to *Newark in the Great War* are:

David Blake AMA, Curator, Museum of Army Chaplaincy, Amport House, Amport, Hampshire SP11 8BG.
Jill Campbell, Secretary, Newark Archaeological and Local History Society.
Adrian Carter, whose meticulously detailed research over almost a decade into Newarkers who died during the conflict, contributed massively. His most comprehensive appraisal of Newark's sacrifices 1914-18 can be found on the Newark Archaeological and Local History Society website.
Tessa Chesney and colleagues at the Newark and Sherwood District Council Museum Archive.
Richard Lees, brother and the manager of the artist Michael Lees, for permitting use of the painting reproduced on the front cover.
Lucy Millard and colleagues at the *Newark Advertiser*.
Patty Temple, curator of the Museum at Newark Town Hall.
Francis Towndrow, Newark Town Football Club historian.
Ruper Vinnicombe, former Principal Librarian, East Nottinghamshire.
Tim Warner, Local Studies Librarian, and colleagues at Newark Library.
Gillian Frecknall, author's able assistant, checker and wife.
Commonwealth War Graves Commission website
Forces Reunited website
Genes Reunited website
National Archives, Kew, Richmond, Surrey, TW9 4DU
The Sherwood Foresters 1/8 Battalion in the Great War 1914-1919, Captain WCC Weetman MC.

Newark's territorial volunteers of the 8th Battalion Sherwood Foresters gather in the Market Place, surrounded by family and friends, on Monday, 10 August 1914 and are sent off to War by the Mayor and Corporation situated on the Town Hall balcony.

The 'circus' prepares to roll out... Some of the vehicles begged and borrowed from local companies to transport the Sherwoods' ammunition and supplies on their march to Derby.

Chapter One

The Circus Moves Out – and the Venue is Hell!

'Roll up, roll up to biff the Boche! We'll have won by Christmas!' Such was the confidence of the territorial soldiers of Newark-upon-Trent marching into the Great War on Monday, 10 August 1914 that one of their officers was moved to note airily that 'few Regimental Transports can have looked more like a circus than ours did as we left'. He was referring to their goods vehicles. Beer barrel floats carried their ammunition. A furniture van was stuffed with blankets. Two Corporation water carts and a bread van with large red crosses on each side completed the 'Transport' that followed the men out of Newark Market Place and southwards along the ancient Fosse Way.

It was the start of the town's most significant military adventure since the Civil War, when Newark's strategic position at the junction of the Great North and Fosse Roads, with its bridges over the River Trent, made it such a focal point for the warring factions that it was besieged. The Vicar, Canon Walter Paton Hindley, was first to liken 1914 with the 1640s:

> 'Newark declared for the King then. It has declared for the King now. We are looking upon this contest as a Holy War. God needs our co-operation for the fulfilment of His purposes. It may mean tremendous sacrifices.
>
> It was so to our forefathers. Thousands are making it and surely every young man and his parents, whom the country has called out, is bound to satisfy his conscience in the sight of God…'

Whereas the Royalist inhabitants of the 17th century developed a system of underground tunnels to go about their business, sheltered from the Parliamentary cannonballs, many 20th century Newark artisans were more than happy to leave their damp, cramped, rodent-infested terraced hovels to fight for a better future.

The Territorials of the 8th Battalion Sherwood Foresters – wished 'God speed' by the Mayor, Councillor John Charles Kew, who earned his crust by publishing the *Newark Advertiser* weekly newspaper and running a coal merchant's business – marched thirty-seven miles to Derby over the next two days.

Many were exhausted. Deciding they were merely unfit, officers ordered route marches over the next three boiling hot days. It caused their first death. Drummer Rowland James Baker, twenty-two, blistered a heel. Blood poisoning killed him on 28 September. By then his mates were in camp at Harpenden, Hertfordshire – all except 270 who had returned to Newark, rumoured unwilling to fight. *The Advertiser* scalded:

> 'It is regrettable that so many of the men who returned are young and unmarried.'

It transpired half of them were found to be medically unfit. Unabashed patriotism was such that Lord Kitchener's call for a Second Army was answered so resoundingly that

300 more Newark district men enlisted into the Sherwood Foresters between 12 August and 10 September.

As many men had only the clothes in which they marched, Quartermaster Arthur Ewin persuaded Mayoress Annie Kew to form a Working Party of her friends, who worked tirelessly for the remainder of the war knitting, sewing and crocheting. Mayor Kew formed a committee of the great and good males of the town to look after 'the interests of the wives and dependents'.

Mayor Kew simultaneously wanted to form a Newark Civil Guard in case Germany invaded the East Coast and rampaged across Lincolnshire. The War Office demurred: it would 'draw young men who ought to volunteer for military service overseas'. Boy Scouts initially guarded the Tubular Bridge that took the main London-Scotland railway line over the Trent north of Newark, until the Army found Territorials. Within days one of them was killed. Private Austin Noland, twenty, who worked in a woollen mill and kept his widowed mother in Batley before joining the King's Own Yorkshire Light Infantry, was hit by a light engine. Nobody had told him to walk beside the tracks, not on them, it transpired at his inquest. The jurymen returned a verdict of accidental death and donated their expenses to the Mayor's Fund for widows – their generosity sparked, perhaps, by the news that both the Sherwood Foresters and Sherwood Rangers Yeomanry had been 'honoured by being accepted for Foreign Service'.

The realities of the War began to strike home on 22 September. George Squires, 64, a coachman, and his wife Mary, in their terraced house, 111 Baldertongate, Newark, received a letter from one of their sixteen offspring, Herbert, twenty-eight, a corporal in the 18th Hussars with the British Expeditionary Force:

'It is a terrible war, I can tell you. We never know whose turn it is next. We are at it night and day. I shall always remember how the poor Belgians welcomed the British troops. They thought they were saved…'

Within days of the 8th Sherwoods marching out, recruiting for another Battalion began.

The Mayoress, Mrs Annie Kew.
[Advertiser cutting]

Buglers of the Sherwoods take a road-side break on the way to war. *[Picture NEKMS: 8755.8]*

He was in the first of the BEF's battles between 70,000 British and 160,000 German soldiers, at Mons on 23 August:

> 'It was my first experience of shell fire … The Germans had concentrated nearly 300 guns and shells were flying about like hailstones.'

He said of a famous charge of the 1st Cavalry Brigade as the British were forced to retreat:

> 'We seemed to be all stark staring mad. All I can remember after the crash is catching hold of a horse galloping by me – my own had been shot under me. When I looked round I saw my squadron officer with a few men rallying round him and I joined them. Then we had to cut our way through the enemy to join the remainder of our regiment. We went into the action 900 strong but when the roll was called at night we only mustered eighty-seven, though a few stragglers came in afterwards.'

On the same morning his letter arrived in September, three British warships – the *Aboukir, Hogue* and *Cressey* – were sunk in the North Sea by the German submarine *U9*. Among the *Aboukir* casualties was father-of-four Gunner Francis John Lloyd, thirty-four, from Newark.

Leading Stoker Walter Stanger, forty-two, of Sydney Street, Newark, was among British sailors who disappeared on land attempting to defend Antwerp as the

Mayor John Charles Kew, *Advertiser* **proprietor.**
[Advertiser cutting]

German Army swept through Belgium and into France. Shot in the head and neck, he crossed into Holland and was imprisoned. It was 1 April 1915 before his widower father Walter, seventy-four, and eight siblings discovered that he was interned at Kroningen.

Hundreds of British lives were lost when Germans pretended to surrender, wrote wounded Private William Maltby, twenty-two, of the 2nd Sherwood Foresters, to his folks in Cawkwell's Yard, off Stodman Street:

'Our regiment has suffered a lot but did some good work, especially after the Germans coming the white flag trick on the West Yorks. Two companies went to fetch the Germans in as prisoners but instead the Germans surrounded them and took them prisoners. Then they came up in thousands only to be driven back with the point of the bayonet. They got through our trenches; and our Battalion, being in reserve, was ordered to go and take the trenches back, which we did ... The next morning we could see the enemy's dead all over the field. We lost a few but nothing to what they lost. I got my little wounds in the battle on the coast not far from Armentières... People in England don't know what the horrors of war are. Take for instance one house we went in. We found ten of the family dead. What touched me was a little child with both its legs blown off but still alive, and it never cried when picked up.'

Private Charles Richmond Dobbs, nineteen and clerk to Newark's Overseer of the Poor – forerunner of Social Services – before he enlisted in the 2nd Sherwood Foresters, wrote to his parents William (a brewery clerk) and Martha in Lovers' Lane:

'I have been doing my bit at a village between Lille and Armentières; or rather, I ought to say what was once a village because it is now ruins. The first time I was under fire was when our Company had been relieved from the trenches. We got onto the high road and then the Germans let us have it for an hour and a half ... We had to lie in a dyke six inches deep in mud and water so you can guess what we looked like when we reached our billets. But it would have been all up with us had not our artillery spoken.'

A few weeks later, he revealed in another letter:

'One night while on our way to the trenches to relieve B Company the Germans attacked our trenches. They set fire to several houses, haystacks, barns and anything that would enable them to locate us but after a struggle we landed safely,

Mayor John Charles Kew's coal business. *[Advertiser cutting]*

BLACK DIAMONDS

FOR BEST QUALITY
House Coals,
Kitchen Cobbles,
STEAM, THRASHING,
GREENHOUSE, or
FURNACE COALS,
TRY

J. C. KEW,

BEAUMOND CROSS, NEWARK
Telephone 152.   Telegrams—Kew, Newark

ANTHRACITE for Malting.
SPECIAL STOVES, GAS PRODUCERS,
A SPECIALITY.
Trucks sent to any Station in the Kingdom.
5183

crossing ploughed fields and mangold fields. When we got settled down in our mud beds they fired at us all night long trying to blow the trench up, but it didn't come off. Although we had no sleep that night, we were little the worse for our experience. I and two more formed a guard for part of the trench; our time was from 7am to 7am the next day. After we had finished the night guard we found 36 bullet holes just behind where the sentry stands.

'It is a pitiful sight to see the people leaving their homes with only what they can carry, the mother carrying the baby on her back, and perhaps three or four following her with as much as they can carry, and some of them are very small. The Germans were three whole days setting a village church on fire. They also destroyed the whole village as well. On the Sunday we saw the clergyman and his congregation hold Mass outside the ruined church. It was a pitiful sight and all through the service the devils were shelling the village. There were several nights when we had to 'get down to it' with a wet shirt for it would hail, blow and snow while we were digging trenches.'

Lance-Corporal George Smith of the North Staffs Regiment, wounded on the Belgian frontier, wrote to his Uncle Joseph, landlord at Newark's Wing Tavern pub:

'I was blown about a dozen yards in the air by one of those great shrapnel shells. I received a wound straight through the calf of my right leg. The bullet has fractured a bone, which makes it all the more painful. Wound No. 2 is a piece

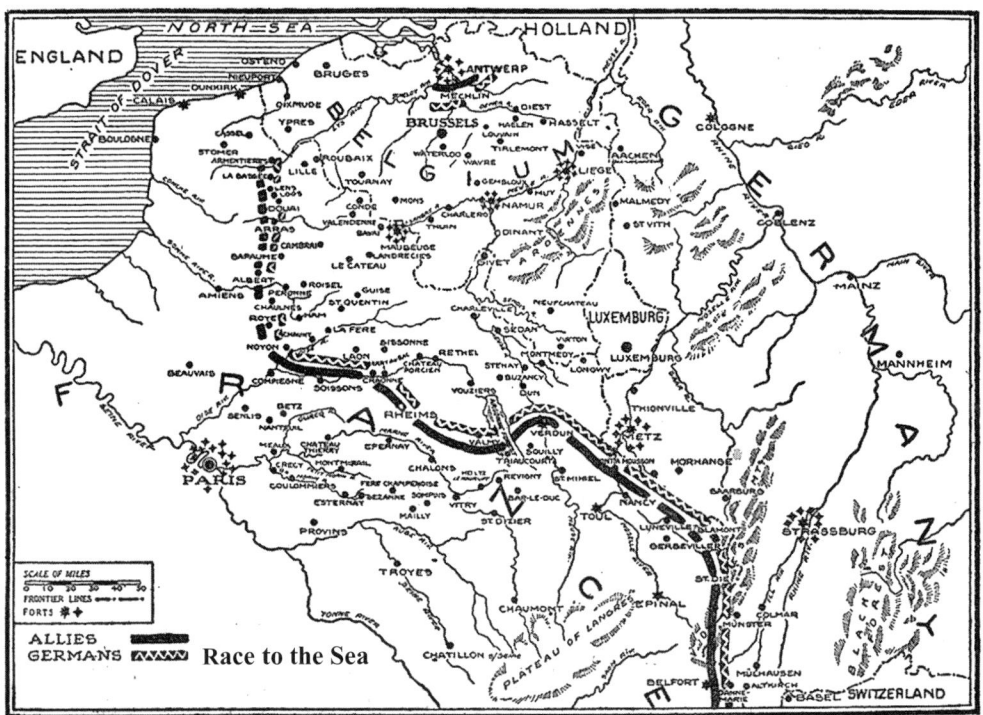

about as big as a man's fist, taken clean out just above my left knee. Wound No. 3 is a piece about the size of a walnut, taken out just below my left shoulder. In addition to this little lot, I received a severe shaking-up, my back and right side being badly bruised internally, which makes it rather difficult for me to breathe properly. But for all that, I am getting on famously and, thank goodness, I can smoke, which is a great solace.

'I am afraid it will be a long job "mending". I suppose I shall have to stick to it, like a Briton. In any case, I am proud to think I have done my little share for my country and ready to do it again, if able, when I am better ... In front of our trenches, which my Regiment held, just before I was hit, there were dozens of dead Germans and the stench was getting a bit awful.'

George recovered to fight again – but was killed in action on 21 February 1915.

John W Gibson, invalided out of the 1st Lincolnshire Regiment in August, went to work as a drayman with grocers Garratt and Hemming in Newark Market Place with haunting memories:

'I saw the Germans shoot women and children in Mons because they would not walk down the street in front of them as a shield.' Of fighting from 12-28 September on the River Aisne, a 170 foot wide river too deep to ford, in which he was wounded, he said: 'We had got the Germans on the run and they were retiring towards Lille. We were in a tobacco field and the Germans started to shell us. I got the bones in my right foot crushed and was hit in my back and arm.'

Private James Davis, thirty, survived to tell the tale of his Aisne battle with the Royal Scots Fusiliers. Invalided home to Beacon Hill with shrapnel in a thigh, he revealed he had to lie in agony on a hillside with shells falling around him. Another soldier sympathetically threw him a packet of cigarettes. A doctor eventually crawled up to him and suggested he try and persuade someone to carry him down the hill. He hitched a lift on a comrade's back before they bizarrely came across a pedal cyclist. Davis was hastily strapped to the cycle and needed no bidding to pedal, albeit one-legged, for his life. Along the way, he recognised another Newarker, Harry Holberry from Sleaford Road, carrying an empty ammunition box.

'Stick at it,' yelled Holberry.

'That took some doing on the bike,' reflected Davis. He reached a house used as a makeshift hospital, only to swiftly realise it was in the German firing line. Patched up, he was put on a train that took three hours to get away from the range of enemy guns.

'One chap with a bullet in his head seemed all right when they put us on the train. What with all the jolting and shaking, he had only just been taken out at Rouen when he died. We were taken on to Le Havre, to a boat home.'

Holberry, twenty-eight, a brewer's labourer, earned

Harry Holberry – posthumous award of the Medal of St George 4th Class from the Emperor of Russia.
[Advertiser cutting]

the Medal of St George, 4th Class, presented by the Emperor of Russia, but did not make it home. His mother Ann discovered three days before Christmas 1914 that he was killed on 11 November. In his last letter he wrote of 'strenuous fighting', confided that he had hoped for a long rest after fourteen days in the trenches, but revealed he was called back into action in less than four hours. He is remembered on the Ypres (Menin Gate) Memorial, one of 54,415 lost in the Salient.

At the same time, Eva Arnold, twenty-three and expecting her first baby, discovered she was a widow. Her husband, Lance-Corporal Charles W Arnold, had been killed 'in the trenches of Flanders' fighting with the 1st Battalion Northamptonshire Regiment on 1 November 1914.

'It's a rough place here,' he had written to Eva in Cross Street. 'But you have to put up with it and don't mind. I hope you will keep yourself quite safe till we meet again...'

The Advertiser cutting that revealed expectant Eva Arnold was a widow, aged 23.

Eva accepted her loss with what the papers at the time called 'Spartan fortitude'. She said: 'There will no doubt be many like me...' Her baby would be born in the first few weeks of 1915. She named him after his father. He died within six months. The resilient Eva was married again in 1918, to one John Crampton of Newark.

In the idealistic atmosphere of 1914, William Hector Mathers Ridley's rapid rise from the ranks of the Sherwood Foresters resembled a chapter from a fictional adventure. He was a champion swimmer while working at his uncle's Newark modern motor company, Mather & Company, and his mechanical training stood him in good stead when he enlisted. He was at the Battle of the Aisne but his moment came in fighting round Lille, where the Sherwoods were surrounded by about 80,000 Bavarian troops who arrived with 'wonderful rapidity' from Antwerp overnight. The Commanding Officer asked for a volunteer to take a message to the General Officer Commanding, acquainting him with the seriousness of the situation. Young Ridley volunteered and successfully carried the message through enemy lines. The Sherwoods were ordered to hang on at all costs. On the return journey he had a narrow escape. The back wheel of his bicycle was shattered by a shell but, unhurt, he dived into a ditch. He sent back to Uncle John a German rifle grenade that pitched near the trench he was in but failed to explode. Another memento was

'a small book belonging to a German musketeer who has finished his part in this or any other war.'

The battles were part of a series of actions that became known as The Race to the Sea and ended with the opposing enemies entrenched for more than 470 miles from the Franco-Swiss border to the North Sea, sparking fears of England being invaded.

Newark's first soldier killed by the enemy was named on 5 October: Hussar Trooper William McLeod, twenty-eight, died on 17 September as the Germans pounded the BEF trenches beside the Aisne with eight-inch siege guns with a range of 10,000 yards. The youngest son of widow Sarah Ann, sixty-nine, a charwoman, living in one of Newark's notorious rows of hovels, he worked at a pork butcher's and then Ransome's woodworks until he joined-up in 1906 and served in India, returning home in 1913. As a reservist, he was recalled on the outbreak of war.

Lance Corporal George Grosse, twenty-six, of the 1st Leicestershire Regiment wrote from a Portsmouth Hospital to his parents, James and Rhoda, and his aunt, Mrs Mary Wheatley, in Water Lane Square:

'I have been so bad – all but kicking the bucket. God knows how I missed being killed on the spot. We had run out of ammunition and they were letting us have it like rain. My chum Lance-Corporal Bob Hough and me volunteered to go for it (the ammunition). We only had about 300 yards to go ... We got there all right, and back to the edge of the trench, but they (the Germans) were waiting for us – and we got it! We dropped the ammunition and fell.

'They pulled us into the trench and dressed my wounds but poor old Bob died two minutes after. There I had to lay until night as it was impossible to get us away. About half past five they retired. I was under an archway out of the way. All at once I heard a scuffle. I turned my head and could see the Germans running for their lives. How I got away, goodness knows. Shot and shell were flying all around me. I could hear someone else on the other side of the railway but didn't know whether they were our men or Germans. I crawled under the trucks and just as I got under, a shell burst in the truck and blew the end out. It was getting too hot so I started off again.

'I was about done when I recognised our Sergeant's voice. I called to him, and he heard me and came back. He carried me on his back until I could not hold any longer. I was done through loss of blood and he laid me down. I thought I was left for good but he came back with another fellow. They started off again with me, and the next thing I remember I was in a temporary hospital. I was put on a train the same night for Boulogne, where I laid for eleven days, and then I was sent home [to England]. It was like being in a new world to be out of the hearing of those mighty guns of theirs, which are doing so much damage to our troops ...'

Lance-Corporal Robert Frank Hough, twenty-two, of Leicester died on 24 October 1914. George Grosse became a sergeant in the Sherwoods and survived the war.

Newark Hospital received its first wounded soldiers on Sunday, 25 October. Twelve Belgians and eight Britons were ferried from Newark Midland Station in a fleet of borrowed cars. The Belgians were given red jackets by the Mayoress's Committee. The British were 'inclined to be somewhat reserved,' reported the *Newark Herald*.

While Newark's menfolk rushed to serve King and country – the 2/8th Battalion Sherwood Foresters was formally founded as a second line unit on Friday, 11 September and the inaugural meeting of the Newark Volunteer Reserve on the following evening

A murky November day in 1914 and trainee Royal Engineers proudly pose on a temporary bridge constructed across the Trent. *[Advertiser cutting]*

attracted five retired soldiers ready for an invasion – there had been two influxes.

The first 400 Royal Engineers arrived on 25 September. The town's Chief Constable, Albert Wright, a thirty-nine-year-old Lancastrian, arranged billeting in private houses, announcing the billeting allowance of 23s 4d per week per man would be 'of immense benefit to the town'. Weekly concerts were arranged for them at the Ossington Coffee Palace, an ornate temperance hotel built as a memorial to a former Speaker of the House of Commons; the Wesleyan Hall on Barnbygate became a writing and reading room; and clothing manufacturers Mumby's let the REs use baths at their Osmondthorpe Works, in which they also established smoking and card rooms. The Licensed Victuallers' Association ordered landlords not to serve the men after 9pm. Newark hosted the Royal Engineers' No.8 Depot to 1919. They learnt to maintain railways, roads, water supplies, bridges and transport; operate railways and, inland waterways; maintain telephones, wireless and other signalling equipment; and in the heat of battle, design and build front-line fortifications to provide cover for the infantry and positions for the artillery. They would also need to develop responses to chemical and underground warfare. Little wonder that the Royal Engineers grew from 25,090 officers and men in 1914 to 295,668 in 1917. By 1919, it was estimated that sappers had contributed an incredible £1 million to Newark's coffers.

The good ladies of Newark conduct a flag day to raise funds for Belgian refugees who had arrived with virtually only the clothes they were wearing. *[Advertiser cutting]*

The other incomers were fifteen Belgian refugees, who arrived mainly from Antwerp in early October with few possessions but many tales of German atrocities. Newark Town Council housed them in three empty houses and warned-off large numbers of inquisitive children who caused 'considerable annoyance' by gathering noisily each night to glimpse their new neighbours. 'This must be distracting to the refugees who, after their trying ordeal, most require quietness and rest,' said Mayor Kew.

When a German soldier's cap sent home to Newark by veterinary surgeon Captain Frank Baker Gresham went on display at his old school, the Mount, headmaster Herbert Speight, a no-nonsense Yorkshireman, charged 1d a time for a look at it, aiming to raise £1 for the Belgian Refugees' Relief Fund. A sister of Gresham, Mrs Maud George, organised the town's first 'Belgium Day'. It received great support: Bainbridge's, the haberdashers with a chocolate box shop frontage in the Market Place, gave 1,000 yards of ribbon in Belgium's colours and tobacconists donated cigar boxes that were rapidly converted into collecting tins. The effort raised £15 for the refugees. Frank went on to receive a Military Cross in the King's Birthday Honours in 1916 for his bravery with the Army Veterinary Corps; was promoted major while commanding a veterinary hospital from 16 February 1918; returned to Newark in peacetime and lived to the age of eighty-one.

One of the refugees, Mademoiselle Marthe Rumes, twenty-one, became a teacher at Holy Trinity Roman Catholic School. She revealed that while she was living in Ghent, a male acquaintance was ordered by the Germans to bury their dead.

'This drove him mad because he was told to bury them alive if he thought they had no chance of getting better. Another man had to drive two Germans to Diksmuide and for three hours was riding in between dead bodies and over them when he could not drive between them.'

The cover and programme for the first of many social events arranged to raise money for the refugees.

It was all nearly too much for the Newark Gas Company. After sixteen workers joined the rush into the Forces, the time it took to train replacements caused 'great dislocation', the company chairman revealed, once the crisis was over: 'Instead of complaining that the quality of gas was not up to standard, our customers ought to be very well satisfied that the Company was able to keep the supply going.'

And the killing intensified. 6ft 3in Trooper Thomas Herbert Helliwell, twenty-one, was felled on 20 November. His parents Barker and Frances Helliwell of William Street, learnt from his friend in the 1st Life Guards, J Victor Bell: 'Tom was shot instantly and he never murmured as he fell ... Please forgive me if I have seemed brutal in breaking the news to you.'

Tom had left the Ransome's drawing office in 1912 to join the military.

Alfred Squires of Mount Pleasant, one of four brothers in the Scottish Rifles, was killed on Sunday, 29 November while moving to the trenches. The news was sent home by his brother Albert, whose letter took six weeks to arrive but still beat official notification. Both had been moulders in a boiler works before enlisting.

With such revelations, it was no surprise that 120 of the 8th Foresters ordered to France on 30 October had asked to be confirmed at Harpenden Parish Church by the Bishop of Southwell. Their Commanding Officer's wife, Mrs Annie Huskinson, wrote a begging letter to the local papers:

> 'They have the winter to face ... They need mufflers, mittens, sleep-in caps and belts. ... £10 is also wanted to buy mackintosh capes for sentries.'

Elizabeth Quibell, whose husband Oliver manufactured sheep dips, sent 110 knitted sleeping helmets collected from friends. Virtually as soon as they landed, one of their leading officers, Major Robert Frank Byron Hodgkinson, 42, a Newark solicitor, was shot in the head. He

Drawing office giant – Trooper Thomas Herbert Helliwell.
[Advertiser cutting]

Patriotic calls to arms appear in the local papers.

survived to earn a Territorial Decoration reserved for officers who 'satisfactorily served twenty years' in 1919; but it was a reality check for the 'circus'.

Simultaneously, the Sherwood Rangers Yeomanry, who were destined for the battlefields created when Turkey entered the war on Germany's side, advertised for 300 more experienced horse riders for a reserve unit but discovered that their Commanding Officer, Colonel Albert E Whittaker, was 'not strong enough' to lead them. Their new CO, Sir John Peniston Milbanke, Baronet, forty-two, had earned a Victoria Cross – the ultimate honour for a British fighting man – with the 10th Hussars in the Boer War. His citation in the *London Gazette* on 6 July 1900 recorded that, although severely wounded in the thigh, he rode back to one of the men whose pony was exhausted and who was under fire from the Boers. 'Sir John took the man up on his own horse under a most galling fire and brought him safely back to camp.'

As the 1914 battles raged closer to the Channel and invasion fears intensified, the Newark Volunteer Reserve grew from five in September to 118 by November. They exercised Monday and Thursday evenings in 'the big room' above the Duke of Newcastle's estate offices in Lombard Street, part of the Great North Road through town. They set-up a miniature shooting range in a loft above Stray's animal feeds shop in Middlegate for rifle practice every Tuesday and Friday evening. But the Wool Hall was out of bounds for drill on wet days.

There was good and bad news from the seas. Bravado on the waves lightened the gloom on 20 October when First Class PO Harold Summerfield, twenty, wrote to his parents at their insalubrious Lincoln Row terrace, off Slaughterhouse Lane, about 'a picnic' with German destroyers. He was 'doing a bit of training' on HMS *Undaunted* alongside four destroyers when they happened across four German ships in the North Sea.

'They didn't have a chance. I didn't take the time but I think it was only about an hour's job [to sink the enemy] and then we went to tea ... I like to give praise where it's due, for they fought like seamen and died as such. You know I've always said there's no Navy in the world can shoot like ours.'

One of the area's biggest engineering works, Simpson's, suffered its first loss on 26 November: Stoker 1st Class Henry Bond, twenty-eight, was on the 15,000-ton battleship HMS *Bulwark* which blew-up while moored on the River Medway at 7.35am on 26 November. Winston Churchill announced in the House of Commons that an internal magazine explosion had rent the ship asunder.

HMS *Bulwark* which blew-up while moored on the River Medway, 26 November, 1914.

> 'I regret to say the loss of life is very severe. Only twelve men are saved. All the officers and the rest of the crew, who, I suppose, amounted to between 700 and 800, have perished.'

Henry's widow Martha, forty, was already taking in boarders to help pay the rent.

As 1914 drew to a close, two Newarkers wrote home with first-hand reports of great naval battles. Herbert Kirk, boiler man in a maltster's, and his wife Annie at 167 Barnbygate received a letter dated 8 November from their son Arthur, twenty-one, an Ordinary Seaman on HMS *Glasgow*:

> 'Dear Mother and Father, just a few lines to let you know I am still alive and quite all right in every way. No doubt before you receive this letter you will have read about the engagement we had in the Pacific Ocean off the coast of Chili (sic) and have been a bit anxious to hear whether I was all right or not. I am very sorry to say that we lost the fight but we were not disgraced, thank God, as we fought superior ships and were out-numbered by five to three – the *Good Hope*, *Monmouth* and *Glasgow* – and we are the only ones left to tell the tale…

Lowfield Works, Newark, suffered first loss of a workman 26 November.

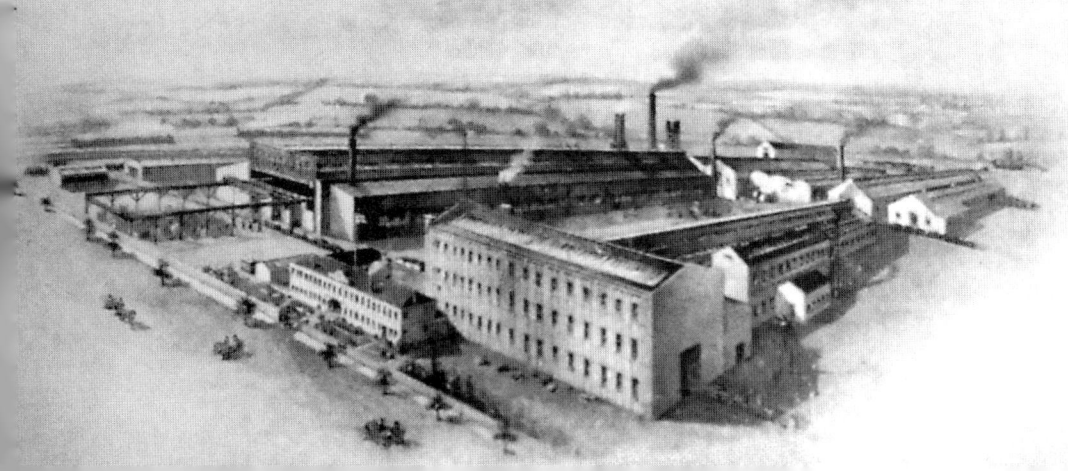

'It seems a miracle that we were not blown to smithereens as when the other two ships went down, all the five German boats concentrated their fire on the good old *Glasgow*, and we owe our salvation to our speed, which enabled us to leave the enemy ships behind when they chased us. I can tell you that all aboard our ship wept like children, and the Captain also, when we fell-in next morning to read prayers … The *Good Hope* caught fire and blew up. The *Monmouth* also caught fire but got it under control all right. But when the engagement was over (it was a pitch dark night) our Captain made a signal to the *Monmouth* asking if they were all right and she replied she was making water very badly and had no hope of keeping afloat for long. Then their brave Captain turned his ship about and ran full speed into the enemy and tried to sink them. They died a noble death and it ought to make us doubly thankful that we are still here.'

The 'good old *Glasgow*' came out on top in its next battle. From the numbingly cold waters off the Falklands in December, William Wade, 33, yeoman of signals on HMS *Kent,* wrote to his wife in Side Row, Beacon Hill:

'About five past eight last Tuesday the signal was made, "Enemy in sight. *Kent* weigh anchor." Our two big ships, the *Invincible* and *Inflexible*, took on the two big German ships, the *Scharnhorst* and *Gneisenau* [the cornerstones of the Germans' East Asian Squadron], and left the other three to the *Kent, Cornwall* and *Glasgow*. We had the time of our lives watching the big ships fighting but we soon lost sight of them as they were steaming much faster than we were.

HMS *Kent*: sank SMS *Nürnberg* off the Falkland Islands.

German cruiser SMS *Nürnberg*: only twelve rescued from icy waters.

'The *Glasgow* started fighting her ship about three o' clock and we started ours just after ... I have often said I should like to go into action while in the Navy, and I have had my wish, but I can't say I particularly like it. In fact I will go one better and say I don't like it at all, although if we had to go into action again tomorrow, I would go eagerly enough. It was one continual crash, bang and groans from the wounded and cheers from the lads all jumbled up together, with a few choice expressions as to the Kaiser and all his disciples.

'Anyhow, we got into action with the *Nürnberg*, a German cruiser and sank her at 7.26 ... We had no one killed outright but six have since died of wounds and one or two others of the wounded are very bad. Mostly all our killed or wounded are Marines although one Able Seaman was struck down while standing close to me; he died the same night. I played a hose over two Marines, who were horribly burnt and have since died, and I didn't go much on it, I can tell you...

'We went and tried to save as many Germans as possible from the *Nürnberg* but we only picked up twelve as the weather was bitterly cold and the sea was rather rough. We only had seven alive out of those when we got into the harbour as the cold weather had polished them off. We might, perhaps, have saved more as there were anything between thirty and forty men clinging to wreckage, but both our sea boats were broken in with shells. It was awful to hear their cries as they floated by the ship; everyone did his best to save more but it was impossible.'

History *[http://www.worldwar1.co.uk/armoured-cruiser/sms-scharnhorst.html]* records that ten British sailors died; 2,200 German sailors were lost; no British ships were badly damaged; the German fleet was destroyed. The Germans stopped raiding ships transporting commerce to Britain. Victory also gave the Allies an immeasurable morale boost. Meanwhile, as the nights and moods darkened, servicemen were deemed in peril on Newark streets. Fifteen clergymen of all denominations wrote to the papers in November telling parents to make their daughters behave:

'Many girls, and especially those who are still quite young, are allowed to linger in the streets and not infrequently are to be seen attracting the attention of young men ... The girls of our town should conduct themselves with becoming dignity. We therefore ask all parents to make such rules in their homes as shall enable them to know where their daughters are in the evenings, and also in whose company they are spending their time ... We would venture to say to all our fellow townsmen: On no account let us ever treat a soldier or a recruit to strong drink.'

Ten days later Chief Constable Wright announced:

'Attention must be given to the prevention of girls under the age of sixteen congregating in the streets or walking with soldiers. In any case where girls under the age of sixteen are seen with men, it is essential that the names and addresses of the girls should be taken and reported to me, when the parents will be communicated with ... Where it is shown that a girl under sixteen, with the knowledge of her parents or guardian, is exposed to the risk of seduction or prostitution, the parents or guardian may be bound over to exercise proper care and supervision.'

Two days later, soldier's wife Edith Blackburn, twenty-three, was fined £3 by Newark Magistrates after being convicted of keeping a disorderly house at her home in Ward's Row.

And the killings on the Western Front were relentless. News arrived on 11 December that a prominent Newark boxer had been killed on 28 October near Armentières. Corporal Thomas Walster, thirty-one, from the same boxing stable as British and

Boxer mourned ... Corporal Thomas Walster.
[Advertiser cutting]

Empire heavyweight champion Bombardier Billy Wells, served in the 2nd Royal Scots Fusiliers.

Christmas Eve brought anguish for Henry Tacey of Northgate who had five sons fighting. One of them, Fred, thirty, was wounded and a prisoner. He was shot through both thighs during the Battle for Mons and was thought to be in hospital in England. In fact he was in Gustrow, in Germany, with nothing but the light summer clothing he wore when he enlisted. He begged them for ten shillings, a shirt and cigarettes. His mum Mary Ann approached Mayoress Kew, who arranged for Fred to be sent shirt, socks, muffler and other comforts plus home-made cake and a packet of cigarettes. He received many more parcels before returning home on 2 January 1919.

And in a far corner of Africa, the Reverend Ernest Frederick Spanton, forty-six, former Vicar of the St Leonard's parish in the northern half of Newark, was imprisoned by the Germans from 1914 until 1916, along with wealthy planters and English ladies, and 'subjected to degradations as revolting as anything in the history of German kultur' according to a report in 1918 by a committee set up by the British Government into *The Treatment by the Enemy of British Prisoners of War in East Africa*. Mr Spanton was

The massive Christmas card sent to 'every fighting man in Nottinghamshire' by civic and political leaders – including the Mayor of Newark, Councillor Kew.

initially asked to remain at the Msalabani church of the Universities Mission to Central Africa in the Tanga District of German East Africa [Tangyanika] to help 'keep the natives quiet'. But on 29 September 1914 the German General Command ordered all English people on an eleven-day march to Morogoro, a hill town on the Central Railway. The prisoners were kept short of food; and nearly twenty native Mission teachers were driven to death by having to carry heavy loads while in chains. The English prisoners in vermin-invested cells were frequently kept without water for up to three days. Floggings took place just outside the ladies' rooms, 'horrid, dreadful; how we shrink from such sights', wrote one in her diary. Mr Spanton survived to continue missionary work; he died in 1936.

With former parishioners unaware of his plight, he was not among the fighting men of Nottinghamshire sent a ten-page Christmas card by the diplomatic and political hierarchy, including Mayor Kew.

'We spent a wonderful Christmas,' Private William Setchfield of the Royal Warwickshire Regiment wrote to his brother Arthur in Northgate about an unofficial truce on the Western Front. 'The Germans came over to us in the afternoon and we had our photos taken with them. But it would be a big task to put everything that happened in a letter.' If William experienced the football match between the enemies that became part of legend, he would have sent a kick-by-kick report given his love of the sport. But if he did it was censored. He merely wrote on: 'Forest made a draw with Derby, I see... Awful weather we've been having, but I'm still in excellent health and so have plenty to be thankful for...'

The message was more sombre from Private Fred Kelsall, a house painter before joining the 1st Battalion Sherwoods. He wrote to his old headmaster, James Trout, at Christ Church School:

> 'It is horrible, sir, to see the devastated villages and homes of the poor people. They will almost worship you for a crust of bread or a tin of bully beef. It gives me immense satisfaction every time I have the chance of wiping out a German.'

There was no thought now that the 'circus' would be back home to England soon.

Christmas Truce 1914: 'The Germans came over in the afternoon.'

Chapter Two

Crazy Horsemen – and Too Much Bravery

The British Army entered the Great War as dependent as circuses on daredevil horsemen. The difference was that in 1915, the horses were taken from the soldiers prior to the 'final charge of England's Yeomen'. It turned into one of three catastrophes suffered by Newarkers in a year in which the infantry became fearless fire eaters in the face of the Germans and the womenfolk played the part of the helpless targets in the knife-thrower's act under the Big Top: tied to the factories and kitchens, ever-fearful of raiding Zeppelins and invading Germans.

The massive blows that rocked Newark were inflicted at the French village of Neuve Chapelle on 10-13 March, the Battle of Scimitar Hill at Gallipoli in Turkey on 21 August and, back in France, at the Hohenzollern Redoubt during the Battle of Loos 25 September to 15 October.

With the 1/8th Battalion Sherwood Foresters decimated in France and Sherwood Rangers Yeomanry shredded in Gallipoli, Newark's response each time was to increase its recruitment efforts.

Charles Henry Dady, 28, one of thirteen children of bootmaker William and Harriett in Kirkgate, in Newark's commercial centre, became symbolic of the Sherwoods' heroism at Neuve Chapelle:

> 'I had a little band of forty men and we were surrounded. When I called the roll afterwards, there were six men ... It nearly broke my heart. I should not like to go through that ordeal again.'

He did go through it, again and again. In the two years before he got home to receive the

SLAYING OF BABES.

Slaying of babes. What classic lore
To place on history's future page.
What noble deed! How nobly done!
True warrior ne'er strikes unarmed foe—
Oft gives to babe his tender care
Would scorn to claim a victory won.

Weaver of sorrow, the scord they loom,
The warp thine ever-ready lie,
To call the warrior would be to mock.
Justice scarce knows thy rightful doom.
   The headsman's stroke would not repay,
Nor traitor's doom o'er Tarpean rock.

Was't not enough that Belgium mourned
Her lisping babes, her noble sons;
Their bleeding forms first felt the blow,
Her reddened fields, her dwellings wrecked,
The deepened rut, where cannon stood—
All, all proclaim a ruthless foe.

History all time shall find a name,
A name for demon fit alone.
Demon thou art, with sickening cant,
These babes are they of whom Christ said
Their angels stand before His Throne.
Where standest thou, base sycophant?

Foul scorpion with serpent's fangs,
No nimbus e'er shall press thy brow;
The widow's curse alone is thine,
For He who marks the sparrow's fall,
For He who said " I will repay,"
Hath He not said, " Vengeance is Mine."
30, Crown-street.   E. H. CAMAMILE.

1915 starts with a Newark resident's poetic assessment of the atrocities in Belgium.
[Advertiser cutting]

Hero of Neuve Chapelle Charles Dady, who received his DCM two years later.
[Advertiser cutting]

Distinguished Conduct Medal from the Mayor, he was wounded 'several times' and spent six months in hospital suffering from, officially, rheumatism. In fact, he was concussed by a shell at Ypres in May 1915, well before steel helmets were issued.

'I didn't come round for about two hours. I was congratulating myself on getting off so lightly when another shell exploded, smothering me again.'

He reckoned he escaped with 'a few scratches and a terrible shaking-up' but a fellow hospital patient said he was dreadfully wounded.

His DCM citation in the *London Gazette* on 3 June was very succinct:

'For gallant conduct at Neuve Chapelle from 10 to 14 March 1915. When his Platoon was surrounded by the enemy, he showed a fine example to his men, whom he handled with much ability.'

Charles regretted more Newark lads had not been honoured:

'I've seen some of them do greater deeds than I have ever done. Some of these poor lads are now – worse luck – underneath. I can tell you this: many of the Newark lads now at rest would be in the land of the living still if it hadn't been for them having such a heart. They showed too much bravery.'

He spoke from the heart: Allied losses in the First Battle of Neuve Chapelle amounted to 12,800 in two March days.

Office clerk W E Chappell, Colour Sergeant of B Company, 1/8th Sherwoods, wrote an overview to his boss at Ransome's factory:

'My Platoon lost seven killed, six of whom marched out from Newark with us in August ... Newark can be proud of those who own her as their native town, for they are all fine fellows. The General Commanding our Division personally came to see the Battalion a few days ago and especially mentioned our Company for the way in which it had carried out its work. So you will see we are getting quite a good name out here. We are getting pretty used to the trenches now, but shell fire takes some getting used to; and as for trench mortars, the least said the better, for they aren't half hot. I am proud to hear that I am the first of the (Ransome's) office staff to come out to the Front, but hope I shall not be the last, for there seems to be room for still more men to come before this great struggle can be brought to a satisfactory conclusion. I am glad to hear that business is still good and hope it will continue to be so. I am writing this letter in my latest new billet, which is part of an old stable but which, with plenty of straw to lie on, is quite comfortable after having had a few nights on a hard stone floor.'

Surgeon Captain Harry Stallard wrote to his surgery partner, Dr Frederick Henry Appleby, at Barnbygate House from 'somewhere in Belgium' with the 1/8th Sherwoods:

> 'We are at last up against the real thing and our men have had one period in the trenches. They are absolutely top-hole and are behaving splendidly. I am really proud to belong to such a body of men. We go in again tonight for another spell. I have been up to the trenches once to see A------, who was sick, but it is no treat as the bullets were flying about pretty freely and in order to get to the trench in question, one had to pass through a cross-fire. They are rather particular about medical officers going into trenches and prohibit it unless by a direct order of the CO, as we appear to be scarce and there is some difficulty as to replacements.

> 'I have a very good dressing station and am able to do fairly good work there. My routine is thus ... I see the sick of the reserves (two-and-a-half platoons) at 6.30pm then the sick from the trenches come in to see me as soon as may be after dusk. I thus clear the way for any wounded who may be brought in. They cannot be moved during the day so when dusk, if necessary, the stretcher parties are detailed from the dressing station to fetch them in but, of course, not the 'walking' cases. I don't go to bed before dawn so as to be ready to deal with any emergency which might arise during the night. As to bed, I go about 5 and stay until 11, then breakfast at my quarters. My other meals I have at the Battalion headquarters about 80 yards away. I am afraid you will think this all about ego, but I thought it might interest you to know how we carry on.'

Dr Stallard's next letter to Newark was to widow Hannah Copley – to inform her that her son, William Richard, 21, had become the first Newark Territorial killed at the Front. Billy grew up through the Church Lads' Brigade, the Scouts and the Churchman's Club; enlisted as soon as the September 1914 appeal was made; and was killed on 13 April 1915. Dr Stallard's words to horror-struck Hannah were to be repeated regularly over the next three years and more:

> 'I sympathise with you in the loss of your son ... so good a soldier and a credit to the Battalion ... He did not suffer any pain as he was instantly killed ... body was brought down from the trenches by my bearers and he was buried in the military cemetery where a pretty cross marks the spot.'

The Reverend John Percy Hales, the Sherwoods' Chaplain until 1919, also wrote:

> 'We laid your dear lad to rest last night by the side of many brave comrades who have laid down their lives for their country and the cause of righteousness for which we are fighting.'

Private 2362 Copley rests among 1,131 comrades in Kemmel Chateau Military Cemetery.

A week later, Mayor Kew persuaded the local papers to publish a begging letter from Dr Stallard:

> 'I have to attend to the wounded by the light of two or three candles (the wounded can only be brought out of the trenches at night). Could you get me for the dressing station two Axol hurricane acetylene lamps with, say, four spare burners, a spare cleaner and, say, seven pounds of calcium carbide for the same. I do not think that the total cost of the lot would be more than £2. The possession of these would be

a great boon to me and, incidentally, to the poor wounded fellows of our Battalion.'
The requested equipment reached him within a fortnight. Stallard added:

> 'The men of this Battalion are simply splendid and I am proud to be their medical officer. Life in the trenches is very strenuous but the men are always cheery and bright. I only wish the people of Newark could see them; they would be proud of them, and we should have more recruits.

> 'The scene of devastation here is appalling and it is, to my mind, exceedingly necessary for every young man to try and realise to some slight extent what would take place in England if the Germans once affected a landing, and then we should have no shirkers. Finally, the surgical haversacks, which the people of Newark so kindly provided for my stretcher-bearers, have already proved of great value, and the bearers have been able to do good work with them. The lesson I have learnt out here, Mr Mayor, is – send us more men, and yet more men!'

Within a week he was asking for two more surgical haversacks to replace a couple that had been 'destroyed by fire' in the trenches.

Mary Marsh, thirty-one, in tiny Shamrock Cottage beside Cafferata's plaster works on Beacon Hill, was quickly informed that her twin brother was killed and her husband wounded in 'the great British victory'. Her spouse, Arthur, forty-two – an employee at a plaster works for eleven years before he became a private in the 2nd Lincolns – was shipped to hospital with shrapnel in his legs. Beside him was Sergeant W Chart of the 1st Sherwoods, who earned a Distinguished Conduct Medal for 'laying breastwork across a road under heavy rifle fire' and proving himself 'a good leader'. As they talked, Marsh showed Chart a picture of himself and his wife. Chart recognised Mary's resemblance to his pal, Private Jack Fincham. Once Marsh confirmed they were twins, Chart settled to the sad task of writing to Mary:

> 'Madam – I had your brother in my Company of 'Bombers' and regret to state that he was killed in the charge of our Regiment when we retook our trenches.'

Jack, thirty-one, worked in Mumby's cutting department before enlisting. On 21 April – almost six weeks later – the twins' parents, retired groom John Fincham, aged seventy-six, and his wife Sarah of 6 Hospital Cottages, among Newark's alms houses, received confirmation that John was not dead after all. It arrived in a letter from Jack himself! He married in 1919 – and lived to the age of eighty-two.

Others were less lucky. Fanny Inwards, thirty-four, at home near Mary on Beacon Hill with her six-week-old baby Joan and daughter Kathleen Mary, not quite two, learnt in trembling detail how her husband Ralph was killed. Serving with the 1st Lincolns, he had written at Christmas that he thought his time had come when his pack was shot through four times and he lost all his possessions including some china he had been saving for her. Later he was struck by shrapnel but continued fighting with the metal embedded in his shoulder. On 28 March the Reverend E F Campbell, Chaplain, 84th Field Ambulance, wrote to Fanny:

> 'He was very badly wounded in the stomach in the trenches last night, and was brought into this Field Ambulance this morning. Poor fellow, he was very far gone

when I saw him. He asked me had he any chance and I told him. Then he said, "Ah, then it can make no matter. Let me have a drink of water." We gave him some. He then gave me your address, asked me to write, and said three times over, "I love them." He never spoke after that but I held his hand and he went off at just a quarter past 12 ... Oh, Mrs Inwards, I cannot tell you how sorry I feel for you, and how much I sympathise with you in your great trouble. He died a hero's death; but I know that thought won't comfort you at first. And the only comfort I can give you is the thought that always comes to me when my friends and dear ones are called home. And that is the thought of the Resurrection morning when we all shall meet again.'

Fanny lived to the age of seventy-three. Kathleen died a spinster in Newark in 2000. Joan married in 1948 and lived until 1996.

Private Harry Gregory, son of a horse dealer and hawker in Porter's Row off Middlegate, near the homes of some of the Belgian refugees, was killed beside his best mate in the 2nd Sherwoods, Richard Gill, who was buried alive but dug himself free and wrote to his wife Mary Ellen:

'Will you tell Mr Gregory that his son Harry died with a good heart and was very cheerful up to the time of his death. He was singing a song to his pals in the trenches when he was shot.'

Gill was himself killed in action 9 August.

Private Arthur Andrew, twenty-two, son of a pub landlord on Lincoln Road, Newark, was thrown rooftop high by a shell explosion – and landed impaled on his own bayonet. He was repaired at a base hospital in France and returned to the 1st Sherwoods until severe frost bite in both feet incapacitated him again.

Sunday School teacher A W Iliffe, clerk at the Great Northern Railway Company's Newark Northgate Station before becoming a corporal, wrote from a London hospital about his brush with death:

'We received the order to advance and I scrambled over the parapet of my trench (which I had dug under fire the previous night) to meet a perfect hail of lead from the Germans. I had only doubled a few yards when a piece of shrapnel struck my left arm and did considerable damage to the muscle. It had previously passed through my Prayer Book and Testament and had been turned aside by my watch, all of which I keep in my breast pocket."

Charles William Combes, twenty-eight, suffered a head wound – but recovered quickly enough to write defiantly to his parents, George and Caroline, and eleven siblings at 1 Charles Street:

'The Germans attacked … and they did catch it. They fell in dozens. I do not expect they will try it again in a hurry. We repulsed them and took their trenches from them.'

A paragraph in the *Advertiser* on 7 April spelt-out the scale of casualties: Lieutenant Edward Lionel Scales, heir to his father's corset manufacturing business, was home in London Road 'for a few weeks' well-earned rest' – 'the only officer in the Brigade who has survived six months' service in the War.'

He became a captain in the 4th Middlesex Regiment and would be killed, aged twenty-four, on 11 November 1918, minutes before peace arrived.

Ironmongers John Howitt & Sons unveiled a unique window display in their Stodman Street stores: photographs of their twelve employees in the Forces and souvenirs they had sent ... a mirror that stopped a bullet and saved a Newark officer's life, a French '75' shell, the time fuse of a 'Jack Johnson' [large artillery shell named after the then world heavyweight boxing champion], clips of German and French cartridges, a German infantryman's belt picked up at Neuve Chapelle, and the time fuse of a German shrapnel shell.

On 24 April, Harry Trickett, twenty-one, a foundry worker before joining the Sherwoods, got a letter to his mum Kate: 'We had one or two Newark lads wounded last week ... God be with you till we meet again.' Two days later, another note arrived, from Wesleyan Chaplain, the Reverend A Stanley Bishop: Harry was killed on 20 April and 'laid to rest in a cemetery behind a castle where lie many of his comrades ... The spot is at present under fire.'

The spot was Kemmel Chateau. One of his comrades, Sergeant George Thomas Percival Wilmore, was killed on 14 April when he stood up in a trench. Reared from the age of nine by Mrs Jennie Wilson, fifty-four, wife of a groom, he was a maltster, played cricket for Newark Castle and volunteered as soon as war was declared.

Another sniper's victim, Captain Robert Frank Byron Hodgkinson, a solicitor and Registrar at Newark County Court, suffered a head wound and was removed from the Front Line.

Private George Shepherd, 23, a moulder, wrote to his parents in Mary's Row, Eldon Street, late in April:

> 'We have had a rough time of it this journey and a few boys have been put out of action. A few of them are Newark boys. Charlie Redmile, Vernon Street, and Dick East out of Chatham Street, have been killed. I am sorry to tell you these are not

The early war cemetery near Mount Kemmel.

all of them but they have died like heroes. These men are true British heroes. They are better men than those staying at home. Dear Mother, I am proud of my battalion and the men I am with. This war is drawing men to God every day; men who did not believe there was a Supreme Being before. The country is beginning to realise that the Lord is watching over them. I know He is watching and guarding me from danger because I have put myself in His hands and I do not fear death ... I shall always think of the day I enlisted as the Red Letter Day of my life. I could never sit at home and hang about and see our country the same as Belgium is.'

It transpired a few days later that that five Newark Territorials were killed when a German mortar exploded in their trench on 24 April. Private Richard East, twenty-three, a moulder at Nicholson's, supported his widowed mother Fanny Louise. Private Charles Ernest Redmile also worked at 'Nicky's'. Private William Godfrey, twenty-two, was a maltster's analyst at Bishop's, living with his parents in Bowbridge Road. Private Walter Hunt, twenty, an iron moulder at Simpson's, had written to his parents in Grove Street, New Balderton, only two days earlier that he was 'all right' and about to go into the trenches. Private Bert Sketchley, of Alliance Street, possibly had a premonition: he asked Lance-Corporal William Hurt only a few hours earlier: 'If anything happens to me, will you make sure my sister hears it first so that she can break it gently to Mum, who is so ill.' His widowed mother, Charlotte, was eighty-five; she passed away early in 1919.

One of Newark's best-known anglers, William Markwell, endured a double tragedy. His son Ernest, twenty, a lance corporal in the 1/8th Sherwoods, was killed on Friday, 1 May while on sentry duty. His wife Mary suffered a heart attack on hearing the news and died within a fortnight.

An even younger lance corporal, Fred Priestley, nineteen, was killed on his wife's birthday, 9 May. The former Ransome's apprentice, recently promoted to lead a group of 1st Sherwoods, was showing them how to throw a hand grenade when it exploded. Only five days earlier, his young wife Ellen, living in Egglestone's Yard with their young son, received 'a most affectionate' letter from him, telling her that her latest parcel 'went down a treat' and revealing he had already had at least one narrow escape:

'It was about 7 o' clock in the morning when the Germans were sending a few shells over, but not so many to bother about. I went up and drew the bacon for my section and call my men to fetch their bit. They were standing each side of me when a shell dropped at the back of me, killing one man and wounding three more. Thank God I escaped with only being buried with sandbags, which were soon removed. Well, I must stop talking about the war and think about 9 May, your birthday. I am sending you a card as this is all I can get out here, but I wish you many happy returns of the day and I pray God will keep you and my son from all harm and bring me safely home to you so that we can live happily together again.'

Ellen eventually remarried and moved to Halifax with her new husband.

Police Constable Thomas Cupid Rose of Newark Borough Police Force lost his twenty-three-year-old son Albert, a Rifleman in the King's Royal Rifles, to a bullet that killed two at Ypres. It happened after they had been sent to repair a trench damaged by shell fire. Albert had already experienced one narrow escape: blown into the air by a shell and almost buried alive, he managed to crawl to safety despite his back being so badly injured that he spent weeks in hospital. News of his death was first received by his former head teacher, Samuel Ashbourne Hildage, at Barnby Road County School, in a letter from another ex-pupil, Sergeant A W Wilson:

> 'Many thanks for parcel. I am very sorry to inform you that one of your old boys, Rifleman Rose, was killed in action on the 29th ult. He was with me the same afternoon and read your letter. I had given him some of the cigarettes. He said he was writing to you. I am writing this letter in the trenches; in fact, the trench that Rose was killed in … I was on patrol duty when I received the news that he and a corporal had been killed – both shot by the same bullet … Both were killed doing their duty.'

More heartbreak awaited the Rose family. Albert's youngest brother, Thomas was killed in August 1917; and his middle brother, Arthur Edward, a corporal in the King's Own Yorkshire Light Infantry, badly wounded.

Barley room labourer Joseph Nicholson, nineteen, was hailed in mid-May 1915 as the first 8th Sherwood Forester to win a bayonet duel with a German soldier:

> 'I am in good health and all right except for a very small wound in the shoulder. My officer and myself were out in front of our trenches patrolling when we were surprised by a group of Germans. The officer shot two and wounded one. A German struck me in the shoulder but it was only small and did not matter a deal as I managed to kill him. Dear parents [bricklayer's labourer William and Eleanor in Tenter Buildings, Appletongate] I am all right now so don't be alarmed if you see my name in the papers shortly. It will be about this small affair.'

The officer involved, Lieutenant J S Oates, son of Colonel William Coape Oates, of the 2/8th Sherwoods, also wrote to the Nicholson's, confirming Joseph

> 'has the distinction of getting the first bayonet wound in the Battalion … On this and on other occasions he has behaved very well, and his name has gone in for mention … He has had the satisfaction of sticking a German.'

In virtually the same post, widow Sophia Elizabeth Kirk, forty-six, who ran a confectionery shop, heard her son Herbert, nineteen, had been killed – 'shot in the trenches this morning by the Germans as he was firing over the parapet'.

The notion that life in the trenches was a lottery maybe also occurred to blacksmith Joseph and Elizabeth Brewster of Mount Zion Square, Eldon Street, who had four sons serving. William, twenty, a brewery worker, was killed in action with the 1st Sherwoods at Bois Grenier near Armentières on 9 May 1915. Harry survived in the 2/8th Sherwoods until April 1918, but then perished on the Western Front, aged twenty-two. Their other two sons, Joseph and Alfred, survived in the 2/8th Sherwoods and the Navy respectively.

Sergeant Edwin Cecil Coy was killed at Béthune, an important French railway centre, on 21 May. He lodged with his sister at the Bowling Green pub near Northgate Station and worked in Nicholson's foundry before emigrating to Canada in 1910 and founding a flourishing plumber's business. He joined the 15th Battalion Canadian Infantry on Guy Fawkes Day 1914.

There was some light relief on 6 June: Rifleman Harry Francis wrote to his family in Barnbygate about a tea party at the Front with fellow Newarkers of the Sherwoods:

'We had cake, biscuits, jam, butter and bread, eggs and some lovely tea, which I enjoyed immensely. Fancy being invited out to tea in the War area! ... I am very pleased to say we have left [censored]. My word, we had an awfully rough time of it while we were there ... I was on brigade guide and had to carry messages through all the awful shelling, but I got through without a scratch! I'm sorry to say that the men who were along with me were not so fortunate, some of them being killed by shells and others badly wounded ... The gasses used by the Germans are indeed awful. I have been through it once, when my eyes ran so much that I could not see out of them, and the smell was awful. But our respirators are not so bad as they do save some from penetrating into one's lungs.'

Tom Massey, eighteen, youngest son of the former licensee of the Queen's Head in the Market Place and a Parish Church chorister, was killed on 1 June while on patrol with the 1/8th Sherwoods.

A fortnight later, the Newark Company of the 8th Sherwoods, 'somewhere in Belgium' faced their biggest battle yet. The Germans mined their position but incredibly there was loss of life in only one trench, held by H Company. A terrible bombardment followed: heavy artillery, 'Jack Johnsons', machine guns, mortars and rifles belched out shot and shell for over an hour. The Newark lads, however, held on and inflicted heavy losses on the enemy who were 'hopelessly defeated' in their endeavour to break the battalion lines. The Newark Company lost only two men, who shared a surname. Private William Richardson, twenty-three, only son of John and Ann Richardson in Baldertongate, was a foundryman and Congregational Sunday School teacher. Private George Richardson, twenty-one, of Wright Street, worked at Ransome's.

Sergeant C W Chappell wrote to Newark relatives of 'our hottest time so far' ...

'[It] started with the Germans blowing up some mines in front of our trenches. Then followed a perfect rain of shells, trench mortars and bullets including machine gun, which went on for about an hour. The battalion, you will be pleased to hear, acted splendidly and effectually stopped the attack which was made on several of our trenches. Of course we lost a good few men including several more from Newark, but I am very pleased to say I came out of it all quite all right, and have a lot to be thankful for in doing so. The General Commanding the Brigade personally came and congratulated the battalion on the work it did that night, which is the second time he has acted in a similar manner, so you will see we are still keeping our good name up.'

With verve and nerves thus tested, it was as well that Miss Della Ray, the popular vocalist, who had appeared at Newark Picturedrome the previous week, presented 1,200 cigarettes for the Mayoress to forward to the 1/8th Sherwoods. It was far from the only example of Girl Power: Newark was undergoing revolutionary changes in its labour force. Quibell's were employing females to pack their soaps in attractive wrappings. At Warwick's & Richardson's Brewery, women and girls replaced boys washing bottles. Female labour was established at Cafferata's gypsum works and Associated Portland

Spot the smile ... Wounded men of the 8th Sherwoods report for duty again, June 1915. *[Advertiser cutting]*

cement works. And Ransome's were following suit in their new ball bearing department. An important meeting of senior representatives of Newark's engineering firms on 25 June, chaired by Mayor Kew, formed a committee to co-operate with the National Munitions Factory at Nottingham in the rapid production of more munitions. Twelve Newark firms were represented: what a powerhouse the town was.

The 1/8th Sherwoods asked the Mayoress's Working Party on 25 June to begin preparing warm winter clothing for the troops. Two days later, Newark Town Council turned down requests by four married police constables to be allowed to join the Army and sent two single PCs instead.

An official list of 8th Sherwoods' casualties thus far in the *Advertiser* on 30 June revealed that the Newark Company had suffered most: eighteen killed and fifty-nine wounded. On the same day the Germans used flame throwers for the first time against the British lines at Hooge, Ypres. Josephine Gilstrap, a spinster living on private means with seven servants in a twenty-four room residence in Winthorpe, north-east of Newark, became a heroine of the Sherwoods who had taken over a part of the British Front in Belgium. She sent three galvanised iron baths, complete with boiler, so that the men could bathe at their own billets in Locre village rather than scramble four miles to the next-nearest baths at Bailleul.

Newark's Belgian refugees experienced joy and grief. Baby Albert George Tote was born on 11 June; and would be joined in October by a cousin, Adrian Albert Martin Tote, born to Martin Francis Tote and his wife in Middlegate. Alas one of their leaders, widower Emile Volkaert, fifty-nine, died on 18 June while living in Lower Sleaford Road with his daughter, Madame Pateet, whose husband Leonard was a Cafferata's engineer. A chair-maker in his native Malines, Emile fled through Ghent, Ypres and Ostend before sailing to London. He found sanctuary with his daughter and son-in-law but never seemed able to forget the awful sights and sounds he had witnessed while being driven so savagely from his own country.

The death of the Reverend John Garrett Bussell, thirty-three, grandson of a former vicar of Newark, came as a shock even to those somewhat dehumanised by war news. He had failed in a bid for the headmastership of the Magnus Grammar School a few years earlier, became assistant master at Marlborough College and was serving as a captain with the 7th Battalion Royal Sussex Regiment when he fell near Plugstreet Wood, Belgium, leaving a widow, Dorothea, thirty, and children aged four and two.

Mayor Kew took on the sad task of visiting Cawkwell's Yard on 12 July to inform William and Martha Maria Pond that one of their eight children, Private John Turner Pond, twenty-two, had been killed fighting with the 1st Sherwoods. Three weeks earlier, the Mayor had a letter from John, who worked at Quibell's until a few months earlier, asking for Woodbine cigarettes. He sent six dozen packets. A postcard dated 4 July arrived at the Town Hall acknowledging receipt and promised a letter would follow. The letter was not from John but from Corporal J Blythe, asking the Mayor to break the news gently to Mr and Mrs Pond that 'he got killed this morning (5 July) at 6.15 ... He was the jolliest chap in our section.'

A few hours after Mayor Kew consoled the Ponds, William and Mary Catherine Smith of the Spread Eagle, Middlegate, received a telegram: their son William, twenty, had been thrown from a horse, only three months into his training as a Driver with the Royal Engineers 106th Field Company at Aldershot. They caught a train south – and at Finsbury Park station were handed another telegram: William had died.

Police Sergeant William Taylor and his wife Emma lost their only son, Christopher William, eighteen, while he was firing a machine gun at Ypres on 21 July. The news came in a letter from Leslie Tyers, eighteen, who would himself perish in 1916.

Rifleman Albert Duckworth, twenty, of the 1/7th West Yorkshire Regiment wrote to his parents, labourer George and Fanny, and seven siblings:

> 'I should just like to come home to England and let someone else have a go. The Germans are fond of sending gas over the trenches we are in and it is rum stuff, I can tell you ... It's all right for those blokes who go walking with girls up the Muskham road and never think about their comrades out here. But never mind. Wait until they come to cheer me up at the station. I will [censored] them up. I was in a nice race the other day. Just as we were digging a trench, the Germans started to shell us. It was a panic moment.'

By coincidence, Old Magnusian Lieutenant Claud Davenport, in charge of 1/8th

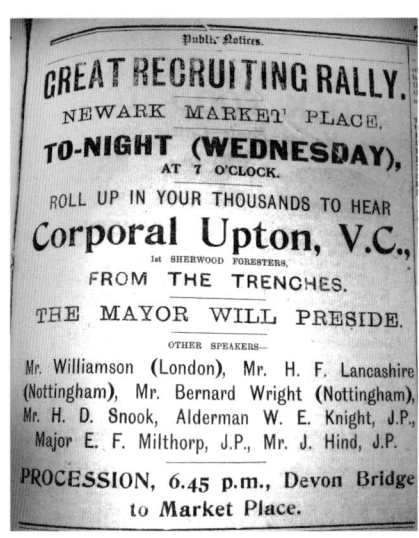

> **Public Notices.**
>
> **GREAT RECRUITING RALLY.**
> NEWARK MARKET PLACE.
> **TO-NIGHT (WEDNESDAY),**
> AT 7 O'CLOCK.
> ROLL UP IN YOUR THOUSANDS TO HEAR
> **Corporal Upton, V.C.,**
> 1st SHERWOOD FORESTERS,
> FROM THE TRENCHES.
> THE MAYOR WILL PRESIDE.
> OTHER SPEAKERS—
> Mr. Williamson (London), Mr. H. F. Lancashire (Nottingham), Mr. Bernard Wright (Nottingham), Mr. H. D. Snook, Alderman W. E. Knight, J.P., Major E. F. Milthorp, J.P., Mr. J. Hind, J.P.
> PROCESSION, 6.45 p.m., Devon Bridge to Market Place.

The newspaper advertisement that urged Newark men to join forces with VC hero James Upton.
[Advertiser cutting]

Corporal James Upton VC (seated) awaits his turn to address the gathering.

Sherwoods transport, was in Newark appealing for goggles for his motor cyclists, explaining: 'They would be a great protection from the German gas.'

It was hardly surprising that a great recruiting rally in Newark Market Place on 29 July fell flat. Victoria Cross hero Corporal James Upton, 26, from Lincoln made regal progress through the town in a parade from Sconce Hills – and found time to praise Newark's own DCM winner, Charles Dady.

Upton, 5ft 4in tall, was deemed too small to join-up initially. He earned his VC on 9 May near Rouges Bancs, displaying the greatest courage in succouring the wounded while exposed to heavy rifle and artillery fire, going close to the enemy's parapet regardless of his own safety. One wounded man was killed by a shell while Upton was carrying him. When not carrying in the wounded, he was engaged in bandaging and dressing the serious cases in front of the regiment's parapet, exposed to enemy fire.

Dady earned his DCM in the same drama. Once Upton and his entourage reached the Market Place, it was crammed with crowds. He spoke. So did wounded soldiers. None minced his words. Upton said:

> 'I have come here tonight to see how many of the young fellows of Newark are coming back with me to see Sergeant-Major Dady ... I don't want to get back to Dady and a lot more of the boys and say, "Well, it wasn't much use going to Newark." I can certainly tell you this: if the Germans get to England, there won't be a great deal of Newark left. I have seen nine months of it. Every possible mark they will have down. I have seen little children, four and five years of age, with one of their hands off. Are we going to see that in Newark? No! Not while we have some of the boys here who are going to enlist and give us a lift.'

The net result of his martial bravado and eloquence..? Two men recruited.

By gruesome coincidence, as the crowd dispersed from the Market Place the newest 8th Sherwoods to reach the Front were entering the trenches for the first time. At 3.30 the following morning they were attacked with 'liquid fire' [flame-throwers] followed by bombing parties, which they beat off, with the loss of 'a number of good men'. In the evening the 7th Sherwoods were brought up on the left of the 8th and suffered 'considerable loss' from enemy shellfire while digging themselves in to cover a gap in the trenches. News of Newark casualties seeped home...

Fred Parker, thirty-two, one of eight offspring of a builder's carter, poked his head above the parapet to gaze at the approaching fire and was killed by a sniper. Frank Walster, twenty-three, one of Nicholson's volunteers, was bayoneted while on patrol. Private Herbert Moore, twenty-two, from Bradley's foundry, was buried alive by a shell burst and killed. Private Robert Huckerby, nineteen, son of a brewery cellarman, was killed on patrol. It was Friday the 13th of August when mother of eight Harriett Gumsley discovered her nineteen-year-old son, Thomas Frederick, had perished. He had written in his last letter: 'Keep a sharp eye open. I might be home on leave at any time!'

Another Private Fred Parker from Newark, who survived while his namesake perished, composed on his sixteenth consecutive day in the trenches a letter to the *Advertiser* overflowing with dignity and defiance:

> 'We have been up against it pretty hot but we have repulsed every German attack. The Huns have made five or six attacks on our positions just lately, and one was very severe. They tried to get through our lines by sending us some of that liquid fire they so often use against the French, and we withstood the bombardment very well under the circumstances. If that liquid fire drops clean on the parapet, it not only sets the sandbags on fire but the men as well.
>
> 'A few odd Germans managed to get in one of our trenches but they didn't reign

Corporal James Upton VC. *Taylor Library]*

very long, I can tell you. Our bombers bombed them out quickly with their own bombs, which they were throwing at our chaps. Some of our men were picking them up and throwing them back again before they exploded. It was a fine feat and very plucky ... It was here that the Barnbygate Parker got killed. I saw in the paper that it was thought to be me who had gone under but, thank God, I am still alive and well and am able to get a bit of my own back for those poor Newark chaps.

'The Germans have tried their utmost to break through to the coast, but they can't do that – they've got to get past us first before they can get to England. Our chaps hang on and stick to it too well to let them through. We had General Sir Charles Fergusson [Commander of the II and later the XVIII Corps in France] to speak to us one day and he told us that he couldn't wish to have any better troops ... We have earned some fame since we have been here and I hope we shall bring it back to Newark with us some day.'

A few days after returning to the Front from Upton VC's recruitment rally, Lieutenant Hector Wilson Ridley, twenty-three, was killed in the trenches with the 2nd Sherwoods. He was so respected that his widowed mother Elizabeth received a letter from Buckingham Palace: 'The King and Queen deeply regret the loss you and the Army have sustained by the death of your son in the service of his country. Their Majesties truly sympathise with you in your sorrow.'

A small picture in the *Advertiser* of seven prisoners of war in Doeberitz Camp, Germany, brought a degree of comfort to some Newark families who had been worrying for almost a year about missing menfolk. Among them were George E White, a railway shunter and local cricketer before he joined the Duke of Wellington's (West Riding) Regiment, who was captured early in the hostilities at Mons, and Private E Bullard, formerly an insurance agent. US Ambassador James W. Gerard wrote in his book *My Four Years in Germany* in 1917:

'In the beginning of the War the Germans were surprised by the great number of prisoners taken and had made no adequate preparations for their reception. Clothing and blankets were woefully wanting, so I

NEWARK PRISONERS IN GERMANY.

Three of the soldiers in this picture belong to Newark. They are at Doeberitz Camp, Germany, and in the original photograph White looks emaciated, his clothes ragged and hanging loose upon him. Standing in the back row, on the extreme left of the picture, is Geo. E. White, of the Duke of Wellington's (West Ridings). He was taken prisoner at Mons. He was formerly a shunter on the G.N., and a prominent member of the Wesley Guild Cricket Club. Standing on the extreme right of the picture is Private E. Bullard, who was formerly an insurance agent, and resided at Barnby Crossing. The third Newarker is Pte. A. Stevenson, 7, Trent-villas, Farndon-road.

Newark's first glimpse of locals captured by the Germans.
[Advertiser cutting]

immediately bought what I could in the way of underclothes and blankets at the large department stores of Berlin and the wholesalers and sent these to the camps where the British prisoners were confined. I also sent to the Doeberitz camp articles such as sticks for wounded men who were recovering, and crutches, and even eggs and other nourishing delicacies for the sick.'

Within a few weeks, auctioneer's wife Edith Pink launched a Working Party to send food parcels to Newark's PoWs: she would be lauded as a life-saver.

Little wonder the town became more anxious! Ellen Martha Hense, fifty, wife of a German-born musician, was sentenced to six months' gaol with hard labour by Newark Magistrates on 3 August for being 'an alien enemy'. She was a native of Newcastle-on-Tyne but Police Chief Wright called her a woman of 'questionable moral character, travelling from camp to camp'.

And 'quite a sensation' erupted the following Saturday morning: a gas explosion in Cartergate, one of the main shopping streets, shattered hairdresser Harold Southern's ceiling. Zeppelin fears ended when he explained he had only just moved in and had asked a plumber to locate 'a whiff of gas'. The plumber lit a match! No one was injured and the flames were subdued by a PC who was proceeding along the street as the windows blew out.

With more and more wounded fighters being shipped home from the Western Front and Turkey, Newark opened a depot in mid-August to provide supplies to extra hospitals being established locally. Staffed by volunteers on only two days a week, it provided 3,167 bandages by Christmas.

Yet the bizarre continued: Albert Jollands, fifty-five, who made such a substantial fortune while he ran the imposing Clinton Arms in Newark Market Place – from which William Gladstone had launched his political career – that he owned a string of race horses, died while in camp in Norfolk as the South Notts Hussars' letter carrier. He often lay on his bed in a little wooden hut at the end of each day reading by the light of a candle balanced on his chest. On 25 August, he burnt to death.

On the same night, the *London Gazette* announced the award of the Medal of St George, 4th Class, by the Emperor of Russia to Drummer William Bernard Robb, eighteen, son of the Spring House landlord; the first member of the 1/8th Sherwoods to be honoured. At Kemmel on 21 June he and Drummer J W Newton, under heavy rifle fire, carried to a casualty station Cambridge University graduate Second Lieutenant John Radley Eddison, twenty-three, from Retford, who had been so severely wounded that he died.

Cook Edith Alice Elvidge, 31, was expecting her fiancé Thomas Tournay, thity-four, home on special leave for their wedding early in September. Instead she learnt he had been killed by a sniper at Potijze, near Ypres, on 25 August while on fatigue duty. In his last letter, he had marvelled at going through so much brutality without a scratch; he looked forward to getting home to marry his sweetheart.

In another family tragedy, Private George William Jex, thirty-two, was given compassionate leave to console his three children at the funeral of their mother, Nellie, thirty-three. The children, all under ten, were looked after by aunties until dad returned from the War. Father-of-seven Private William Thomas Marshall, twenty-seven, clung to life for three weeks before succumbing to shrapnel wounds in the head and neck. His wife, Mary Ann, left to rear offspring aged sixteen years to four weeks, received conflicting information from the Australian Hospital, Wimereux, near Boulogne. The Reverend R A Gibbs attempted to console her: 'He was delighted with your letter and photograph of the baby.' Nursing Sister Gertrude Taddy wrote: 'He was always too ill to read your letters but we read them to him.'

Mother of seven, Sarah Ann Guy, in Chester Place off Bowbridge Road, discovered that her husband Private William Henry Guy, forty, of the 12th Sherwoods had been killed five days after he wrote that he was working safely with the cooks. A Trent gravel dredger, he lied about his age to enlist, for Army records aged him thirty-six when he was killed on 26 September, by a German shell.

Landscape gardener Joseph Robert Dench and his wife Katherine lost their son, Sergeant Alfred Charles Dench, who had joined the King's Company, 1st Battalion Grenadier Guards aged fourteen nine years earlier. Sergeant Major H Young wrote: 'He had just got into a German trench with his platoon and was telling his men to pass along when he fell forward and died in less than two minutes on the evening of 27 September.'

Alfred Savage, twenty-two, a brewery worker, was killed on the Front with the 9th Leicestershire Regiment – while his parents were visiting his wounded brother, William, twenty-five, in hospital in Bury St Edmunds.

Charles Harrison, the popular Newark Football League secretary who had built the competition from four clubs to twenty, was killed when a shell exploded in his trench on 5 October. Barely six weeks earlier, he had been home on leave to his wife, Eleanor Ann, thirty-four, and son John, three, with souvenirs: a German rifle and bayonet. Now all they had were memories of a man so patriotic that, having voluntarily served during the Boer War, he was one of the first to respond in 1914, giving up his job as a brewery clerk.

Amid the grief, widow Elizabeth Killingley – a neighbour of the Marshalls and Guys in the Bowbridge Road area – received a massive shock in the post on 10 October: a postcard from the son she thought was dead. Two days later a letter arrived from him. Both were dated

Died in German trench – Sergeant Alfred Charles Dench.
[Advertiser cutting]

Souvenirs then death ... football inspiration Charles Harrison.
[Advertiser cutting]

well after she was assured that Private Harry Killingley of the 9th Leicestershire Regiment had been killed. He explained he was one of the bearers at the funeral of another Newarker, Alfred Savage, twenty-three, from Newnham Road, who was at Mount School with him. Someone must have mixed them up.

More good news came from PoW Fred Tacey, last heard from on Christmas Eve. He wrote thanking his parents for 'the parcel with the cigarettes in ... We are away from headquarters now, harvesting, and ten of us are billeted at a manor farm. We are having a splendid time, plenty of food, and a little money; but we cannot get on owing to the weather.'

With the Western Front so deadlocked, the Allies attempted to open a backdoor to Germany via a sea route to Russia by taking control of the Dardanelles Straits: a new battlefront was opened in Gallipoli, north-western Turkey. A naval bombardment of entrenched Turkish positions from 19 February failed. But that did not stop Newark's first Dardanelles gallantry medals being earned at sea.

Old Magnusian Arthur Edward Dunn, thirty-eight, commanding mine layer HMS *Gazelle*, was congratulated by Vice-Admiral John M de Robeck, Commanding the Eastern Mediterranean Squadron, for mine laying operations in the Gulf of Smyrna and then received the Royal Naval Reserve Officers' Decoration from the Lords Commissioners of the Admiralty. Pre-war, he was Marine Superintendent in London for the New Zealand Shipping Company. He said of *Gazelle's* mine-laying and the French mine-layer, *Casa Blanca*:

> 'The work had to be done on very dark nights and no lights were allowed. The first expedition passed off all right, but on the second one we were alone and had to lay eight mines across the entrance to the Gulf. We had just begun our work when a searchlight from one of the forts picked us up, and the guns opened fire. In addition, they kept revolving the searchlights on us so that we were almost blinded, and should have been done for if the *Doris* had not come along and blazed away with her big guns while we dropped the rest of our mines and sneaked away.
>
> 'On the next trip the *Casa Blanca* laid several and then one exploded but, luckily, clear of the ship. Of ours, the first three lots floated away all right, but the next lot exploded as soon as they touched the water and blew up several of the others as well. The noise was awful and bits were flying about in all directions. Several of the men were hit by pieces. We were recalled to Mudros for a doctor and gave the reminder of our mines to the *Casa Blanca*.

Mine-laying bravery – Arthur Edward Dunn.
[Advertiser cutting]

> 'A few hours later she struck one of her own mines and went down with a loss of eight officers and eighty-nine men. We were now the only mine-layer attached to the Allied Fleet and they kept us busy. We used to lay over fifty mines every night that we could go out.'

On 30 May 1915 Signalman Isaac Overton, twenty-seven, became the first Newarker awarded a Distinguished Service Medal in this War. While on HMS *Wear* seeking enemy submarines, they espied a Turkish sailing ship *Aynsmata*. Eight crew, including Isaac, went off in a whaler. There was 'a fierce scrap', for there were many hands on the Turkish vessel. The tars had only rifles with penetrating bullets, which were employed with such good effect that the Turks surrendered, and they towed the enemy ship to one of the isles in the Gulf of Smyrna. It was months before Isaac was informed he was being honoured ... during which time he returned home in August and married his childhood sweetheart Rose Tyler, twenty-eight. The many privations he suffered in serving his country culminated in his suffering paralysis down his left side in November 1916. He was discharged from the Navy, returned home in a bath chair and was bedridden for so long that his medal was posted rather than presented to him. The loyal Rose pushed him around town frequently. But after they got home to Barnbygate on 2 July 1917, he fell seriously ill at around 8pm and died twelve hours later. He became the first man ever to be buried in Newark Cemetery will full Naval honours.

Meanwhile, the Rangers became part of a huge Allied land Army massing in Egypt in mid-1915. Their ancient barracks in Cairo 'were built by Napoleon', Old Magnusian Thomas Rowland Smith asserted to his uncle, Jonathon Henry Smith, a chemist who had reared him from the age of nine in Bridge Street.

'We shall soon melt with the sun glaring ... Most of the Australians have left for the Dardanelles ... We get plenty of work, but not so much food as we did at home. The Government rations per man is 1lb meat and 1lb of bread with tea and ½oz of rice per day. We get about 6d a day extra and that buys bacon, a sausage or eggs for breakfast and 1oz jam and butter for tea.'

The Allies landed two divisions at Suvla Bay on 6 August 1915. The commanding general opted not to strike immediately for strategic heights overlooking the beaches; so they became pinned to the coast by Turkish troops entrenched above them.

Sergeant T H Brown, third generation of a Newark family of butchers, wrote from the trenches of his hair-raising exploits with D Company, 9th Worcestershire Regiment:

'We went out at 10pm to try and discover any useful information about the enemy. We were only eighty yards from the Turks' first line trenches, and the wire in front of theirs and ours left about fifty yards to be covered. We had crept up to within about fifteen yards of their wire when we encountered a patrol of the enemy, and just to the left they also had a large party of men digging. The enemy patrol was lying quite still and, thinking they had not seen us, I decided to try and capture them without having to shoot, which would have made our presence known to the large party close by us. I then made a half circle, intending to close in on them and capture them silently if possible. When, however, we had made the half-circle (we were on our knees by now) they suddenly opened rapid fire on us. We, of course, dropped flat at the risk of capture, and remained so until they had ceased fire for a time. We could hear them creeping forward to look for us or our bodies, and we started to creep backwards until we reached our lines. We then reported and the line opened fire in the direction I gave ... I had as narrow an escape as it

Sherwood Rangers Yeomanry with horses before they left England.
[Advertiser cutting]

Newark men of 'A' Squadron, Sherwood Rangers Yeomanry, in training for the infantry role, Abbassia Barracks, Cairo, June 1915.
[NEKMS T15854]

would be possible to have: a bullet penetrated my great coat, tunic, jersey and shirt from left to right, and just singed the skin a little but did not even draw blood. An eighth of an inch nearer and it would have gone through my chest. The Commanding Officer, Adjutant and my Company officer congratulated me on penetrating so far into the enemy's quarters, also on my escape and the escape of my party, saying that had I tried to get my party back under fire, we should surely have been bowled over. It was only my giving the order to lie flat and let the enemy think we were shot that allowed us to escape. It made us pretty sick at the time, but I am pleased to have gained a little distinction, particularly on work that is considered one of the more nervy jobs.'

Pioneer R Heath, who trained with the 68th Field Company in Newark, wrote to his parents a spine-chilling account of how he played dead while being stripped:

'One of our officers, two infantry fellows and myself volunteered to go out to see if we could shoot a sniper ... I was the only one to come back alive. We were surprised by five Turks who opened fire on us. All the rest were shot down. I feigned death and dropped too. The Turks took my rifle, boots, puttees, braces, watch and all my private belongings. They dragged me about 200 yards and I lay there for about two-and-a-half hours, afraid to move because I did not know where the blinking Turks were. Eventually some of ours [most likely the Chester Regiment] came up and I got safely back.'

The Rangers, arriving on 18 August, found the terrain inhospitable: rocky and scrub-covered, with little water. The steep hills were cut into deep gullies and ravines. Shopkeeper Elizabeth Dring in Portland Street received from her thirty-four-year-old son Harry, a bricklayer, a letter that could have been a holiday postcard:

'It is very hot with no shade at all, but it is on the sea front and surrounded by mountains. It is very nice for a bathe, which we have every day. Some say they heard big guns firing last night but I didn't. You can buy melons at 3d and 4d each, but they are green. There are plenty of hawkers around but you have not got to buy any drink off them, lemonade, etc., for fear of cholera ... Don't forget to send some salts and a bit of tobacco.'

When their Officer Commanding, Lieutenant-Colonel Sir John Peniston Milbanke VC, 10th Bart, revealed they were to attack a redoubt blandly named Hill 70 on 21 August, he shrugged: 'I don't know where it is and I don't think anyone else does, either. But in any case we are to go ahead and attack any Turk we meet.' He was among the 5,000 killed. It was 'a textbook example of how not to introduce troops into the line or to make an attack,' Captain William Wedgwood Benn, 1st County of London Yeomanry, 4th Mounted Brigade, 2nd Mounted Division, would write in his memoir, *In the Side Shows* (published by Hodder & Stoughton, 1919).

It was almost dark 'when suddenly the Yeomanry leapt to their feet and, as a single man, charged right up the hill,' war correspondent Ashmead Bartlett reported at the time in *The Globe* newspaper.

'They were met by a withering fire which rose to a crescendo as they neared the northern crest, but nothing could stop them. They charged at amazing speed without a single halt from the bottom to the top, losing many men and many of their chosen leaders, including gallant Sir John Milbanke. It was a stirring sight, watched by thousands in the ever-gathering gloom. One moment they were below the crest, the next on top. A moment after, many had disappeared inside the Turkish trenches, bayoneting all the defenders who had not fled in time, while others never stopped at the trench-line, but dashed in pursuit down the reverse slopes.

'From a thousand lips a shout went up that Hill 70 was won. But night now was rapidly falling. The figures became blurred, then lost all shape, and finally disappeared from view ... and as one left Chocolate Hill one looked back on a vista of rolling clouds of smoke and huge fires, from the midst of which the incessant roar of the rifle-fire never for a moment ceased.

'This was ominous, for although Hill 70 was in our hands, the question arose: could we hold it throughout the night in the face of determined counter-attacks? In fact, all through the night the battle raged incessantly, and when morning broke Hill 70 was no longer in our possession.

'Apparently the Turks were never driven off a knoll on the northern crest, from which they enfiladed us with machine guns and artillery fire, while those of the Yeomanry who had dashed down the reverse slopes in pursuit were counter-attacked and lost heavily and had been obliged to retire. In the night it was decided it would be impossible to hold the hill in daylight, and the order was given for the troops to withdraw to their original positions. Nothing, however, will lessen the glory of that final charge of England's Yeomen.'

The heroism of stretcher bearer Bert Colton, twenty-one, Newark's first death among the Rangers, was reported by Major Harold Thorpe in a letter to his grieving mother, written from a crowded dug-out with shells still flying around:

'Your brave son brought no less than fourteen men out of one patch of burning gorse and personally dressed the wounds of ten of them. Unfortunately he was struck by a shrapnel bullet in the head and fell mortally wounded ... He has always been the pattern of what a soldier should be.'

Educated at the Magnus, Bert worked for an auctioneer's and was a scoutmaster. To underline his selflessness, Private Frank Robinson, twenty-two, son of a photographer in Lombard Street, part of the Great North Road through Newark, wrote to their mutual friend, Ivy Lees, 22, in Portland Street:

'He [Bert] died like a hero. His duties took him right into the firing and there is no ducking as they have to carry the stretcher. Anyway, he and his chum carried in thirty-four cases before he was shot.'

Rescued fourteen from burning gorse ... brave Bert Colton.
[Advertiser cutting]

The *Advertiser*, 25 August, reported the 9th Sherwoods' casualties included

Quartermaster Arthur Ewin, forty-three, recipient of a Distinguished Conduct Medal in the Boer War, who arrived in Newark eight years earlier, ran the Newark Militia, and had persuaded the Mayoress to form her Working Party. He left a widow, Helen, who moved along the Fosse to Montague House in Syerston, and eight children. In 2004, his grand-daughter Christine Ditcham would move into Montague House and compose *A Soldier's Story – Lieutenant Arthur Ewin DCM 1872-1915* [NEKMS 2006-61-1 in Newark Museum Archives].

The *Advertiser* of 1 September reported 'alarming rumours' about the high numbers of casualties in the Royal Engineers and Newark Squadron of the Rangers. Of the RE 67th and 68th Companies that had quartered in Newark, Major Francis Wilfred Brunner, forty-four, was missing, along with Lieutenants Edward Pearce Elworthy and Louis Rees-Mogg. Lieutenants Feranti, Crawhall and B T James were 'merely wounded'. Major Brunner was indeed dead, as were many of his men. Mother of six, Sarah Ann Quiningborough, was so saddened by the loss of Pioneer Maurice H Dare, who had been billeted at her home in Harcourt Street, she ensured that he was recorded on the Roll of Honour in Newark Charles Street Methodist Church alongside her own sons, Frederick and Herbert, who were killed in France.

'It's like hell,' wrote Sergeant Frederick Gabbitas in the aftermath of the charge.

> 'There is a continuous rain of shrapnel and high explosive shells all the day through. We have to lay like rats; can't move. I have pulled through up to now, but don't know how ... After we landed, we entrenched ourselves and started our advance next day, and we were not long before we knew because they picked us off a bit. All our leaders got knocked out and we finished with about six officers and a couple of Companies, but we had to hold our own. We got entrenched again and could not advance any more until the next Saturday; but they kept us on the move. On about the 21st we had to advance again and the Sherwood Rangers Yeomanry advanced with us, but they soon had some laid low. It was their christening under fire and I bet they knew it. I have not come across them any more ... We came out of that squabble with three officers and 380 men,

Arthur Ewin ... brave in the Boer and Great Wars...
[Advertiser cutting]

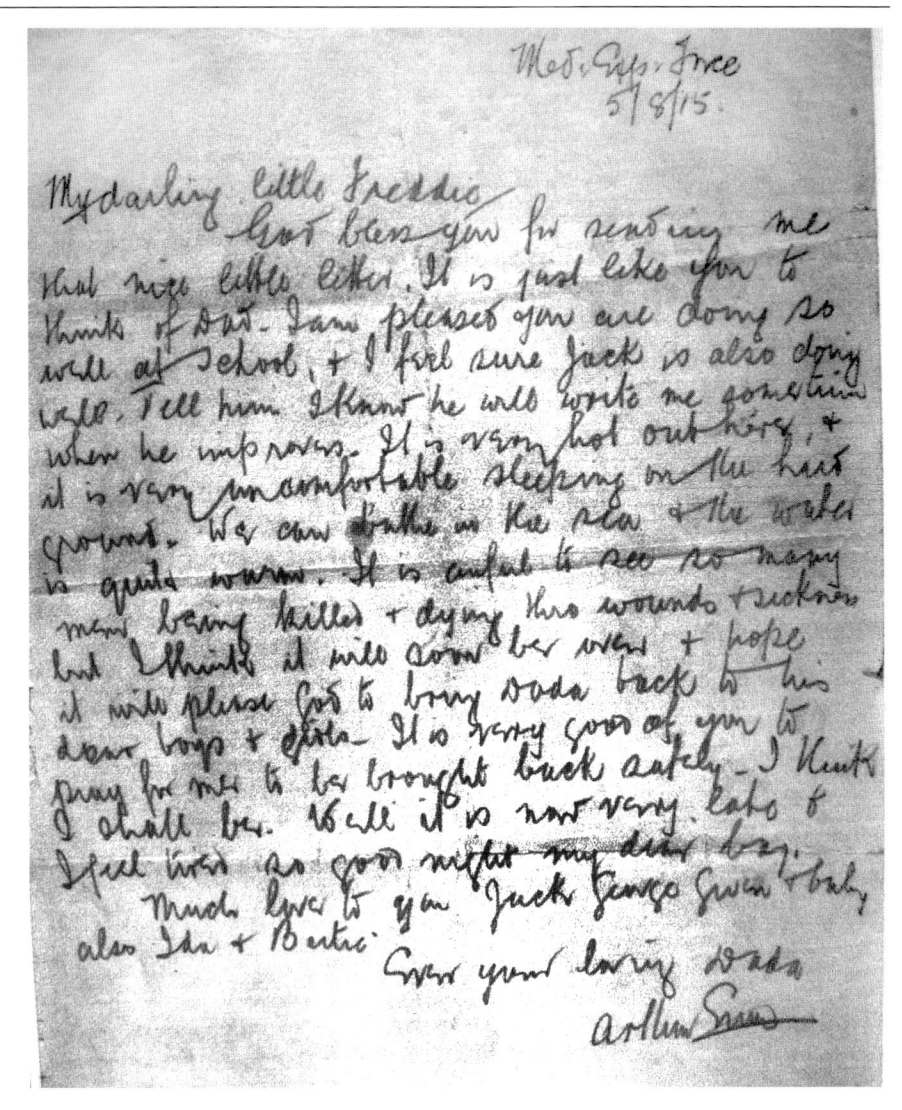

...and gentle father: to his son, darling Freddie.
[NEKMS: 2006.61.2]

and we cannot do any more until we get reinforcements ... I am ready for home any day now. We are having to live on very short rations – biscuits and bully beef ... I can't write any more.'

Some were literally scared stiff. Trooper George West, twenty-eight, popular in the Rangers' Newark Squadron, suffered a 'breakdown and has unfortunately lost the use of his limbs'. Prior to the war, he was living with his uncle John and aunt Flora at their boot making and repairing shop in Bridge Street, working as a draughtsman at

Ransome's and playing football. Doctors diagnosed: 'There is still hope of improvement.' George died a bachelor in 1934 aged forty-seven.

Other troops rotted away. Archie Robb, 23, reared in Newark, left a good job in a shipbuilding yard in Barrow-in-Furness to join the 6th King's Own Lancasters; he died of dysentery, 23 October, despite being shipped back to hospital in Alexandria.

Nine days earlier, the next great action of Newarkers had begun on the Western Front. Solicitor John Pickard Becher, an acting major who had become the first 8th Sherwoods officer to earn the Distinguished Service Order a few months earlier for his leadership near Kemmel and in the flame throwers' attack at Ypres, strapped a lamp to his back when ordered to lead a bayonet charge at the Hohenzollern Redoubt before dawn on 14 October. He wanted to make sure his men could see where they were going over shell-pitted ground in their part of the Battle of Loos. He made himself a beacon for the German snipers. 'It was a noble deed,' commented the Bishop of Southwell, Dr Edwyn Hoskyns, at a memorial service for Becher, the clerk to Newark County Magistrates.

Becher's DSO citation had been for 'conspicuous gallantry and good service on several occasions. On 24 April 1915 near Kemmel, when part of his trench was blown-in, he organised the defence of the breach under heavy fire, and personally assisted in repairing the parapet and digging out buried men. On 15 June near Kemmel, when part of his trench was blown in by mines, shells and trench mortars, he displayed great gallantry and coolness in reorganising the defence. On 30 July and on subsequent days at Ypres, he displayed great coolness, cheerfulness and resource under trying circumstances when in temporary command of his Battalion.'

Shining example ... Major John Pickard Becher.
[Advertiser cutting]

Two of his inspired men earned Distinguished Conduct Medals. Lance Corporal Harold Tyne, twenty, a grocery boy before joining the 8th Sherwoods, picked up unexploded German grenades when his own failed to explode and threw them, killing several of the enemy. Later he held his trench with great coolness and bravery under heavy bomb and machine-gun fire until reinforced, performing a similar action the following day. What the citation did not say was that German machine gun-fire had killed all eight of Harold's comrades, leaving him alone in the trench. He threw bomb after bomb at the advancing enemy and, after his supply was finished, picked up the Germans' unexploded bombs and threw them back at them. Running from one end of the trench to the other, tripping over the bodies of his comrades, he kept the enemy at bay until help arrived. Lance Sergeant Arthur Sheppard, twenty-five, earned his DCM leading a bombing party on his own initiative under heavy bomb and rifle fire against the attacking enemy. Having thrown all his grenades, he brought up a fresh supply; and

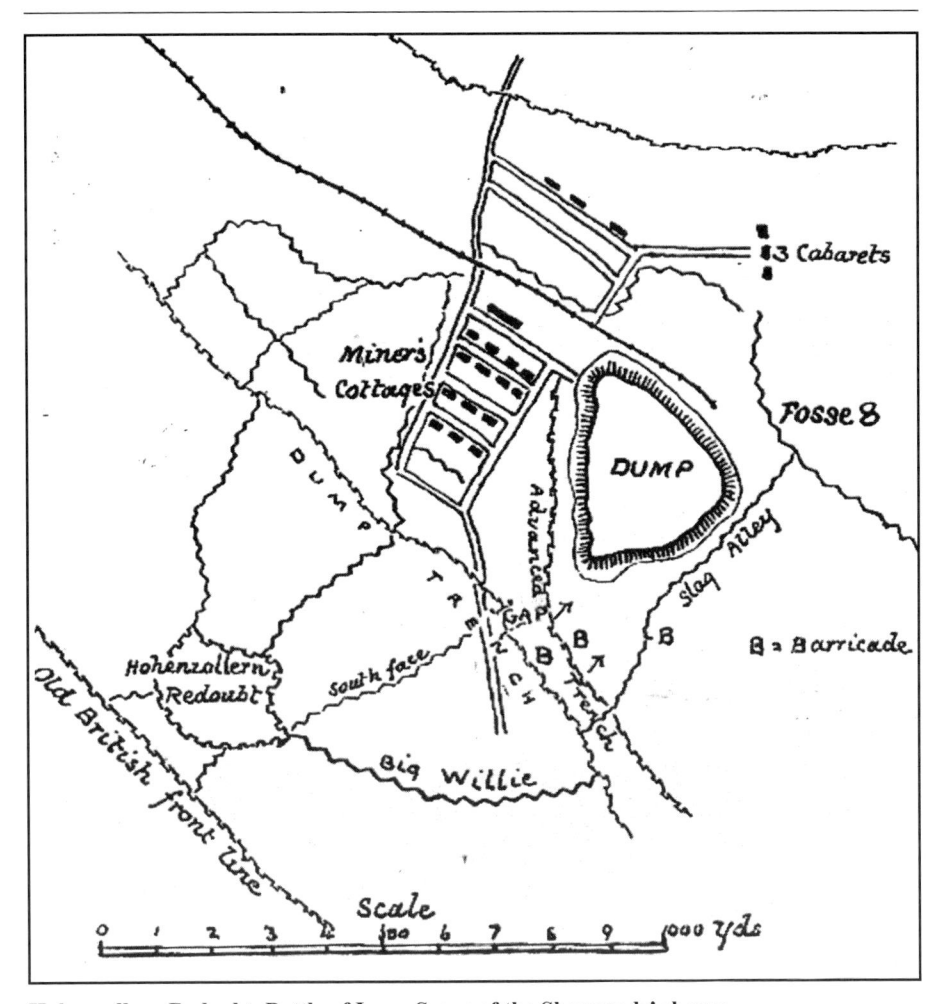

Hohenzollern Redoubt, Battle of Loos. Scene of the Sherwoods' charge.

later, having lost five men, he led up reinforcements.

October began in Newark with a massive recruiting rally: the Army had 'noticed that the recently taken National Register reveals that there are many men in the town eligible for service, but who are holding back for some reason or other'. More than 2,000 in the Market Place heard patriotic speeches. Several stepped forward. Two were passed fit for service: another commentary on living conditions?

But Becher's boys unhesitatingly followed his guiding light in the charge on the Hohenzollern Redoubt. The 1/8th Sherwoods lost forty-nine officers and men killed; forty have no known grave. The rest of 139 North Midland Brigade of the 46th Division had sixty-three killed; fifty-four have no known grave. The action, which carved a significant hole in German defences, was part of The Battle of Loos (25 September –

Brothers killed alongside their brother-in-law Becher ... Henry and Edward Handford.
[Advertiser cuttings]

Killed seeking Becher ... Lieutenant Colonel George Fowler.
[Advertiser cutting]

18 October), an attack by six divisions. Taking place before stocks of ammunition and heavy artillery were sufficient, the opening of the battle was noteworthy for the first use of poison gas by the British Army. The wind turned and blew it over British troops, causing seven deaths and 2,632 casualties.

Despite the casualties, there was considerable first day success in breaking into the deep enemy positions near Loos and Hulluch. But the reserves had been held too far from the battle front to be able to exploit the successes and it slowed from a flashing advance to attritional warfare for minor gains. The Historical Section of the Committee of Imperial Defence determind in its analytical report the following year, that the most important episode was the attempt on the Hohenzollern Redoubt. The Lincoln and Leicester Brigades launched a bayonet charge straight up the heavily-defended hill towards 'Fosse Trench', aiming to send bombing [grenade throwing] parties along entrenchments called 'Little Willie', North Face and South Face. They turned the Germans out of their defences but were halted by machine-gun fire just short of 'Fosse Trench'. Desperate fighting and bombing went on for hours. The 7th and 8th Sherwoods joined in and 'played a leading part in the bombing encounters which went on all night'.

About 4am on the 14th a fine effort by the 8th Sherwoods dislodged a party of Germans who had established themselves in the eastern corner of the Redoubt. It was most timely: the Germans were pressing hard, advancing across the open ground and bombing along the communications trenches. The Sherwoods held the Germans at bay, with much difficulty, until the night of 14-15 October, when they were relieved by 2 Guards Brigade. By then the Redoubt had been wired by the 1st North Midland Field Coy RE, and the position made fairly secure. In the middle of the relief, the enemy made another counter-attack in force, their last serious effort as it turned out. Although they reached the wire, the steady fire of the 5th and 6th Sherwoods was too much for them, and the attack was repulsed with heavy loss. 'The recovery of the Hohenzollern may be taken as the final act in the great battle which had begun on 25 September.'

The first hint of this drama arrived in Newark on 16 October. Mrs Veronica Becher received a telegram: Major Becher DSO was 'seriously ill'. His thigh had been shattered early in the charge. He had to lie for hours within thirty yards of German trenches. In darkness, he managed to slither into the cover of a trench and was discovered hours later by one of the Royal Army Medical Corps. The next news to reach Mrs Becher was that her two brothers, Captain Henry Basil Strutt Handford, twenty-one, and Second Lieutenant Edward Francis Sale Handford, twenty, were killed in the same attack.

The Sherwoods' Commanding Officer, Lieutenant-Colonel George Herbert Fowler, a director of his father's coal mining company, was killed next day when he ventured into No Man's Land looking for Becher.

The *Advertiser*, 20 October, reported:

'A thrill of pride must surge through the hearts of all in the county when it is realised that it was the intrepid Territorials from this district who, in face of a withering fire from machine guns, doggedly fought their way to the front the Germans thought impregnable and, at the point of the bayonet, ousted the enemy from its lair.'

What the report did not reveal was that the Sherwoods had to charge across 300 yards of open countryside at the start of the action, giving the German machine gunners clear sight of a massed target – partially illuminated by the light on Becher's back. Such unimaginable bravery and self-sacrifice was commonplace in this unprecedented conflict.

The *Morning Post* reported:

'The history of our capture of this formidable position, which incidentally breaks up the enemy's line and opens a way to Haisnes, Douvrin and so round La Bassée to the south and east, is one of pure and simple heroism, unsurpassed in the story of the British Army. At no period and in no corner of any battle in which our men have ever been engaged has the demand upon individual courage been greater or more nobly responded to.'

Corporal Arthur Sam Kettle, twenty-six, a tinsmith pre-war, was one of the bomb throwers who survived the 300-yard charge. Allowed home to Newark to recover, he conceded that they had 'a very stiff job' turning the Germans out of a trench in which they were securely set with machine guns, trained onto the advancing British soldiers. He insisted the Newark Terriers lost 'a comparative few killed' but conceded 'a good number' were wounded or gassed. Among the dead was Lance Corporal Bernard Vick, nineteen, a novice monk in the Society of the Sacred Mission at Kelham, just outside Newark, before he became a bomb thrower.

Charlotte Lowe, struggling to bring-up children aged eight and two in one of Newark's infamously unhealthy 'yards', lost her husband, Lance Corporal Frederick James Lowe, twenty-nine, a moulder at Ransome's. First she was told he had been wounded but it was hoped he would recover. Then she heard he had lost his left arm. Six weeks later she was officially informed that he passed away four days after being hit. Charlotte went on to give birth to a third child in April 1916 and suffer a triple tragedy in 1926. Her second husband died; her eldest child was killed in a railway accident on the Northgate sidings; and a new born baby died 24 hours later.

Lance Sergeant Thomas Turgoose probably knew not how he survived. He suffered seventeen wounds in his legs and neck that required hospital treatment in England – but only after he helped organise the defence of the Redoubt so effectively that he earned a Distinguished Conduct Medal 'for conspicuous gallantry and devotion to duty in holding for 24-hours the right barricade [at Hulloch], which was under continuous rifle and bombing attacks, in which he showed marked courage and determination.' Amazingly, this happened some years after he was invalided out of the Lincolns with rheumatic fever. He went to work for Ransome's and regained his strength by playing football for them in the local league. In 1914 he was fit enough to join the 1/8th Sherwoods. Though his Hohenzollern wounds terminated his active service, he was promoted to sergeant and took inspirational roles in the recruiting offices in Newark and Nottingham before being moved to a clerk's role in the Lichfield Records Office. After the war he returned to Ransome & Marles, which grew into one of the world's foremost ball-bearing manufacturers, and eventually became Mayor's Officer and Town Hall Keeper for twenty-five years. He died on 19 June 1952.

Much-wounded, bemedalled Thomas Turgoose...
[Photograph reproduced by kind permission of Rupert Vinnicombe]

...and opposite the thanks he received, with his townsmen.
[Diploma reproduced by kind permission of Rupert Vinnicombe]

Corporal Albert Eason, 24, was shot in the head and lost his left eye. His parents Seth, a farmer and carting contractor and Eliza, who had lost three of their eight children to natural causes, found him 'in the best of spirits and as well as can be expected' in a Manchester hospital.

Insurance agent Frank Kirkby and his wife Sarah Elizabeth got a letter from their son, George Henry, on 14 October: 'I have been under one operation, when the doctors had to take a piece of bone off my brain. It was a success'. Private George, 26, an iron turner pre-war, was in hospital in Camiers, 'laid low' by German shrapnel. 'I have had the best medical skill Canada can produce.' He lived until 1947.

BOROUGH of NEWARK

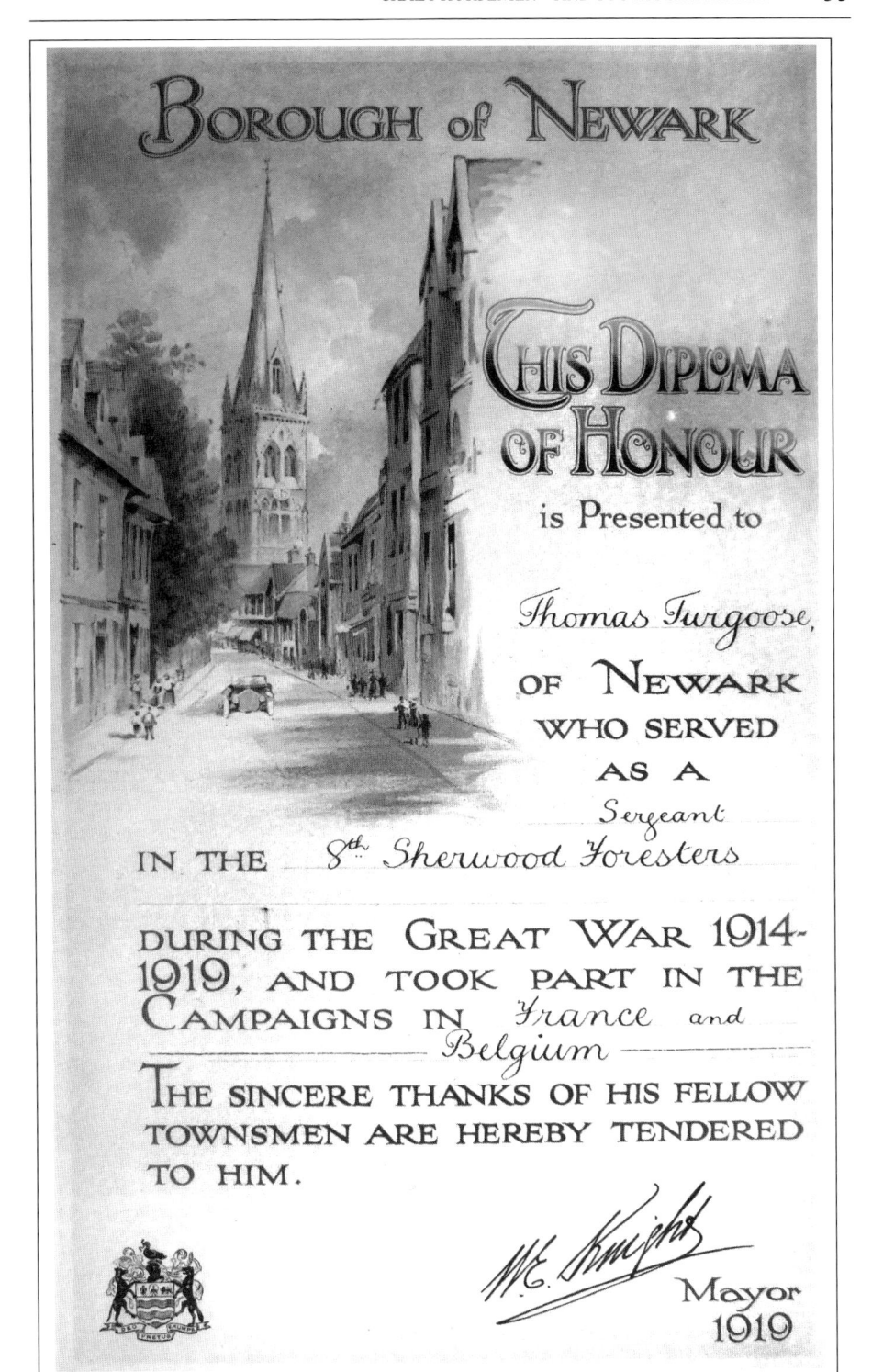

This Diploma of Honour

is Presented to

Thomas Turgoose, OF NEWARK WHO SERVED AS A *Sergeant* IN THE *8th Sherwood Foresters*

DURING THE GREAT WAR 1914-1919, AND TOOK PART IN THE CAMPAIGNS IN *France and Belgium*

THE SINCERE THANKS OF HIS FELLOW TOWNSMEN ARE HEREBY TENDERED TO HIM.

W.E. Knight
Mayor
1919

It was 29 October before blacksmith Charles Lawrence and his wife Emma received a letter from their nineteen-year-old son Charles Sydney – proof that he was not killed, as previously reported. He suffered a cut face and had his eyes 'filled with sand and powder' by a shell burst but he was recovering so well at the No. 6 Base Hospital in Rouen that he looked forward to more action. He lived to the age of 85.

Corporal William Gilbert Moore, twenty-three, one of nine children of a family living on Farndon Road, was recommended for a Distinguished Conduct Medal by Major-General E Stuart-Wortley, General Officer Commanding the 46th Division:

> 'When one of a small party in West Face, after a retirement had begun, he remained on the German side of the barricades alone for threequarters of an hour holding the trench before getting help, after which he continued to bomb the enemy for eight hours.'

Major-General Stuart-Wortley lost no time in turning the heroism into a recruiting drive, writing home: 'I trust that their example may arouse enthusiasm … and that the result of their gallant efforts may be to bring every able-bodied man into the ranks.'

The *Advertiser* printed a more humble appeal from Lance Corporal James Edward Munton, a general labourer, fish fryer and member of the St John Ambulance Service before joining the 2nd Sherwoods:

> 'We need more men urgently out here to face the great struggle which is before us. We want some Newark chaps to fill up the gaps. You know the Newark boys are good fighters and there's a chance out here for them to show their pluck. We all like to see Newark faces; it cheers us up, in fact, nearly as much as coming home. We are having some lively times round here and the Germans do not like the 'Sherwoods' as they know we are too good for them. When the war is over and we all get home, that will be the time when they [the stay-at-homes] will wish they had done their little bit.'

James Edward Munton would not get home: his death was reported on 5 November 1916.

Alfred Doncaster, 'somewhere in Belgium' with the Canadian contingent, wrote to mum Annie in Appletongate from a trench within 300 yards of the Germans: 'The Germans are shelling a village quite close to us … It is quite heart-rending to see some of the scenes … girls of twelve or thirteen years of age with their parents killed and the place they called home shelled day after day. Yet the poor beggars won't move. It's only hearth and home on fire that fetches them out.'

The stiff upper lips at home trembled with pride, among other emotions … Vicar Paton Hindley proclaimed from his pulpit on 24 October:

> 'While we deplore the losses to the 8th Battalion of the Sherwood Foresters and the other battalions of the great North Midlands Division, we thank God for the splendid spirit which has been displayed by officers and men worthy of the best traditions of the English Army.'

Bricklayer James Robinson in William Street, who lost his wife Ann in March, learnt that his youngest son had been killed on 29 October. Sapper Albert E Robinson, thirty-five, left a widow and three young children.

There was much subdued emotion two days later at Newark County Magistrates' Court when a letter was read from the gallant Major Becher, thanking them for their congratulations on his being awarded the DSO. It was, of course, written before he was dangerously wounded.

The King inspected heroes of the Hohenzollern Redoubt at Hesdigneul the following day; it rained, but his thanks were undiluted.

A memorial service in Newark Parish Church on 2 November was all the more impressive for the message delivered by the 8th Sherwoods' chaplain, the Reverend Hales, from the chancel steps. Having returned from the Front only a short time earlier, he told the packed congregation:

'We have known that you were praying for us. And we have been strengthened again and again and again and again – sometimes on the parade ground, sometimes with half-a-dozen men around the camp fire, sometimes in the hospital as we did the other night after the attack with forty or fifty men in the ward with perhaps two candles burning – we have known that you are supporting us by your prayers. It may seem that this is a sad service but the message I have for you is just this … It is all light and not dark. It is all life and not death. I have just come back and it is my privilege to speak these few words to you. It is a message of comfort that I have got to give you that when the Dayspring from on high hath visited us He giveth light to them that sit in darkness and in the shadow of death. He guides our feet, even in sorrow, in the way of peace. If I had never believed in the Resurrection before I went out, what I have since seen and learnt would have convinced me of it. It is all life and as we lay them together, one by one – and sometimes many at a time – it always seemed to me that it is life; just life. Sometimes I have hardly heard my own voice for the noise of the guns and yet nothing has ever put out that light, even in the dark. Nothing has yet silenced the wonderful message of hope and life which is given us in the last service which we say for our loved ones, who love God as our refuge and strength. We know that he has supported us in strength, and now that in His keeping they are alive. They have just got promoted to a higher job. When I have seen the great sacrifices our men make, I can only thank God that the sacrifice is accepted by the God of Love. Their sacrifices – with all their imperfections – I do not say they are perfect – are received into His keeping and perfected until at last "They serve Him as they ought".

'I wonder how many of you who saw us go out from Newark on that morning [10 August 1914] have any idea how few there are, comparatively speaking, of the officers and men who still remain. Two officers are at present here on leave and there is one still out there. The proportion of men who remain is about the same … I will not individualise – my greatest friends are not merely officers but some of my best friends are among the non-commissioned officers and men of other ranks – and I know they have all done their best. But there is one I must speak of. Only one. You who have got loved ones out there – or have had – have much to thank God for that the men have been under the influence of Herbert Fowler, and have been helped and strengthened by his example ... Every man who had the privilege of serving under him is a better man and thanks God for such a leadership.

'For those who are to carry on the work I know you will especially pray that they may have the courage to endure, and for the mourners I would especially say ... "I believe in the resurrection of the body, and I also believe in the Communion of Saints." What a wonderful message this is to us today: we on this side; they who have served and honoured the King of Kings have gone on to see his face. We can only try to seek for it, learn to serve and find the strength to endure ... Go back to your homes – it may be to great suffering – but go back knowing that God is giving you light and giving you strength and keeping them safe.'

Days later, Samuel Whitten, 25, a whitesmith who helped Bradley's football team win the Hospital Cup a couple of winters earlier, wrote to mum Emily Louisa and dad Samuel, a maltster's labourer, in Cross Street: 'I've got shrapnel in the leg. A bullet went clean through the calf'. A sapper in the REs, he recovered to earn a Military Medal for repairing communication lines under fire before being discharged as 'unfit for service' in May 1918.

Gardener Thomas William Rains George and his wife of forty-four years Mary discovered a fortnight before Christmas that the meekest of their nine children had been killed on 25 September. The news came to their son's wife, Eliza Annie, from a Middlesex Regiment sergeant who had picked up a pay book and photographs from beside the body of a dead corporal of The Queen's (Royal West Surrey) Regiment. They belonged to Arthur William George, thirty-four, a gentleman's butler before he volunteered.

Four days before Christmas, Private Cyril Bennett Copley, a maltster's clerk, was officially reported missing, believed killed on 18 November. Aged twenty-four and the son of the former manager of the Singer Sewing Machine Company's Newark branch, he joined the Sherwoods, and was transferred to the Warwickshires after arriving in France. On 28 December, his family's Christmas wish came true: Cyril was not dead but a prisoner in hospital in Germany with a wounded leg. He recovered to live to be sixty-eight.

Almost inevitably, Newark suffered a killing on Christmas Day. And, as if to further tense the heartstrings, he was an orphan aged twenty. George Walter Martin, reared from the age of twelve by his aunt Gertrude and uncle John Henry Martin on Northgate, volunteered in 1914 but was rejected. He tried again in 1915 and was accepted in the Lincolnshire Regiment. He had been in France for a year before his best mate in the Machine Gun Corps, Lance Corporal Wilfred Gelsthorpe, another Newarker, wrote to Aunt Gertrude:

'I am sorry to say the news I have is not good. I come from Newark, the same as your boy, so I thought it best that I write to you and let you know that he met his death on Christmas afternoon. It is not a job that I like, but I know you would get to know sooner or later, so thought it best to write. I feel very sorry for you and

CRAZY HORSEMEN – AND TOO MUCH BRAVERY

all at home. Your boy and I left Grimsby [training camp] together and we were great friends. It was your boy's wish for me to write if anything happened to him. I was first on the spot when he fell and I will tell you more when I come home and see you.'

Wilfred Gelsthorpe, twenty-two, was killed on 11 April 1917.

Christmas 1915 was dreadful, too, for Mary Ellen Gregg. Her sweetheart, Sydney Hunt, twenty-two, was killed by a shell on 17 December. On 31 December, she went to his memorial service in Albert Street Baptist Church, where he had been Sunday School teacher before enlisting in the Royal Field Artillery in January 1916. He was transferred to the Royal Horse Artillery, went to France on 13 July, 1915 and died in the Somme village of Mailly-Maillet.

Major Becher's battle for life ended at Abbeville Hospital, France, on New Year's Day 1916. His wife Veronica and widowed mother Alice attended his funeral in Abbeville Communal Cemetery on 4 January. Simultaneously, Southwell Minster was filled for a memorial service. Among the mourners were fifty wounded men who had served under Major Becher.

After the troop service in Newark Parish Church on 4 June 1916, there was 'a splendid ceremony' in the Market Place. The Distinguished Conduct Medal was presented to RE Sapper G H Johnson:

'On 8 October, at the counter-attack after the Battle of Loos, 63212 Sapper G H Johnson was one of a party of five who, under fire, succeeded in cutting the barbed wire entanglements and enabled the troops to attack the enemy. The officer in charge was wounded and Johnson, although still under fire from the Germans, assisted him to return to safety.' Johnson was also wounded yet 'persisted in an attempt to cut the German wires in front of their trenches in the Laventie area'.

Viscount French's last despatch as Commander in Chief in France (published on 21 August 1916), conceded that the Hohenzollern Redoubt attack failed: 'The whole attack died down without attaining the objective aimed at, and the situation in that part of the line remained much the same throughout the period covered by the present despatch (15 October to 19 December 1915).'

Defiance glowed, though. Newark Corporation lamplighter Sam Bowers, thirty-five, wrote to his wife Sarah, rearing their children aged six and four in Victoria Gardens, so

The battlefield at Loos with the distinctive twin towers of the coal workings, called 'Tower Bridge' by the British troops.

primitive that the locals called it Botany Bay:

> 'From the bottom of my heart, I say, whether rich or poor, no man ought to want enticing to enlist because an Englishman should say, "My place is at the Front along with my comrades" instead of loitering about with a halfpenny cane and about two keys and a penny in his pocket.'

Sarah had already lost her brother, Private Levi Sibcy, on 15 January 1915: only sixteen, he had managed to join the 2/8th Sherwoods in training but he died of pneumonia. Sarah's younger sister Mary Ann was widowed: her husband, Private Edward Harry Mutton, 23, of the 1/8th Sherwoods was killed by a sniper in France. And ultra-patriotic Private Sam Bowers himself would be wounded with the York and Lancashire Regiment in 1916 (but recover and live to 1940).

Patriotism seemed to have faded since early in 1915 when Nicholson's engineering works reported that forty-three employees had joined the Colours and emphasised others would have followed had they not been on 'urgent Government work'. Of Newark Rowing Club's ninety-five members, twenty-eight enlisted.

With the Trent flooding West Newark in January, one of Britain's most famous officers, Major General Sir Reginald Pole-Carew, poured high praise on the new volunteers in the Reserve Battalion of the 8th Sherwoods after a drill and inspection. He was 'astonished to see what good progress has been made in so short a time ... If you continue to improve as you have begun, in a very short while you will be able to hold your own against any battalion in England.' As he spoke, the Bishop of Southwell arrived in a horse-drawn milk float to conduct a service for 1,000 servicemen in Newark Parish Church after his car was marooned in floods.

Sir John McCraith, chairman of Nottingham Watch Committee, warned Newark would be inundated by refugees 'in the event of invasion'. He explained:

> 'The population of Lincolnshire have been ordered to come into Nottingham. Certain roads have been barred to them which the military will want to use. So our duty may be – and although it may seem far away now, we must be prepared for it – to receive ten or twenty thousand or a hundred thousand Lincolnshire people for whom we will have to make provision. We must be prepared for this!'

A week later schools were commandeered by a thousand troops from Lincolnshire on manoeuvres in and around the town.

The mood darkened further when the Newark *Advertiser* listed 119 soldiers of A Company 2nd Battalion Sherwoods who were prisoners of war. Among them was Major William Harold Collier Davy, thirty-seven, brother of the head of the Devon Brewery, whose 'noted ales and stouts' were brewed in Barnbygate. A century later, the National Army Museum had among its artefacts 'Group of four medals: Queen's South Africa Medal 1899-1902; 1914 Star with clasp: 5th Aug - 22nd Nov 1914; British War Medal 1914-20; Allied Victory Medal 1914-19; awarded to Major W H C Davy, Duke of Cambridge's Own (Middlesex Regiment); associated with the Boer War (1899-1902) and World War One (1914-1918).'

The Mayoress's Working Party met a request for mittens and flannel shirts for the newest Sherwoods training at Newark Barracks: they had sent 400 men to the Front already and expected to be up to 2,000 again 'very shortly'. And sixty Newark men of the National Reserve guarding an eight-mile stretch of railway in Hampshire urgently begged for oilskin capes and leggings. All of this charity was being sought at a time when it was announced that, in the last twelve months, wheat had gone up 72%, flour 75%, sugar 72%, British meat 8%, foreign meat 12% and coal 15%, with wages pretty well frozen.

The first airborne attack on British soil – Zeppelins bombed Great Yarmouth and King's Lynn, killing five civilians, on 19 January – led to widow Mary Fitchett in Lime Grove receiving a letter from her daughter Betty, twenty-five, head of a King's Lynn school:

'We all feel so wibberly wobbley today and cannot settle to anything definite. Well, the old Germans and their bombs have arrived and gone, I hope never to return. Nobody feels like settling to another night's rest after last night. I had just gone to bed when on the stroke of 11 I heard the approach of what seemed at first to be a motor cycle...

'I sprang up in bed but it was not until one or two bright flashes had occurred that it dawned on me what might be taking place. Then after hearing explosions and collapse of buildings, there was no doubt that the Germans had really arrived. We had joked about it so often but when they did come it was far from a joke. I haven't done trembling yet and if I live to be 150 I shall not forget it. We made the best of our way downstairs but the bombs were falling quite near and we expected the place to go any time, and doors and windows were rattling away as fast as they could go. The thing must have circled round us two or three times. It seemed endless and even when we heard it going away, we were not relieved...

'Of course, the town was plunged in entire darkness as soon as the danger was upon us but that precaution should have been taken before. There were people in Lynn who knew the airships were over Yarmouth at 8.30. The special constables were called out by the fire alarm after the airship had gone, but no attempt at firing was made at the time. The thing went on its own way unhindered...

'The sights are dreadful: streets and streets of houses with every window smashed. My school had three windows smashed, and the explosion was some distance from there ... I suppose we must prepare for a bombardment next and if that starts I shall surely flee, for the worry is too awful ... The streets are in entire darkness tonight; I am writing this by candle light... I hope you are prepared at Newark!'

Within two days the Newark Emergency Committee was set up 'to deal with any invasion'. It hurriedly arranged to receive telephone and telegram warnings from other towns of imminent air attacks. The townspeople would be alerted by the Fire Bell being clanged at intervals of half-a-minute. The Gas Company would cut off supplies within five minutes. Audiences at 'houses of entertainment' should make their way quietly and without panic to their homes. The public were warned against congregating in the streets which, in night time, would be in darkness. Special Constables would assemble at 'key points'.

Death almost arrived on a pitch-black Monday night, 8 February. Sapper Albert

Tolworthy, eighteen, from Ealing in London, dived into the Trent to rescue a fellow Royal Engineer trainee who could not swim but was knocked into the swift current while dismantling a pontoon bridge. Tolworthy went in fully clothed and saved him, then had to run three miles back to his quarters in dripping clothes. To emphasise the dangers, seven REs were drowned in a similar accident downstream at Gainsborough eleven days later. With more REs arriving, extra huts were erected around a treasured Civil War relic, the Sconce Hills. The War Office agreed a monthly rent of £2 1s 8d but the huts proved to be inadequate – 1,200 trainees were crammed under canvas intended for 600 – so half the schools were taken over as billets in September 1915, meaning children would have part-time education for the rest of the war.

Private William Warriner, proud to have been 'born and bred in the good old Botany Bay', wrote cheerfully about life in the trenches with the Royal Scots Fusiliers:

'I have got frost-bitten feet but we have to stick it out until we fall down ... If the Allies have a victory we forget about our sore feet and jump and shout with joy ... I have had two narrow escapes from snipers' rifle fire, and a Lance-Corporal in the Section next to us in the firing line put his valise on the top of the parapet; a sniper's bullet went through it, a tin box and a match box and lodged in a second box of matches. He now carries it about with him as a souvenir. We get some very dirty work out here. Sometimes we are sitting up to the knees in water and slush all day and night long when we are in the trenches. It's awful in some places. I think this letter will get through [the censors] as I have only put the bright side of things in it.'

A week later, the *Advertiser* carried a picture of Warriner, thirty, a father of two. It was captioned: 'Killed in Action'. He died on the day his letter arrived, 10 February 1915.

Bizarrely amid invasion fears, the 'arrest' of a large prize American steamship suspected of carrying foodstuffs to Germany gave its radio operator, Rex Merry of New York, a chance to visit his auntie in late March. While the ship was anchored at Hull, Rex hopped on a train to Nora Merry, thirty-one, a milliner in the Arcade, Newark's undercover shopping lane. He was 'rather surprised to find the war has made so little difference to the Mother Country. There is a great dislocation of trade in the States.' Little difference? His memory must have played tricks!

Even odder, Trooper Frederick Cox, oldest of seven children of a Newark cattle dealer, was shot while training with the Sherwood Rangers Reserve Regiment in Retford. Police traced the gunman: Henry Roberts Dodman, forty-five, manager of the Corporation Baths, who was aiming at a bird in his garden. While Cox recovered from thigh wounds, Dodman continued working ... as an instructor of the Volunteer Force on Retford's Miniature Rifle Range!

The Newark Legion of Volunteers went on anti-invasion manoeuvres on 5 April. One section defended the town while the other section attacked from the east. The attackers would have won but for the signallers of the defence, stationed on each of the Great Northern railway bridges, who summoned-up reinforcements. The umpires, Commandants Ringrose and Wright, declared a draw: hardly confidence-building. Two days later, more precautions were introduced against Zeppelin raids. Gas lights on streets and bridges were switched off or shaded and a general 'black-out' of windows introduced. Underlining the need for discipline, William Ward Gardener, licensee of the Wheatsheaf Inn, Slaughterhouse Lane, was fined £2 at the Newark Court for supplying two soldiers with intoxicating liquor at 10.15am on a Saturday.

Simultaneously came a reminder that unrest was spreading worldwide. Old Magnusian Cyril Foster, twenty-three, in business at Kuala Lumpur, wrote to his parents that he had completed a month's musketry training with the Singapore Rifles Volunteers and left the day before a riot broke out in which thirty-five Britons were killed. Cyril went to work each day in khaki and armed. He had to be on parade at 5.30am and after business in the evenings; a far cry from his early working experiences as the delivery lad in his Dad's grocery shop.

Back home, half a dozen 'Jolly Boys' of the 2/8th Sherwoods posed in the *Advertiser* on 14 April with a day's rations at their training camp: a leg of mutton, bread, bag of peas, jam and cheese (they had eaten the bacon). Surely this whetted shirkers' appetites!

Training – never mind marching – on their stomachs ... Jolly boys of the Sherwoods with Luton rations.
[Advertiser cutting]

Lost at sea ... Stoker Samuel Asman...
[Advertiser cutting]

...Newark's acknowledgement of his sacrifice...
[NEKMS 2005.22.1.2]

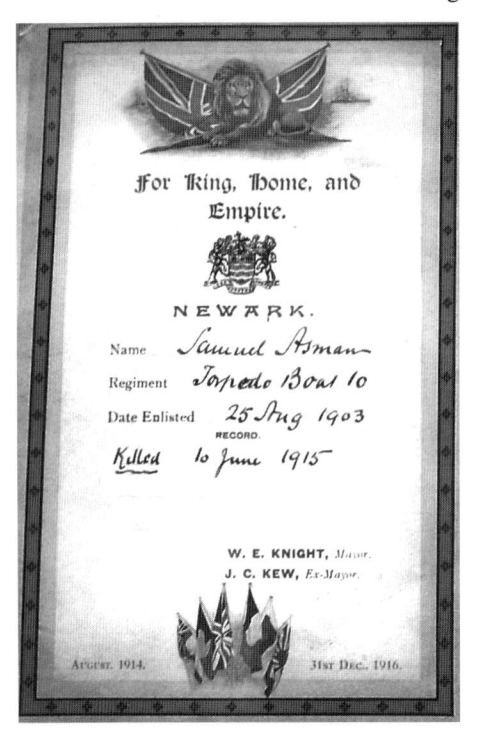

For King, Home, and Empire.

NEWARK.

Name: Samuel Asman
Regiment: Torpedo Boat 10
Date Enlisted: 25 Aug 1903
Killed: 10 June 1915

W. E. KNIGHT, *Mayor.*
J. C. KEW, *Ex-Mayor.*

August 1914.   31st Dec. 1916.

The boys were H S Moran, S Scott, C Layhe, J T Bellamy, H Groves and J Asman. Private Joseph Asman had a tragic war. His brother, Stoker Samuel Asman, was lost in the sinking of Torpedo Boat *11* in June 1915. Joe was discharged in 1917 after being wounded twice and losing his right eye; and died of pneumonia in October 1918, leaving a three-week-old baby orphaned.

Responding to Britain's need to modernise, Newark's biggest employer, Ransome's, primarily engineers in wood, announced they were building a new workshop to meet the unprecedented demand for ball bearings 'not only for motor cars, but for all machines which have to run at a high rate of speed'. Most of their ball bearings in the First World War went into aircraft.

When the British liner *Lusitania* was torpedoed by a German U-boat and sank in the Atlantic on 7 May with the loss of 1,201 lives, 159 of them Americans, it created a diplomatic crisis between the USA and Germany – and an incredulous escape for non-swimmer Miss Queenie Benjamin, thirty, daughter of the licensee of the Cross Keys, London Road. She recollected:

'I had just gone to my cabin when the boat was struck. I heard a terrible commotion and ran up on deck, and went to the high side of the vessel. When the order was given we all got into the boats, and somebody yelled to cut the boats away. It was a good job this was not done or the wooden boats would have dropped thirty feet into the water and we would all have been smashed up. The vessel seemed to be floating all right and we all got out of the lifeboat again. No doubt she would have been all right, but then another torpedo struck us. In a second I scrambled back into the lifeboat and others came on the top of me. In a very little while the vessel went down with the lifeboat fastened to it. I went down in the lifeboat with somebody holding me down and I wondered if I should be drowned. Yet presently I came to the top of the water. Chairs and trunks and all manner of things had been thrown overboard and I clung to something which kept me afloat. I could see a boat but between us were numerous

RMS *Lusitania*, escorted by tugs on her way out of New York Harbour.

> packing cases, trunks and things floating. I shouted to a man in the boat, "Do you mind picking me up? I can't swim." He replied, "Hold on, girlie, you're not dead yet!" Eventually they got to me and pulled me into the boat. The American in the boat said, "You are a brick. Can't you swim?" I said I could not and he replied, "You're more than lucky" and I really I think I was.'

After two hours, they were picked up by a fishing smack and landed at Queenstown at 11pm. It took her another three hours to find a hotel room.

Old Magnusian Bertrand Hayes, eighteen, wrote on 17 May to his parents George and Clara about a Zeppelin raid on Ramsgate:

> 'My word, what an exciting time we have had! We heard a tremendous roar out to sea and a heavy gun firing at about 7pm on Sunday. I was just returning from the post and saw a very fast cruiser steaming north at a tremendous pace. It was firing incessantly. Far beyond it in the mist was the cigar-shaped form of a Zeppelin. After about half an hour's chase the cruiser drove the airship back, but we were soon to know that it had not gone for good. About midnight we were aroused by gunfire from the straits and about 2.15am this was joined by the rattle of the small guns of the patrol boats, some of which were in and others just outside Ramsgate harbour. Then about five minutes later terrific explosions were heard and we then knew that airships had arrived and were bombarding Ramsgate. Just then our telephone bell rang and the commander of the Marconi station, about 100 yards from the school, warned us that one was coming our way. We hurried out to the dug-out in the grounds. It appears that there were two Zepps over Ramsgate. One went south to Dover and the other north to Margate. Only a few minutes elapsed before the roar of the engines told us she was near. She passed

right over us and the Marconi station and the lighthouse but, strange to say, dropped no bombs. We looked out and could see her with lights in her cars (of which there are two) all twinkling like stars. I heard that a good deal of damage had been done at Margate Twenty bombs were dropped in Ramsgate but fourteen failed to explode. One hotel, the Bull and George, was practically reduced to dust.'

Willow merchant Horace Mills and his wife Marion, of Rushcliffe, Farndon Road, Newark, received a telegram on Thursday morning, 27 May: one of their daughters, Mrs Florence Smith, 25, was critically injured in a Zeppelin raid over Southend the previous night. Her husband Frank, who worked in Southend Corporation Surveyor's Department, thought danger had passed after the first bomb dropped, and opened their front door. Another bomb landed on the street – and Flo, standing at her husband's shoulder, was struck by flying fragments of iron and stone. One penetrated her chest and lung. Her parents rushed to her hospital bedside but she died on 15 June. A huge crowd mourned at her funeral in Newark Cemetery on the following Saturday. The floral tributes were headed by a wreath from Frank and their baby daughter Mary, who would never know her mother.

A stark reminder of Newark's ill-health shook the town on 3 June. Private John William Shaw, forty-four, of the 3rd Lincolns was allowed home to Lindum Street to tend his five children after his wife Louise, forty-two, fell seriously ill. Louise recovered; John caught double pneumonia and died. Louise struggled to cope and on 29 November was sent to prison for two months, with hard labour, by Newark Magistrates for neglecting her children. The War Office agreed to pay the NSPCC 27 shillings a week to keep the youngsters.

The financial cost of the War came to the fore in July. Newark Town Council agreed to invest £3,000 in 4½% war loans. At a meeting to launch a War Savings campaign throughout the town, the Mayor explained that the War was costing £2,083 a minute. 'It is vital that we all accept thrift is a small price to pay when compared with the sacrifices of the men at the Front.' Committees were formed to target works, schools and women.

The first hint of a dispute among the town's hierarchy emerged at Newark Court on 15 July when the licensee of the Exchange Hotel, Carl Parkin, was charged under the Defence of the Realm Act with serving intoxicants to three RE corporals after 9pm. One of the most venerable magistrates, Joseph Gilstrap Branston, 77, condemned the case as 'a persecution not a prosecution'. Chief Constable Wright responded: 'I consider I used sufficient discretion, sir.' The other magistrates – Mayor Kew, Colonel Nicholson and plumber John Hind – agreed with him. Parkin was fined five shillings.

Police Chief Wright was busy. When not training Special Constables sworn in to replace full-timers going into the Forces, running his depleted organisation and acting as prosecutor of cases at Magistrates' Courts, he was also second-in-command of the Newark Volunteer Reserve, 100 strong and the only Company of its kind in Nottinghamshire drilling with arms. The men had begged and borrowed shotguns, obsolete rifles and carbines. They took over guard duties on railways, at munitions works and of RE stores and equipment from younger men, who were thus released for war service.

The local MP, Captain John Ralph Starkey responded to income tax rising from 9d to 1s 9½d in the £– all with annual incomes over £130 would be taxed – by returning the £400 salary he had received since the War began, asking for the money to go to the war effort. He added: 'I am convinced that in this supreme crisis some real sacrifice in the interest of thrift and economy is demanded from every member of the community, and Parliament should at once give a lead.'

Lord Derby, Director-General of Recruiting, announced on 16 October a programme, often called the Derby Scheme although its official title was the Group Scheme, for raising the numbers in the Forces. Men aged eighteen to forty could continue to enlist voluntarily or attest with an obligation to join if called up later on. Voluntary enlistment was ending; the last day of registration would be 15 December. Newark responded on 20 October by amalgamating the Mayor's Recruiting Committee, which had concentrated on the town, and the Newark Parliamentary Recruiting Committee, which had also covered the surrounding villages, to organise a canvass of eligible men, warning: 'This is the final effort to make the voluntary system supply the men needed for our fighting forces. The only alternative is conscription.'

'The King's Message to the Nation – a moving personal appeal', complete with his signature appeared in the Newark newspapers:

'To my people. At this grave moment in the struggle between my people and a highly organised enemy who has transgressed the Laws of Nations and changed the ordinance that binds civilised Europe together, I appeal to you. I rejoice in my Empire's effort, and I feel pride in the voluntary response from my Subjects all over the world who have sacrificed home, fortune

King George V.

and life itself in order that another may not inherit the free Empire which their ancestors and mine have built. I ask you to make good these sacrifices. The end is not in sight. More men and yet more are wanted to keep my Armies in the Field, and through them to secure Victory and enduring Peace. In ancient days the darkest moment has ever produced in men of our race the sternest resolve. I ask you, men of all classes, to come forward voluntarily and take your share in the fight. In freely responding to my appeal, you will be giving your support to our brothers, who for long months have nobly upheld Britain's past traditions and the glory of her Arms.'

(signed) George R.

There was more than a hint of controversy when the MP for Wakefield, Arthur H Marshall, gave addresses – which some felt inspiring and others condemned as insulting – to munitions workers at Ransome's, Abbott's, Bradley's and Farrar's. He was quoted as saying they were doing a more valuable job than even the men at the Front; they must strain every effort to ensure maximum output. This was music to the ears of the single men being criticised as shirkers for not enlisting.

Yet there were already so many men in Army training, barracks were inadequate. On 19 October, the Newark Board of Guardians offered to accommodate fifty-three inmates from Gainsborough Workhouse, which had been taken over by the military, 'subject to the net cost being paid for their maintenance and to the necessary adjustment of staff'. The Board received a similar request from Retford and replied that it would be happy to help. Within a week, Newark had to rescind its offers: the Local Government Board had approved military occupation of the west wing of Newark Workhouse. Soon, Royal Engineers occupied all of Newark Workhouse; the inhabitants were found shelter at Derby.

At the same time, Newark Trades Council campaigned against 'rapacious property owners' increasing rents which families could not afford. They gave three examples: a widow with three sons in the Army facing a 3d per week increase; a wife with two children, husband in France, 8d increase; a wife with nine children (all under 14), husband wounded in France, 6d increase.

Voluntary fund raising in Newark in the first year of war amounted to £2,182 19s 4d for the Prince of Wales's Fund, £926 14s 8½d for the Local Belgian Relief Fund, £288 8s 1d for the Mayoress's Working Party and £52 5s 4d for the relief of Belgians in Belgium – 'magnificent generosity' said the auditor, Thomas Harrison, the Corporation accountant. But more was needed. Annie Kew, showing no sign of resting after her stint as Mayoress, wrote to the local papers: 'Captain Davenport [of the 8th Sherwoods] has asked me if I can procure him twenty-five woollen sweaters of any colour for his men who have to drive the transport to the firing line these winter nights in all sorts of weather ... It occurs to me that there are tennis, cricket and golf players, rowing men and others who will be glad to spare their sweaters...'

Her husband was succeeded as Mayor in November by Alderman William Edward Knight, seventy, the 'father' of the Council, a devout Methodist who was an agricultural merchant – and remained in office for the duration of the War, handing £5 cheques from

Mayor William Edward Knight … and his wife Hannah, who died in 1918.
[Advertiser cutting]

his personal account to every Newark man who received a gallantry medal from him. He established his priorities immediately after the traditional Mayor-making ceremony on 14 November: instead of giving refreshments to the VIPs in the Town Hall, as was tradition, he donated £10 to the Parish Church Reparation Fund, £10 to the Newark Company of the Volunteer Training Corps, £10 to the Mayoress's Working Party; £5 to the local YMCA, £5 to Newark Hospital, £5 to the Lombard Street Red Cross Hospital, £5 to the Sherwood Rangers Yeomanry Comforts Fund and £5 to the 8th Sherwood Foresters Fund. He hoped the money might 'relieve some of the suffering and discomforts of the War'.

As more and more of Newark's grand buildings were taken over by the Army in general and the REs in particular, Victoria Cross recipient Frederick Henry Johnson was feted in late November at Northgate House, his temporary billet. The diminutive Londoner, a second lieutenant with the 73rd Field Company, won the highest bravery honour in the attack on Hill 70, near Loos, on 25 September. Despite leg wounds, he stuck to his duty, led several charges on the German redoubt, and at a very critical time, under very heavy fire, repeatedly rallied the men who were near him.

'By his splendid example and cool courage he was mainly instrumental in saving the situation and in establishing firmly his part of the position which had been taken. He remained at his post until relieved in the evening.'

Second Lieutenant Sydney Carlin received his Distinguished Conduct Medal for 'conspicuous gallantry' on 18 May 1915 at Ypres after the RE's church parade in Newark Market Place on 28 November.

'Under heavy shell fire, although severely wounded, he refused to leave the firing line and kept the troops together in a very exposed position. With the trenches on both sides demolished, and after all his seniors had been killed, he gave a true example of courage and devotion to duty.'

This was but the start of the Yorkshireman's heroics. He lost a leg in action in 1916, insisted on fighting on with a wooden leg, earning him the nickname 'Timbertoes'; joined the Royal Flying Corps and became first a pilot and then an instructor. After the Great War, he went farming in Kenya but returned in 1939, joined the RAF, became a gunner in Wellington bombers and lost his life in anti-climactic circumstances when his unit's base at Wittering, Cambridgeshire, was bombed on 9 May 1941.

Josef Tailliez, the first Belgian refugee to be housed in Crown Street (and who taught English in Newark), wrote to Annie Kew from his Hampstead abode having taken a job in London:

'Dear Mistress Mayoress – I cannot find words enough to thank you and the ladies of the committee, and also Mister Mayor for all that you have done for us ... When I remember me the first day we came to Newark, I have a sort of contentment because I could remark that every person there present did all that was possible to make us happy. Never we saw such a kindness, such a sacrifice to help the fugitives, who would not live under German rules. Not only that day, but all the time we were at Newark we saw the same kindness and sacrifice, and that was the reason why we forgot that we were refugees. We regretted that we must leave that nice little Newark and the English friends we made there. Never we shall forget the so praised English hospitality. We hope to come back for holidays as soon as possible.'

Newark Town Hall could have burnt down on the night of 25-26 November. A lighted cigarette dropped through a radiator grating during the weekly whist drive to raise money for war efforts and smouldered among the accumulated fluff and dust. Hall-keeper (and market superintendent) Dennis Gabbitas Peet was startled to see flames darting up one side of the ballroom next morning. He rushed for buckets of water from the kitchen, simultaneously calling to his son Dennis Joseph, fourteen, to run for Fire Brigade Captain Harrison. It was 'due in a great measure to the promptitude and energy of these two men' that more serious damage was not done. That said, in probing for the seat of the fire, Harrison almost fell through the floor into the Butter Market below.

Another speedy job was carried out early in December. Six baths with hot and cold running water were provided for Royal Engineers in a Corporation-owned building in only four days. The lightning provision was helped by Nicholson's donating a boiler. There were 800 baths a week; and after the War the facility was made available to 'the working class of the neighbourhood'. More immediate improvements in living conditions were on the minds of the Newark Women's Thrift Committee: they invited American-born Alys Russell BA, secretary of St Pancras School for Mothers (and first wife of Bertrand Russell) to explain why saving youngsters was vital for the future health of the nation. As if to underline the importance of her campaigning, Olive Mary Gravell, eight, died a day later in Newark Isolation Hospital, attached to the Workhouse.

The slaughter of the innocents continued in the war, too ... Wicker chair-maker William Cliffe and his wife Fanny learnt of the death of their youngest, Cecil, twenty-three, from his best mate in the 8th Sherwoods. Private William Fields wrote that they were on sentry at dawn on 2 December. Cecil whispered: 'Look at them Germans carrying that wood' – and fell dead, shot by a sniper.

A Newark airman, Captain Henry Dalby Dryden Smith, twenty-three, was burned to death on 15 December when his plane crashed at Farnborough. He worked in the drawing office at Simpson's, where his father Henry was a director, before joining the 17th Durham Light Infantry and being transferred to the Royal Flying Corps.

Christmas gifts were practical ... The Newark Habitation sent sixty pairs of socks, nine scarves, nine pairs of pyjamas and fifty bandages to British wounded; fifteen pairs of socks to French wounded; fifteen pairs of mittens to the 2/8th Sherwoods; and twenty pairs of socks, ten scarves, twenty-eight pairs of mittens and eleven body belts to Lieutenant Colonel Henry Branston Warwick, thirty-nine, Commanding Officer of the 12th Northumberland Fusiliers, who had recovered from wounds received in the battle for Hill 70 at Loos to the relief of friends and relations in the Newark brewery business.

Mrs Ellen Cafferata, gypsum mining company matriarch, took over Newark Town Hall for a whist drive and raised the 'splendid sum' of £53 for wounded Russian soldiers in Petrograd ... Newark's REs were given a full-time Chaplain: the appropriately named Reverend A G Battle ... And more than 700 Christmas parcels went from the Mayor and Mayoress to Newark families with a man in the Forces, honouring a promise by Charles Kew when the 8th Sherwoods marched out of town: 'We will look after your families'. Each received ½lb tea, 1lb sugar, a plum cake and a packet of sweets ... Every wounded soldier in Lombard Street Red Cross Hospital awoke to a sock containing pipe, tobacco, cigarettes and Lett's Soldier's Diary provided by the medical staff ... Every wounded soldier in Newark General Hospital received a treat from under a tree from Captain and Mrs Walter Need.

There was even a hint that food was plentiful. Newark's Christmas Fat Stock Market sales totalled 192 beasts (one fewer than 1914) for £4,950; 183 sheep for £592 15s; and 105 pigs for £859 16s 6d. All that was missing from most families' Christmas table was the man of the house ... But they were not forgotten. All nineteen employees of Abbott's boiler works who were in the Forces received a box of comforts and letter: 'The directors and employees, mindful of those who have gone forth from their midst to serve actively in defence of King, of country and of humanity, ask your acceptance of the enclosed comforts as a small tribute of their warm-hearted admiration and affection. Although far away from your former associates, it will be some comfort for you to know that you are constantly in their thoughts. They know that in the difficult and dangerous tasks which lie in the performance of your duty, you will acquit yourself worthily, and they earnestly hope for your speedy and victorious return.'

One of Newark's best 1915 Christmas gifts arrived on 6 February 1916: the landlord of the Boar's Head, Middlegate, finally got word home that he had survived being torpedoed. Thomas Spray, forty, a sergeant in the Army Veterinary Corps, was in the water for four hours after the merchant ship *Ivernia* was struck on 27 December and thirty-six lives were lost. After three days on a hospital ship, he was taken to hospital in Alexandria with 'shock and immersion'. He recovered to appear in the 1918 Absent Voters' List.

More families took comfort that their menfolk were away from peril, at least temporarily: a few days before Christmas, the Allies evacuated 83,000 troops from Suvla Bay and ANZAC Cove in Gallipoli. Not one was killed. The Turkish, entrenched overlooking the beaches, remained unaware of the evacuation. It truly was a circus act of Houdini proportions. The prayer was for more magic in 1916…

Chapter Three

From Slapstick to the Somme

In true circus fashion, slapstick mingled with high wire dangers in 1916. While war spread from the Western Front to Dublin, Italy and the Middle East, and there were more sinkings at sea, those at home were increasingly under pressure to put patriotism before personal feelings, leave their safe jobs and join the fight. The bitterness generated was best illustrated when Newark Council considered in May whether to employ conscientious objectors. 'We could manage with one or two,' mused a councillor who was also a magistrate. 'Yes,' retorted a colleague, 'put them down the sewers.' Amid guffaws of laughter, the discussion ended; there was no place in Newark for 'shirkers'.

What Newark wanted was more boys like George Collett. He was not yet fifteen when he volunteered for the Warwickshire Regiment. But he stood 5ft 9in tall and found it easy to persuade the authorities he was nineteen and a half. He had completed his training and was in France before his father Joseph, a tailor and ex-Councillor, discovered that he had left his job in Birmingham (having given up a scholarship at the Magnus to do war work). Joseph asked the Army to send the boy home. George demurred. In March Joseph received a letter from the military authorities stating that George 'has been medically examined and found physically fit to bear the strain of active service and, as he has expressed the wish to remain with his unit in the Expeditionary Force, he is being retained.'

George wrote to Frances Hines, seventeen, daughter of a butcher:

> 'I think it is my duty to stop out here. I assure you that the wet, muddy trenches are no attraction – it is no delight to sit in two-foot of water all night long. Nevertheless, why are we all sticking it so? Supposing all us chaps were to give in? Then the Boches would get through. We have seen and heard what the Germans did to the peasants when they advanced in the early part of the War. And we know they would do their work just as well on the English civilians provided they got through and overran England. There are plenty of chaps not much older than me doing the same.'

Schoolboy hero George Collett ... 'my duty'.
[Advertiser cutting]

Private 3279 George William Collett perished in the Battle of the Somme on 18 July 1916, aged sixteen, and is remembered on the Thiepval Memorial among 72,192 British and South African troops with no known grave.

The number 72,192 – that was the equivalent of the populations of more than four Newarks being wiped-out. Add the losses on all Fronts, and it was obvious why conscription was introduced to maintain a regular flow of men to the Army – and equally obvious why men were no longer rushing to volunteer. So Tribunals set up under the Derby Scheme sat long into winter nights to determine who should, in effect, be given a possible death sentence. Its impact was perhaps best illustrated by Newark Council's budget for the year: police £83, weights and measures £15, education £261 – implementing the Registration Act £403.

No wonder the year 1916 in Newark started with an earthquake. It happened on Friday evening, 14 January. The walls of Councillor Redmond Barton Cafferata's properties on Beacon Hill shook for a couple of seconds around 7.30pm: extra spooky, as he was about to spy for his country. Antique dealer's wife, Eliza Ford, was startled when the table and chairs in her dining room begin to rock in Appletongate. And Workhouse Master Harrison's flower pots shook as he sat at his table in Bowbridge Road. So the tremors were felt all the way across town: nature's reminder that 'we're all in it together'.

The Workhouse Master had just disciplined a nurse [never named] for insubordination. She wanted to go out on a 'rough' night. He asked who she was meeting. 'The soldier boys,' she replied. He refused permission, 'treating her as I would my own daughter'. She still went out. The Guardians gave her the choice: resign or be dismissed for 'gross disobedience'. She wrote to the *Herald* that she was pleased to leave the oppressive place.

This was at a time when unity was demanded. Mayor Knight took to the pulpit of Barnbygate Wesleyan Church to announce the Mayoress's Working Party had a War Office request for 480 pairs of mittens and 100 mufflers, 30 bed jackets, 50 pairs of bed socks, 20 dressing gowns, 50 draw sheets, 50 pairs of slippers and 24 pairs of operation stockings by the end of January; not for soldiers sleeping snugly. The wounded were freezing in makeshift casualty stations. And Newark Hospital was about to be filled by military patients. But its annual report revealed that 'the satisfactory amount' of £530 19s 6d had been subscribed during the year; there had been 55 military patients, 340 in-patients, 476 out-patients, 368 casualties and 302 dental cases.

The Notts Territorial Forces Association revealed that, up to 10 January, there had been 1,648 casualties among county units, with the 8th Sherwoods worst-hit:

	Officers killed	Officers wounded	ORs killed	ORs wounded	Grand total
Sherwood Rangers Yeomanry	3	4	8	39	54
South Notts Hussars Yeomanry	–	2	10	44	56
Notts Royal Horse Artillery	–	–	–	1	1
7th Sherwoods	6	22	101	451	580
8th Sherwoods	11	24	147	756	938
North Midlands Division Cyclists' Corps	–	3	1	7	11
MBF Ambulance	–	–	1	–	1
Totals	**20**	**55**	**268**	**1,298**	**1,648**

With all single men aged eighteen to forty-one expected to be available for conscription, Newark Tribunal began hearing appeals on 17 January. In the first case of a tradesman failing to register, butcher James Staples Tustin was fined £1 by Newark Magistrates on 16 February; but three days later was allowed by the Tribunal to remain in his shop rather than enlist. By 23 March, the Tribunal announced it did not wish to send married men to fight until it had exhausted the supply of single ones.

Many married men felt they should never go. On Sunday afternoon, 26 March, the REs based in town sabotaged one of their protest meetings. Every time their supporter, Sir Arthur Markham, Liberal MP for Mansfield, attempted to speak, the REs broke into song – 'We don't want to lose you, but we think you ought to go' … 'It's a long way to Tipperary' … 'Keep the home fires burning'. The meeting was abandoned.

There was a bitter argument in the Tribunal on 17 April. Miller John T Parnham's attempts to hang onto his sons Hugh, twenty-two, and Harold, twenty-five, were condemned as 'a public scandal' by military representative Herbert Downes Cherry-Downes. Parnham said his alternative was to shut his mill; he could not turn out 1,600 bags of flour per week without them. It would take a year to train men over the age for military call-up. The Tribunal decided Hugh must enlist. His father reacted angrily: 'You might as well take the lot because I shall shut down'. Another Tribunal member, Councillor G A Lacy retorted: 'If one of your sons had died, the business would still go on'. Cherry-Downes had another success minutes later. He hauled farmer and milk seller Horace Bird, thirty-eight, back before the Tribunal having heard he boasted that he had 'done the Tribunal' by earning exemption. Bird insisted he would never say such a thing but he had plenty of enemies who would swear he did. He was ordered to enlist on 1 June.

The *Herald* was saved from extinction on 11 May: the Tribunal granted exemption to its editor, Fred T Jones, thirty-six, after the paper's owner, Mrs Jane Stennett, fifty-seven, pointed out that since her son Jesse had to join-up and two reporters were about to go, there was no one else to produce the paper. It survived until 1960, when Jesse was killed in a road accident.

On 13 May, Quibell's earned exemption for two men engaged in manufacturing disinfectants and sheep oils by assuring the Tribunal that 'women have been found to be susceptible to arsenic poisoning when tried on this work'.

Three evenings later there were heated exchanges when the Home and Colonial Stores were told that their relief manager, Stanley H Sharman, must enlist; they should replace him with a woman. The firm's representative was applauded by other appellants when he said it was as important that a man stay in charge of their shop as of 'the Co-operative stores or beer'. He went on: 'Newark has gained notoriety…' but was silenced by the Mayor, who stated: 'We don't want any remarks. The case has been decided.'

The Newark Trades and Labour Council on 21 August strongly protested against 'the compact made between the Borough Tribunal and the publicans that a married licensed victualler liable for military service may be exempted providing he could displace a single man from munitions, and send to the Tribunal the name of the man to be the said publican's proxy.

'While we do not complain if, in the interests of the country, the Minister of Munitions releases such men for the Army, even to the last man, we do object to a class privilege which must lend itself to the greatest abuse and cannot do other than cause serious friction in any works where it is carried out.'

The Tribunal learned on 14 October that its policy appeared to be at odds with that of the Labour Exchange regarding the availability of young, single men for military service. The Labour Exchange wanted some of them to work in munitions. Military Representative Cherry-Downes insisted they should be firing bullets, not making them.

Meanwhile, the Newark Volunteer Reserve had gone from strength to strength and, they had a great day in the pouring rain on 11 November: national recognition of their zeal. Commander in Chief Home Forces, Viscount French inspected the Nottinghamshire Volunteer Regiment in Nottingham. The Newark Company paraded at their Drill Hall at 8.45am almost at full strength, 'a striking testimony to the keenness of all ranks', great coats were worn and pocket rations carried. Headed by the Bugle Band, they marched to the Midland Station and caught a special train at 10am to Nottingham, accompanied by Newark members of the St John Ambulance Brigade and 5th Newark Boy Scouts Troop. They marched through Nottingham, still the only Company in the county to be fully armed. Rain continued to pour throughout the inspection and the march back to the Midland Station. It was nearly 5pm before they were dismissed at Newark Drill Hall, 'very tired, drenched to the skin, but still cheerful, full of enthusiasm and very proud of the part they have taken in a great occasion' – a memorable day on what in far-off peacetime would become Remembrance Day.

Invasion fears had resurfaced on 31 January. After a meeting in London, Mayor Knight took a train from London King's Cross at 5.30pm. The biggest air raid so far halted his train so frequently, he did not arrive in Newark until 5.30am. Nine Zeppelins – tasked with attacking Sheffield, Manchester and Liverpool – hit several West Midlands towns and Loughborough, killing sixty-three. The Newark Gas Company's lack of a telephone was exposed as a danger. A constable had to be despatched from the Market Place to warn them of the alert. He took five minutes to cycle there – vital minutes in which a Zeppelin could have struck before the gas supply was turned off. Within days, Newark Magistrates ordered the Midland Railway Company to turn off two lights at the Castle Station that could be seen two miles away; Chief Constable Wright demanded a black-out of all tradesmen's buildings; and the Newark Board of Guardians insured the Workhouse against aircraft in the same way as it was insured against fire after Catholic priest Father Hadican estimated: 'A few pounds should cover it'.

Newark Watch Committee and the Local Emergency Committee arranged to receive early warnings of hostile aircraft and announced the public would be alerted by three blasts on factory hooters at Ransome's and Simpson's while a klaxon was fitted on to the roof of the Town Hall. All gas, electricity and lights must be turned off – and private subscribers must not use telephones, leaving the lines clear for emergency services. An inquest in Lincolnshire on 21 February explained Newark's sudden concern. A young farmer had been killed by a Zeppelin bomb fuse that exploded after being taken into the house by his sister. She had found it in a grass verge and they had 'played with it' for a week. The Coroner condemned the cowardice of the Germans, advised the jury to return a verdict of accidental death – and asked the police and military authorities to search for the bomb. On the same day Newark Magistrates fined baronet's daughter Dorothy Brockton, twenty-five, £1 for having two 'naked electric side lamps' on her motor car: she should dim them with her handkerchiefs.

Another of Newark's leading families lost a son in action on 5 February. Major Samuel Boyd Quibell, at twenty-five, said to be the youngest Major at the Western Front, succumbed to wounds suffered on 5 January. The War Office telegram to his parents in Shalem Lodge, London Road, arrived only a few hours after they had received a postcard assuring them he was progressing favourably. The eldest son of Oliver and Elizabeth Quibell, being groomed to inherit the family business before he joined the East Yorkshire Regiment, was hailed as

> 'a keen and alert officer who inspired confidence and quickly gained esteem owing to his unassuming character and the wonderful initiative he displayed on many occasions when his Regiment was in a dangerous position.'

At a memorial service in Barnbygate Wesleyan Church on 13 February, the Minister, the Reverend T W Bisseker, emphasised the selflessness that drove Sam to return to the Front swiftly after he was first wounded, rather than taking a few weeks' leave to recuperate fully. 'This is war,' he told friends. 'I must get back to my Company.'

Youngest Major ... Samuel Boyd Quibell.
[Advertiser cutting]

On 22 February Mayor Knight discovered that one of his nephews had been killed at Ypres – a tragedy witnessed by another nephew. Private James Walter Hammond joined the King's Shropshire Light Infantry with his brother Frederick when war broke out. They were moving up the trenches on 10 February to reinforce the front line during a thirty-six hour bombardment. A shell burst in the communication trench, killing James before Frederick's eyes. The Battalion Chaplain wrote to their mother:

> 'We had a great attack upon us ... It was successfully repelled and the Shropshire lads acted magnificently ... Many gave their lives to prevent a German advance, many were wounded. All Sunday we were at work carrying them out and attending to them. Among those who had given everything, even life itself, was your lad. His brother Fred was also with him and remained amid the dropping shells for hours, and then the dear boy was quietly laid to rest in the trenches he had helped to save. Be brave and comforted about him.'

Sergeant Thomas Claude (Tom) Carter, twenty-five, succumbed on 6 March to wounds received on 3 February. His parents Joseph and Mary visited him in hospital in Rouen and thought he was progressing well from his leg wounds. What they did not realise was that, as in many cases, infection had set in.

Newark's magnificently militaristic Turgoose family was in mourning the following day. Petty Officer Frederick Birkett Turgoose, thirty-seven, was among twenty-four sailors killed when His Majesty's Torpedo Boat *No. 11* was mined off the East Coast. Fred joined the Royal Navy aged fifteen; and in 1902 served on the ship that brought home the body of the first British Ambassador to the USA, the Right Honourable Julian, Baron Pauncefote, GCB, GCMC, for his grand funeral at East Stoke near Newark. Fred's eldest brother, Thomas, was involved in the Relief of General Gordon at Khartoum. Another brother, First-Class Petty Officer Albert Turgoose, was chief wireless operator on HMS *Cyclone*. Tom's brother-in-law, Sergeant-Major Israel S Steptoe, died serving in India. Of Tom's sons in the Army, Thomas earned a Distinguished Conduct Medal at Hohenzollern; Joseph was on special duty with the 2/8th Sherwoods.

Brothers who worked at Quibell's were killed within eight days in April. The Footitt boys Fred, twenty-one, and Harry, nineteen, lived in Slaughterhouse Lane with their parents, Fred and Fanny. The *Herald* reported: 'The grief of the stricken parents is exceedingly great; it is a credit to those living in the vicinity that they do their utmost to bring comfort and consolation to the bereaved.'

Parents of ten children, Henry and Mary Ann Hill lost their fifth son, Ernest Alfred, twenty-one, a motor mechanic before he joined the Sherwoods and was attached to the Grenade Section. Jack Leader, twenty, Old Magnusian son of Newark's former Baptist minister, Reverend George Charles Leader, was set for a bright future in journalism before he joined the Durham Light Infantry. Both fell at Ypres.

As winter turned to spring, widow Mary Atkinson, fifty-four and working as a nurse, resigned herself to never knowing how her eldest, Arthur, thirty, died in Salonika with the Sherwood Rangers after surviving service in Egypt and Serbia. On 28 September 1915 she was informed that Arthur had volunteered to take a message under fire to two comrades in danger of being cut off by the enemy. He was seen approaching two men in some bushes. Three Bulgars fired at him. He began to return but disappeared in some bushes. The squadron was then pushed back a short distance by the enemy and it was night before they realised Arthur was missing.

Twenty-four hours after church clocks and bells were silenced during hours of darkness under the Defence of the Realm Act, Newark had its biggest air raid fright on 31 March. Klaxons clanged. Special constables took to court householders responsible for any chink of light. They were fined 2s 6d per light and warned by the Mayor: 'Future punishments will be much more stringent'. He was as good as his word: fish fryer John Henry Lamb, thirty-eight, complained it was 'robbery' when he was fined 10s on 11 May, but he had previously been warned. Horse and Jockey licensee Henry Brown was also fined 10s and ordered to install better window blinds.

Newark Watch and War Emergency Committee met Newark Hospital governors and the town's doctors on 2 April 'regarding air raids'. The hospital was full, so supplementary provisions and equipment were necessary. The institution could not afford them. A public appeal was launched for 90 sheets, 60 pillow cases, 60 pillows, 12 blankets and 30 waterproof sheets. Extra bandages had 'partly been promised'. Dressings needed to be purchased. Extra mattresses had been hired from Wilkinson's furniture shop.

Amazing danger loomed on the Great North Road through town on Saturday night,

1 April. A policeman halted a munitions steam lorry towing two trucks and discovered the driver, Richard Dooley, was operating the pedals while his mate was steering. Both were inebriated. Dooley was fined £1 – but the report in the local papers neglected to reveal whether the trucks were loaded.

Seventy-eight Newark children were affected by a measles epidemic in April – George Henry Ford, fifteen, died shortly after passing the Cambridge junior examination while his father was soldiering in the Middle East; but there were bright intervals. Machine Gunner Jim Henderson, twenty-three, was labelled Newark's luckiest bridegroom on 24 April when he married Grace Lillian Stafford, twenty, youngest daughter of the nine children of George and Grace Stafford. He had been wounded no fewer than three times while fighting with the 1/8th Sherwoods. The best man, the bride's brother, Machine Gunner Harold Stafford, twenty-three, of the 2/8th Sherwoods, went on to earn a Military Medal in March 1918 for rescuing wounded under heavy shell fire.

Former Newark Town footballer Charles Robinson distinguished himself for his signalling work as a Royal Field Artillery corporal. He was presented with a card headed 'For gallant and meritorious service' and inscribed:

> 'The Major-General Commanding has noted with pleasure the gallant and meritorious conduct of No. 99881 Corporal C Robinson between May 1915 and February 1916, which has been brought to his attention by his Commanding Officer.'

It was signed by Major-General V Couper, GOC 14th (Light) Division. Charles explained that it was earned

> 'during the scraps, one in which I was on duty with the infantry, the first time for keeping communications, and the second for getting a flag message through to my battery when all wires had been broken, the enemy being successfully countered. My officer has already been decorated with the Military Cross. We had never tried to send a visual message before. We should have been stopped at any ordinary time, but things were hot at the time and I suppose the enemy were too busy elsewhere. Fortunately for us, my own Officer Commanding saw the signal, and he was the only one who spotted it. We sent 'SOS' first and then ran back into cover after we had repeated it several times. The officer then brought a message and we sent it several times. Imagine my joy, and also the officers and the other signallers, who had also sent the message, when an orderly came along and said the Captain had received my message. The Officer Commanding another battery complimented me on my work during the scrap. He said my flag message was great.'

Charles, a former altar- and choirboy at the Catholic Church, worked for Abbott's before joining up. His heroics followed Lieutenant Henry Higgs of the RE Engineer Training Centre at Newark, who earned the Albert Medal 1st Class in February for 'a grenade incident'.

In the same month the President of the French Republic bestowed the 'Medaille Militaire' on Lance Corporal James Richard Coupe of the RE Newark Training Centre (formerly 86th Field Company) in recognition of his distinguished service. *The London Gazette*, 21 June, announced DCM awards to Company Sergeant Major 52852 E Lockwood and Sgt 40008 W T Foster of the RE Newark Training Centre. Lockwood's award was for 'consistent good work in the Front Line, frequently under fire' with the 89th Field Company. Foster was honoured for 'conspicuous gallantry and determination on several occasions when carrying out dangerous work' with the 63rd Field Company. His citation added in the military's matter-of-fact way: 'He lost his leg when performing such work'. There was another hint of the pain being endured on 5 July: RE trainees staged a concert in the Town Hall in aid of Sapper Benson, 'who has become totally incapable of employment in civil life owing to blindness and wounds received in action'.

Newark Market Place was lined by crowds on three sides and massed ranks of locally-based soldiers on the other flank on 10 September when Sergeant 44888 VD Harvey of the 74th Field Company REs received the Distinguished Conduct Medal for 'conspicuous gallantry when he rallied a working party and got the wounded into safety during a bombardment by trench mortar shells'.

There were exhilarating tales from the Middle East. Private George Hopkinson of the 2nd Light Battery Armoured Cars in Egypt wrote to his father, whitesmith James Hopkinson, of experiences 'among the Senussi' (a Muslim political-religious Sufi order and tribe in Libya and the Sudan) in April:

'I think our first scrap was 27 February. Well, the infantry and cavalry had set out from [place censored] about five days before us. They marched about seventy miles out, and we set off the day before the fight. Next morning, we came in touch with the infantry about half past eight and found the enemy were on the left of the road. So we went after them with the cars but could not go fast because of our infantry and cavalry having to keep up with us. We found the enemy entrenched

A Rolls-Royce armoured car similar to George Hopkinson's in Egypt.

in some soft sands and were only able to make the advance party retreat to their main body.

'The main body of our troops came up about an hour afterwards, and they got well into it. The cavalry had quite a few casualties. We were not able to do much, really, for the sands. Four of the cars out of the six got stuck. But still we were a great help and helped put a few out of the way. My car got within threequarters of a mile from the enemy before I got stuck. We were the best part of an hour there before the infantry came up to us and, my word, the bullets weren't half wizzing [sic] about!

'Anyway, the enemy got a good position and to stop them retreating, we had to go right through them. We had orders to kill all on horseback, for those were sure to be officers of some sort. It was 11am when we first started to fight. Our car spent the best part of an hour chasing these sort, and then came back to where the other cars were having their sport. Then we got into it. The Turkish leaders stuck it well. One party killed the crew of a machine gun, opened fire on us from our rear, and the bullets were spluttering up against the sides of our turret, making an awful rattle. We turned round and finished them off, but they stuck to their guns to the last. The whole lot were wiped off the map.

'One of the cars fired at some of their camels early on in the fight, the load on one of which burst into flames and, as the gun traversed, the whole caravan of them were not killed instantly but ran about actually on fire, for they were carrying ammunition and petrol. But we soon put a few merciful shots into them.

'We were at it until 1pm and I should think had killed about sixty or seventy and wounded lots more. But they always have their women with them when they are fighting; and they carry the dead or wounded away. After the fight we found we had captured about 300,000 rounds of rifle ammunition and lots of boxes of shell besides nine machine guns and three 10-pounders. One 10-pounder opened fire on us at about 400 yards range, but they all went over us, for a good job, and we were on them before they could do us any damage. We all had to go before the General. He said a lot of things; you know the style. He made quite a fuss of us.

'We set out on the 17th at 3am, went seventy miles along the coast, and then across the desert forty and fifty miles. I showed 230 miles for the whole trip on my speedometer, but it is not quite correct. We came up to the place at 3pm. I was in the first car up to take poor prisoners. The prisoners told us their guard had fled as soon as they saw us on the skyline, so we made off after them. Our car accounted for eight and the other for the rest. We set off back at 4pm, and it was 1.30am the next morning before we got back to camp. I had twenty-two hours at the wheel and fell asleep three times coming back, you know, just for a second or two; time to go off the road and wake up by hitting a bump. We went again before the Colonel and had some tongue wag (worse than before) all praise, you know.'

A bizarre link with Newark was reported from Mesopotamia by Private Gerard Alfred Oldrini, twenty-three, of the South Notts Hussars to his parents, Basil and Emily. In an attack on Turkish positions he was held up by heavy enemy fire while crossing a ploughed field. He dived into a furrow and dug in as deeply as he could, along with his comrades. A night passed before anyone dared move. Then one of his friends crept up to him and whispered: 'You come from Newark, don't you?' Oldrini answered: 'Yes.' 'Well, just crawl along the furrow and you'll find something of interest.' Off he went and came across a plough bearing the maker's name: 'Geo. Stephenson and Son, Newark'. How incredible that this plough from his home town should cut the furrow in which a soldier found refuge! Stephenson's professed no idea how the implement got there.

It was early May before Newark began to learn about the high local cost of an Irish Rebellion in Dublin over Easter. 'Newarkers have suffered grievously,' reported the *Herald* on 6 May. 'Up to the time of going to press information has been received that three local lads have been killed by the fanatics and several wounded.' The report explained that 2/8th Sherwoods were ambushed the previous Tuesday week while marching line abreast along the road from Kingstown towards Dublin. It was the new Battalion's first taste of battle. Several fell in the initial onslaught. Surviving troops boldly closed-up ranks and brought their machine gun into play, taking summary vengeance for their losses. Four officers were killed and fourteen wounded, including Arthur Holmes Quibell, twenty-two, a captain who quickly recovered from his 'scratch'. The son of Oliver and Elizabeth Quibell received the Distinguished Service Order for showing 'fine presence of mind and leadership to A Company' but insisted: 'The honour is for the Company. They did their work splendidly.' (Mrs Quibell was also doing splendid work: the Newark Nursing Association, which she ran, was making almost 800 visits annually to 'pauper cases' with the help of a ten-guinea subscription from the Newark Board of Guardians.)

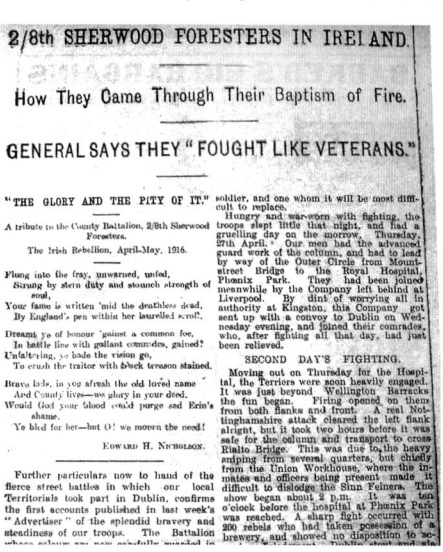

The Advertiser tribute to the 2/8th Sherwoods' baptism of fire in Dublin.
[Advertiser cutting]

Another Distinguished Service Order went to Lieutenant-Colonel Frank Rayner, Trent Navigation Company engineer since 1896. The Distinguished Conduct Medal was earned by Sergeant-Major John Lacey, a veteran of the Boer War, who was a police constable in Newark before returning to the Colours. He and his wife Emily lost an eighteen-year-old son in action on 26 April 1915. His citation commended his conspicuous gallantry and devotion to duty: 'He carried several important messages under heavy fire ... a fine example of courage and determination.'

The three killed were Company Sergeant Major Henry Charles Dixey, twenty-two,

British troops firing from behind a barrier of overturned park benches during the Easter Rebellion in Dublin, April 1916. *Taylor Library*

a schoolteacher whose last letter home to his parents strengthened them by telling them he had been posted to Ireland, not the Western Front, 'so you are not to worry'; Lance Corporal George W Barks, nineteen, an apprentice at Simpson's; and Private Albert James Kitchen, twenty-four, another of Cafferata's men. Among the wounded, Company Sergeant Major Herbert Lawrence wrote that a bullet 'went right through me. It pierced my left lung but I'll be back in action soon.' Private John Cecil Belton, who worked in his father's hairdressers before enlisting three months earlier, was shot in the nose during a bayonet charge. Dixey and Lawrence both had the distinction of being mentioned in despatches 'for gallantry and coolness in the field'.

Corporal Thomas A Pykett, twenty-seven, serving with the military police on the Dublin streets having been wounded in the Dardanelles and judged unfit for active service, wrote to his parents George and Ann:

'It has been hell on earth and I have had some narrow escapes. They had two shots at me but they were rotten bad shots, they could not hit me. These were the first shots that started the affair. Of course I had to run to get out of the road of them, as I had not got my revolver, but when I got back to the Castle I jolly soon got it and plenty of ammunition, and took up position at the Castle gates, where we held them at bay until the troops arrived. I had a good many shots at them, killing two Sinn Feiners and capturing three rifles ... Things are quiet again but the city is in awful ruins, 150 places having been wiped out by fire. I can tell you it's been an awful week for us.'

The Notts Territorial Association president, the Duke of Portland, and chairman, Henry Mellish, wrote to the Sherwoods as

'an expression of our great appreciation of the manner in which the officers, non-commissioned officers and men of your Battalion carried out the very difficult duties assigned to them in connection with the recent disturbances in Dublin, thereby winning for themselves the admiration, not only of this County, but the whole of England. Their conduct shows that they well deserve to share the high reputation which has already been gained by the County units in France. The Association deeply regrets that these duties have involved the loss of so many brave lives.'

Newark Council wrote 'congratulating and complementing the Regiment on the gallant services so ably rendered by them during the recent rebellion in Ireland and condoling with them in the heavy losses of officers and men thereby incurred.'

There was dissent in the House of Commons on 29 May. The Irish Nationalist MP for Leitrim, Francis Edward Meehan claimed 200 soldiers of the Sherwoods 'under the command of Captain Jackson, without asking permission, which would have been feely granted, took possession of St Clare's Hall in Manor Hamilton, County Leitrim, last week and, while in possession smashed several instruments, tore scene screens and did other damage to the hall and goods contained therein, belonging to the temperance club. He asked whether they would be held responsible for such damage; and, if not, to what source should the club apply for compensation. Under Secretary of State Harold Tennant replied that sixty NCOs and men of Captain Jackson's company, 6th Sherwoods, were billeted in St Clare's Hall on 13 and 14 May. The billets were arranged by the district inspector, Royal Ireland Constabulary, and the caretaker opened the hall for the troops. The NCOs in charge were prepared to state on oath that no such damage was done by the troops.

As a postscript, or even an after thought in that male dominated era, the surviving Sherwoods were intrigued to learn that two of the nurses who tended their wounds – Misses Nora and Jennie Fitzpatrick – received Red Cross decorations at Buckingham Palace in May 1918.

A female gesture, bordering on slapstick, did not go down well at Newark Court on Monday, 22 May 1916. Emma Boothwright, thirty-three, was fined five shillings with two shillings costs for 'bringing a soldier's uniform into contempt'. She proudly put on her husband Thomas's uniform in the Swan and Salmon, run by her parents Amos and Hannah – but was spotted by a policeman when she marched across Castlegate to have a drink with her mother at the Exchange Hotel. Emma apologised, explaining that with her brother and husband both fighting, the last thing she would do was insult their uniform. She was celebrating Tom being on leave.

Increasingly, shortage of money was forcing wives of serving soldiers to move back to their parents. On 22 May, Newark Council considered the subject, though not from the little woman's perspective. With men 'compelled to vacate their houses on account of having joined His Majesty's Forces', the Council asked their General Purposes Committee to make arrangements for storing their furniture.

Councillor Henry Cubley's youngest daughter Ethel appeared in the King's Birthday Honours. As a member of Queen Alexandria's Nursing Reserve, she was among twenty awarded the Royal Red Cross Medal of the Second Class, having already received a monogram brooch from the Queen of the Belgians.

Buried in column four of page five of the *Herald* on 15 April was news about a member of another prominent Newark family which launched the town's best spy story of the War: Councillor Redmond Barton Cafferata, gypsum mining company chairman, had left Newark 'to take up an appointment under the War Office'. A century later, it

Face of a spy ... Redmond Barton Cafferata on his passport, 1916.
[https://europeana1914-1918.s3.amazonaws.com/attachments/54631/4929.54631.large.jpg?1359842643]

was reveled that he had an interesting war. As Chairman of an Advisory Committee on the Derby Scheme, he found it impossible to get married men to join-up. In disgust, despite being in his thirties with a wife and children, he 'chucked all up and volunteered' for a career with Military Intelligence in the predecessor of MI6, under the command of Sir Mansfield Cumming, who always signed himself 'C'. Charged with intelligence gathering from abroad, mainly about troop movements, he travelled 'for my health' on 20 June 1916 to 'join family in Switzerland' settled in Pontarlier because it was on Allied soil. Thus he respected Switzerland's neutrality while being able to use links with Berne only seventy miles away. Travelling as a Ministry of Munitions representative and codenamed Zulu, he bagged 'twenty or thirty Hun agents' operating in Switzerland and France over the next two years; discovered that the German Consul General employed 122 in espionage compared with ten by France and eight by Britain; built a network of twenty agents and, among other things, trained them to avoid detection with advice such as: 'Never confide in women'; 'Never give your photo to anyone, especially a female'; and to escape being followed 'Get on a tram and, as soon as the agent gets on, get off yourself'. He continued to operate until April 1918, when he was moved to the British Legation, Athens.

Of his twelve siblings, Bernard, obtained a commission in the Motor Transport Branch of the Army Service Corps and returned post war to help run the companies. Another brother, Clement Chamberlain Cafferata, a rancher in Canada when the war broke out, joined the Duke of Connaught's Own Irish Canadians, survived the hostilities but died of pneumonia early in 1919 and was interred in Newark.

Not that the ruling classes were entirely in unison in mid 1916. There was forthright disagreement at the Newark Division Conservative Association AGM between the MP, Captain Starkey, and the prospective Unionist candidate, Henry Arthur Colefax, a London-based barrister. The Captain defended the coalition Government, arguing that there had been a shortage of munitions but an immense industry had been brought into action; on recruiting, he was satisfied with the voluntary system pre-War but current circumstances showed compulsion to be necessary. History always showed that when a country was at war and did not win great victories, the government was unpopular; but preparations were being made to win the greatest victory. The barrister was 'disappointed': he expected the war to be fought with more vigour and greater strength and wisdom. He did not accept it was unpatriotic to criticise the Government; the country and Empire had behaved splendidly and deserved a responsible, reasonable Opposition.

One of Cafferata's managers, Louis d'Ascanio, celebrated his son-in-law's James Hickman, twenty-nine, escaping from the Battle of Jutland despite being wounded. One Newarker died: Ernest Kelham, twenty, a gunner on HMS *Invincible* when it sank on 31 May. A century on, Naval warfare experts continue to debate who won: Britain suffered greater losses but was left in possession of the sea when the Germans ran for home; thereafter the German High Seas Fleet rarely left harbour, the main reason for low morale which culminated in mutinies in October 1918. None of this was consolation for Ernie's parents, bricklayer Arthur Robert Kelham, forty-six, and his wife Harriett, who had five other children. In contrast, nurse Hannah Flower was justifiably proud in

September when it was announced that her son John Edward Flower, thirty-five, of the Royal Marine Artillery had been commended for 'good service in action' and promoted from Warrant Officer to Lieutenant in Sir John Jellicoe's despatch giving the Naval Honours List for the Battle Jutland Bank. A marine since 1897, he had earned a medal for conspicuous gallantry in Somaliland in 1904.

Newark suffered deaths on the Western Front almost daily from mid summer. Private George Edmund Harold Coulsey, a Church Lads' Brigade drummer and fruiterer's errand boy, who was one of the few inspired to join up by the visit of Corporal Upton VC to Newark in 1915, died on 14 June.

Shattering news for the Tye family arrived on 15 June. Cousins John, twenty-two, and Harold, twenty-five, who enlisted in the 1st East Yorkshire Regiment together, had died on the Somme. Percy and Betsy Norval, who reared John after his parents died while he was a baby, and Harold's widowed mother Eliza mourned for ten days before another official missive arrived. A mistake had been made by office staff given the awful task of notifying next of kin: John was alive and fighting on. Even worse for Eliza, she lost another son, Frank, nineteen and another of Cafferata's workers, on 25 February 1917 at Cambrin.

Railwayman's son Harold Barling, twenty-three, was also killed on 15 June, a fortnight after returning to the Front from a three week furlough. He was building a career with the Daimler Motor Works in Nottingham before he joined the 8th Leicestershire Regiment, rapidly rising to second lieutenant.

Two more Newark lads – Privates Leslie Tyers, nineteen, a Ransome's apprentice, and Albert Edward Pulford, nineteen, a Simpson's apprentice – were among six from the 8th Sherwoods killed by an enemy shell as they carried rations to troops in the front line trenches on 20 June. The first intimation was received in Newark by fish dealer George Cross in a letter from one of his twelve children, Ernest, a corporal. He explained the Battalion had been in the trenches for eighteen days. They expected to have a month's break but were recalled after ten days – and: 'I have been upset today as I have been having to dig graves for six men. They were carrying dinner up the trench when a shell dropped amongst them.' Tyers' folks had only just received a letter saying: 'The Battalion is in the trenches but my Company is in reserve, taking up the rations, which is better than being in the Front Line.'

Newark Tribunal, under pressure to identify more and more potential conscripts, agreed on 19 June to meet the Newark Licensed Victuallers' Association to seek consistent treatment of pub landlords; within months Newark Magistrates were urging them to transfer licences to their wives and join 'the patriotic struggle'.

When Joseph Warriner appeared before Newark Magistrates charged with attempting to commit suicide, he was discharged when the military authorities revealed he had to join up that week.

A special Children's Court was convened after a Belgian refugee, Francois Moens, eleven, stole five oranges from a market stall. Francis said his brother, fifteen, told him to take them. On hearing that the boys' father was of good character and working nights, the magistrates dismissed the case.

A severe shell-shock case appeared before Newark Magistrates on 25 July, not for the last time: Lance Corporal Coaten was fined 10s for stealing a bicycle. He had been discharged from the RE: 'on account of mental shock and epilepsy in France. I've not been altogether myself since I came back. I'm very sorry to find myself in this position. I can't remember what I did with the bike. I've never been in trouble before.'

The agonies became more frequent at the Front, particularly around the Somme ... Private Thomas Cope, 1st Sherwoods, was killed on 24 June 'by a shell which dropped in the trench just where he was sitting', according to a letter to his widow, Sarah in Wood Street. With his parents Henry and Ann still mourning, his twin brother Henry was killed on 25 September, leaving a widow and a baby a few months old whom he never saw.

Mountna Johnson, an apprentice joiner before he became involved in most of the Sherwoods' scraps over the first year of War, was killed by a shell on 25 June – thirteen days after celebrating his twenty-first birthday in the trenches. Sergeant Ernest Marshall wrote as comfortingly as he could to his parents in Warburton Street:

'Being a Newark man myself, I thought it my duty to let you know how deeply we feel the loss you have sustained, but he died without the slightest pain, a shell bursting quite near him, and a piece passing through his heart. He is now laid beside many of his own comrades who have also fell fighting for right and justice in this great struggle...' [Foncquevillers, a village about ten miles south-west of Arras].

Walter and Emily Moore on Farndon Road discovered that their son was killed on 26 June. Lance Corporal Walter Gilbert Moore, 1/8th Sherwoods, had been recommended for a bravery award in November 1915: Major-General Stuart-Wortley, GOC 46th (North Midland) Division, wrote: 'Your Commanding Officer and Brigade Commander have informed me that you distinguished yourself by conspicuous bravery in the field. I have read their report with much pleasure, and am bringing your conduct to the notice of superior authority.' He never told his parents what he had done. He was promoted to corporal before he was killed on the Somme.

Ernest Judson, nineteen, killed on the same day, wrote in his last letter to his mother Mary Jane, in Cawkwell's Yard: 'Dear Mum, Please do not worry... but I shall never see England again.'

The killing by another shell of Lance Corporal Alma Adolphus Grant, twenty, on 27 June, sparked perhaps Newark's most touching story of love and enduring devotion of the century. His fiancée, Daisy Vanns, a kitchen maid at the Ossington Coffee Palace, which had been taken over as RE officers' quarters, was as devastated as Alma's parents, accountant Joshua and Mary, and his five siblings.

Alma, named after one of the Crimean War battles in which his maternal grandfather fought, had written defiantly in his last letter home: 'We were blown-up three times within five days, but still the old 8th Battalion came out on top. I am proud to belong to it, although it brings us many trying times.'

His comrades were equally proud of Alma; Captain J W Turner wrote: 'He never knew what fear was and always did what was asked of him with a smile ... We shall all miss him very much indeed.' Alma had made a huge impact in his short life: apprenticed at Ransome's, a Parish Church choirboy, his early military training was in the Church Lads' Brigade. He became county champion during a roller skating fad, was secretary of Newark Harriers and won their Christmas Day six-and-a-half-mile race just before he joined the Sherwoods.

Struggling to accept his loss, Daisy grew closer to Alma's kindly big brother, Robert, who also worked at Ransome's. They married in 1926. By an outrageous twist of fate, Robert was killed in 1941 during Newark's only air raid of the Second World War. Daisy was left to raise their son Christopher, six at the time. He grew to study and teach at the Magnus, become Mayor of Newark – and frequently conducted tours to The Great War battlefields, always taking in the trench in which Alma fell and the cemetery at Foncquevillers in which he is remembered.

Rifleman Bertram Stevenette, twenty-two, raised in Newark before finding work as a timber merchant's clerk in Peterborough, was killed nine months to the day after the death of his father. He was among six comrades of the Rifle Brigade machine gun section to be wiped-out by a shell on 30 June, his aunt, Beatrice Cooke of Pelham Street learnt.

Love and devotion ... Alma Adolphus Grant.
[Advertiser cutting]

One of a family of eight, Private Ernest Priestley, a chemical works labourer before he enlisted in the 1/8th Sherwoods, survived eleven months on the Western Front but died in camp at Marsh Chapel near Grimsby in June 1916 when a scratched lip became gangrenous.

In the same week, a memorial service was held at Parliament Street Chapel for Private Ernest Allison, twenty-one, whose step-mother Elizabeth Beckett, only thirty-three, was working as a charwoman to look after five more children aged seventeen to five. He was a Primitive Methodist Church lay preacher before joining the 6th Lincolnshire Regiment and was in the landing at Suvla Bay. He was reported wounded and missing on 9 August 1915; but it was June 1916 before the Army Council was 'regretfully constrained to conclude that he is dead'.

The dangers to schoolchildren working on farms were made brutally apparent in a field near Quibell's works. William Ellis, fifteen, was leading a horse with a hoe when suddenly the animal reared, kicked him in the stomach and trod on him as he fell. His cries were heard by workmen who rushed to him. He recovered in hospital, but the incident gave impetus to teachers' objections to pupils as young as thirteen replacing farm labourers sent to war. Newark Hospital could have done without the extra patient, too; with wounded soldiers flooding in, the Mayor led an appeal for more voluntary funds to keep it solvent; it was three decades before the creation of the National Health Service. Teachers also had money on their minds: they called Notts Education Committee's offer of a war bonus of 1s 11d per week 'miserably inadequate – further proof that the national importance of the work of the teacher is not yet appreciated'.

As if purses were not stretched enough, a meeting in the Town Hall to determine how best to maximise war savings in Newark led to sub-committees being formed targeting maltsters and brewers, engineering works (including munitions), education, general trades works, and religious and philanthropic sections. To help people get in the habit of 'putting a bit aside every week', the Newark Borough War Savings Association met every Saturday evening, 7-8pm, to receive applications for membership and subscriptions.

Respite from terror abroad or duty at home was rare; and controversy raged when the Government 'asked' rather than 'ordered' workers not to take Whit Monday off in June. Men at Abbott's, Simpson's, Bradley's, Farrar's and the Midland Ironworks obtained time-and-a-half rates and went in. Ransome's refused to pay extra and so their men stayed at home while the management blamed 'the actions of the Trades Unions'.

During August Bank Holiday Newark Magistrate John Hind, fifty-six, and the youngest of his six children, Vincent, thirteen, were charged at 'an East Coast Police Court' with flying a kite 'which might be used for signalling purposes'. The case was dismissed but the Bench warned that kite flying would not be tolerated during the war.

Of those 'on holiday from the trenches', having been taken prisoner, Private Richard Billyard, twenty-four, a turner in an engineering factory pre-war, wrote:

> 'My boots are very bad and you cannot get them repaired here. So if you can get me a pair of boots or clogs, it would be very good of you. My feet are very wet every day, and the work we are doing would be bad if we had no more rain for six months. We are cutting peat out on the moors and it is all bog and it has rained every day for six weeks, every day since we have been here.'

William Henry Allen, twenty-four, was sent to Hanover after being captured on 26 September. It was merely his latest trauma: wounded in the Dardanelles, he contracted enteric fever while recovering at a base hospital, was sent to fight in Egypt and then transferred to France. His parents George and Sarah, who had fifteen children, had plenty more to worry about at home in Lindum Street. Their eldest, Tom, twenty-six, a private in the RE, was convalescing from chest wounds. George, twenty-one, suffered a 'poisoned leg' in the Sherwoods' trenches and was in hospital. John, eighteeen, was training with the next line of Sherwoods. And Joe spent twelve months in the Territorials before his parents claimed him back: he was under sixteen.

With his son Thomas, twenty-two, a prisoner after being wounded three times and gassed once with the 1st Lincolns, builder's labourer Joe Beckett sold copies of the following lines for a penny for the Prisoners' Relief Fund:

> Daily we read of the great conflict that's raging / Of deeds great and noble of our men good and true / Fighting for our Homeland, our Freedom they're making / Under the good old Flag, the Red, White and Blue.
>
> Daily we read of deeds that's fiendish and cruel / Committed by German kultur that's failed in its tests. / But as sure as the great Eagle's engaged in this great duel, / As sure will the Lion prove itself greatly the best.
>
> Often we think and wonder what will it all cost? / Why, a price that money can never repay! / Thousands of dear lads' lives already that's lost / Through one who must answer to his Maker one day.

In Belgium your career of destruction first started. / Your deeds remain fresh as the ages roll by. Oh mocker of God many loved ones has parted. / 'twould have been a great blessing if you'd had to die.

Christianity and the Kaiser must be strangers to each other / Although as we know, he is born of high rank. / Cathedrals and churches, the fine work of the sculptor, / Has he reduced to ruins, this fine Potsdam crank.

But all honour to those brave lads who have fallen; / Who fought side by side, by day and by night. / They fought for the cause that is true to their calling; / A cause that is Just and Right, and not Might.

But 'tis hard for the widows and orphans / Of the loved ones that's bravely fell for their King. / For how sweet it was when husbands and sons / Could all join together at home and sing.

But when, oh when, shall I see thee... / Oh, the words of that beautiful hymn! / If not on earth, in Heaven it may be / When life's light has lost all its joy and glim.

Now, when you have read these few lines above / If you can spare a small mite and will give it / To the poor prisoners of war whom we love, / You will have the best thanks from Joe Beckett.

Appletongate confectioner Mrs Sophia Elizabeth Kirk, who had already lost her son Herbert in action in May 1915, had her eldest, Charles, twenty-four, her sugar boiler, called up on 27 July 1916 – but defiantly assured customers the business would carry on 'as usual, as far as possible'. Charles, too, perished in action but life went on for resilient Sophia: she remarried in 1919.

By then the Battle of the Somme raged: the 'Big Push' by the Allies began on 1 July 1916 and ended in November with the German Army thrown back without a decisive breakthrough but with great casualties.

How bravely the Sherwoods acted in the first great advance was told graphically by Sergeant W Cole, one of the Newarkers of the 1/8th involved. The men had a hot breakfast at 5am while waiting for the word to attack,

'but don't imagine we were left there as if we were waiting to go to the theatre, for the Huns had been dropping shells at different points all along our Front Line and stretcher bearers were beginning to have a busy time of it, but not so busy as they got afterwards. Our artillery had been giving their Front Line all they wanted and everything seemed ready.

'The men were joking with one another and on all sides you could hear such remarks as, "Never mind, Bill, we'll get our own back soon." Our officer shouted as we had word to stand, "Are we down-hearted?" You can imagine the response. Just then all other sounds were drowned by the crackle of machine guns which seemed to come from all directions but mostly from our left flank.

'I shall never forget the way our boys went on... just as cool and regular as in the early days when they were taught to do it. It was just pluck. I saw them go right across and although our losses were heavy, they still went on, line after line, just like a huge machine at work; and it seems I can see it over again as I write. Our

British infantry attacking on the first day of the Battle of the Somme, 1 July 1916.

Second in Command shouted, "Come on the Foresters!" and doubled along, revolver in hand, but I am sorry to say I saw him fall just in front of the Hun first line, and someone was "going through it". I have since seen that our Second in Command was wounded and I am glad he got back safely because he was so fearless.

'I daresay you wonder how I was able to see all this. Well, we did not go more than fifty yards before the officer in charge of the platoon got one from a machine gun and he almost fell into a shell hole. I just rolled him in and got on the go again when I had a shock like a thousand volts of electricity going through my shoulder and out at the top of my right arm, and I knew I was finished for a bit but not done. I crawled back to that same friendly shell hole and by this time about eight men were there. Anyhow, I got my arm dressed and my officer gave me his revolver as I could not use my rifle. I had no sooner got out of the hole than I went down again with one through the top part of the left arm which quite put me out for the count. I am glad to say my wounds are going on splendidly and I shall soon be about again, thanks to the special treatment in hospital [in Kent].'

Cafferata's worker Arthur Fell, twenty, a Lincolnshire Regiment private who had been invalided home to Newark from the Dardanelles with dysentery, disappeared in the opening bayonet charge: it was Friday 30 March 1917 before his widowed mother Elizabeth was officially informed that he was dead. There were good reasons for the delay: losses were the heaviest ever suffered by the British Army: 19,240 men killed in one day and more than 40,000 wounded.

Private George Seagrave, thirty-eight, one of Abbott's engineers in the Sherwoods, was another killed in the first charge. It was 31 August before Elizabeth Howitt – looking after son John, seven, and daughter Edith Adelaide, five – discovered her husband George also disappeared in the opening moments.

Reg Porter, son of the president of Newark Tradesmen's Association, was also one of the first to be 'knocked over' when the order was given to 'Advance'. Reg, born in 1897, joined the 7th Sherwoods aged eighteen and went to France on his nineteenth birthday. Shot in a leg and arm, he crawled to a shell hole and, while bandaging his own leg, had a lucky escape when a sniper's bullet pinged off his steel helmet. He had to stay in the crater for fifteen hours before stretcher bearers reached him but he wrote home in a most cheery spirit – and survived to appear in the 1918 Absent Voters List.

Lance Corporal Percy Andrew, twenty, a Home & Colonial Stores errand boy, had a narrower escape. Shrapnel seared into the right side of his chest and lodged about six inches to the left. The surgeon told him if it had gone as far into him as it went sideways, he would be dead rather than in bed writing to his father, Ranby, foreman porter at the GNR Goods Depot at Newark, and mother, Sarah Hannah, who had seven more offspring.

Old Magnusian Andrew Robson, only eighteen and too young to be at the Front, reported his 'wonderful escape' in the school magazine:

'We went over the top and I came safely back through an absolute hail of bullets, without a scratch. I had two narrow escapes. A piece of shrapnel pierced the brim of my tin hat. And a bullet from a sniper entered my tunic below the second button, went into my right breast top pocket, through my pay-book and mirror, and the lid of a cocoa tin. It cut all my cigarettes in half, and the bottom of the tin turned the bullet out again. I also had two holes in my wool waistcoat and a smaller one in my shirt. It was a wonderful escape as I ran 300 yards across No Man's Land with a machine gun turned on me and sundry shells bursting. I never expected to reach our lines again. I am out of the trenches now and many miles behind the line. I am to stay here until I am nineteen years old next February.'

Former Newark Golf Club professional William Stephenson was struck by shrapnel and died in the Sportsmen's Battalion charge on 1 July, leaving a widow, May, twenty-eight, and four children between seven years and six weeks.

Postman's son William Brunt, twenty-seven, a private in the King's Own Scottish Borderers, wrote about being an accidental film extra in Martinpuich, which was bombarded for three days. They started for the trenches at 6pm and arrived three or four hours later, but came under fire and had to withdraw to the second line of trenches. Soon they were warned gas was coming and donned their helmets. They were in the first line trenches from 3.30 am until 6.30 am before being ordered over the parapet. The man immediately to William's right fell dead instantly but the line advanced 800 yards. William received personal orders an hour afterwards: he was given a flag and laid on his back in exposed country, awaiting orders to wave it as a signal for the artillery to fire. An officer told him to hold the flag out. Instantly a shell exploded, showering him in bricks, earth and stone without putting him out of action. Eventually tanks appeared in support. He thought it a joke when told a film had been made of the drama – but was astonished on leave back home months later to visit Newark's Beaumond Hall and see the action replayed: 'I recognised many things which happened, but could not see myself.' In November 1916 he went down with trench fever, was surprised and delighted to be treated at the Front by his Newark doctor, Councillor Stallard; he spent time in hospital in Leeds and convalesced in Castleford; and was then allowed a furlough with his parents, Joseph, nearly seventy, and Mary Ann, who had a total of twelve children. Four had died over the years but four more sons and a son-in-law served in the war.

Arthur West, who struggled to persuade the Army he was fit enough to fight, was killed on 2 July. The Chaplain of the 6th Battalion Wiltshire Regiment, the Reverend A A Davies, assured his father, a widower on Boundary Road: 'There was no shirking, no turning aside in the day of battle. He died the death of a gallant soldier – in action and for a good cause.' Arthur sang in the choir of Christ Church, where his father was verger, was a Post Office telegraph boy before joining-up at sixteen but was discharged after two-and-a-half years with sciatica. When war broke out, he was rejected for service twice but was eventually accepted in the South Staffordshire Regiment.

A neighbour rushed to James and Edith Jean Harper in Sleaford Road to say how sorry she was that their eldest son had been killed – and discovered that they did not know. She took it for granted that they, too, had had a letter from Sergeant Major R Mayfield, who wrote: 'I've just seen poor Jim Harper dead on the battlefield.' He was a Ransome's apprentice before joining the 3rd Leicestershire Regiment and wrote home regularly, always cheerfully. His last letter ended: 'I am hoping to see you soon'.

Ernest Mountney's exceptionally painful war ended 3 August, a month after he suffered his final wounds. He was twenty-eight; a plumber, and a willing 1st Sherwoods private. Within a month of going to France in November 1914, he was in a Nottingham hospital with frost bitten feet and rheumatism. After recovering, he was shot in the left hand in April. A month later, he suffered bad head injuries and was critical for months in Colchester Hospital. He was again returned to the Front, only to contract blood poisoning in both hands in February 1916. Yet he battled back sufficiently to take his place in the Big Push, where wounds to his head, arm and both legs proved fatal.

Cecil Sefton, twenty-five, assistant in a gents' outfitters, was killed by a shell on 5 July while a private with the 20th Battalion Royal Fusiliers. Lieutenant Stuart Rawson told his parents in Lime Grove: 'We have lost one of the cheeriest and best workers one could ever hope to have.'

Corporal Alf Parry, thirty, regularly in boxing action at Newark's Queen's Head and Imperial Buildings before joining the West Yorkshire Regiment (Prince of Wales's Own), was killed after volunteering to take another man's place carrying ammunition to the Front Line. He left a young wife, Emily, and girls aged two years and two months. He had been at the Front eighteen months and was mentioned in despatches for bravely rescuing a wounded man under fire.

Fred Thurman, not yet seventeen, was killed in action on 7 July – after volunteering to take soup to the firing line. He got to within twenty yards before being hit. Private Fred May wrote to his mother: 'I ran out to Fred and got him under cover and did what was possible, but it was too late. There was no chance for him living. It might be of some consolation to you that he said goodbye to all before he passed away, and to know that he died a noble death. My heart is too sore to say any more.'

A hint of the chaos emerged when father of five Ralph Shepperson, a gypsum miner with the 10th Sherwoods, was officially reported 'killed between 5 and 11 July'. Of his brothers, the youngest, William, lied about his age to enlist and celebrated his sixteenth birthday during five months in the trenches before being sent home; Herbert, a lance corporal, was wounded 'somewhere in France'.

General HQ of the British Army in France reported on 11 July: 'After ten days and nights of continuous fighting, our troops have completed the methodical capture of the whole of the enemy's first system of defence, on a front of 14,000 yards.' Six hospital ships a day were arriving in Southampton packed with casualties.

Amid the dire news, Alice Pride in Farndon Fields was relieved to hear from her son Ernest, nineteen:

'We are resting now, just behind the trenches... 8 July: Had to leave off yesterday as we moved nearer to the firing line. It seems years since I last saw you, but the time will come, dear Mother, when we shall all meet again. I am about deaf with the roar of the guns. The bombardments are sometimes terrific. If you were here, you would wonder however men live through it.'

Ernie was killed on 13 July by a trench mortar.

Lance Corporal Hassell Ernest Robinson, twenty-one, was reported wounded and missing during a Royal West Kent Regiment victory at Trônes Wood on 13 July. The Old Magnusian, a draughtsman, only went to the front on 22 June. It was two months before his mother Florence heard from the battaltion's Chaplain that her only son went over the parapet with the bombers and was feared mortally wounded; it was 4 June 1917 before his death was officially confirmed. Hassell thus joined George Collett and 72,000 more on the Thiepval Memorial.

Among the many letters Mrs Hannah Cavey received in Bullen's Buildings off Boundary Road after the death of her eldest, John William, twenty-five, on 14 July was a photograph of her. He carried it with him everywhere; and one of the stretcher bearers who carried him from the Somme battlefield kept a promise made in the heat of the mayhem to send it home. It was one of many pledges made by the over-worked bearer, Private Scarborough, as the shells rained down. By the time he had time to post the photograph to his sister in Cambridge, he was not entirely sure whose it was, but he thought it might be Mrs Cavey (who had lost to natural causes three of the nine children of her marriage with farm labourer William). So Miss Scarborough wrote to Mrs Cavey:

'I have a brother in France and he sent me this picture of somebody's Mother and I, thinking you might value it, have sent it to you. My brother said in his letter that your son, as I expect it would be, was killed, poor fellow. Would you be kind enough, if it does not belong to you, to send it back to me as I shall treasure it with care.'

She did not get it back; it was treasured.

Lance Corporal Joseph Kelly of the 1st Lincolnshire Regiment wrote to the *Herald* on 29 July

German machine gun team in action during the Somme battle.

'Just to offer my sincere sympathy with the relatives of the Newark lads who have gone under. I have been out here since May 1915 and have seen a bit of hard scrapping around Ypres and St Jean where I was wounded in August 1915. There is plenty of excitement out here, I can tell you, especially just now and, when you come to talk about the advance [on 1 July], well, it was simply grand. After a bombardment lasting seven days, our lads rushed the German first line trench on a long front. Of course we had a few casualties caused by the German machine gunners who showered a hail of lead across No Man's Land but nothing could stop the rush, and the first line was won.

'Our artillery had played sad havoc amongst them, as the Germans lay in heaps; a mangled mass. One part of the trench on the right of Fricourt was simply a fortress with dug-outs thirty foot deep, and some deeper. Right in the bowels of this hill the Germans lived in luxury as no shells could penetrate to that depth and nothing but a mine could blow them up, and as our lads entered the trench some of the *Allemand* seemed rather loathe to come out. Our bombers threw hand grenades amongst them. Oh yes, I think we shall win.'

Joseph, 15765 Kelly was destined to die in 1918, aged thirty-seven, leaving a widow, six children and a recently widowed mother in the Millgate area. Through three operations after his body was shattered by shrapnel, he kept his family informed of the biggest personal battle of his brave life. His first letter, to mother Matilda, revealed he was in the Australian Hospital, Rouen, with broken legs, a smashed jaw and other wounds. After two operations, he wrote that he didn't know what the future held because he needed another and could not take any nourishment. A telegram warned he was dangerously ill. Another wire came two days later: he passed away on 14 June.

The last man to climb the 236-foot Newark Parish Church steeple was killed on 14 July aged forty-three – so old, he would not have been allowed to enlist if he had stayed in England. John James Gravell scrambled up the church before breakfast as a teenager. As evidence, he scratched his name on the top before returning to earth. He continued his adventures by sailing to South Africa, worked as a joiner for De Beers' diamond miners for almost twenty years, but left his Newark-born wife in Kimberley in October 1915, and had been in France for three months. He was alone in a dug-out in Delville Wood when a shell exploded on the parapet.

Oliver Farrance, reared in a Dr Barnardo's home, had all the makings of a truthful and reliable citizen; and unhesitatingly joined the Army rather than stay in the safe service of the Newark family who took him in four years earlier. Having obtained a 1st class certificate in machine gunnery with the 8th Battalion Queen's Own (Royal West Kent) Regiment he was killed on 15 July aged twenty at Ypres.

One of the few Newark bakers to volunteer when war broke out, Private David Proctor, died on 16 July, aged twenty-five. He had spent five months in hospitals with frost-bitten feet before being sent back to France with the 1st Leicestershire Regiment.

Two Old Magnusians perished on 21 July. Archibald Gordon Ford, twenty, a sapper, helped in the Dardanelles evacuation, fought in Egypt and died near Albert. William Derry, twenty-seven, fourth son of a former licensee of the King's Arms, served a plumber's apprenticeship in Newark but he went farming in Australia in 1910. He joined the 1st Battalion Australian Infantry and went to Egypt, where he was reunited with Sherwood Rangers who had been with him in Newark Rowing Club. Transferred to France, he was killed around Pozières when a shell struck his mortar.

The Lawrence boys from Sleaford Road were in the wars again. Only a few days after Herbert, twenty-seven, a company sergeant major in the 2/8th Sherwoods, left the Dublin hospital that had extracted a bullet from his chest, his brother Albert was wounded near the French town of Albert. A joiner at Ransome's before joining the REs, Albert saw action at Loos, Hohenzollern Redoubt, Hill 60, Givenchy, Armentières and Hulluch. He had had several narrow escapes, especially when a sniper's bullet grazed his lip.

Police Constable Charles William Smith, twenty-two, was killed on 1 August, the first fatality among volunteers from the Newark Force. He was a sergeant in the 17th Foresters.

Corporal Albert Peet, 32, whose wife Bertha and seven children lived in Crescent Place off Cherry Holt Lane near the Sherwoods' new drill hall, received a surprise birthday present on 9 August: a Military Medal for 'gallantry and devotion to duty during a raid on the enemy trenches near Givenchy on the night of 31 July-1 August 1916'. The Slater's fishing tackle shop assistant was rejected as unfit for the 8th Sherwoods when war broke out so enlisted in the 17th Sherwoods (Welbeck Rangers).

George Nicholas Harvey, nineteen, a gentleman's valet before joining the 1/8th Battalion King's Liverpool Regiment, was killed on 9 August while being carried to a dressing station with a head wound. What happened to his stretcher bearer(s) was not related to his mother, Charlotte Harvey in King Street.

George Cobb, twenty-seven, Newark Midland Railway Station porter, initially rejected for active service because of poor eyesight, became the best stretcher bearer in his company of the King's Royal Rifles and died, 19 August, in Delville Wood. Writing to his parents, Lieutenant GH Gibson paid tribute to George's 'high degree of true courage', adding: 'There are so few of my old Company left that I feel the loss of your son more deeply.'

Christopher Winn, twenty-two, reared in two Newark hotels, The Midland and Old White Hart, passed away in the renowned Wharncliffe Hospital, Sheffield on 21 August – a victim of cruel fate twice over. He was wounded while walking with friends far behind the front lines: a German shell landed among them, killing one and wounding three. After treatment, Christopher was shipped to England for an operation on his right ankle but, after a haemorrhage, lost his leg. This appeared a success until gangrene supervened.

A letter in the *Herald* on 2 September from Private G Clarke of the Machine Gun Corps revealed the bravery of Frank Bentley, thirty, a Quibell's labourer and sometime boxer before he joined the 4th Sherwoods, aged eighteen:

> 'Private Bentley and Sergeant Poole went out to the Front to look for a better position for their machine gun, and got such a good position that they were able to fire straight up and down the German trenches. They took their bearings before it was dark and then came back in the trench for ten minutes or so, then they took the gun out and got it mounted and laid. As soon as they had got everything ready the Huns started dropping 5.9s around them and we expected to see them get blown up any minute. But we saw both of the men sitting smoking and laughing till it was pretty quiet again and then they let the Germans have a lively ten minutes of it. Then Fritz started again with his heavies so they came back into the trench again with the gun. I have seen Private Bentley fight in the ring and have a great liking for him, and I have seen him fight in the trenches, always cool and laughing; no matter how heavy the straffing is, he is always the same.'

Frank continued to move elusively: he does not appear among the 1918 Newark Absent Voters List or among the war dead.

John Charles Judson, twenty, a star schoolboy footballer before he worked for Quibell's and then joined the Sherwoods, was posted missing on 5 September. It was July 1917 before the authorities told his parents Joseph and Emma that he was killed on 3 September at Beaumont-Hamel, one of the villages the Germans had turned into a fortress. Even later in July, 1917, carter's widow Elizabeth Daubney, fifty-nine, of Eldon Street, would be told the nephew she had raised as her own, George Henry Pilsworth, thirty-two, had also perished on 3 September 1916, with the 17th Foresters.

Walter Vacey, twenty-four, who worked for Gilstrap's in Newark before joining Leeds City Police in 1912, was killed at Gorré on 6 September. His parents, Joseph and Lucy, received a caring letter from a comrade in the Royal Garrison Artillery:

> 'He was a good mate … We worked as policemen together and enlisted together and I feel it very much as he was a soldier and a man and did his duty well. He

got his wish as he often told me that if anything happened to him, he wanted it to be quick and it was.'

Of his five siblings, Lance Corporal Robert Vacey, twenty-seven, would be killed at Arras in spring 1917.

Robert Welch, twenty-two, was writing a 'thank you' letter for a parcel he had just opened when a shell exploded beside him at Bouzincourt on 9 September. Of his brothers who had been fighting alongside him in the Lincolns, John William, thirty-one, was home in Tolney Lane with shell shock and Lewis, eighteen, had such severe arm injuries that he was limited to home service.

William Grocock, thirty-nine, left winger during some of Newark Town's most successful football seasons, was killed on 14 September at Authuille, near Albert, leaving a widow Ellen, thirty-six, and children aged eleven and nine. A boilerman, he was a lance corporal in the Duke of Wellington's (West Riding) Regiment.

Lucy Davis, twenty-nine, was starkly informed on 15 September she was a widow. Announcing the death of William Henry Davis, a private in the Lewis Gun Section of the Sherwoods, his Sergeant Major wrote:

'I hope you will not let this sad news trouble you too much. I know it is very hard, and you must excuse me putting it so straight and plain, but I have had this sad and painful duty to perform so often. I have always found it better to let the relatives concerned know the exact facts.'

Barclay's bank clerk Percy White went 'over the top' on 15 September with his Royal Fusiliers' platoon officer, Sir William Blount – and disappeared. Sir William was wounded. Percy was officially listed as died on 18 September.

Mother of three Elizabeth Smith received news that her forty-year-old husband, Corporal-Farrier Alfred Smith, was 'accidentally killed by an explosion' at Millencourt near Albert, on 20 September. 'I cannot tell you how sorry I am,' wrote his captain in the 23rd Division Ammunition Column, Royal Field Artillery. Alf played the organ at St Agnes' Mission on Beacon Hill and carried on the family farrier's business before enlisting. He had no trouble remembering that he went out to France on 24 August 1915: it was the tenth anniversary of his father, Richard's, death.

Spinster Elizabeth Gale, fifty-five, provided Newark with a rare titbit of cheery news on 22 September: her nephew, Second Lieutenant J H Baker of the Royal Field Artillery Special Reserve, had earned a Military Cross for keeping a forward gun in action within 300 yards of the enemy throughout an attack, despite heavy shelling of his exposed position. 'He showed the greatest coolness and determination.'

On the same day Arthur L Smith, one of the clerks in Mayor Knight's business before he became a drummer in the 1/8th Sherwoods, earned a mention in despatches during a successful raid on enemy trenches. While lying in a hospital bed in Wharncliffe recovering from bullet wounds to his abdomen and right side plus bomb wounds to the left knee and thigh, he received a message from the Major General Commanding the North Midland Division: 'Your Commanding Officer and Brigade Commander have informed me that you have distinguished yourself by conspicuous bravery in the field. I have read their report with much pleasure.'

With so much good news, the day simply had to end badly – and hansom cab proprietor Francis Swann in Boundary Road discovered that his son William, twenty-two, had been killed in Greece. A sergeant in A Squadron of the Sherwood Rangers Yeomanry, William was looking for a position from which fire could be brought to bear on the enemy, who were 'making things rather too warm' when a Bulgarian bullet hit him in the neck. His Commanding Officer, Lieutenant Colonel Harold Thorpe, called William 'a most promising sergeant, keen and capable, and absolutely fearless. There is no man to whom I would entrust a difficult task with more confidence.' Major Hugh Tallents added that William was 'full of courage and always ready for any duty, however dangerous.' Quite a transformation from when the Simpson's apprentice was a choirboy and in the Bible Class at Christ Church.

Back on the Somme, Leonard George Simpson, twenty-two, a cashier at the London City and Midland Bank's Newark branch before joining the Royal Fusiliers in March 1916, disappeared on his way to a dressing station after being wounded while fighting with the 12th Middlesex Regiment on 26 September. Almost three months later he was officially confirmed killed. He had been performing so gallantly that he had been recommended for a commission.

Private John Henry Atkinson, twenty-six, a brewery worker before enlisting in August 1914, was wounded in the ear and shoulder during the taking of Thiepval on 27 September, as he had been during the Suvla Bay landings in Turkey. He served in three regiments: the Lincolns, Lancashire Fusiliers and Northants; and was in three hospitals at Alexandria, Zig-a-Zag and Sittingbourne, before getting home to Sydney Street, marrying Florence Seymour in 1919, and living to the age of eighty.

Sherwoods Private Thomas Gardner, thirty-eight, who went unscathed through the Dardanelles and served in Egypt before being shipped to France, lay for thirty hours where he had been hit by shrapnel before comrades found him. He underwent two operations on a shattered thigh – and returned home to Barnbygate to live into his sixties.

Former Newark Town footballer Walter Wilson, thirty-one, who had emigrated to Holland to teach football and cricket but became a sergeant in the Leicestershire Regiment (one of four sons and two sons-in-law of jobbing gardener Frederick and Eliza Ann Wilson to serve), wrote:

'I am in dock, am to undergo an operation for a broken cartilage in the right knee … so I thought it would interest you to hear of the fighting on the Somme by someone who has been through it.

'I am going to refer to our Division's last success there on 25-26 September 1916, the taking of the village of Guedecourt. We were having rather a decent time in part of the Arras sector and had been there for about three weeks roughly when it came through we were for the Somme – we were off on the march – we arrived on the sloping ground in front of Bernafay Wood about 2am. Shelters there were none and this ground was under constant shell fire, so we had to make what cover we could. I, with a party of my men, made several journeys over to Trones Wood and brought back material from Boche dug-outs for that purpose. (I might add that our first morning here I saw [Prime Minister] Mr Asquith's son buried

[Lieutenant Raymond Asquith, of the Grenadier Guards], also the grave of an unknown soldier that the King saw.)

'The weather set in very bad, rained in torrents for two days; it was awful for the boys who had no cover. The weather delayed the attack for two days. We had a surprise: Horace Twells of the REs, late of Ransome's, walked into our camp. I was just issuing out the rum. Of course, we had to treat our visitor.

'Well, it was Sunday morning when the order came. We were off up to position that night, so there was plenty of work to do. We left camp at 6.30pm and marched along, leaving the town of Longueval and Delville Wood on our left. Roughly we were two hours reaching position. The Durhams and the KOYLIs were holding this trench and were to file out for us to occupy it.

'As we filed along on top of the parados, Fritz started shelling us. One shell fell just in front of me and put a few of our Battalion out of mess. We had to make a scramble in the trench and get the wounded men bandaged up. Here it was difficult getting the stretcher bearers up owing to the trenches being full. I had to dress one bombing officer up: he got his right arm smashed to bits – hard luck for us as we were short of officers. Fritz shelled us pretty heavy that night, also the next morning. I had the unpleasant experience of being buried but one of our stretcher bearers dug me out. Afterwards I went and found my boys and everything was all right.

German artillery men loading their gun.

'We got our orders that we were going over at 12.35 midday. The morning passed pretty quiet up to 12 o' clock and all the boys were happy and anxious. We were all just awaiting our gun barrage and then once over the top we had orders to advance in files of sections, artillery formation as far as possible, then deploy if enemy fire too heavy. We hadn't gone fifty yards before we had to extend. The German barrage and machine guns played the devil.

'Men were falling like sheep. But it didn't stop us. We had to take the village if it took a week and all our men. We had one mile of open country to advance over and owing to the heavy fire we had to get into a sunken road and dig-in. Tommy Bentley was shot down just a few yards in front of me. Well, we had to lie down here for a time as Fritz was giving us some of all sorts. It was in this road at one particular spot a German machine gunner was sniping the poor wounded chaps who were crawling to safety. Shelled as we were at this point, we were almost

British troops moving to the Front Line along a communication trench.

non-combatants, but it was impossible to do anything other than wait. There was no officer and I found myself in command of men of all units.

'We waited until dusk and then filed into a trench and reorganised for another push. This took place on 26th and here we first saw a tank in action. At 8.30am we had just got rations issued when a cheer went up and all jumped on the top of the parapet to see the land ironclad. It came waddling along the trench and firing down, driving the Germans in front of it. They came out in droves, holding their hands up and crying: "Mercy!" We took 826 of them and for this we have the tank to thank. Afterwards it was an easy matter. We chased over the ground and held the village until a reserve battalion of ours and the KOYLIs came and dug themselves in. We had achieved our object, although it had taken longer than time allowed, but Fritz was far stronger than estimated. But the chief factor in the success was the tank.

'Of course we are all proud of our units. But the casualty roll tells what the Tigers had done. There are some Newark boys of the Tigers who will never return. But I am proud to think that I have had many of them with me. When we came back for a rest, I met an old pal, Charlie Aslin [33, a millwright]. Also we saw young Gelsthorpe from Barnbygate [most likely Wilfred]. It's surprising who we meet from Old Newark!'

Hubert Everard Clifton, twenty-five, only son of the former Wesleyan superintendent minister at Newark, succumbed to pneumonia on 4 October, having twice overcome war wounds. The Old Magnusian and Cambridge University student set aside ambitions in the legal profession and enlisted in the 1st Battalion Devonshire Regiment in 1914.

Sergeant Charles William Crowder, thirty-one, died of wounds at a clearing station at Meaulte on 12 October, three days after revealing he had nearly reached the top of the roll for leave and looked forward to popping in to Bowbridge Road. His big brother George, thirty-four, of Sleaford Road also went missing in October, but it was August 1917 before he was officially listed as killed. The oldest of seven children, George was a Ransome's coal porter before joining the North Staffs in May 1916, went to France in August and was transferred to the Lancashire Fusiliers a fortnight before his death.

The *London Gazette* of 20 October, announced that former Newark Baptist Church Minister, the Reverend Thomas William Hart, forty, had been awarded the Military Cross:

'On two occasions he has shown great devotion to duty under heavy shell fire in assisting to collect wounded. His work and assistance in attending to the wants of the wounded, both in the front trenches and in the advance dressing stations, have been invaluable and worthy of the highest praise. He has carried out his duties under shell fire in a cool and resolute manner.'

He had been in France since September 1915, as a chaplain to 75 Infantry Brigade and 76th Field Ambulance of the Royal Army Medical Corps.

Private Frederick Harry Jepson, twenty-seven, was killed on 13 October – nineteen months after his brother-in-law, William Copley, died in action in 1915. Fred had been married barely a year before being ordered to leave the Newark Clothing Company and join the Sherwoods. He was transferred first to the North Staffordshire Regiment and finally the Lancashire Fusiliers.

James Edward Munton, 27, became Newark's first St John Ambulance Brigade volunteer to be killed in the war, on 21 October, a year after pleading with fellow fit Newarkers to enlist. His family heard about his demise at Meaulte in agonising stages. First a letter from a comrade in the trenches told his parents:

'Jim has been wounded ... he got rather a nasty smack. It is very hard luck as he had just been made Sergeant and they all tell me he had just done some very fine work before he was hit.'

Then came an up-date from a Wesleyan chaplain:

'His condition is, I think, serious. The wound in his head has affected his speech but he can understand a little when spoken to.'

And finally the sister in charge of a clearing station informed his wife Ruth:

'We did all we could but the brain was injured and he died. He was unable to send you any message.'

More prolonged suspense was suffered by Thomas Brown's family: his young wife Emily, three children aged ten to six plus his parents Harry and Emma. Tom, thirty, was reported missing at Bancourt on 23 October, only days after being rushed to France to join the 2nd Lincolnshire Regiment from a massive munitions factory at Chilwell, Nottingham. It was 19 June 1917 before he was officially declared dead.

The boy who would become Sir Donald Wolfitt, the Newark area's most famous actor, lost his big brother Philip to war wounds on 1 November. A scholarship from the Mount School earned Philip education at the Magnus until he was fifteen. Then he sailed to Canada, joined his grandfather, JH Tomlinson, in Victoria, British Colombia, and began to learn surveying before patriotism led him into the 88th Battalion CEF at Victoria in December 1915. He had a few days' leave with his parents and siblings before he volunteered to join a draft of the 43rd

Big brother of a famous actor – Philip Woolfitt. *[Advertiser cutting]*

CEF sent to France early in August.

He was in the firing line for a month before he was severely wounded in the right arm, left hand and head on 9 October. Severe shrapnel wounds in the hip caused complications. He was shipped to England on 17 October and underwent several operations at King George's Hospital, London. Septic poisoning and haemorrhage conspired: there was no hope of saving the young life. His parents, William Pearce Woolfitt, a brewers' accountant, and Ontario born Emma, were at his bedside when he died, aged nineteen. The hospital chaplain wrote:

> 'All of us who have come in touch with the dear boy have felt that it was fitting that he should be called away on All Saints' Day. His sheer goodness has inspired us all. His patience and cheerfulness were wonderful all through, for he has been suffering much pain. We have lost a lot of boys since July, but in no case do I remember such a widespread feeling of sorrow and sympathy in the Hospital as was felt today.' (When Donald opted for the stage, he dropped one of the o's from his surname.)

The panic in Private Charles Salmon's message was clear when he wrote to his parents Walter, a bricklayer, and Mary early in November:

> 'Do you know what has become of Jack Abbott? I told him that I would look for him and bring him in, dead or alive, but he crept away, shell-shaken. I was in the thick of it on the 3, 4 and 5 July – shells bursting all around me. I fetched in 100 wounded men in the three days. I worked that hard that I laid down about 600 yards behind [the front line] and had a rest for a bit. I have been in another big fight since then. We helped to capture Combies. We are the lads who fought at Mons, on the Aisne and the Marne. We fought them to a standstill when quite a small Army.'

Charles survived to appear among the 1918 Absent Voters and so did his Lincolnshire Regiment mate, John Thomas Abbott.

Wesleyan lay preacher Herbert Caunt, twenty-three, a butcher's assistant before he joined the Royal Army Medical Corps, was commended for bravery. Not one to boast, he merely forwarded to his parents a letter signed by the Major General commanding his division:

> 'Your Commanding Officer and Brigade Commander have informed me that you have distinguished yourself by conspicuous bravery in the field on 13 to 16 November 1916. I have read their report and, although promotions and decorations cannot be given in every case, I should like you to know that your gallant action is recognised and how greatly it is appreciated.'

Herbert wrote:

> 'I would love from the bottom of my heart to be with you for Christmas but that doesn't seem possible so I must make the best of it out here. The officers have kindly purchased two pigs and other things for us. The last time we were in action we had a pretty rough time of it but our boys did fine. Of course I am pleased to try and get honour for our ambulance... but I only realise how little I can do

without the aid of our Saviour and friend Jesus. He won it for me – I hope and pray that this terrible war will soon be over so that I can return home again among you.'

Herbert returned eventually and wed Ada Woodforth in 1924.

Butcher's boy Charles Frederick Titchener, nineteen, was killed on his second venture into the Front Line on 13 November. He joined the Sherwood Rangers six months earlier, was in the West Yorkshire Regiment when he went to France in October, and died at Colincamps near Albert.

Private Ernest Barton, twenty-six, was posted missing at Thiepval by the 1/7th Northumberland Fusiliers on 14 November. On 10 July 1917 his mother Kate, in Lombard Street was told that he must have died.

Amputations were in the news on 3 December. Joseph Cutts, twenty-seven, a willow worker before he became a signals sergeant, lost a leg after being wounded in the right knee. A sister in the 10th General Hospital, Rouen, assured his wife:

'He is doing as well as can be expected and, considering everything, he is wonderfully cheerful. If he continues to make the progress that he is doing at present there is no reason why he should not eventually get back to you in England.'

His father had already been invalided out of the army after fighting in the Dardanelles and France. Also on this Sunday, Sapper George Wright, twenty-six, had his left leg amputated in Southampton University Hospital after being wounded while on road-making duties with a Scottish regiment. It was his fourth operation; devastating for a young man who loved to play football and cricket and was a bricklayer.

Barnby Road Council School teacher Walter Holmes, thirty-four, returned to Newark on 8 December after being wounded in the Somme while with the Liverpool Pals: shrapnel 'entered his temple and destroyed an eye'.

Sergeant Joseph Naylor, twenty-one, was buried at Newark Cemetery on 18 December. He worked at Simpson's, enlisted in the Leicestershire Regiment in 1914 and was at the Front for seventeen months. He fell ill in the trenches with pleurisy and pneumonia and was sent to Guildford Hospital. Consumption supervened, he lost the power of speech, but was still able to recognise his parents and sisters May and Rebecca when they visited to say their 'farewells.'

On 21 December, lengthy and heart-wrenching worry ended for two Newark mothers. Mother of ten Annie Bryan was told that her football-mad younger son, Fred, posted missing more than fourteen months earlier, had finally been reported dead. He celebrated his twenty-third birthday in the trenches in August 1915, was allowed home on leave the following month and had only returned to France about a fortnight before he disappeared. Simultaneously, mother of six Mary Jane Hardy, in Rowbotham's Row off Water Lane, learnt she was officially a widow, eleven months after her thirty-year-old husband Adolphus went missing.

The Sherwoods' performance on the Somme was warmly praised by 'a British general holding an important command on the Western Front' in a Newark *Herald* review months later:

'No Regiment I know of has acquitted itself better on the Somme than the Old Sherwood Foresters. On one occasion our success in very difficult and important operations over a wide front depended on our ability to carry a position that had proved a stumbling block for days past. Several attempts had been made to carry the position. They had failed, and it was the general impression that the position could not be taken by mortals.

'As a forlorn hope we decided to let the Notts and Derbys men have a try. The Battalion selected was made up of new army men [the 2/8th, raised in Newark]. They had had no previous experience of such terrible work. But when I saw them parade for the attack on the morning selected, I knew at once that if mortals could command success in this enterprise the "Fearless Foresters" could achieve it. The Battalion went over in fine spirits. They were met with a terrible storm of projectiles from all kinds of guns, and it looked as though they were going to be swept out of existence. Yet they never faltered, never wavered for a fraction of a second even. Men went down under the terrible hail of fire. But the survivors pressed on with a steadiness that veterans might have envied.

German infantry counter-attacking positions with the aid of a flamethrower and hand grenades.

'They crossed the ground separating them from the enemy's position in record time and flung themselves on the foe like a mountain torrent rushing downhill. The enemy had reckoned their position impregnable, and they were astonished that it should have been rushed in the way our brave lads from Nottingham and Derby districts rushed it. They brought up every available man and spare gun they had. They directed on this small front a big gunfire of unparalleled violence, and flung against the attacking force horde after horde of their finest troops. All to no purpose.

'Sheer weight of numbers and metal forced the Notts and Derbys to give way, but their recoil was only temporary. Quickly rallying under the leadership of one of the finest officers, they threw themselves on the foe with the bayonet. The Germans strove their hardest to withstand the attack, but they might as well have tried to smash the force of Atlantic breakers with paper walls. The Notts and Derbys men fought their way into the trenches in spite of all opposition. Quickly they took possession of the whole section, and settled down to withstand the inevitable counter-attacks which were delivered by enemy forces eight to ten times as strong as ours. The first attack broke down under the withering fire of the lads of Nottingham and Derby, but the second gained a footing in our advanced trenches.

'The Foresters gave ground again for a few moments, but again they rallied, and by one of the finest bayonet charges I have ever seen they swept the foe out of the position once more. After that they held their ground in spite of all the enemy could do. Poison gas, liquid fire, torrents of bombs, massed machine-gun fire, and shells by the thousand; all were tried in the desperate aim of the Huns to break our line and undo the damage that had been done to their cause by the fine onslaught of the Foresters. All was in vain. In spite of everything the foe could do, the line held firm. Our advance was made possible in other directions, and that was entirely due to the splendid valour of this glorious regiment. I think it right that the people at home should know.'

While the Somme became a blood-soaked struggle in the mud, Newarkers had wished 'Godspeed' on Sunday 24 September 1916 to a pair of wealthy neighbours on London Road whose exploits on the Carso (Italian) Front – a barren limestone plateau of about fifty square miles – became a deadly version of the Keystone Cops of silent movie fame. Councillor Frederick Richmond, forty-four, and retired wood merchant Roland Hadfield Smith, sixty-eight, manned a motor ambulance of the British Red Cross Society, operating up to the firing lines. Smith was killed on 1 December (leaving an impressive £27,048 12s 3d net in his will). Richmond returned home after three 'very arduous months' during which 58,000 Italian allies and 55,000 of the Austrian enemy were killed or wounded.

Richmond had been turned down for Front Line service because of defective eyesight in 1914. In Italy he drove himself to exhaustion (and his colleagues to distraction). Most driving had to be done at night because vehicles were easy prey for snipers during daylight. The twisting mountain roads, along with incessant snow, proved a great strain on his poor eyesight. Richmond persevered until the commandant of his unit insisted that he saw a renowned Italian oculist, Professor O Parisotti, in Rome. Richmond was forbidden to drive again and ordered home 'for quiet and necessary rest'. He rejected the verdict, insisting on a second opinion from Sir Alex Ogston, the King's physician who was in Italy with the British Red Cross. Sir Alex confirmed Richmond was suffering from 'abnormal refraction' of the eyes. Richmond returned reluctantly with the thanks of Commandant F Alexander 'for the excellent way you carried out your duties, transporting the wounded from the Front Line, often under trying and dangerous circumstances.' His Commandant, Kenneth Cookson, told him:

> 'You have worked here under the most trying conditions with great courage and willingness. The constant driving, especially at night, to the Front, without any light on black nights, over the crowded and bad roads, often under fire, is a very hard test, which only the young and fit can stand. It is beyond the endurance of those over military age, as I know well by experience.'

As winter set in and moods darkened, a hundred wives or widows of our soldiers and sailors were entertained to tea in Newark Salvation Army Hall on 25 October and exhorted by Mayoress Hannah Knight and a lady officer from the Salvation Army to be careful where they found companionship, and 'if in severe trouble and anxiety not to fly to drink but to seek help and guidance from Almighty God'. It was announced that during the past year, the Mayoress's Working Party had sent to the troops: 3,874 pairs of mittens, 979 mufflers, 670 pairs of socks, 161 handkerchiefs, 125 pairs of slippers, 104 bed jackets, 78 shirts, 64 splints (various), 59 dressing gowns, 50 draw sheets, 40 pairs of operation stockings, 20 pairs of pyjamas, 35 helmets, 12 bed tables, 2 invalid chairs, 62 hospital bags, 50 pairs of bed socks and 20 'helpless-case' jackets.

Next came fears that Newark would run out of bread. Mill owner Parnham, furious in February when one of his sons was called-up, announced weeks before Christmas that he would have to close because so many of his men had been conscripted. Newark Tradesmen's Association resolved to offer 'whatever help he requires to find the experienced labour to operate it'.

The landlord of the Boar's Head pub, Thomas Spray, forty, a sergeant in the Army Veterinary Corps, survived the sinking of the merchant ship *Ivernia* on 27 December, when thirty-six lives were lost. He was in the water for four hours, on a hospital ship for three days and taken to hospital in Alexandria suffering from 'shock and immersion'. He recovered to live to the age of seventy-two.

For all its traumas, Newark had behaved pretty lawfully in 1916: Chief Constable Wright reported 201 people were prosecuted, forty-seven fewer than in 1915. The value of property stolen was £50 18s 8d of which the police recovered £22 2s.

And the future..?

From the trenches, Herbert Frederick Wilson, a wheeler by rank, who had a son and two brothers serving in France and more brothers in India and Ireland, wrote home to 21 Harcourt Street:

> 'Let us hope the New Year will bring lasting peace among nations and a happy reunion for all our boys. We arrived here after a long, cold journey of three days

and two nights, hungry and tired out, on Saturday night, 23 December. We had our Christmas dinner: roast beef and ham with vegetables, plum pudding with sauce, bon-bons, etc. The dining hall had been prettily decorated by some of the boys. Every man appreciated the hard work which had made our Christmas such a success.'

At home, Newark Tradesmen's Association invited Borough Engineer Joseph E Wilkes to explain his vision for the town. He foresaw Newark and district growing like Birmingham as a major hub in the centre of England, utilising the 1,400hp from the flow of the Trent for a power electricity generating station; emphasised the importance of coal substitutes; and opined that within fifteen years the Government would prohibit the wasteful process of burning raw material.

So much for circus mystics with their crystal balls!

Chapter Four

Tarnished Gold of Hard-Won Victory

As every circus-goer knows, all that glitters is rarely gold. When Newarkers flocked to the 1917 May Fair in the Market Place, packed with cunning inventions created to separate them from their hard-earned cash, a gold watch awaited the dexterous person who could knock over a dice by swinging a ball on a rope. Or, if the winner did not want the watch, he/she could pocket 2s 6d instead. The many soldiers training in town preferred to throng the shooting galleries.

It was just as well: the Territorials of the 1/8th Foresters, who had marched so optimistically from the same cobbled square in August 1914, were on that very weekend again counting the high cost of their latest hard won victory and absorbing the realisation that it counted for little. In the Second Battle of Arras, from 9 April to 16 May 1917, the British, Canadian, Australian and New Zealand forces clawed several miles eastward over muddy, blood soaked territory taken from the Germans including the tactically important Vimy Ridge. There were about 84,000 British killed while the German count

Vimy Ridge, 1917 and the Canadians are seen here 'going over the top'.

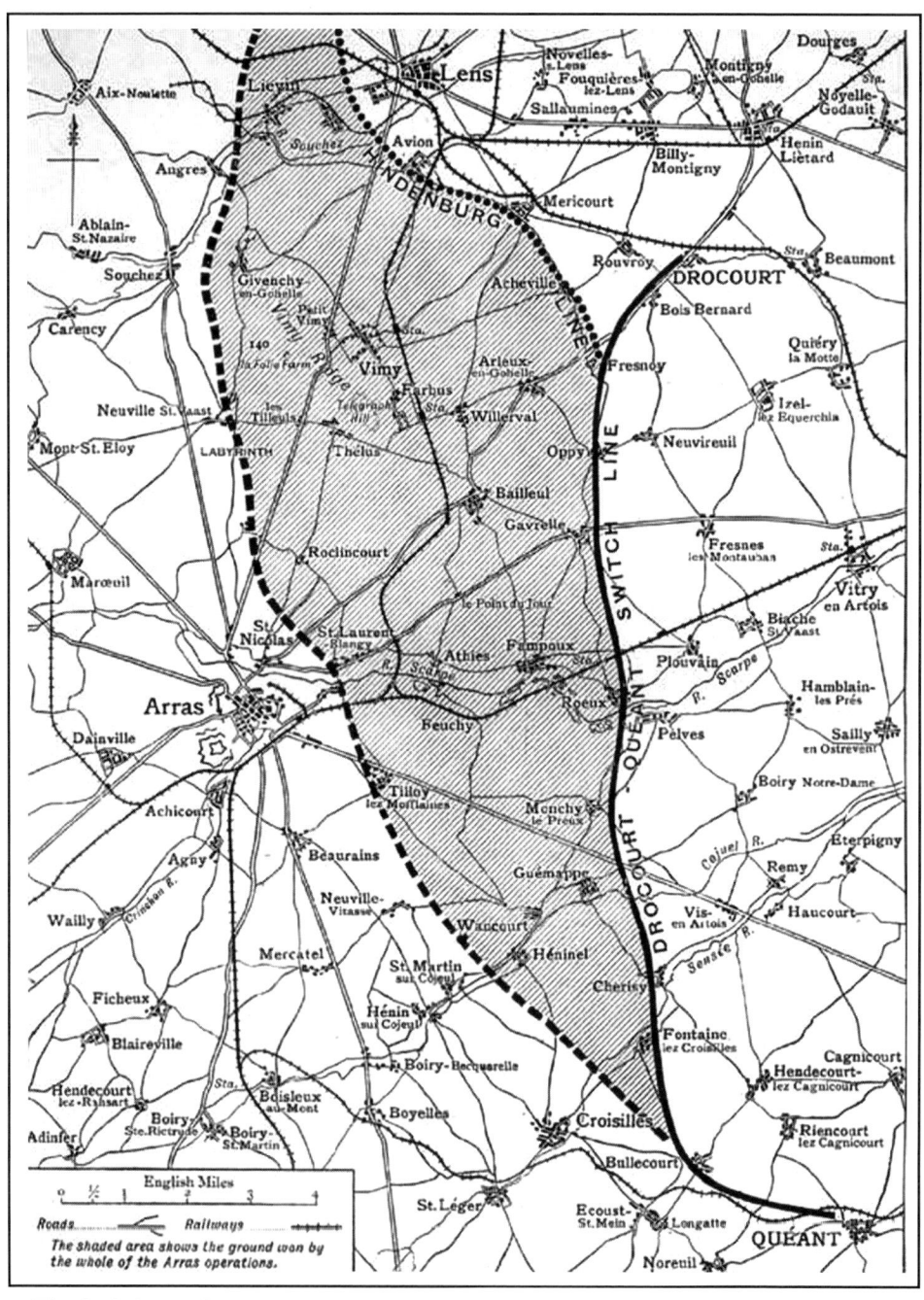

The shaded area shows ground won by the Allies in the Second Battle of Arras, 9 April to 16 May 1917.

was over 75,000. And its value was limited because the almost simultaneous Second Battle of the Aisne failed with huge French losses and a mutiny in the home camp.

The *Newark Herald* alerted the heroes' relatives on 21 April:

'The Sherwoods have taken part in the splendid advance at Arras and have worthily maintained the high traditions of the glorious Regiment, both officers and men displaying the greatest gallantry under the most trying conditions. Alas it is feared that the casualties are heavy, several of our brave lads having paid the full price of victory while many others have been wounded.' It explained why the postmen had been extra busy over the previous few days with doom-laden communications to tearful recipients.

Maltster Christopher Smith and his wife Emily, in Elgin Place, off Appletongate, who had four sons serving, got a note on 17 April from their youngest's best mate in the Sherwoods: Walter, nineteen, was killed 'during the early hours of Easter eve'. Having lied about his age, he enlisted along with fellow iron-workers from Nicholson's foundry on 9 November 1914; emerged unscathed from the Dublin Rebellion; and had only been in France six weeks. It was to become a repetitive pedigree.

Laundress Fanny Catley, fifty, in Mount Pleasant, off Millgate, heard from an officer:

'I deeply regret to have to tell you that your boy, Private William Catley, fell in action on Good Friday in well and bravely doing his duty in an attack. Your lad was always such a cheerful, willing soldier and I had a great affection for him. Words do not express what one feels at all but please accept my most heartfelt sympathy for you in your great loss and may God comfort you in your trouble.'

William, twenty-one, drove a traction engine before joining the 1/8th Sherwoods. There was, of course, heroism among the horrors. On 17 April the *London Gazette* announced a Distinguished Conduct Medal for brewery clerk Harold Wilson, twenty-one, from Spring Gardens for:

'Picking up a trench mortar bomb which fell into the emplacement owing to a defective time fuse and, by unscrewing the time fuse, undoubtedly saving the lives of the whole detachment.'

He had previously done fine work as Gunner 32358, Royal Garrison Artillery. Such news was as rare as a real gold watch.

Ada Cragg was dressing her two children, aged four years and twelve months, when the postman arrived on 19 April with two letters. The first told her that a shell burst while John Thomas Cragg, her husband – their father – was in his billet. The second spelt out the impact: the shell killed him. The youngest of eight children of a brewery drayman, he was twenty-eight, the sugar boiler's assistant at a confectioner's before he enlisted eleven months earlier; gone before his children knew him.

Parents of thirteen, George and Caroline Combes received a letter on 20 April, from Chaplain Hales about their boy Roland, a bandsman, two months before his nineteenth birthday:

'I am very sorry to tell you that your son was killed in action in the early hours of Saturday 7 April. I should like to express my deep sympathy with you in your loss. At the same time I know you will be very proud that he has met his death in so fine a way.'

Roland, who played the bass in Abbott's Band, was one of four patriotic brothers:

Charles had been wounded three times; George was invalided home; and Albert, of the Royal Marines Light Infantry, had fought in Arabia, Egypt, Persia, Somaliland and the Dardanelles.

Ellen Haywood received a happier letter from her husband, John, thirty-four, part-time agent for Newark Liberal Party: his pack saved his life when he was shot on Easter Monday. He was still wounded in the body, but it would have been much worse if the bullet had not been cushioned.

Private Percy Charles Pratt, twenty-nine, an insurance agent like John Haywood before enlisting in the 2/8th Sherwoods, perished while sending signals. His officer wrote to his parents:

> 'I have not been able to find out how he met with his death but the Chaplain told me that the expression on his face was calm and happy with no sign of pain. I am sure you will be glad to know this.'

Borough Surveyor Wilkes arrived to begin overseeing the laying of light railways. He found it 'a weird experience to rush from London to the Front', he wrote to the Town Hall on 23 April. A powerful car was waiting at the French port and they drove straight ahead in the night. It was not long before they 'saw fireworks and heard guns'. There were many sights for which he would have preferred more preparation. The men were working tirelessly but there was so much to be done.

George Henry and Ann Cope, who lost four of their ten children to illnesses pre-war, were informed on 25 April that three of their sons had now been killed in action. The third was Lance Corporal James Cope, twenty-three, whose twin brother Henry was slain at Loos on 25 September 1915, and whose other brother Thomas was killed on 24 June 1916. A chaplain, presumably unaware of the magnitude of the family's sacrifices, wrote: 'I know that you will be very proud that he met his death in so fine a way.'

Two days later, decorator Joseph Smith and his wife Sarah Ann had two letters about their only surviving child, Frank, twenty-four, being killed thirteen months after leaving his hairdresser's job for the 8th Battalion Leicestershire Regiment.

Hairdresser and tobacconist John Cook Belton and his wife Mary Jane were enjoying tea on 3 May when notification arrived that their only son, John Cecil, twenty-two, had died of wounds. He survived horrific injuries in the Dublin Rebellion: he was shot in the nose and a hand grenade smashed one of his knees; but he recovered to go to France with the Sherwoods in February. News of his death came from Sister A Lloyd: 'He was admitted on the 27th suffering from a gunshot wound in the abdomen and, although everything possible was done for him, he passed away the same day at 2.30pm.'

Harry Revill heard on 6 May that he had lost a second son. Harold, twenty-eight, who worked for Gilstrap's for fourteen years before joining the Northumberland Fusiliers in March 1916, had been wounded twice previously. His brother Robert was also twenty-eight when he was killed with the Border Regiment in 1915.

Eleanor Nicholson, whose husband and award winning son were in the Foresters, feared the worst when a shoal of letters arrived on 8 May. All were about her boy, Joseph Henry, whose fearlessness had earned him the Distinguished Conduct Medal – and Newark's first bayonet wound – in 1916. The first message, from a casualty clearing station, was that Joseph was wounded ... 'He wished me to send you his love and tell you not to worry about him.' Then the clearing station Chaplain wrote: 'Your son passed away in the hospital last night [26 April] ... His wounds were very severe and he gradually became weaker ... Your boy died as a hero and gave his life for his country.' The Foresters' Chaplain followed-up with more detail:

> 'On Monday last your son was with others heavily engaged with the enemy. He was severely wounded in the lungs by a flying piece of shell. He was a good man and a brave soldier; it will be difficult to fill his place. I know that you must be proud of the work that he has done and I hope that in time to come it will be a source of pride to you to remember that he met a glorious end.'

His sergeant, E Crooks, despatched 'the deepest sympathy of the boys in the Platoon'. He added:

> 'We can hardly realise yet that he has gone; he was always happy and cheery no matter what hardships we had. He got his wound whilst firing at the enemy who had surrounded a lot of our fellows, but we were unable to save them.'

Of the letters John William and Elizabeth Cox received about the death of the eldest of their nine children, Arthur Edward, thirty-two, they most cherished the one written by Private A Stewart on behalf of his 1/8th Sherwoods platoon:

> 'You may not realise what a tower of strength Sergeant Cox was. Dangers did not disturb nor frighten him and if anything terrible happened, one could feel more confidence if in his presence. You will understand that we cannot at present tell you everything about his death but can certainly assure you that he was doing his duty nobly and fell fighting for King and Country, which is such a great honour for any soldier.'

Arthur's Sergeant-Major added:

> 'He was my greatest friend. It was in a shallow length of trench this happened. He had got all his men in a small dug-out and was standing on the top of the steps to make more room when a shell came over and burst in the trench, and a small piece hit him on the side of the head.'

Private William Charles Savage, twenty-two, a shoe salesman with Freeman Hardy and Willis before he joined the Foresters, suffered shrapnel wounds in both legs.

Five children of school age were left fatherless by the death on 28 April of Charles Cobb, thirty-four, the second son among the thirteen children of his own parents, William and Mary. A Lincolnshire Regiment chaplain wrote to his widow, Lily Mary Ann, thirty:

> 'Your husband took part in an attack in which the Battalion won great praise and he has entered the higher life through the glorious gateway that is opened for those who have laid down their lives for their country.'

Brewery worker Fred Wright, nineteen, disappeared from the Northumberland Fusiliers at Arras on 28 April. It was 9 February 1918 before his death was confirmed to his parents, iron foundryman James and Harriett in Queen Street.

Private Harry Smith, of Barnbygate, was also killed 28 April 1917. He was in the 11th Suffolks Regiment, which attacked the village of Roeux on the north bank of the

River Scarpe, to the east of Arras. Many men were lost as they were beaten back; it was a year before the authorities confirmed he was presumed to have been killed. His wife and children contributed to the *Advertiser's* In Memoriam column:

It's sweet to know we'll meet again / Where partings are no more / And the one we loved so well / Has only gone before.

The Times newspaper on 14 May reported the death of Lieutenant Philip Townsend Crowther, thirty-three, who took part in many entertainments for war charities while attached to the RE at Newark. He had been in France for barely two months before he was killed on 5 May whilst serving with the 211th Field Company.

The Mayor, doubtless recognising that so many deaths were depressing the town, put the cost into stark perspective: of the 1,416 Newark men known to have gone to fight, eighty-six had been killed.

The 87th was named the following day. Arthur Grocock, thirty, who had left his wife Mabel to run the Robin Hood and Little John pub near Northgate Railway Station when he joined the Sherwoods, had been chatting cheerfully to a doctor and nurses at a Casualty Clearing Station at Lijssenthoek near Ypres about his tiresome troubles with 'the screws' as he called his rheumatics when he keeled over. His lungs, ruined by gas, had haemorrhaged. He was the fourth son of Samuel Grocock, President of Newark Trade and Labour Council. Another son, father of two George, thirty-four, of the Lincolnshire Territorials, was wounded and in a Torquay hospital; and five other boys were working in munitions. Arthur's brother-in-law, Joseph Maull, would go missing on 10 July; it would be 20 March 1918 before his death was confirmed.

Harriet Turner, twenty-one, discovered on 17 May that she had been widowed with baby Thomas to rear. Her husband Tom, a hairdresser before being conscripted seven months earlier, was 'killed instantly on 4 May', said a letter from a fellow King's Own Yorkshire Light Infantry private. Official records give his date of death as 3 May – another indicator of the confusion.

Former Magnus teacher and Newark Town footballer William Victor Cavill, a lieutenant in the 1st Battalion West Yorkshire Regiment, was awarded the Military Cross: he entered the enemy lines and, single-handed, captured several Germans. He would live until 1959.

Joiner Walter Kay, whose twenty-seven year marriage to Elizabeth Ann created a family of eleven, learnt on 23 May that their son Harry, twenty-six, had been killed in action, 29 April, leaving a wife Louisa and daughter, eight.

A telegram on 24 May told Florrie Carter she was a widow, aged twenty:

'Regret to inform you Officer Commanding Field Ambulance France reports No. 89960 F J Carter RE died 18 May of wounds. Colonel, RE Records.' Frank James Carter married Florrie on 31 July 1915 while training with the RE in Newark. She had seen him for only ten days since the end of 1915, though according to his last letter 'I think I'll be back in Newark soon'.

Pleasant shell shocks (excuse the pun) arrived as spring gave way to summer. Charles and Elizabeth Lawrence's son Herbert, recovering from two operations after being shot near Arras, got an unexpected perk from home for breakfast – an egg. It was one donated by Cyril Dickinson, twelve, son of a baker and grocer less than half a mile from Herbert's home; one of 214,560 distributed from Newark since the conflict began. It could have gone anywhere in the war torn world. Herbert, a Company Sergeant Major, replied:

> 'Well, Master Cyril, I enjoyed this egg immensely – because it was sent by a little fellow who is doing his bit to assist and comfort we wounded Tommies and, last but not least, because it came from dear old Newark.'

Even more coincidentally, Daisy Musgrove sent from Christ Church School an egg that was gobbled up by an ex-pupil of the same school. 'Perhaps the headmaster will remember me, although it is a few years since I saw him,' wrote wounded Bandsman George William Turner, one of eleven children of tailor's cutter George and Mary Jane. He was a butcher's errand boy and recovered to appear in the 1918 Absent Voters' List.

On 14 June Florence Edlin learnt that her husband George, twenty-five, a brewery cellarman, was among three Sherwoods privates killed by a shell while digging a trench after an attack on 8 May. A fellow private wrote:

> 'I was not far away when it happened. The shell came over and dropped close against your husband, so he could not get out of it no-how. Several other fellows were wounded, and very badly too. I had a narrow escape myself, but I got through again, thank God. I don't know how I shall go on without him. He helped me along at all times. All the fellows will miss him. He was such a nice lad.'

Another letter, 'from comrades', said: 'We loved him for his ever-cheerful and generous disposition.'

A year after pneumonia killed her husband, Eliza Walker heard on 21 June that her second son, George had died on 3 May. Only twenty-two, he could have remained a railway platelayer but enlisted eighteen months earlier and was sent to France in the Rifle Brigade after three months' training.

The postman heaped more misery on widower Frederick Gray, sixty-nine, on 27 June: his third son, Harry, had been killed on 28 April, aged thirty-six. The farm labourer had been in the Lincolnshire Regiment for a year and was last in Newark two months earlier for the funeral of his mother.

Postman and former Newark Town footballer of repute, Charles William Statham, thirty-three, of Harcourt Street, was killed at Arras with the Yorks and Lancs Regiment on 28 June. But it was not confirmed until 3 August; a harrowing interlude for his wife, Nellie, twenty-nine, at home with three children aged seven to one. Nellie first received a letter from a comrade:

> 'We gained our objective with very slight losses but when we got formed up in our proper sections your husband could not be found. I have waited a few days to see whether I could gather any further news but am sorry to say I have not been able to do so.'

A few days later, he wrote again:

> 'I'm afraid he was killed. I feel certain he was not taken a prisoner as none of our fellows met opposition.'

Desperate to find out exactly what had happened, Nellie wrote to the chaplain, who replied: 'I am sorry to say we have no news of him at all'. Eventually the Records Office announced: 'Information has reached this office of the death of 31515 Private CW Statham.'

No wonder the town felt besieged by grief, not to mention hunger, poverty and toil. A public meeting in the Town Hall 28 February had pretty much set the home tone for 1917: Mayor Knight said between 1,200 and 1,400 Newark men had gone to fight. The principal speaker, Sir Richard Cooper, MP for Walsall, added that everyone must help the war effort by rationing their food intake, giving financial support to the War Loan scheme, and straining brain and muscle to do the work that had been carried out by the men in the Forces.

As they were exhorted to make greater sacrifices, Newarkers were absorbing the horrors of two sinkings.

Wireless Officer Edward J Dench, a keen cricketer, returned to his parents who ran the Mechanics Institute in town, confessing that he was 'lucky to be here'. He was on the cargo steamship *Vedamore* heading for Liverpool from Baltimore, when it was torpedoed twenty miles west from Fastnet at 6.10am, in darkness on 7 February with the loss of twenty-three lives. The explosion blew the engine room to pieces, killing its occupants and reducing to splinters all but two of the lifeboats. The *Vedamore* sank within seven minutes. Edward, fast asleep in his bunk when the U-boat struck, awoke as he was hurled to the floor. Quickly dressing, he hurried on deck, discovered what had happened, dashed back to his cabin for his life jacket, and eventually scrambled onto the bridge of the boat, which was listing so alarmingly that the lifeboats could not be launched in the usual manner but merely cut away. A wave brought a lifeboat within a few feet of the ship and Edward leapt for it. He fell into the freezing Atlantic and clung desperately to wreckage. After several minutes in peril, he was hauled into the lifeboat. Twenty-two were rescued and took turns at rowing for ten hours to keep warm. They were picked up by the steamer SS *Wyvsbrook* and then transferred to a warship, which took them into an Irish port.

Councillor Henry Cubley's son Basil, 34, was among the heroes who saved lives after the troop ship *Tyndareus* was mined on 9 February off Cape Agulhas, the southernmost point of Africa. The *New York Times* was awestruck to report that a battalion of the Middlesex Regiment on board 'were paraded on deck and, after roll call, began to sing while they waited for the ship to sink. The *Tyndareus* however was saved and the troops were transferred to two rescuing steamers.' King George V sent a message to the Admiralty and War Office: 'Please express to the officers commanding the Battalion of the Middlesex Regiment my admiration of the conduct displayed by all ranks.' Lieutenant Colonel John Ward MP, commanding officer of a battalion in the Middlesex Regiment, wrote to the *Tyndareus* Captain George Flynn: 'We felt so safe with you and the good old *Tyndareus* that we would have preferred to have continued the journey with you and her. Give not my regards but my real manly love to every one of your officers and crew, especially to your chief engineer (Mr Wregg) and first officer (Mr Cubley). If we never meet again, we shall still be lifelong friends.' After the troops were transferred, the *Tyndareus* crew worked for forty-eight hours in rough weather before reaching port. Every minute, death stared them in the face: they were prepared for the vessel to take her final plunge. Yet the *Tyndareus* continued to serve as a troop ship through World War II, was converted into a peacetime liner carrying 2,000 people, and was not scrapped until 1960. Basil Cubley was promoted Captain of the steam ship *Tantalus* in September 1917.

Belgian refugees Madam and J Delfosse appreciated civilian Newarkers' efforts. Having moved to live with relatives in Gravelines, close to the battlefields, they wrote to the Newark Belgian Homes Committee:

> 'We realise now more than ever, now that we are away, what a great work yours has been. For nearly two years we have lived in a nice comfortable house. You have made our stay in England so happy and pleasant that we almost forget our exile. During all that while, we have been able to notice that your generosity and kindness have been boundless and that Newark people have been as charitable as you. We wish to express our gratitude to the Mayoress and the ladies of the Committee, and we beg you to thank in our name the inhabitants of Newark.'

The Newark Tribunal, meeting on virtually every Saturday night to hear appeals by men not wanting to enlist, gave considerable time to Post Office employee Arnold Evans Dixon, eighteen, a conscientious objector whose convictions emanated from his reading the Bible as a fourteen-year-old. Asked what would have happened if every Englishman had held his view, he said: 'The war would not have happened if everyone had obeyed God.' Military representative Nicholson retorted: 'You would have been in the German Army by now'. The Tribunal refused his appeal.

In a heart-rending case at the Borough Police Court on 8 January, Corporal Coyne of the Military Mounted Police applied for his motherless son of eleven to be sent to 'some institution'. He explained the boy had been put in good homes but repeatedly ran away. He walked to Nottingham once and, when apprehended by the police, said he had eaten nothing for three days and nights. It was decided to send him to an industrial school for two years. Records available a century later reveal that the corporal was Ernest Charles Coyne, forty-three, an Army pensioner living in Harcourt Street and working as a boilermaker's planer, a widower since his wife, Fanny Elizabeth, thirty-five, died in 1914. He rejoined the Forces, despite having sons George William and Owen. The runaway appears to have been none the worse for his traumas. George William Coyne, born 20 September 1906, was seventy-five when he died at Newham, Essex, in 1982. Owen Coyne, born 4 December 1908, lived until 1990 in Peterborough, where his father died in 1920. Corporal Coyne's patriotism is acknowledged on the Charles Street Methodist Church roll of honour.

George Stanley, twenty-six, a maltster at Gilstrap's before he became what his officer in the Manchesters called 'in all senses, a splendid soldier', was killed by shell fire during an attack on an enemy trench on the morning of 11 January. Gilstrap's lost another man two days later: Fred Norton, twenty-five, who had finished fifth of 500 men in a bomb-running competition in training with the North Staffordshire Regiment, was killed beside the River Tigris in Mesopotamia, leaving his wife Edith widowed and with two young children.

Retired Army Captain Tom Harrison, Newark Fire Brigade Captain, and his wife of forty-three years Emma, who had nineteen children, feared the worst on 29 January when the postman called. One of their daughters lost her life in 1906 while endeavouring to save the life of a child; an act that led to the erection of a fountain as a memorial on the Great North Road heading south of out of town. Their son Cyril, twenty-one, made the supreme sacrifice at the Hohenzollern Redoubt along with his workmate at Ransome's, Horace Steemson Wilkinson, twenty-one, who was so determined to 'do my bit' despite suffering acute rheumatism in the knees that he made several attempts to pass the medical to get into the 8th Sherwoods. Another Harrison son was in hospital suffering from German gas. Another was in the 9th Staffordshire Regiment. Yet another was working on munitions. But the new missive was joyous: the oldest of their fourteen surviving offspring, father of four Thomas Ernest, forty, had earned a Distinguished Conduct Medal with the 6th Lincolnshire Regiment. One of his privates, E Martin, wrote excitedly to their old Wesleyan School Head Master, Samuel Walker:

'It was a very brave action that he performed. A post of a certain regiment was captured by the Germans and Sergeant Harrison, without a moment's hesitation, volunteered to go in search of them. I am pleased to inform you that he found the lost men and also captured the Germans.'

The official citation said he 'led a party into the open under heavy enemy fire and succeeded in capturing five prisoners. He set a splendid example throughout.' When Tom returned home, a large crowd was allowed into the Town Hall on 15 May, to see his medal pinned on his tunic by the Mayor. Tom was seriously wounded on 9 June by a stray shell. His Commanding Officer, Lieutenant-Colonel Slater, wrote:

'Don't worry about him as, although his wounds are serious enough to keep him quiet for a time, I don't think any of them are bad. I was quite close to him at the time he was hit, and during the time he was being bandaged I was talking to him. He was as cheerful as possible and his only regret was that he was leaving us. I know you must be very proud of him and you have every reason to be. He is obviously fearless and ready to volunteer for any risky undertaking. We all have the highest admiration for him, and his Company Commander and I will miss him very much. I hope he will get a good rest for there is no one in the Battalion who has done more hard work. The men in his Company were ready to follow him anywhere…'

A chaplain of the 8th Stationary Hospital in France, wrote:

'He is seriously wounded in the back, both legs and left arm. His condition will

Gallantry at 40 – Thomas Ernest Harrison.
[Advertiser cutting]

be critical for some time.' Tom lived well past retirement age.

Factory worker William Knee and his wife Rosa, who had lost three of their six children to illnesses, received three letters on 30 January, informing them that their only surviving son, Reginald, nineteen, a Ransome's machine hand, had been killed by a trench mortar bomb that 'caused a number of casualties' at Foncquevillers. His machine gun officer in the Sherwoods praised him as 'a very keen, intelligent and trustworthy lad. I had great hopes of his advancement and was on the point of giving him a responsible position in his team.'

Back home, Arthur Stephenson Perry, twenty-one, walked into Newark Police Station on Thursday night, 1 February, to explain he had undergone an operation in hospital and wanted leave to pop home to 'the north of England' before returning to the Front. He was arrested for being absent without leave, appeared before a special Police Court the following morning, and was remanded in custody to await a military escort.

On 4 February the Newark Market Place crowd watched an unprecedented ceremony after Church Parades: nine fine sappers received gallantry medals won the previous autumn. Sergeant 49308 G C Hill, No. 4 Company, earned both the Distinguished Conduct Medal and Military Medal. DCMs went to Sergeant 40299 Sergeant G W Heath, No.4 Company; Lance Corporal 63297 H Binnington No. 11 Company. MMs to Corporal 66290 A E Bailey, No. 9 Company; Corporal 40428 R L Crawford, No. 4 Company; Lance Corporal 63124 R James, No. 11 Company; Sapper 61516 J Holt, No. 4 Company; Sapper 96110 T Churchward, No. 11 Company; and Sapper 41865 T Hannah, No. 11 Company. Hill's DCM was

> 'for conspicuous and consistent gallantry during operations. He has over and over again shown great bravery when in charge of working parties under heavy fire. He took out his section on ten consecutive nights and did fine work under heavy fire though suffering very heavy casualties. He was finally wounded himself.'

Heath's DCM was for conspicuous gallantry during operations. When his officer was wounded he led his men daily to work through the enemy's barrage. He constructed the wire of a strong point under heavy shell and machine gun fire. He set a fine example.'
Binnington's DCM was:

> 'for conspicuous gallantry and ability in the construction of an observation post under heavy shell fire. During the work a shell set alight a pile of boxes of bombs in a trench twenty yards away. Lance Corporal Binnington at once proceeded to extinguish the flames though once knocked down by an explosion while doing so. Two days later he was wounded while engaged in the same work.'

Bailey's MM was gazetted on 11 October 1916; Crawford's on 14 September 1916; James's, Holt's and Hannah's on 14 September 1916; and Churchward's on 1 September 1916.

The King, accompanied by Field Marshal Lord French, the Duke of Rutland and Major-General Sandbach, presented gallantry medals earned in 1916 to Captain Quibell DSO, Captain Hewitt MC, Sergeant Major Lacey DCM and Lieutenant Colonel Rayner DSO. The King asked Lacey how long he had been with the Regiment. 'Two years, Your Majesty.' Noticing his ribbons, the King inquired to what regiment he previously belonged. 'The Grenadier Guards, Your Majesty.' The King smiled: 'Ah, I thought so.

You can always tell a guardsman by his smartness.'

The RE attended a different ceremony on 17 February. Sapper Walter F Collins, twenty-five an agricultural engineer pre-war, was buried with full military honours at Newark Cemetery. He enlisted in the 1/8th Sherwoods in September 1914, went to France and was transferred to the RE Inland Water Transport. After a furlough with his wife Lily, twenty-seven, he left to return to his military duties, apparently in good health, but was taken ill within a fortnight, rushed to hospital and expired.

Widow Rachel Day, sixty-five, was too ill to trudge to Newark Cemetery on 22 February to bury her third and last son. Private John Thomas Day, thirty-eight, a

Sign of the times ... workforce in Ransome & Marles' new bearing department.
[NEKMS 11181]

groundsman at Newark Golf Links before joining the Sherwoods, died and was buried a year to the day after his sibling Arthur, forty, of the Leicestershire Regiment.

With the RE entrenched in Newark Workhouse early in 1917, the Board of Guardians accepted Mrs Angene Ellissa Price's offer to lodge and feed Newark's tramps for 6d per head per night in Rowbotham's Row. Within three months, she sought – and received – an increase to 9d per tramp. And with food prices rising, the Guardians agreed to pay Derby Infirmary 10s 6d per head per week to keep paupers and infirm inmates displaced from Bowbridge Road Workhouse: most were 'very infirm'. The move cost a total of £901 8s 5d.

The relentless pressures on the fit were emphasised in mid February: A Ransome and Company Limited of Stanley Works formed a new enterprise, Ransome and Marles

Bearing Company Limited, to extend their bearing department 'to cope with further urgent contracts for war material'. It would earn a worldwide reputation by the end of the Second World War.

Another enterprise had a stinking reputation. Captain C T W Finch RE penned a letter to the *Herald*:

> 'Hundreds of officers and all ranks now stationed in Newark have had various experiences of gas attacks overseas. Is the Newark Gas Company desirous of poisoning their own countrymen? The whole gas system and the stench therefrom is abominable and a great menace to health.'

A month later a mystery that had exercised Newark's chattering classes for two months was solved with the discovery of the body of Gas Company chief cashier Robert Thorpe in the River Trent. Oh, the conjecture since he went missing just after Christmas. But Coroner Foottit announced that the company's books were 'entirely in order'. Thorpe, severely overworked since two clerks were called-up, 'committed suicide during temporary insanity' aged fifty, leaving a wife of twenty-six years, Annie, fifty-four, and four children aged twenty-three to seventeen. One of the gasworkers, Private James William Morton Sooley, twenty-one, was killed in action with the 2nd Sherwoods on 10 March at Philosophe.

Newark made 'magnificent' contributions to the War Loan Scheme. The Council subscribed £17,000 in January. Abbott's bought £5 loans for workmen prepared to pay for them at 1s a week. Thorpe's maltsters bought loans for fifty men who took them at 2s 6d a week. Within six weeks Newark had contributed £329,155 of 'new money' to the war chest. And on 19 March, Newark War Savings Committee received a letter from admiring officials in London: its sub-committees had been so successful at persuading workers to save that they also ought to 'carry out a campaign with the object of reducing the consumption of food'.

A Great Patriotic Sale, involving virtually every organisation and individual for miles around, on 1 March raised £3,664 10s 1d, comfortably exceeding the £2,799 9s 10d from the 1916 effort. The sale encompassed everything from sheep and cattle to soups and kettles; the list of donated items stretched to a page and a half of the broadsheet weeklies. Grants were made to: Mayoress's Working Party £150, Southwell Voluntary Aid Detachment Hospital £100, Newark Prisoners of War Fund £100, Newark Branch War Hospital Supply Depot £100, St Dunstan's Hospital for blinded soldiers and sailors £50, YMCA huts £50, Newark Primrose League Ladies' Working Party £50, Mayoress's Egg Collection £30, Collingham War Funds £30, Lombard Street VAD Hospital £30.

Among nurses 'brought to the notice of the Secretary of State for War for valuable service rendered in connection with the war' on 2 March were ME Cheetham, of the Lombard Street VAD Hospital, and M Edwards, Newark General Hospital. May Shepherd, twenty-six, daughter of gent's outfitter Joshua Shepherd in Victoria Street, became the first Notts VAD member selected for service abroad: she spent eighteen months in Salonika.

Mayoress Knight received a letter from Sir Edward Ward, Scotland House, New Scotland Yard, London, urging her Working Party to keep up their good work:

'Our business is to win the War, and it is essential at this grave moment of national crisis that not only every Association, but every individual forming that Association, should work as he or she has never worked before so as to ensure a continual and adequate supply of all those comforts, both for men in the Field and for the sick and wounded in Military Hospitals at home and abroad, which means so much to the well-being of our Army, and the necessity for which will be even more urgent than hitherto in the near future.'

As proof, Dublin Rebellion hero Captain Quibell DSO wrote to his mother: 'Can do with any amount of socks for the men.'

More rewards for Somme soldiers were announced – H Wilson from Crown Street was recommended for a Military Medal and promoted to corporal in the field for 'a fine act in leading a bombing party' with the King's Own Yorkshire Light Infantry. Even more impressively, ten Sherwoods earned Distinguished Conduct Medals 'for conspicuous gallantry and devotion to duty'.

Sergeant Drummer 2543 R M Cooper: 'On several occasions he collected small bodies of men without a leader and took them forwards. Later he led an attack with great gallantry. He was wounded.' Acting Sergeant Major 9188 T Cumming 'made three journeys in daylight in an armoured car under heavy fire and succeeded in rescuing 350 rifles'. Corporal 3886 J Hill 'acted throughout the day with great courage and initiative, and set a fine example to all ranks'. Company Sergeant Major 2505 M W H King 'greatly assisted his company commander during the storming of various buildings. He set a splendid example throughout.' Sergeant Major 4096 J Lacey 'carried several important messages under very heavy fire. He set a fine example of courage and determination.' Company Sergeant Major 3415 S H Lomas 'erected barricades under very heavy fire, and set a splendid example throughout'. Private 4045 F Snowdin 'although twice wounded and in considerable pain, continued fighting in a most gallant manner'. Private 4871 J Spencer 'remained alone at his post and continued to fire his rifle with good effect. He set a fine example of courage and determination'. Company Sergeant Major H J Toulson 'assumed command of two platoons and led them forward with great gallantry'. Corporal 3894 A E Walker 'displayed great courage and determination during an assault on an enemy barricade. Later he held the enemy back by skilful bombing.' Sapper Sam Whitten, a whitesmith who won medals playing local football pre-war, earned a Military Medal, explaining to his proud parents Samuel and Emily Louisa: 'Me and a Corporal, who has been killed, have been recommended for good work in repairing lines under heavy shell fire.' Then came an update: 'I won a Military Medal on the Somme.' He would be invalided out of the RE in May 1918. Second Lieutenant John Gray, a cadet with the RE in Newark in the summer of 1916, was awarded the Military Cross for conspicuous gallantry in leading a demolition party when raiding enemy trenches near Ypres-Comines Canal on 8 February 1917 and helping to capture ten prisoners.

A letter which arrived in Newark on 13 March was even more poignant than most. It was written by Harold Percy Seager, thirty-one, who lodged at 6 Spring Gardens with widow Jane Huckerby and her three grown-up children. He began the war as joint secretary of a recruiting committee, joined the 7th Royal West Kent Regiment as a private, was commissioned in March 1915, transferred to the Machine Gun Corps in 1916, proceeded to France, endured 'arduous and thrilling times' on the Somme when his company was 'badly cut-up' with the loss of all but four officers and twenty men, and returned to England shell-shocked. In hospital, Lieutenant Seager composed 'The Soldier's Question'. (Opposite.)

Harold P Seager not only survived the War; he reached the age of seventy-three before dying in London.

Three days before Harold's thoughts appeared in the *Newark Herald*, Cafferata's labourer William Brown and his wife Sarah Ann Brown lost their son William, twenty, a painter in a Newark brewery before he volunteered for the Sherwoods. He was sent home with frost-bitten feet in November 1915. His right arm was hit by shrapnel on the opening day of the 1916 Somme 'push'. In mid-February 1917 his worst injury was 'from the back into the chest'; doctors removed part of his ribs. Alas, the matron of a hospital in France wrote on 11 March: 'Your son died this evening. He had been fairly well all day, till about 5pm, when he had a severe haemorrhage.'

Successive Sundays brought sombre messages. Builder Joseph Wright learnt on 8 April that the workman he treated as a son, William Wright Thacker, twenty-two, had been killed at Philosophe. He had become such a valued worker that he moved in with Joseph and Phoebe Wright, who had seven children of their own. He joined the Sherwoods in September 1914, and listed Mrs Wright as his next of kin so affectionately that he was recorded as her adopted son. William and Mary Francis, who had six sons serving, heard on 15 April that the oldest had died aged twenty-nine. Lance Corporal Henry Francis had written that he was very ill in Salonika.

With so much doom to deliver, some postmen were suffering breakdowns so there was quiet understanding when the *London Gazette* on 10 April announced an Imperial Service Medal for Joseph Stanfield, fifty-nine, of Newark Post Office in recognition of long and meritorious service since 1885. Joe sought relaxation as an enthusiastic member of the Newark and District Fanciers' Society (for owners and admirers of exotic birds).

Acutely aware of the need for more soldiers, Newark Tribunal had already adopted a ruthless policy against young men wanting to finish apprenticeships. On 26 March, John Brown, eighteen, was refused two months' exemption to qualify as a plumber; Leslie Francis Twidale, eighteen, an apprentice chemist, was also told to enlist immediately though J H Smith protested he was the only assistant left in his dispensary. Alfred Ernest Stroud, twenty-eight, a wagon loader on the Midland Railway with a widowed and crippled mother, was given a month to find someone to look after her.

Newark was, of course, already choked by trainee soldiers. Half year exams proved the children were adversely affected by half day teaching while the military occupied schools; Newark Education Committee pronounced the results 'satisfactory in the circumstances'. Ex-Mayor Kew demurred, wanting the military out of schools. The Newark Tradesman's Association president George Porter insisted the children could be 'usefully employed for half-days if properly organised'.

In the midst of this contretemps, the RE staged a military funeral in Newark Cemetery

The Soldier's Question

As I trudged one day
Through the mud and clay
A horrible sight I spied
Twas a man in grey
Who had fallen that day –
A bullet had pierced his side.
Twas the battlefield
And my mind did yield
To thoughts of pity and shame
In the heat of the fray
My aim was to slay
With steady and careful laid aim
As my work I surveyed
I knew I had laid
With an accuracy dead and true
For the gun I had fired
With hatred inspired
Had laid out the Bosch – not a few
Then I saw with a frown
A lad in light brown
(Or khaki it's called by the crowd)
Laying close beside
The Bosch; he had died
By the fragments which flew in a cloud
I knew too well
What an absolute hell
These 'sons of their lands' had passed
Ere they gained that peace
Where all troubles cease
So I stopped, I thought, and I asked:
What has become
Of those two, now dumb
Both sodden in bloody clay?
Were they both of them right
In God's own sight?
Will they meet at the Judgment Day?
When Christ shall come
Will they cease to be dumb
And sing of His glorious praise?
Will they cease to fight
In the dazzling light
Of His heavenly sunlit rays?

I had killed fellow men –
My enemies then –
At the sound of my country's call.
My enemies, too,
Had done all they knew
By their fire to make me fall.
I continued my way
Through the mud and the clay
To the trenches just on ahead
Not heeding the shells
Nor the horrible smells
But just thinking of duty instead.
For a while I'm at home
At least, sitting alone
Where it's ever so quiet and still
In a hospital snug,
Round my feet there's a rug
For they tell me I've been rather ill.
As I sit here tonight
In the lamp's bright sunlight
My heart is troubled and sore.
Could I look in His face?
Could I take up my place
And dwell in His light ever more?
Is the Gospel all true –
Proclaimed old and yet new –
Of redemption for those who repent?
E'en though they fight
With the Devil's own might
For us, it was surely not meant!
He declared: 'Peace!
'All warfare shall cease.
'Peace, honour and glory I bring.'
But the Devil says: 'Nay!
'Man shall quarrel and slay,
'Live forever in hatred and sin.'
So my head's all aflame
For I've seen strife and pain
And I've wallowed in dastardly sights.
And my thoughts go astray.
I feel I can't pray
Or decide on the wrongs and the rights.

for Sapper Thomas Asher, twenty-three, eldest son of the nine children of postman John and Eliza of Eldon Street, who contracted blood poisoning in training, had a leg amputated, yet still died. Tommy worked in a foundry pre-war.

One young victim of the RE takeover of Newark Workhouse, aged thirteen, appeared before the town's Guardians, having escaped from Derby Workhouse and walked to a relative's house in Newark. The trek took twelve hours; he did not know the way, but kept asking for directions. The Guardians acknowledged his preference for his relations and arranged for him to remain in Newark and attend an elementary school, part-time of course.

Food became scarcer than schooling. While bread went up to 5½d for a 2lb loaf in March, a sample of barley meal at the Workhouse was found to contain 'a large proportion of cat husks, a substance worthless for feeding purposes'. The supplier, Samuel Ellis, apologised. His next sample revealed too much moisture. He blamed a blizzard that blew snow into his mill but was fined £2 with £2 2s costs by Newark Magistrates for selling barley containing 18 per cent of moisture. He retorted a week later: 'I have since ascertained from Newark maltsters that the moisture in the English barley that they received during February was over 20 per cent. I therefore leave the public to judge whether this was a reasonable case for prosecution.'

Newark Councillors were confounded by a Food Control Order under the Defence of the Realm Act. It identified Wednesday each week as a meatless day (and potatoes could be served only on Wednesdays and Fridays in restaurants and hotels). As Wednesday was Market Day, councillors changed Newark's meatless day to Tuesday. Newark Food Control Committee staged a three day exhibition and gave lectures on how to make the best out of smaller rations. And when it obtained a ton of cane sugar plus a ton of glucose for jam making, there was nearly a stampede in the New Market Hall.

Increasing numbers of prisoners of war in Germany needed food parcels. On 24 April, 240 kind-hearts contested a whist drive to buy supplies for twenty-five men from the Newark area: eighteen Sherwoods, four Lincolns, one West Yorks, one Suffolk and one Northumberland Fusiliers. New regulations forced the local fund to work on a larger scale: 440 boxes were sent in 1916 at a cost of £125; 114 boxes a month were required now at 7s each; almost £480 annually. They included a selection of 2lb corned beef, 1lb treacle, 1lb condensed milk, 1lb Quaker oats, 1lb jam, 1lb salmon, tin herrings, tin tomatoes or beans, etc., 1lb plum loaf, ½lb plum pudding, soup squares, figs, raisins, cigarettes, tobacco, soap, salt and mustard.

Railway signalman's wife Mary Gammage received a grim letter from her son, Frederick, twenty-three, dated 25 May: he and his Sherwoods pals were being very ill-treated and starved by Germans convinced that this was how Britain was treating their prisoners. They were forced to work within range of the Allies' shells. Rifleman John Mayfield of the King's Royal Rifle Corps wrote to his parents, James and Annie Mayfield, in Farndon Fields, on 28 May, that he was a PoW: his letter arrived on 4 July.

Newark Public Health Committee feared that a shortage of doctors was imminent, too. Medical Officer of Health Dr Galbraith and another GP had been called up into the

Army, joining Dr Stallard. The Secretary of the War Committee of the British Medical Association visited to insist that they 'put no obstacle in the way of the military' if more were conscripted.

The townspeople remained so law-abiding that there were no cases to be heard when Newark Quarter Sessions sat on 12 April. But a young widow, Emily Evans, appeared before Newark Police Court on 7 May accused of loitering and was given arguably the town's first ASBO. The Chief Constable labelled her 'one of many women of loose character and unclean' accosting soldiers. She said she could not work as she had only one arm. She was given fourteen days in prison 'with such hard labour as you can do'. Police also obtained an order under the Defence of the Realm Act barring her from residing in Newark.

Good news came to Gunner Adam Fenton, thirty-four, a professional artist, on 19 April in a letter from Lieutenant W Russell, Officer Commanding 1st Section, B Company, Royal Marine Artillery, AA:

> 'You have been awarded the Distinguished Service Medal. Lieutenant Sawyer and I very heartily congratulate you and take this opportunity of telling you how very highly we appreciate your unvarying willingness and good work in the Section, often under very trying circumstances and at great personal risk.'

Almost a century later, the worldwide web reveals that the 'scarce Great War DSM awarded to Gunner A Fenton, Royal Marine Artillery, serving with the Anti-Aircraft Brigade in France' was sold for £500 at auction in 2000. Auctioneers Dix Noonan Webb of Piccadilly said:

> 'Gunner Adam Fenton served with the Royal Marine Brigade which was part of the so-called 'Flying Column' at Ostend and was slightly wounded between 27 and 31 August 1914. After the disbandment of the Royal Marine Artillery Battalion, Fenton again went to France with the main RM Brigade. He was again slightly wounded at Dunkirk in the fighting between 7 and 18 October 1914. After the formation of the Anti-Aircraft Brigade, Fenton joined B Battery, which formed part of the British Mission in Belgium, serving with the RN and RMA Siege Guns.'

Bad news continued to far outweigh the good. The son of a former Magnus headmaster, Captain Cyril Edward Spencer Noakes, twenty-three, of the Sherwoods, was 'dangerously wounded in the chest and shoulder by the accidental explosion of a bomb.' He lived to the age of sixty-five.

There were heartbreaks at home, too. Hannah Brownlow in Pelham Street, whose husband Charles was a regimental sergeant major in Egypt, lost their son, Thomas, seventeen, to double pneumonia.

Full military honours were accorded at Private James Riley's funeral in Newark Cemetery on 23 May. Only twenty-one, the factory labourer, who had joined the Duke of Wellington's (West Riding) Regiment, lost a finger in the Battle of Loos, had a kneecap badly damaged on the Somme, yet was still deemed fit for home service – and was in Halifax when he contracted fever and died.

A memorial service was held in Charles Street Mission four days later for their former

Wilfred Gelsthorpe, second from left, with his brothers Arthur, Ernest and George.
[NEKMS 8763.3]

scholars who had fallen: Privates Frank Tye and Wilfred Gelsthorpe, plus their latest victim, Sapper Walter Hanson. Aged twenty-two, Walter was killed on the night of 6 May by a shell at Beaulencourt, near Arras. His parents, Fred and Harriett, who had lost two of their five children to natural causes, learnt of the death of their only boy from Lieutenant E G King: 'He often acted as my orderly and on many occasions accompanied me on duty in various parts of the line. He was one of the best of soldiers.'

Harry James Stibbard, released as head of Lover's Lane Council School to take charge of the RE Depot Messing Department in Newark, lost his younger brother, Captain Sydney Stibbard, twenty-seven, near Vimy Ridge on 3 June. One of seven brothers engaged in the services, he was living in Winnipeg, Canada, and working as assistant secretary of the Grand Trunk Pacific Railways Company before joining the Manitoba Regiment in April 1916.

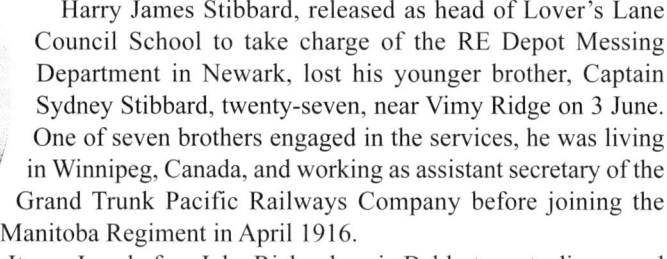

It was June before John Richardson in Baldertongate discovered that his adventurous brother, Arthur Ellis Richardson, had been wounded in the head on 27 February so badly that the right side of his body was paralysed. It happened a few weeks after he joined the Egyptian campaign with the Machine Gun Section of the 3rd South African Infantry. He had been in hospitals in Alexandria, Tooting, Richmond, Durban and Pretoria; and was 'making a slow recovery'.

Memorial service – Frank Tye.
[Advertiser cutting]

Keen sportsman Edward J R Rich was killed with the 8th North Staffordshire Regiment on 7 June. Ted was sent with four others for ammunition for a Maxim gun at Ypres. He was the only one to return. Warned that there was a sniper about, he crept around trying to locate him. A shell burst within a yard of him.

On the previous evening a special supplement of the *London Gazette* listed locals decorated in the King's Birthday Honours. Major Hugh Tallents joined his brother, Major Godfrey Tallents, of the Lancashire Fusiliers, and his brother in law, Lieutenant Colonel Harold Thorpe, as holders of the Distinguished Service Order for bravery with the Sherwood Rangers in the Dardanelles and on the Eastern battlefields; and was about to return home to succeed his late father as Newark Town Clerk. Corporal Drummer Charles Hagues, thirty-seven, who marched out of Newark with the 1/8th Sherwoods, earned a Military Medal:

> 'At Uti de Risement on 23 April 1917, during the house to house fighting, he was continually sniping, accounting for at least twelve of the enemy from an exposed position, which was continually under heavy artillery fire. Notwithstanding this he continued to fire calmly and by this greatly encouraged the other Battalions and his to hold their positions and continue sniping. On another occasion at Gommecourt in June 1916 he selected a sniping post in No Man's Land and remained there throughout the day, doing considerable execution at great risk to himself.'

A bugle captured by the 1/8th Sherwoods from the 2nd Prussian Guard at Gommecourt on 4 March appeared in Harry Cook's jewellery shop window in Chain Lane before the summer was out.

Lance Corporal John Henry Ayto, 20, buried with military honours in Newark Cemetery on 23 June, survived the Dublin Rebellion but waas sent home with consumption from France. On the same day, the 1/8th Sherwoods lost at Loos Private Horace Buckler, 'a promising lad' who had considerable scholastic achievements before becoming apprenticed to Smith's chemists.

Harry Sanderson, nineteen, was killed in France exactly a year after his brother Private Ernest Stanley Sanderson, of the South Wales Borderers, drowned in Mesopotamia and four months after the death of his maternal grandfather, a Crimea War veteran. His parents, Joseph and Eliza, received the news from a hospital sister who thought a War Office telegram would reach them first:

> 'Dear Mrs Sanderson, my thoughts are with you for I know how keenly you must feel the sad news about your son. He was brought in this hospital dangerously wounded in the abdomen. Everything that could be done was done.'

Other sons gave them more worry: Thomas had been discharged with a badly wounded arm; Joseph had been wounded twice; and James Arthur, twenty-two, was hospitalised with rheumatic fever.

Widow Harriet Graveney heard from the War Office that her son, Sergeant Albert Edward John Graveney, nineteen, was killed on 7 June. A Patrol Leader in the 2nd Newark Scouts, Albert left his pattern-maker's job at Ransome's in 1914 to join the Sherwoods, was wounded in the Irish Rebellion but went to France with his mates and died in the village of Metz-en-Couture.

Midway down the REs Notes on the back page of the *Herald* of 9 June, it was revealed that Corporal J Patterson of the Corps' School of Instruction had been awarded the Military Medal 'for gallant conduct in the fire at RE Farm (France) on the night of 6-7 May'.

There could have been a massive disaster in Newark early on Sunday, 15 July. A fire at Quibell's works, containing 'grease, benzene and other inflammables and combustibles' for munitions, was confined to one building thanks to the eagle eye of railway signalman James Hydes, fifty-eight. He called the fire brigade at 4.45am and they had it under control within an hour, saving surrounding factories.

Military Representative Nicholson espied 'shirkers' on his way to a Tribunal hearing on 17 July. He counted thirty-five men 'hanging over the Cattle Market wall looking at the cattle'. The inference: they should be working or, better still, fighting.

Watchmaker William Edgar Rawlin and his wife Mary, who had seven children, discovered that their son Bert, twenty-one, had not been killed, as they had feared. The Sherwoods private, missing since 23 April, was wounded at Lens and taken prisoner, said a War Office telegram.

A moving letter from one-time Newark grocery boy Private W Seaton told foundryman John Lyndon Fox and his wife Sarah Ann they had lost their third son, James Harold, twenty-one, a tailor's presser at Mumby's before he joined the Sherwoods in 1915: 'I expect by this time you have received some intimation of the death.' They had not.

> 'It happened on the night of the 27th [June] whilst he was on a working party [at Loos] a shell burst, wounding four and killed Harold and another lad from Newark, I believe by the name of Willingham. He died as he lived, a true and noble Christian soldier, one who did his duty always, in the face of great danger, who was never ashamed of his colours.'

The soldier who died with Harold was Drummer Somerville Willingham, 19. His mum Martha received a letter from him, written on the morning before he died; 'he sounded cheerful as ever'. Somerville was an apprentice French polisher and Patrol Leader with the 5th Newark Scouts before enlisting.

Joseph Chapman, captain of the steam tug *Little John*, and his wife Eleanor Annie, feared the worst when an envelope was delivered on 3 July. But the letter was written by the eldest of their seven offspring, Harry, twenty, a baker's errand boy, who became a Gunner in the Royal Field Artillery:

> 'I have a bit of good news this time. I have been awarded the Military Medal ... While the Battery was being shelled heavily, a corporal and I ran to put fires out and save the ammunition which had started to go off. Guns were disguised by netting with grass tied to them, which we call Camaflower [sic]. The enemy had been shelling for about half an hour when a gun-pit caught fire and an ammunition dump was hit. This Camaflower burns quickly and it had got well hold, starting the shells going... corporal and I ran to put the fires out, and turned our attention to the ammunition dump. We got the worst out and slacked it well with water and earth. That's how we got it, and neither of us was hit. Our major thanked us for what we did. We have not been withdrawn to rest yet, but we still keep smiling. I saw Harry Joynes [from Tolney Lane] the other day, and Jack Hoe [from Millgate] is in his Company. But the latter was in the trenches so I did not get a chance to see him. The same night I saw two of the Mellors out of Queen Street. Best wishes, and luck for us all.'

British 9.2 inch howitzer under camouflage netting in the Ypres Salient, 1917.
[Taylor Library]

Although the 1/8th Sherwoods began eighteen days of rest and recuperation at Chelers on 4 July after nearly three months of incessant and strenuous fighting, back at home the people battled on.

William and Betsy Walker in Portland Street lost the eldest of their eight children, Percy, thirty-one, two days after they had a telegram warning them he had been so 'dangerously wounded' at Estaires near Armentières that they could not visit him. A casualty centre sister wrote that he died from wounds of the abdomen, arms, chest and legs: 'He did not suffer very much as he was unconscious and died quietly.' Percy ran his father's barber shop on Beaumond Cross before becoming Private 357483 in The King's (Liverpool) Regiment.

Parents of nine Edward and Emma Bentley in Lindum Street were informed by telegram on 5 July, that their football mad son 'Dass', twenty-six, had been 'grievously wounded' by gunshot in the chest. He was their third war victim. His brother Thomas, twenty-four, a Leicestershire Regiment private, was recovering from wounds at Ripon and his brother-in-law, Sapper William McQuiston of the RE, who had married Caroline Bentley a couple of months earlier, had been invalided out of the front line. 'Dass', who was christened Henry, could have stayed at home, playing football for Simpson's: having completed five years in the Territorials, he had 'done his time' before the war, but joined the Sherwoods with his mates and was transferred to the Machine Gun Corps. He survived the war but died, aged only thirty-seven in 1929.

Eliza Brown of Water Lane heard on 6 July that she had been widowed after barely six months' marriage. A letter from a 2/8th Foresters chaplain said that her husband, Andrew, 'was at his duty by the Company kitchen when some shells began to fall nearby and he was hit by a piece while running to a trench to take shelter'. He was twenty-nine, a maltster at Gilstrap's, and got married after the Dublin Rebellion.

As if enemy fire was not causing enough carnage, widow Harriett Bond, seventy, of Shepherd's Row off Northgate was informed by the War Office on 7 July that her son, Ernest, twenty-nine, a Sherwoods private, was 'accidentally killed' on 16 June at Ypres.

On 12 July, bewildered Isabel Grosse, thirty-two, in Pelham Street, received a third version of how her husband, 1/8th Sherwoods Private Thomas Grosse, died on 23 June in Aix-Noulette, a village near Arras. A Wesleyan chaplain wrote: 'He was wounded in the head by a bomb. They got him down to the field ambulance but he passed away as the medical officer was dressing his wound.' The War Office version was that Tommy, thirty-four, died in hospital from wounds. And his parents, Joseph and Ellen, in Northgate, had a letter from his cousin, Private Percy Grosse, twenty-one, of Beacon Hill asserting that Tommy died in the hospital where Percy was being treated for a sore throat.

Father of three, Henry Hurst from Water Lane, died on 3 July. Formerly in the old Militia, he settled to work in the Midland Railway grain sheds but could not resist enlisting in the Sherwoods in March 1915. A chaplain wrote: 'He made a brave fight for life and was cheerful to the last; but his injuries were very severe and pneumonia supervened. England has lost a brave and gallant soldier.'

Fred and Alice Amelia Ansell in Kelham Villas – proud that their farm worker son, William Edward, twenty-two, had become 'very clever at his Lewis gun work' during the 1/4th Lincolnshire Regiment's hard fighting – received a letter from his lieutenant on 20 July: 'It is with deep regret, he was on a post with four other men when a shell hit the post, your son and another being killed, and two more severely wounded.' Thomas White, thirty, of 16 Sheppard's Row, was posted missing on the same day, 1 July, by the Sherwoods. Nine months later his widowed mother Ellen was told he must be dead.

Attempts by the trainee RE to transform Newark into Joy Town proved a damp squib. Rain forced the postponement of opening night by twenty-four hours to Tuesday, 31 July, and attendances through the week were lower than expected. But the RE Dramatic and Operatic Society went through its full repertoire; the display of captured German helmets attracted interest; and the bridge-building demonstrations were impressive.

Back in the real world, a year after she lost her eldest son George, widow Charlotte Howitt, sixty-two, of Field House, Bowbridge Road, was going through a month of agonies over her youngest, Albert, twenty, a corporal in the King's Royal Rifle Corps, who enlisted aged only 17½ in December 1914. A letter from his best chum, Lance Corporal J Munro-Kyles, alerted her: 'I am returning to you the small pocket book belonging to your son who, as you have doubtless been informed [she had not], was reported missing on the 11th … The Army has lost a fine soldier and I have lost a firm friend and true chum.' On 28 August a note from Albert arrived: 'I am quite well but a prisoner of war. I was captured on 10 July with several of my pals. Do not trouble too much. I will drop you a letter and address first opportunity, then I shall look out for cigs, etc.' By then another son, Henry, a sergeant in the Leicestershire Regiment, was in hospital with an eye wound. He explained: 'We were giving the Boche a strafe with the rifle grenades to celebrate my two years in France when one exploded at the end of the rifle, wounding an officer and myself. It was a lucky shot: there were eight of us all round it; it was a wonder none was [sic] killed.'

Gertrude Arnold, at home in Lincoln Street with toddler son Jesse, was advised her husband John Richard, twenty-four, manager of Higgs' tobacco shop on Bridge Street before he became a Middlesex Regiment private, had been missing since 31 July; he was never found. Gert married again in 1920 to Leonard Barker, who fought with the Sherwoods. Jesse would married Phyllis Bates in Newark in 1940 and lived to the age of sixty-three.

While the third anniversary of the start of the Great War was being marked on 4 August by services in all the Newark churches, eighty-three-year-old Joseph Lambert, whose extended family was so big that it occupied both 5 and 6 Collingham Row, off Queen's Road, received War Office notification that his son, Private George Lambert, thirty-six, of the Labour Corps, died in hospital at Étaples on 17 July from 'suspected cerebro-spinal fever'.

Herbert Taylor, twenty-four, of 1 Eldon Place, assistant in a gent's outfitters before joining the 1/8th Sherwoods in 1916, disappeared on 4 August 1917. It was exactly a year before his death was confirmed. 'Much sympathy' went to his widowed mother.

The Sherry family mourned two bereavements on 7 August. Sarah Sherry in New Street heard from two sources that her husband, Albert George, twenty-five, died at Ypres on 1 August, only four months after being called-up and five weeks after crossing the Channel with the 17th Sherwoods. Albert's brother, Private 66344 Walter Sherry, who lived in Northants and fought with the 12th Battalion Royal Fusiliers, also perished on 1 August at Ypres.

Police Constable Thomas Cupid Rose and his wife Eliza discovered on 8 August that they had lost another son. Also christened Thomas Cupid, he was only eighteen but had earned a Military Medal on the Somme in October 1916 and was on his way to promotion in a Grenadier Guards Machine Gun Section. The Records Office said he was killed on 1 August – and an officer's letter praised:

'No better, more willing a man I have ever had in my section, not only in this advance but in everything connected with soldiering. Many times has he commanded a gun team in the trenches, and very well, too. So well, indeed, that had he lived I would have made him an NCO.'

His second brother, Arthur Edward, twenty-three, a King's Own Yorkshire Light Infantry corporal, had been wounded: 'his right arm is useless'.

Florence Cree refused to believe that her husband Jack, a pigeon fancier who worked at Warwick's brewery, was dead, aged twenty-nine. She received the news in a letter from one of his pals in the Sherwoods on 10 August but insisted it was a case of mistaken identity. Her defiance was shattered days later by a captain's letter: 'I found the dead body of your husband. These are sad and trying times.' Jack was killed at Ypres on the night of 28-29 July. His stunned parents, Ruth and Henry, widow Florrie and son Frederick, inserted a death notice in the *Herald* of 25 August:

No mother's care did him attend
Nor o'er him did a father bend.
No sister by to shed a tear
No brother his last words to hear.
Dying in a foreign land
No father by to take his hand
No mother by to close his eyes
But in a hero's grave he lies.
Sleep on, dear Jack, and take thy rest
In a grave we may never see
But as long as life and memory lasts
We will remember thee.

From his sorrowing Father and Mother, sisters, brothers, Bill in India, Frank in France and George wounded in Hospital.

A glimmer of brighter news came from the other side of Europe. Battery Sergeant-Major William Wade, thirty, from Tolney Lane, had earned a Meritorious Service Medal. He left Stephenson's to join the Royal Field Artillery fifteen years earlier, went to India in 1903, fought alongside General Townsend in Mesopotamia and was wounded before arriving at Kut. He was back with the forces in Mesopotamia. The Newark celebrations of his medal were led by his sister, Elizabeth Kirkland, whose husband, Frank, was in the Royal Army Medical Corps.

There was surely never a sadder Sunday in Newark than 12 August 1917. Lizzie Allen, twenty-eight, discovered that her fiancé, Sapper Michael Scullion, had been killed less than a week before their wedding day. The devastating news arrived by special delivery as she prepared to go to St Leonard's Church, where arrangements had been finalised for their wedding. Lizzie was one of fifteen children of labourer George and long-suffering Sarah in Lindum Street. Michael, from Port Glasgow, swept her off her feet while training in Newark. A domestic servant for Post Office Superintendent William Thompson and his wife Mary Jane in Wellington Road, she could not even attend his funeral: he had already been buried in Potijze Chateau Lawn Cemetery, Ypres.

Sunday 12 August was also Joseph Henry Harrison's twenty-second birthday – and his parents, John Henry and Emily, in Vernon Street got a card from a chaplain:

'It is with profound regret... I saw a good deal of your splendid boy prior to his death and prayed many times with him. His pluck was magnificent, never a murmur, though he was in great pain. Such a splendid boy, you may well be proud of him. Dear lad, I thought he would pull through all right and never thought he would not survive his wounds.'

Joe worked on the Great Northern Railway until enlisting in the Sherwoods in May 1915, went to France in February 1916, was gassed in September but returned to action in February.

The 13th brought news of another sad Sunday. Arthur George Musgrove, 18½, had been killed. A comrade wrote to his parents, Arthur and Ivy, in Albert Street:

> 'We were climbing from one trench to another in the night (29 July) when he got struck with a piece of shell. I ran to him but he was dead. He took a liking to me and said he would stick with me. But on the Sunday night he got about 20 yards away from me and I had not missed him until he got hit. There were two killed and five wounded with the same shell.'

Arthur worked in a fishmonger's before joining the 2/8th Sherwoods in November 1914 and, in France, was transferred to the 3rd Battalion Manchester Regiment.

Disabled Lucy Clayton received two letters in William Street on 15 August. One contained a new portrait of her husband of four years, RE Sapper George H Clayton, smiling pensively. The other was from his Commanding Officer: 'I very much regret having to inform you of the death of your husband … on 28 July [at Ypres]. He was struck by a piece of shell.' George, twenty-eight, manager of Coombes' boot repairers, could have done with staying at home, because Lucy had the misfortune to lose her right leg a few years earlier. But duty insisted on calling.

Gamekeeper's widow Emma Sentance of Lindum Street had suffered the heartaches of three of her boys being in serious scrapes – but the worst news came on 16 August. Her fourth son, John, nineteen, was killed at Ypres on 31 July. His lieutenant praised him: 'He proved himself a splendid soldier, willing, cheerful and always ready to do some good turn.' John worked at Farrar's boilerworks before enlisting six months earlier and went to France in May. Of his brothers, Fred, twenty-six, was in hospital with trench fever; George, twenty-eight, had been wounded twice and gassed; and Henry, thirty, was with the 2/8th Sherwoods.

Dusk was falling on 18 August when a telegram arrived at 21 Appletongate with black news for Frederick and Annie Doncaster: their son, Percy, was killed on 31 July at Boezinge, near Ypres. Worse, they had to tell Percy's wife Ellen and two children aged eight and five. Percy, thirty-five, a Coldstream Guards private, was about as unwarlike as a man could be: a musical talent; organist at his Methodist chapel; highly esteemed travelling salesman over in the North of England. He was equally admired by his comrades. His platoon sergeant wrote:

> 'We are all very sorry that such a thing should have happened. He was a very good man while he was with us and he died as he lived, "a man". He was killed with a shell … I feel sorry for his little ones…'

Another Sunday, 19 August, and Newark prayed for one of its original 1/8th Sherwoods. Drummer William Bernard Robb, twenty-one, whose father, Harry, had run the Spring House near Sconce Hills, earned the Medal of St George by going into No Man's Land and rescuing a wounded officer (who later died). He was granted leave from 4 July to 2 August and had only been back in France eight days when he was gassed and wounded; an amazing war for a meek butcher-boy. He recovered and lived until 1966.

Leonard Wakefield died in the army on 19 August 1917, twenty-one years after being born in it. And maybe he had a premonition. The son of the late Colour Sergeant Thomas

Wakefield of Baldertongate perished while attacking at Thiepval. The news reached his widowed mother Elizabeth from a comrade in the Sherwoods and a chaplain. The pal explained:

> 'We went to take a German trench and were assembled on a sunken road when I saw Leonard. He asked me to write to you in case anything happened to him and, of course, I asked him to do the same for me. We were both in the same attack. He was a good and fearless soldier and died the death of a gallant young soldier.'

The chaplain added: 'The Battalion has accomplished a very fine piece of work and your son's gallant conduct contributed very largely to the success of the attack.' Born in Normanton Barracks, Derby, while his father was in the Sherwoods, he joined the Territorials' band in Newark, aged fifteen, and never hesitated about joining the war.

Private George Stoakes from Cross Street informed George Henry and Sarah Ann Smith on Beacon Hill of the death of their fourth son Joseph, nineteen, of the 1/7th Sherwoods. A builder's apprentice, Joe frequently wrote home cheerfully and hopefully during his seven months in France. George was only able to pass on the news because mutual friends had mentioned Joe's death as they exchanged places in the Front Line.

One of Newark's best athletes, Ernest Lees, was gassed with the 3rd Sherwoods. He survived to the age of fifty-five, passing away in 1939. But one of Newark Cricket Club's finest bowlers, Frederick Herbert Northen, twenty-six, made the supreme sacrifice on 12 August. He was a clerk at Barclay's Bank in Castlegate before he enlisted in the Lincolnshire Regiment in 1914.

Newark's Schools Attendance Officer, Evelyn Edgar Golland, 37, was killed. His wife Florence heard the news on 25 August at home in William Street from a comrade in Kensingtons, Sniper Charles Jeeps: 'I have no doubt the War Office has notified you officially of the death of your husband, my friend.' It had not; official word arrived a week later. Evelyn – whose parents, pipe clay dealer William, eightyß-two, and Eleanor, seventy-seven, lived in Northgate – became a music teacher, helped with the annual Methodist Sunday School Union Festival, enlisted in April 1916 only a few weeks after marrying, and fell in fierce fighting on the Somme.

From the blood and bravery of the trenches, a pencilled message from Sergeant Edward Thompson, twenty-nine, from Grove Cottages, Barnby Road, arrived with his sister:

> 'Dear old Dolly, just a few lines to let you know that I hope to be back with you very shortly. I have just stopped a small packet in the arm and leg, which has raised my dander somewhat as I was awaiting very much on leave. Tell Dad to chin-up as I shan't be long before I see him when he comes to see me, although I am not out of the wood yet. Please forgive me for not writing before, but I have been very busy. Best love to you all. Your affect. brother Ted.'

There follows a full line of x's – 'a few kisses for the kids'. In the same hand-writing beneath this note is another:

> 'Dear Mrs Evans, Sergeant Thompson dictated this letter shortly after he was wounded. I got to him about half-a-minute afterwards and helped dress him, and I have never met a pluckier chap. We are all sad that he has to leave us for he was

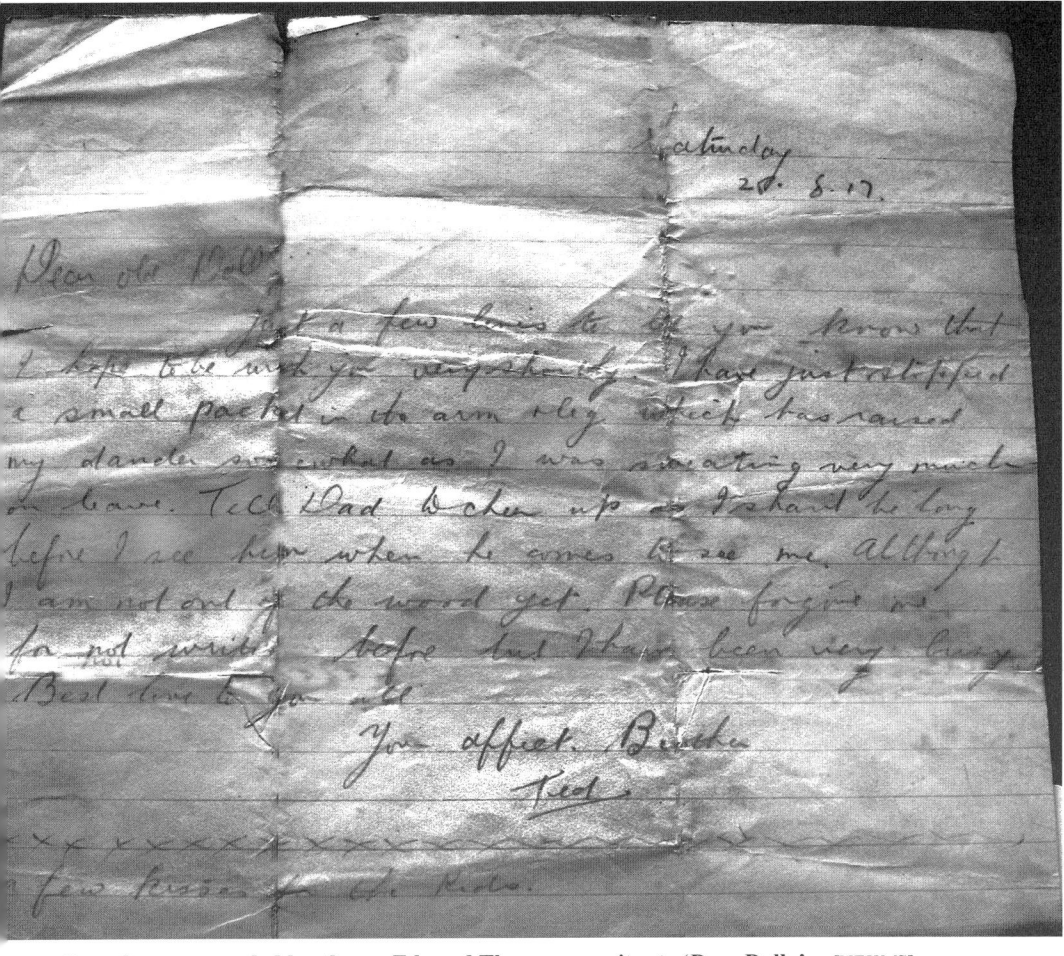

Love from a wounded brother... Edward Thompson writes to 'Dear Dolly'. *[NEKMS]*

immensely popular. Please tell him that I have arranged that little matter for him successfully and am enclosing twenty-two francs that were in his pay book...'

'Dad' was Joseph Thompson, foreman on an estate a few miles up the North Road at Carlton-on-Trent.

Edward John Probert's painful war ended on 22 August. He aimed to serve in the South Wales Borderers as had his grandfather, Adam Orlopp, a captain and quartermaster, and father, John Henry. Aged only 18½, Edward was in the retreat from Mons and was invalided home with such frozen feet that a toe was amputated. He was sent to East Africa in February 1917; and died during an operation for appendicitis.

Newark's former Borough Surveyor, Thomas Pierson Frank, thirty-five, an RE captain, was in hospital in September after a road accident in France. He was unconscious for some hours after a car crashed into his motor cycle and, despite wishing to return to duty, was shipped to England as a cot case.

Brighter news came in the shape of five Military Medals in the first half of September: to hairdresser James Harold Smith, twenty-nine, a private in the Loyal North Lancs, for 'great gallantry in carrying despatches under very heavy shell fire' and grocery assistant William Watts, twenty-one, a private in the 1st Sherwoods for 'gallantry and great devotion to duty during operations east of Ypres on 31 July and 1 August'; bricklayer George Henry Parr, twenty-eight, for dressing and attending wounded for forty-eight hours under heavy shell fire near Langemarck in mid-August; Richard Henry Walster, twenty-three, a bombardier with the Royal Garrison Artillery, who had been wounded five times and gassed once since he quit working in Branston's kilns; and auctioneer's clerk William Eastgate Alcock, thirty-one, who went into No Man's Land at Ypres under shell fire to repair telephone wires. He wrote to his wife, Ada, at home with their three-year-old son, William: 'It was my duty to go. I had no thought of honours.'

Thomas Butler, twenty-nine, wrote to mum Annie and dad Joseph in Chatham Street:

'I won the Military Medal in the big Battle of Ypres on 25 September. The General put the ribbon on my breast and made me Lance Corporal in the King's name, so I am King's corporal and no one can take it from me!'

Tom's 25 September in fact had lasted three days or more:

'We were under very heavy shell fire and many of our men were killed before we reached the Front we had to hold. On the 24 and 25 September the Germans started to bombard all day and night, and about this time most of our men were wounded or killed. My officer and sergeant were killed, and that left me in charge with twenty men. Then the bombardment lifted and over came the enemy in large numbers. Most of our regiment were killed or captured but I hung on with my few men, throwing bombs for about an hour, killing most of them and capturing those who were not killed. All the trenches but ours were captured, so we were in for a bad time, as we had no water or food for three days. We still, however, hung on. My twenty men had now got down to fourteen, and the lads were done up with hard fighting and nothing to eat. Then came the order to counter-attack to take back the trenches which had been lost. That did not take long, and we also took the big ridge beyond it. The worst part about it was to get more men. None of my men were fit to go for any because it looked like certain death to go through the German shell fire, so I went myself and got a Company of Australians. All that day, I was wounded but stuck to my post until I got relieved.'

It was the fourth time Tom, twenty-eight, a Cafferata's labourer, had been wounded since he enlisted as a private in the 2nd Sherwoods and later transferred to the Middlesex Regiment. He had suffered injuries to his back and feet, been buried alive and survived gassing. He lived to 1951.

What a difference a month made to Second Lieutenant Walter Bilson Easterfield, a bank clerk before joining the Sherwoods. Four weeks after being seriously wounded while attached to the Machine Gun Corps, he learnt on 27 September that he had earned a Military Cross.

'for conspicuous gallantry and devotion to duty. He brought his guns into action in the open within 100 yards of a fortified house held by hostile snipers and machine guns. It was due to his coolness and courage and the accuracy of his rapid fire that the garrison were compelled to surrender.'

Three days later, one of Newark's five battling Brunt brothers sent to proud parents Joseph and Mary Ann a Card of Honour he had earned:

'Gunner George Brunt, your Brigadier has reported that during operations near [censored] on 9 September 1917, whilst acting as linesman on the line from Battalion Headquarters to the Battery, you displayed great gallantry and devotion to duty in working continuously on the wire and in maintaining an almost uninterrupted communication during an intense bombardment.'

George, twenty-five, was a corn porter before becoming a War hero.

Autumn's golden glow at home was accompanied by strict restrictions on sugar distribution; local provision dealers Garratt & Heming opened a jam-making factory; and Newark Butchers' Association fixed prices per pound of every morsel – beef: neck with bone 1s 1d, neck without bone 1s 4d, blade chine 1s 4d, best chine 1s 6d, sirloin 1s 6d, steak 1s 6d to 2s, flank 1s to 1s 6d, rounds 1s 3d to 1s 6d, aitch bone 1s to 1s 6d, shin of beef 8d, shin (whole meat) 1s 4d, brisket 11d to 1s 3d, ribs 1s to 1s 6d, clod 1s to 1s 2d, suet 1s, bones 1½d; mutton: suet 8d, legs 1s 6d, loin 1s 6d, chops 1s 10d, neck 1s 6d, breast 1s 3d, shoulder 1s 5d. These were cash prices; credit cost ½d per pound extra. When the Board of Guardians sought suppliers for what remained of the Workhouse for the second half of 1917, prices were rising so quickly that no tenders were received to provide bread, groceries, milk, wines and spirits, blankets, boots, straw, coffins and barley meal. The Master was instructed to buy all on the open market – no easy task, as every housewife knew. Yet Newark Prisoners of War Comforts Fund despatched 144 boxes of food (and received seventy-six expressions of thanks) in August.

To add to the worries as the evenings grew darker, ex-Mayor Kew articulated on 25 September what many still feared: 'There is likely to be an invasion. Lord French is of that opinion and so are many other military experts.' The Newark Company of Volunteers had already developed to such an extent that, like the RE, they could erect emergency bridges over the Trent; and their motorised division was 'almost full of motor cars and motor cyclists, but has vacancies for vans and lorries of one-and-a-half and three tons'.

The thoroughness of the enemy and the ravages of an occupied country were emphasised by Tank Corps Company Quartermaster Sergeant PA Watford, a surveyor, writing to his father, a former Newark Midland Railway Station Master:

'I had the opportunity of examining a system of trenches from which the Germans had been recently driven, and very interesting I found it. The enormous amount of labour the Germans spend on some of their underground work is simply marvellous. At one point there was a complete chemical laboratory for the manufacture of explosives. One also found spacious rooms hollowed out and capable of sleeping 200 men, luxury apartments for the accommodation of officers and even a large wine cellar. The occupants of this system of trenches had obviously quitted them in haste as everything in the last apartment was smashed and the floor was covered to a depth of six inches in slush, made up of the wines of the country and the local mud. Every department was lit up with electric light. On the surface there was no indication whatever of the wonders to be found below.

'I also passed through a town which was being shelled daily by the Germans. It was a strange sensation to pass along the deserted streets and see the empty houses from which the civil population had long ago departed. Here was a house not touched, perhaps a little further along one had been hit by a large shell and almost entirely demolished. Another had the front blown away, disclosing the whole of the furniture, and each room in section. In another house was a room where everything had been destroyed save a solitary picture which still hung in its place on the wall.

'A few miles outside the town was a small village with almost every house levelled to the ground. A small fragment of the church tower was still standing. The gardens and shrubs and the avenue of trees leading up to the entrance were all cut to pieces by shell-fire, and the whole presented a scene of desolation. Not far from this last place was a large wood, looking from a distance for all the world like a large shipyard as the branches of the trees were all shot away, and nothing remained but the straight trunks, stripped of everything. In the wood the ground was full of bomb holes, and had evidently been the scene of fierce hand to hand fighting.

'In a deep dug-out not far from the wood was a steel tube extending to the surface. On the walls of the dug-out was written-up the names of different villages in the neighbourhood, and the exact range. The Germans evidently had a big gun located here which was fired through the steel tube. This was one of the cleverest gun positions I have ever seen as it was practically impossible to discover, situated as it was some thirty feet below ground.'

Newark had to be prepared for anything, especially as Kew's fear was aired at the very moment the town received a first-hand account of Russian revolutions that ended centuries of imperial rule and set in motion the political and social changes that would lead to the evolution of the Soviet Union. Janet Cubley, a daughter of a Newark Councillor and sister of sea hero Basil, was a teacher in the capital, Petrograd (which would become St Petersburg) and thought it all 'beastly'. Her first letter home generated such sympathy that, within a month of the first revolution in March, Newark raised £44 9s 10d for Russian Red Cross funds through a flag day and sent

To Russia with love – plaque on bed bought by Newark for the Russia Red Cross.

The Red Guard preparing to storm the Winter Palace at Petrograd during the second Russian Revolution in October 1917.

£100 to endow a bed in Petrograd Hospital.

On 30 June Janet penned a pessimistic letter, which arrived at her parents in Millgate in September:

'Things do not improve here at all: one day they seem to promise well; and the next day, they are worse than ever. People in England do not realise at all what is going on here. I know the censorship is supposed to be abolished, but I can't help laughing at the carefully prepared reports in the English papers, though at the same time they make me furious. I feel so sorry for the intelligent, really patriotic Russians, who are ashamed of what is going on here, but they form such an infinitesimal part of the millions in this country that they are practically helpless. Certainly the old regime sowed better than they knew when they imagined they kept the masses so ignorant. What will happen this next winter I don't know.

'Already we are on the verge of famine. It seems to me prices are preposterous, and even then very little is to be had. This is owing principally to the enormous wages demanded by the working people. Whether I shall be able to stick it out I don't know. It is not that I mind the prospect of heavy privations in the coming months as the utter disorder and lack of discipline among the people. To get a tram nowadays you must generally behave like a regular hooligan, or wait for hours: trams are very few, and mostly filled with soldiers, who pay nothing and practically do nothing but amuse themselves by going about in the trams. I have seen no end of them get on a tram to go from one stopping place to the next. The fares for the paying public are now 15 kopeks instead of five, and will probably soon be 20.

'I lose so much time in going to and coming from lessons and, above all, in getting provisions. The servants will not undertake that now. For one thing, you never know what there is to be had, and for most necessaries you have to wait in the queues. This ticket system is terrible: I hope you may escape it in England. We have meat tickets, also bread, sugar, butter and egg tickets; and even then it is impossible to get things. For ten months I have not had a bit of beef. For five weeks I was without butter, but managed to get a little last week. In September we shall have 30 or 40 per cent added on to the rent of our rooms because heating, lighting, etc. is so dear. This letter is not very cheerful but I am only writing of life as it is right now. Yet, in spite of all, the places of amusement are doing a roaring trade, so some people are making money out of disorder.'

By September Janet had become a refugee and had moved from regal Petrograd to deepest Siberia:

'Life was getting impossible. All necessary provisions had to be waited for hours and hours, and even then were often unobtainable, and standing for food meant giving up lessons, so we were in a difficult position. Even here things are pretty bad; just after I came the card system for many things was introduced. All the same, life is easier here at present. I have taken a room in the house of Mr Whittle, also a teacher of English, who has come here from Mongolia. I have the use of his classroom. Another Englishman here, Mr Grant, passed on one of his pupils to me and wants to give me two others. I have had an offer to go to Hartarovsk [now Khabarovsk, the largest city and the administrative centre of Khabarovsk Krai, Russia, less than twenty miles from the Chinese border], where I could have lessons, but I shall wait and see how things go on here.

'We had the greatest difficulty in finding rooms as the place is full of refugees like ourselves, and more coming every day. Yesterday I had tea with a Russian lady, the wife of an English Captain in India, who has come to live with her own people because her husband is under orders to go to Mesopotamia. Irkutsk is a curious place, very advanced in some things and half-civilised in others. This house is like a barrack with white-washed walls, yet we have electric lights and bells! It is not safe to be out after dark, as many robberies and even murders happen. Fortunately all my pupils at present come to me. Our luggage did not come till a fortnight after we arrived, and then it was difficult to receive it. One of my pupils is on the Railway Administration, and he got it for us. Even he was hunting for it all one afternoon, and then kindly brought it up from wherever he found it.

'All materials and manufactured goods are terribly dear: calico, etc. only obtainable by cards at the rate of four yards a month for each card. I had to buy a bed; and for a simple iron bedstead and straw mattress I had to pay 70 roubles. The weather is very cold. Last night there were 25 degrees of frost. They say in December and January there are between 40 and 50 degrees. But the air is splendid. This is a good place for consumptives. The sun is dazzlingly bright from eight or nine o' clock till three or four. In winter you have to buy milk in blocks.

I hope you will get this letter. I fear many have gone astray.' The letter reached Newark in five months. Janet eventually returned home, where she passed away aged fifty in 1928.

One daughter who could not return from revolutionary Russia was Laura Talbot, 38. Mayor Knight took it upon himself on 3 July 1917 to visit her widowed mother Emma, seventy-one, in Friary Road with devastating news for her and her other daughter Mary, curator of Newark Museum. He had a cablegram: 'Please inform Mary Talbot, Newark Museum, her sister drowned at Kluga. Result of bathing accident 17 June. Funeral, Moscow, 26 June. Letter following. (signed) Lockhart, British Consul.'

The bad news continued from the trenches. First Air Mechanic Clement Holmes Kingston Hogg, twenty, was in his dug-out on 18 September when, Captain W Pratt of the Royal Garrison Artillery wrote, 'an unlucky shell struck the dug-out and killed him; at the same time wounding five of his chums. Your son was the cheeriest of the cheery, a splendid example to all men, and even in a Battery which has suffered many losses, his passing away has produced a profound depression.'

One of Newark's intrepid pilots, Lieutenant Duncan MacRae, was captured in October. Eventually a fascinating letter arrived from his observer, Lieutenant Blake, from a prison camp in Asia Minor:

'We were on a job of work on 4 October in the morning when our engine went wrong and we had to land in the desert on the right bank of the Shat-el-adhain, a small tributary of the Tigris between Samarra and Baghdad.

'We were surrounded by a large and very violent crowd of Bedouin Arabs, who stripped us most unkindly. I was annoyed! We were promised by signs that our throats would be cut, but we were eventually taken to their camp in the riverbed. We were separated at night and chained down. It was very hot in the day but cold at night. Early the next morning I was taken out and discovered a new Turkish cavalryman had appeared. Duncan was with them. We started on the backs of camels and travelled all day till about 4pm over the desert to the Diala. We had no water or food and I had given my topee (what was left of it) to Duncan as he had a headache. We were jolly glad to reach Deliabour on the Diala, where a decent officer took charge of us and gave us tea. We had some dinner at another camp, where we were given a jacket each. We had our shorts, but nothing on our feet. Then we went on that night in a cart; and travelled for a fortnight by mules, horses and carts till we got to German lorries. We spent a week at Mosul and then moved on by lorries to a rail-head. We arrived at Aleppo 5 November, and the Spanish Consul gave us £40 each (in paper). We had been given a suit of Red Cross clothes by an Indian Army doctor ... I am still wearing it! We travelled on by railways through the Taurus Range, changed at Airon-Karabissar and at Ouchak, came on here by road in two days. Other details I will tell you anon.'

Good news – of a kind – reached three families who had missing loved ones. Father of five Tommy Abbott, Alfred Sleights and Sidney Osborn were all wounded PoWs, three more hungry mouths for the PoW Comforts Fund to feed while food restrictions were tightened in Newark. Employees having meals at their business premises were ordered to take sugar supplies with them. Hotels were denied sugar 'for use in sweetening hot liquors' while works canteens, clubs and public houses had their rations drastically reduced on the grounds that their customers should take their own.

A potato growing scheme initiated by Ransome's director Japh Mason reached a climax with a show in the Town Hall, followed by a dinner for the committee and workers at the Clinton Arms Hotel. His offer of a £25 trophy led to entries by schoolchildren, displays by the Newark Horticultural Society and advice from the Newark Panel of Gardeners – all leading to a vital increase in production. The Mason Cup was won by Borough Police Constable F Smith, who pledged a hundredweight of his crop to the hospital. Classes winners: allotment, G Gumsley, Princes Street; novices, QMS Walker, Victoria Street; virgin soil, E Winter, Harcourt Street; labourers, W Wright, Farndon Fields; ladies, Miss N Gumsley; girls, Miss M Hopesmith; boys, A James, Appletongate. Acknowledging a shortage of flour and a glut of potatoes, Mayor Knight, as Chairman of the Food Control Committee, offered a recipe for potato bread: take 7lb flour, mix 1oz yeast with flour, add 1½lb boiled washed potatoes, thoroughly mix and work-up. The dough should be allowed to stand for twelve hours.

The *Advertiser* on 10 October returned the focus back to foreign soil:

'Our local Battalion of Sherwood Foresters have taken a prominent part in the great advance in Flanders. In the face of a stubborn resistance they carried out the task which was entrusted to them and successfully attained all their objectives. They have added new lustre to the name of a famous Regiment, and we tender our heartfelt congratulations.'

It explained a sudden increase in casualty news from Ypres. Bread roundsman Arthur Hutchinson, thirty-four, went missing after only a month in France with the Royal Scots. Officials eventually decided that he must have been killed on 22 August.

On 7 October news reached Frederic Wilson Boulton and his wife Elizabeth that their youngest boy, Fred, twenty-one, a milk roundsman before enlisting in the Lincolns, had been killed. A day later, widower William McKears received a letter revealing his son Walter, twenty-eight, an auctioneer's assistant before enlisting in the Yorks and Lancaster Regiment, got 'more than my fair share of a mustard gas shell' on 27 September, causing intense pain and affecting his eyes. Private Walter Edmund Twigg, twenty-three, accustomed to dealing with hot metal as a linotype operator at the *Advertiser*, had a piece of shrapnel in a wounded shoulder that doctors in France and Blighty had failed to remove, he wrote to his mum Clarissa in Eldon Street.

Harry Pride, twenty-nine, live-in gardener at brewer James Hole's Westfield House on Farndon Road pre-war, reckoned on 9 October that his cigarette case saved his life. He still had severe shell wounds in a knee and hand.

Blacksmith Joseph Selby was told on 10 October of the death of his son Frank, twenty-one, who helped to reclaim the Workhouse from the Sinn Feiners during the Dublin Rebellion. A Captain in the 2/8th Sherwoods added: 'His loss to me is great as he was one of the original members of the Battery.'

Sergeant George Gregory, an Old Magnusian, who forsook his chemist's job in South Africa to join the London Regiment (Artists' Rifles), was in hospital after being bombed

Fighting in the Ypres Salient: bringing in a casualty during the Second Battle of Passchendaele, November 1917. *[Taylor Library]*

by the enemy while in charge of a listening party on the night of 18 September.

Penelope Hollis discovered on 12 October that she was widowed with two babies under two. Her husband Lawrence, twenty-three, a gas works stoker, had been in the Sherwoods seven months before he died at midnight, 27 September, of chest and abdomen wounds. 'He was too ill to realise that he was dying,' wrote a matron.

Mother of four Annie Catley, thirty-five, was told on 13 October that she was almost certainly a widow. Two letters to her in Side Row, Beacon Hill, said Acting Sergeant-Major Thomas Catley, thirty-seven, had been missing since 26 September 'when the Battalion was in a very hot corner'. His Company Quartermaster Sergeant Glasby, in the 1/8th Sherwoods, added:

'I have tried through enquiries amongst the men to find something about him but I am only too sorry to say that up to the present I have failed. I still hope the worst has not happened but, all the same, I am afraid there is very little hope.'

Major F G Cursham was less optimistic: 'I wish, on behalf of the Company, to convey to you the deepest sympathy with you and your relatives in their sad bereavement.' Long before Tom's death was confirmed on 11 June 1918, it was revealed he had opted to go to France rather than remain in Ireland as an instructor. The children he left behind were aged thirteen to four.

Harold Hutchinson could not wait to do his bit – literally. He enlisted in the Sherwoods and was sent to France on 5 June 1915. The snag was that he was only seventeen; and even Lord Kitchener's enthusiasm would not allow boys to fight until they were 18½. So Harold's parents, Thomas, a brewer's labourer, and Clara had him returned home until he was old enough. Transferred to the Highland Light Infantry, aged nineteen, he was 'seriously wounded' in the stomach. A chaplain wrote soothingly from a hospital in France: an operation had been successful; the boy was getting on splendidly so splendidly that he returned home, married in 1924 and lived to the age of eighty-five.

Horace Mills, embittered by the death of his daughter in a 1915 Zeppelin raid and his basket-making workforce being decimated by Tribunal decisions, discovered on 15 October that his nephew had died a defiant hero. Sherwoods Second Lieutenant Thomas Arthur Reginald Mills, twenty-one, was 'gallantly rallying his men in the face of a German counter-attack, and it was greatly due to his determination and conduct that the enemy was forced back and the whole of the battlefield remained in our hands'.

Lieutenant James Henry William Ford, forty-five, was about to sit down to midday dinner with his wife Sarah on 17 October when a telegram arrived at home in Appletongate: 'Regret to inform you Captain J E Ford KOSB was killed in action on 5 October. Army Council expresses their sympathy.' James Ernest, their eldest son, was twenty-four, engaged to Miss Beryl H Hunter, twenty-four, younger daughter of a retired Army officer, building a career in the Borough Accountant's office; and subsequent letters told how the King's Own Scottish Borderers valued him. The chaplain wrote:

> 'The Battalion was engaged in heavy fighting, your son was in command of his Company. Everybody's testimony is to the same effect – that he did splendidly. That was only what we expected of him from his previous record. He was an excellent officer at all times and did his duty nobly.'

He had been mobilised with the Sherwood Rangers in 1914, went to Egypt but contracted dysentery and was invalided to England. He was drafted to France in November 1916. His last letter, dated 29 September, revealed he was not looking forward to the next move for which they had received orders.

News reached Newark on 19 October that Charles Bradley, twenty-eight, who emigrated to Australia several years earlier, was killed while working as a stretcher bearer under fierce enemy bombardment on the night of 21 September. The youngest son of merchant's clerk George Alfred Bradley and his wife Kate, in Stone Terrace, off Victoria Street, he settled in New South Wales, joined the Australian Army Medical Corps in April 1915 and served in Egypt before moving to France with the 8th Field Ambulance.

Brewery worker James Willows' war ended a month before his twenty-first birthday.

His parents, George and Emma in Farndon Fields, were informed he was killed with the Seaforth Highlanders 'between 19 and 21 September', a phrase that often encapsulated the confusion around Ypres at that time.

Railwayman Alfred Cobb, twenty-seven, twice wounded previously, was killed by a shell that fell in the road while he was unloading ammunition. 'I cannot say how grieved I am,' his Major in the 198th Royal Field Artillery wrote to Alf's parents, Frederick and Annie in Sleaford Road. 'He was doing extremely well, had only been promoted [to corporal] a few days ago and was marked out to go higher.'

George Smith, twenty, was killed 'during a heavy bombardment when a fragment of shell must have caught him in the head,' a Lieutenant in the South Staffordshire Regiment wrote to his mother, Emily Gray Bennett in Eldon Street, on 23 October. 'One of his friends was killed at the same time. I was only a few yards away at the time and I am pleased to tell you that your son died doing his duty as a gallant British soldier.'

Double heartbreak hit a close family in Northgate on 24 October. Three letters arrived at No. 11 to tell Mary Hannah Southerington that she had been widowed with a nine year old son by the death of her husband George, thirty-eight, a Gas Works' stoker before he enlisted in the 2/8th Sherwoods. When she ran next-door to inform George's parents William, sixty-nine, and Susan, sixty-four, she found them already in tears: they'd received a letter announcing the death of George's brother Alf, twenty-six. An eager footballer locally and prolific run-getter for the cricket team at Mumby's, where he worked as a tailor's cutter, he died on 12 October in his first 'tour' of the Royal Scots' trenches.

The Advertiser on 24 October reported the deaths of a son and grandson of James Garnet from Wellington Road. Only eighteen, Second Lieutenant Henry Graham of the 74th Punjabis was killed in Mesopotamia on 27 June while attached to the 67th Punjabis and placed in command of a cavalry patrol. His major explained somewhat casually that he...

> 'went out to drive off, with the assistance of armoured cars, a party of Arabs who were attacking a convoy about four miles away.
>
> 'No cavalry officer being available, and as your son was always extremely keen to go on little jaunts of that sort, he was offered the command and accepted with sparkling eyes. The last I saw of him was when he rode out of camp at the head of the cavalry, looking as happy as a lord. The cavalry drew back and pursued the Arabs but, going rather too far, found the enemy increasing and working round the flank (right). So at 10.30 your son gave the order to retire and he and four men covered the right flank. The main body was able to get back to the road but the right flank party were surrounded and shot down.'

Henry's youngest uncle, Grosvenor Garnet, twenty-three, was killed at Ypres on 9 October leading his company of the 1st Battalion Lancashire Fusiliers into action. Educated at the Magnus, Grosvenor had sailed to Canada in 1910, joined the Princess Patricia's Canadian Light Infantry and been transferred to the Fusiliers after arriving in France in 1916. Second Lieutenant W Addison wrote: 'In spite of many hardships, your son always set us a splendid example in cheerfulness and courage.' James Garnet discovered in the same post that his daughter, Lucy Kate, forty-three, had received an honourable mention as Matron of the Weymouth Isolation Hospital.

Private Ernest Birkett, twenty-eight, was killed on Sunday, 21 October, while preparing to take wounded men for treatment. His great friend Jack Hunt, thirty-five, who joined the Army Service Corps Motor Transport Section with him, wrote to his own wife Edith:

> 'I don't know how to tell you that five of our men were killed and two wounded, one of them being my old pal Dick [as Ernest was always known to his friends] ... After he was killed another shell came and blew his motor to pieces.'

Dick's wife of eighteen months, Esme, received a letter from an officer:

> 'He had been for just over a week on a detachment conveying "walking wounded" from an advanced dressing station to a casualty clearing station behind the line. Several of them were unloading their petrol and rations off a lorry when a shell burst amongst them.'

A stunning letter arrived in the post on 29 October for Eleanor Smith, thirty-one, of Hatton Gardens. 'Before you receive this, you will have received the sad news of the death of your husband, Sergeant FH Smith.' She had not. The sister of a hospital 'somewhere in France' added: 'He was admitted at 1.30pm very ill with severe wounds in back, a penetrating wound in abdomen and a fractured left thigh. He passed away at 2.40pm. He was far too ill to talk but seemed very grateful for what little could be done for him. I told him I should write to you and he sent his love.' Frank, twenty-nine, a maltster's chemist, joined the Sherwoods in May 1916. Eleanor, still deeply mourning a fortnight later, received a letter from Frank, detailing one of his escapades (and giving her an inkling of what a hero she had lost). He and another Newarker, Private Lowe, volunteered to take an important message 300 yards through heavy enemy fire. They got there in ten minutes. It took six hours to return. They had to crawl in the mud beneath ceaseless fire. Once they found themselves in a German dug-out. 'Luckily' all the occupants lay dead. So the Newark boys huddled there until dark and then completed their hazardous journey.

Florence Turner of Cross Street was called from her bench on the Ransome's night shift on 29-30 October to meet her brother-in-law Private George Turner, home on leave. She dashed out of the workshop – to be told of the death of her husband, John, thirty-one, a peace-loving pigeon fancier. George carried an explanation from a chaplain: 'Our Battalion took part in a big attack up here on the Flanders front and in the advance your husband was killed ... He was bravely attacking when he was killed...' By coincidence, John's partner in the pigeon world, Private Ernest Bryan of Bottom Row, Beacon Hill, was killed on 2 November, his 31st birthday, leaving widow Daisy, twenty-nine, and children aged five and two. Ernie, a maltster's labourer, survived the Sherwoods' Big Push in October but fell victim to a shell. One of his brothers, Fred, of the 1/8th Sherwoods, had been missing for more than two years: authorities eventually conceded he must have been killed on 15 October 1915.

Postman Albert Andrew's death, aged twenty-one, was reported to his brother Ernest on 30 October by the sister in a casualty clearing station:

'He was dangerously wounded yesterday in the thighs and left leg. He had every care and attention but all was to no avail and he died peacefully at 11.15 this morning ... May God give you courage and grace to bear your sorrow bravely.'

On Guy Fawkes' Day Maria Burrows heard she had lost the youngest of her four fighting sons. Private Ernest Burrows, twenty-two, a worker at Abbott's before joining the 9th Leicestershire Regiment, was struck by a shell on 1 October.

Dr Harry Stallard returned to Newark for garrison and hospital duty – a sure sign that wounded soldiers were filling local beds as never before – having 'seen much service' in the hospitals and on ambulance trains on the Western Front as well as with the 1/8th Sherwoods. His return was necessitated by another of Newark's valued and respected doctors, Lieutenant-Colonel Appleby, requiring treatment at the age of 73. Shortly after being mentioned in the London Gazette for valuable medical services rendered, Dr Appleby had 'over-worked himself in his zeal and attention to the troops'.

The former Magnus French master, Captain Ernest Harold Robinson, won his third bravery honour while Machine Gun Officer with the 7th Battalion King's Shropshire Light Infantry. He added a Distinguished Service Order in the Ypres battle to the Military Cross and Bar earned earlier. The DSO was

'For conspicuous gallantry and devotion to duty. He led his company in an attack until further advance was impossible. He then reorganised them, and collecting all men available of other companies, successfully repelled two counter-attacks, although the troops on either flank fell back. His skilful leadership and resolute bearing were a magnificent example to the remainder of the Battalion.'

His MC was gazetted on 1 January:

'Finding the Battalion was held up, he immediately organised bombing parties to clear up the objective. When this was found impossible he was of the utmost assistance in re-organising not only his own company but the remainder of the Battalion. His splendid example largely contributed to the success of the operations.'

Old Magnusian John George Harrison, the Newark Workhouse manager's son, earned the Military Cross for conspicuous gallantry and devotion to duty as a second lieutenant with the 7th Battalion Lincolnshire Regiment.

'He took command of his Company in an attack when he was the only officer left, reorganised the men, sited his posts with great judgment and sent in a very clear and useful report on the situation. He was largely responsible for repulsing an enemy counter-attack. He showed great courage and initiative, and his contempt for danger had a great effect on his men.'

At home, Mayor Knight called a meeting in the Town Hall for

Last officer standing – John George Harrison MC.
[Advertiser cutting]

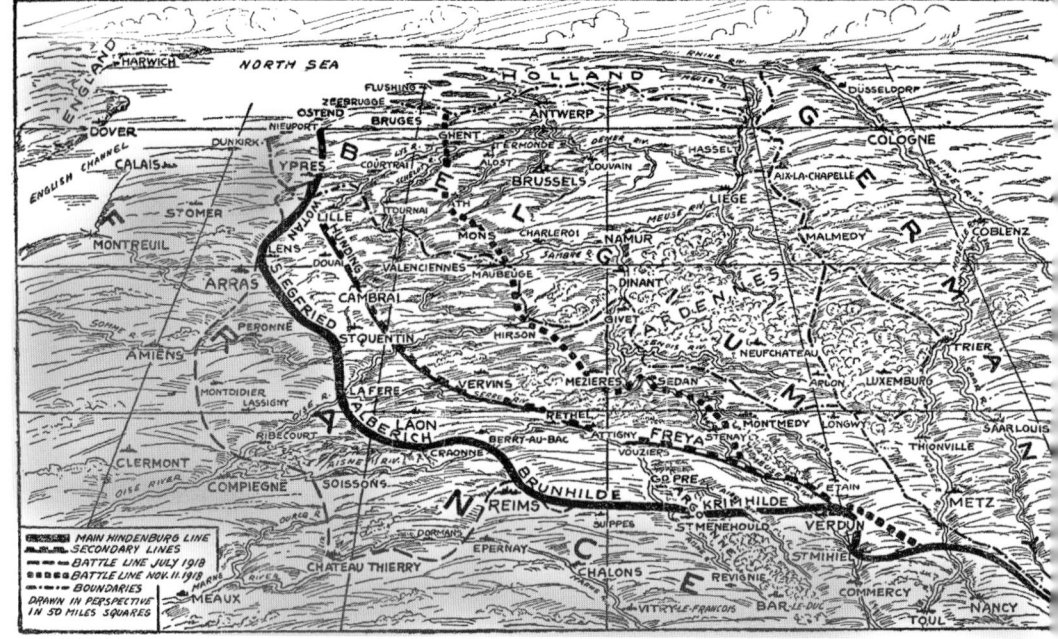

Construction of the *Siegfriedstellung* (Hindenburg Line) began in September 1916 and was intended to straighten the line and prepare for further Anglo-French attacks in 1917.

ladies and gentlemen willing to carry out a house-to-house canvass as 'an important part of the Autumn Food Economy Campaign'. On 23 November 'a new voluntary weekly bread ration' was announced. Men on heavy industrial or farm work were allowed 8lb. Men on ordinary industrial or manual work: 7lb. Men unoccupied or on sedentary work: 4lb 8oz. Women on heavy industrial or farm work: 5lb. Women on ordinary industrial work or in domestic service: 4lb. Women unoccupied or on sedentary work: 3lb 8oz. Other staple foods for all: 12oz cereals, 2lb meat, 10oz butter, margarine, lard, oils and fats, and 8oz sugar.

As food shortages increased at home, so did the number of PoWs in Germany depending on food from the Newark Comforts Fund. Already worried about one son, Walter, who was gassed and another, Charlie, who had lost his left leg, William McKears of Wellington Road heard via a captured German soldier that another of his boys, Harry, was a wounded prisoner. The Red Cross sent Mr McKears a statement found on the German:

> 'Information re English prisoner from whom letters and papers were taken: He was taken prisoner on the 9th inst., having been found lying in a shell hole a few kilos in front of Passchendaele Village. He had three bullet wounds in shoulder

Carefully planned barbed wire obstructions of the Hindenburg Line defences, considered to be nigh on impregnable by the Germans.

and chest, and apparently had been lying about 24 hours. His present whereabouts unknown.'

Harry's letters the German had stolen were sent to Mr McKears; they were 'cheery and optimistic that we will win the war by Christmas'. Harry, a Manchester Regiment private, worked for the Newark Clothing Company before the war.

In November, Newark soberly celebrated the President of France conferring the Croix de Guerre on Engineer Lieutenant Commander William Smith of the Royal Navy for distinguished services. Born in Newark in 1881, he was the son of Charles Smith, the British Temperance League secretary who was born in Newark in 1859. It was amazing how rumours flew in this era of few telephones, no wireless, no television and no internet: it was 22 June 1918 before the *London Gazette* announced the honour.

Widow Maud Parker in Barnbygate discovered on 10 November that she had lost her gentle grandson William, twenty. He was in service to Lord Belper before joining the Sherwoods, went to France six months earlier, was swiftly in hospital with shock, but was returned to the front line and killed 'between 20 and 22 September'.

On 11 November the Reverend William Shaw and his wife Sarah, in Crown Street, were notified of the death of their second son, Frank, thirty-three, on 17 October, leaving his widow, Emma Henrietta, living with her parents, the butler and house steward to Lord North of Wroxton Abbey, near Banbury.

A friend on leave popped round to Lincoln Row, between Northgate and Slaughterhouse Lane, on 12 November to tell seventy-eight-year-old Richard and Esther Ann Stevenson he was sorry but that their eldest, Albert, had been killed. They had not heard. Albert, 38, served ten years in the Grenadier Guards, worked at Simpson's and re-enlisted in 1914. The last time he was home, at Christmas 1916, he was happy to tell every one that he had been fighting for 31 months without a scratch or a day's illness…

Two of the original 1/8th Sherwoods had also been killed. Father of two children aged under seven, Drummer Edgar Sharp, thirty-six, of Trent Villas, Farndon Fields had only returned to the front three weeks prior to his death, having suffered facial wounds. James Allen Christie, a Lloyd's Bank cashier before working his way up from private to second lieutenant, had transferred to the Queen's (Royal West Surrey) Regiment before he was mortally wounded.

Another Lloyd's cashier, John Archibald Frederick Stewart, twenty-two, from Hatton Gardens, earned the Military Medal for repairing communication wires under heavy fire. Back home on leave before he joined an Officer Training Course, he 'acknowledges that he has been fortunate to come through the many engagements without a scratch'.

A lance corporal sent a letter to George and Jane Morley at 4 Lincoln Street confirming that their boy, George, twenty-five, had died between 19 and 24 September: 'Being one of my Section, I always found him a willing and good soldier.' George had been rejected for service three times before he was accepted into the Sherwoods five months earlier.

Mrs Ethel Bailey, twenty-three, of 109 Bowbridge Road, received official intimation from the War Office that her big brother, Edgar Marshall, thirty, a house painter who became a gunner in 186th Siege Battery, Royal Garrison Artillery, was killed on 15 October.

Gallantry medals were presented in Newark Market Place on 15 November: Distinguished Conduct Medal and Military Medal – Corporal R Beswick MGC 'single-handedly killed an enemy machine gunner and silenced the gun and later, when all the remainder of his team had become casualties, still continued to serve his gun'. Distinguished Conduct Medal – Lance Corporal J Hill RE 'has consistently performed good work throughout, particularly rescuing wounded men after the taking of a trench'. Distinguished Conduct Medal – Second Corporal A Ritchie RE 'led a party to repair a bridge under continuous and accurate enemy shell fire. He replaced casualties and completed the work with great initiative and courage. Shortly afterwards, while repairing another bridge, he was blown into the river by a shell, but though very severely shaken he continued to work unceasingly, displaying marvellous pluck and determination'. Distinguished Conduct Medal – Sergeant (Cadet) A C Rodgers RE 'consistently performed good work throughout, particularly when he assisted in destroying an enemy machine gun out in No Man's Land'. Distinguished Conduct Medal – Company Sergeant Major White MGC, no citation. Military Medals – Sergeant E Binney, MGC; Sergeant Boville, RE; Lance Corporal Bowen, MGC; Private J Crane, RDC; Sergeant W H Duffin, RE; Sergeant E Grant, RE; Sapper J S Hall, RE; Sergeant G Howard, RE; Lance Corporal W May, MGC; Private A McPheely, MGC; Sergeant B A Miller, RE; Sergeant T A Newman, RE; Second Corporal Moore, RE; Corporal H Payne, RE; Second Corporal H Shrimpton, RE; Sapper A S Skinner, RE. Meritorious Service Medal – Company Sergeant Major W Statham, MGC. Most poignantly, the Military Medal and clasp were presented to the next of kin of Gunner E Meade, RFA, who had been killed since he was honoured ... a stark reminder that death continued to stalk the battlegrounds.

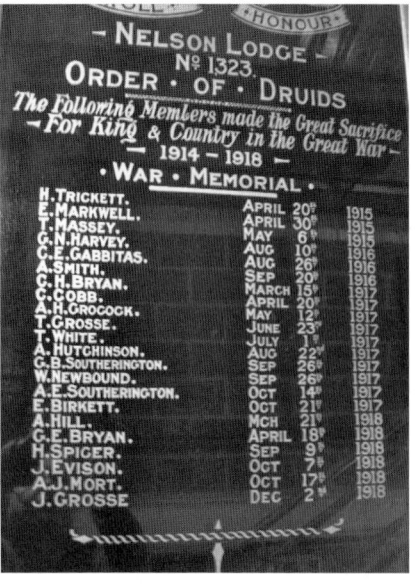

Remembered among Newark's Druids ... Walter Newbound.
[Photograph: Jillian Campbell]

The wife of a soldier serving in Salonika was sent to prison with hard labour for two months by Newark Magistrates on 15 November for cruelty to their three children aged three, five and seven. The relieving officer at the Workhouse, Walter Pearson, said it is the worst case he had seen: the children were insufficiently clad, had scabies and were in a filthy state. Elizabeth Blackburn of Long Row promised to try and do better in future. The children went to the Workhouse.

Baker William Newbound and his wife Fanny at 74 Northgate had three letters on 16 November concerning their son Walter, twenty-three, a saw miller. The first, from the Records Office, advised that Walter was missing. His regiment said he was killed in action. The War Office renewed the heartache: 'It is regretted nothing further has yet been heard of your son. He was reported missing on 26 September. No report of his death has been received and the information you have received was evidently issued to you in error. I am to express the sympathy of the Army Council with you in your anxiety.' It was July 1918 before Private 201405 Newbound of the 1st Royal Scots Fusiliers was officially recorded killed in action, 26 September 1917, during an attack on Hill 40 near Zonnebeke.

Educated at the Mount School, Walter worked initially for Clutterbuck's the butcher in Bridge Street before moving to Smith's saw mill on London Road, all the while attending North End Wesleyan Sunday School and Chapel. His parents had hoped he would return to continue the family business.

Widow Elizabeth Sharp, at 8 Guildhall Street, suffered similarly. Her second son Aaron, twenty-three, a Simpson's labourer, was posted missing by the 2/8th Sherwoods on 26 September 1917. It was 25 July 1918 before the War Office agreed he must have died on that date.

The Druids' memorial contains the name of at least one victim not on the town's official memorial. Private Jim Evison was working as a general labourer and living at 1 Sheppard's Row, off Northgate with wife Elsie Maria and children aged four and three before joining the Sherwoods in 1914, transferring to the Warwickshires, and being killed on 7 October, near Wimille.

Walter Newbound.

Bombardier George Lunn, 31, was mourned in Newark, where he was born and grew up, and Leeds, where he had been a police constable for ten years, when his death was announced on 17 November. He succumbed to wounds to the chest, left arm and leg; and left a widow, Lily Agnes, in Leeds and parents in Newark.

Next it was the turn of an altogether gentler chap: John Edward Walker, thirty-three, was a valet to the lord of a manor near Derby for thirteen years before enlisting in the 1st Battalion Lincolnshire Regiment in March 1915. He went to France five months later, soon suffered trench fever and, despite being wounded in the leg and gassed in the last year, performed so admirably that he was promoted in the field to sergeant.

Jobbing gardener's son Walter Wilson from Barnbygate was honoured and decorated for gallantry with the 16th (Irish) Division on 20 November. A parchment signed by the Major General Commanding stated:

> 'I have read with much pleasure the reports of your Commander and Brigade Commander regarding your gallant conduct and devotion to duty in the field and have ordered your name and deed to be entered in the record of the Irish Division.'

A second recommendation was sent in for gallant conduct in action on the three days that followed. Machine gunners under Sergeant Wilson fired 52,000 rounds per gun in beating off seven counter-attacks that resulted in 670 Germans being captured. Sergeant Wilson, who went out with the original BEF in August 1914, had been wounded in the

1914 Battle of Mons and invalided home; went out again in 1915 and was gassed and wounded, necessitating more hospital treatment; and was then transferred from the 1st King's Royal Rifles to the Machine Gun Corps, with which he distinguished himself. His latest heroics earned him promotion to company sergeant major.

Frank Thompson's wife, Mary Elizabeth, received an emotional letter on 24 November to announce his death in the trenches:

> 'He was the type of man I, as his commander, felt honoured to have had. Owing to his great ability in the use of the Lewis gun, he was sent to a school to receive additional instruction. While there, he won great admiration from his instructors. On his return he took command of my platoon gun and subsequently gave every possible satisfaction. The plain facts are that he was sniped through the head whilst standing in the Front Line trench.'

A letter from a Newark lad she had never met brought awful news to Emma Addis in Railway Terrace off London Road, on 25 November: the nephew she reared as her own had been killed in action. She had heard nothing from authorities. But the writer knew Herbert Wiggins well enough for this not to be a dreadful mistake. Herbert, 23, worked for Ransome's and played football in the local league before enlisting in the 2nd Sherwoods in July 1914. Confirmation arrived a week later from his platoon commander: 'It was during an attack that he was killed (on 20 November). We had reached our objective when he was hit on the head by a piece of shell.'

Solomon Freedman, fifty-eight, a Russian/Polish-born tailor, and his wife Annie in Victoria Street, were advised on 26 November not to hold out much hope for their son, Joseph, thirty-three, a private in the King's Own Yorkshire Light Infantry, who was married with a young family. He had been missing since 4 October; and an NCO wrote: 'Will you forgive me if I suggest that you do not build up hopes too high of hearing of him. If there had been any possibility of his having reached hospital, we should have learned of it by now.' Officials eventually decided Private 235130 Freedman must have died on 4 October.

Mother of six Harriett Johnson of George Street was told on 3 December that her husband, George Henry, thirty-four, was dead – 'killed by an enemy shell yesterday morning at nine o' clock while on his post of duty,' a Sherwoods officer wrote. Their children were all under eight.

Mother of three Rebecca Elizabeth Martin, thirty-six, in Hill Vue Gardens off Massey Street, received official notification on 8 December that her husband, Private George Martin, had been missing for two months. A bricklayer, he joined the 10th Sherwoods in August 1916, went to France in December and months later was deemed to have died on 12 October.

An 'extensive' measles epidemic that began in November led to the Council initially banning from school all children from houses where the disease existed until reported by the Medical Officer of Health as being 'clean' again. When that did not work and a problem with chickenpox arose, all schools in Newark were closed. On 4 December; Sunday Schools superintendents were advised to take similar precautions. Critics argued strongly that places of entertainment should also be closed, but to no avail.

North End Wesleyan Sunday School children heard on 9 December that one of their scripture teachers had been killed. George W Hill, twenty-nine, a Royal Army Medical Corps private, was a grocery assistant in peacetime.

Mother of four Ethel Annie Hardy, twenty-seven, in George Street publicised her desperation for news of her husband Private Joseph Edward Hardy, thirty-one, of the 2/8th Foresters in early December. She was told on 25 October that he had been wounded on 26 September, found his way to a clearing station and what happened next was a mystery. An officer wrote: 'I am sorry to say I cannot tell you in which hospital your husband is. We know that he passed through the clearing station and he was struck off the strength of the battalion. You can be sure of his safety, however…' Mrs Hardy was not so sure. A letter on 14 November left her wondering if he was a prisoner. Since then, nothing... It was 31 August 1918 before he was declared to have died on 26 September.

From the Ypres area, Ellen Haywood in Milner Street, with her twenty-one-month-old son, received a brutally honest letter on 12 December from a chaplain about her husband, John George, a King's Liverpool Regiment private: 'He was killed in action on 4 December and buried in the trenches where he fell. Owing to the machine guns and shell fire I was not allowed to take the burial. We are all sorry for you, for we too have lost a good man…'

Hairdresser John Henry Simpson, thirty-four, was killed while drawing water from a well, his wife Charlotte Beatrice learnt at home in Barnbygate. An officer of the 11th

British dead awaiting burial.

Battalion Royal Scots wrote on 13 December:

> 'It is my painful duty to inform you that your dear husband was called to higher service yesterday morning ... He was near the well with several other men, getting water, when a shell burst among them, killing him instantaneously and wounding three others.'

John was in Gouzeaucourt, a village which was lost on 30 November in a German counterattack at the end of the Battle of Cambrai, and recaptured the same day by the 1st Irish Guards.

The first Newarker ever to earn the Distinguished Conduct Medal, ex-Private John William Spick, heard the RE bugles sound from the Sconce as he slipped into his bed in George Street on the evening of 13 December. 'There goes the Last Post,' he smiled. They were his final words. He died in his sleep, aged only forty-four. He earned his DCM on the North West Frontier, in the Tirah Campaign of 1897: although wounded after trying to save his Company officer, Captain C E Smith, who was fatally wounded, Spick went to the assistance of a Dorset Regiment private whose arm had been shattered by a dum-dum bullet. Brigadier-General Hart recommended him for a Victoria Cross, the highest possible honour, but he was given the DCM. No wonder that, at his funeral, the Newark-based RE afforded him full military honours. But did they have time to ponder whether John's fate would be theirs post-war? On his return to civilian life, he struggled to find labouring jobs in Lincoln and Newark as his health failed.

More worries arose for mums as Christmas approached. Newark Gas Company threatened rationing:

> 'Owing to the great and increasing difficulty of obtaining labour, together with the largely increased demand for gas for munition purposes, the Newark Gas Company request all consumers to exercise the strictest economy in the use of gas for household purposes, otherwise the Company may be compelled without further notice to restrict the hours of consumption.'

Three days later milk rose to 3½d per pint; the Newark Milk Sellers' Association cited 'increased cost of production' and 'a grave possibility of shortage'.

The need to conserve fuel was underlined at the Magistrates' Court on 20 December, when two partners in Mather's esteemed motor engineering company were each fined £24 – a fortune to the working man – for receiving 129 gallons of petrol more than their allowance between July and September. They pleaded they had not become accustomed to their allocation being drastically reduced. The magistrates' message was clear: everyone had better get used to tightening their belts ... in much the same way that they were accustomed to deaths on the Western Front.

The final flicker of hope for Lance Corporal Arthur Stamper, twenty-two, a Simpson's apprentice when he enlisted on 23 December 1914, was extinguished on 14 December 1917. He had been posted wounded and missing four months earlier; and eleven days before Christmas his parents, bricklayer Fred and tailoress Elizabeth, received definitive news at home in Parliament Street from an officer: 'I have been waiting in vain to hear news of your son, who was wounded severely or killed during an attack on 22 August. I am afraid that there is but little hope that he can still be alive ... He was such a splendid and experienced soldier, and so brave that I shall never really fill his place.' The War Office eventually reported the recovery of Arthur's body had been reported by the 9th (Scottish) Division. He was wounded at Loos in October 1915 and Ypres in July 1916, then was transferred to the Ox & Bucks Light Infantry.

The Gumsley family in Parliament Street lost their second son to the war on 18 December: Harry, twenty-four, died from gunshot wounds in his leg. Of his surviving brothers, one was in hospital with frost-bitten feet; the other in a convalescent home with shrapnel under the heart.

With invasion still feared, the Newark Tribunal was ordered on 19 December to ensure men given conditional exemption donated part of their time to the Volunteer Regiment. Robert Henry Vickers, thirty-one, of Barnbygate pleaded that he was too busy carting grain; he was told he would have to enlist if he did not do his bit with the Volunteers. Baker Frank Ernest Nicholson, thirty-one, of the Market Place was excused: he was up until 2am on Saturday mornings meeting weekend orders. Under further orders to call-up four bakers, the Tribunal ordered Frederick Burbridge, twenty-eight, to go because his father could run their Appletongate shop; and withdrew Herbert Wilfred Marriott's exemption 'because he has not fulfilled the conditions'.

Less than six months after being married, Mary J Cooke was told on 20 December that she was a widow: brewery drayman Charles E Cordy, twenty-four, had been killed in action. He rushed through his wedding before sailing off with the 9th Leicestershire Regiment but was killed on 22 November without even reaching the Front: he was in billets shattered by a long-range shell.

Christmas Eve brought news to Joseph and Jane Frisby in Northern Buildings that their eldest, Ernest William, twenty-five, had been killed in Palestine. He worked for Simpson's, was called into the Rangers Yeomanry in August 1914, became a corporal, and died on 28 November on the road from Tel Aviv towards Jerusalem.

Regimental Sergeant Major Herbert Wilkins, forty-three, son of a Newark Post Officer pensioner, received an unexpected Christmas gift – a Meritorious Service Medal for devotion to duty in carrying supplies up to the Front Line trenches held by the Rifle Brigade at Passchendaele.

Newark's contributions to Christmas boxes for servicemen amounted to £276 5s. Each box was valued at 10s – a fair bit more than most people at home could afford to spend on each other; but they could never afford what the men were really worth.

Two disasters at sea spanned Christmas. The *Waverley* merchant ship was torpedoed on 20 December and former Mount School pupil Cyril Smith, only nineteen but Third Officer, was among those drowned. The Second Officer survived to explain:

> 'Cyril got into the starboard lifeboat safely with twenty-two hands but, owing to the terrific weather, the boat was unable to get away clear of the ship and a heavy sea struck her, turning her completely over, and I gather from an eye witness that he was never seen after that. He died doing his duty for his country just as bravely as any soldier or sailor.'

When the transport ship *Osmanieh* was mined in the Mediterranean on 31 December, Sapper Stanley Unsworth, thirty-two – a Newark Post Office telegraphist before joining

HM Fleet Messenger *Osmanieh* which struck a mine in the Mediterranean, off Egypt, on 31 December 1917.

the RE – escaped to tell the tale. Amid 'a sheet of flame and a dense volume of smoke' he helped two nurses to adjust their lifebelts, then plunged into the sea and swam around for eighty minutes before being picked up by rescuers. He lost all his Army kit and some of his most precious personal belongings. Yet Stanley lived to the age of eighty-two. Now that is what any circus escapologist would call spectacular.

Chapter Five

And the Last Trick is... to Achieve the Impossible

Leaving the best until the frenzied final scenes, in the finest tradition of showmen, the last few survivors of the Sherwoods' 'circus' helped the British to achieve the impossible in September and October 1918. Wearing inflatable jackets atop full battle dress, carrying their weapons and in the face of fierce fire, they slithered down a bank of the St Quentin Canal steeper and higher than a house, swam across the waterway, and clambered up the other side to storm one of the Germans' greatest strongholds, the Hindenburg Line. As suicidal charges went, it was the most outrageous and therefore the least expected – which was precisely why it succeeded.

The shock was summed-up by a Prussian officer finding himself face to face with a Sherwoods' Company Commander:

'What are you doing here?' barked the Prussian. 'Don't you know the Canal is a barrier between your troops and ours? You have no right to be here!'

'Well, I am here,' replied the Sherwood, indicating his men emerging behind him, 'so you might as well surrender.'

British troops crossing the St Quentin Canal over the captured Riqueval Bridge. The impossible had been achieved.

German prisoners – their faces tell the story of defeat and pain.

Over 4,000 prisoners and seventy enemy guns were captured; the German Army never recovered from the psychological, and physical, blow of losing a defensive network they believed to be impregnable.

Officialdom was thrilled after so many days, months and years of stalemate. 'The forcing of the main Hindenburg Line on the canal and the capture of Bellenglise ranks as one of the finest and most dashing exploits of the War,' declared General Sir Henry Seymour Rawlinson, head of the effort to break through the multi-storey German defensive line between St Quentin and Cambrai. 'The attacks constitute a record of which all ranks of the Division may feel justly proud. I offer to all ranks my warmest thanks for their great gallantry.'

One of the Sherwoods men took up the tale for the *Nottingham Evening News*:

'After we had gone some time we found ourselves being attacked by fresh enemy troops and by and by we got almost surrounded. Before long our ammunition ran out and the Company was left with no weapons but bayonets and lifebelts. It was the funniest sight in the world to watch our men rush into the fight hammering the Huns over their heads with lifebelts.'

It was such a momentous victory that the Duke of Portland recommended all Nottinghamshire children be given a day's holiday to celebrate. Newark schools could not take advantage: they were already closed by an influenza epidemic that would cause as many deaths at home as was the fierce fighting on the various Fronts.

Among the locally born territorials' most cavalier heroes was Joseph Richard Dench, twenty-seven, son of landscape gardener Joseph Robert and Katherine Dench, who lived in Middlegate – fittingly, in the heart of Newark – who had marched out with the 1/8th Sherwoods and risen through the ranks after being transferred to the 1/5th Battalion. He earned three Military Crosses in the helter-skelter chase to grind the enemy into submission.

Firstly –

'For great courage and dash at Lehaucourt on 29 September, when in command of his Platoon. When his Platoon was held up by direct fire from a 77mm. battery and machine-gun fire, he worked round a flank and captured the battery and two machine guns, killing some of the team and taking the remainder prisoners. He did splendid work.'

In fact, he captured four guns and thirty Germans who had been firing on his men at point-blank range. When the Germans counter-attacked, Captain Dench and a hundred men were ordered to hold the line at all costs, which they did against all odds.

Second –

'At Montbrehane on 3 October, during a heavy enemy counter-attack, he took command of his Company when his Company Commander was wounded. By his utter disregard for personal safety he steadied his men and with great skill he organised Lewis gun fire and inflicted such heavy casualties on the enemy that the counter-attack was completely held on his Front. His cool courage and prompt action at a very critical time saved the situation.'

Thirdly –

'For conspicuous gallantry and resource during the advance from Prisches on 6 November. He displayed the greatest courage and determination in leading his Company over very difficult and thickly wooded country, which was constantly under hostile machine gun fire and, although at one time held up by a broad and deep stream, he skilfully constructed a rough bridge, got his Company across and gained his objective.'

Once the war was over, he was rushed over the Channel to have the honour of ceremonially receiving the 5th Sherwoods' Colours from All Saints Church, Derby, on 8 December.

Company Sergeant Major John Francis Rawding, thirty, a maltster before he became one of the bravest of the brave in the original 'circus', earned a Distinguished Conduct Medal on 29 September at Bellenglise:

'He showed the greatest gallantry and devotion to duty. He reorganised the Company after a difficult advance through thick fog. Before the final assault he fearlessly exposed himself to heavy machine gun fire in his efforts to control the Company more efficiently, and whilst so employed he was severely wounded. He set a fine example throughout.'

The award was announced, alas, long after John was killed on the night of 30 September. His wife of five years, Mary, at home in Tolney Lane with sons Leonard, four, and Lawford, three, received a letter from his officer: 'Your husband was one of the bravest of soldiers, and was respected by everyone in the Battalion.' Months later, Mary discovered John had also been granted the Meritorious Service Medal 'for valuable services rendered in France and Flanders'. Mayor Knight invited her to the Town Hall to receive the medals, pointed out that he was the only Newark man to earn this double distinction, acknowledged it was little consolation to her to know that his life had been lost in service to King and country, and hoped she would show her little boys the medals from time to time, and 'tell them of the bravery of their father in the service of his country'.

Lance Corporal James North, 1/8th Sherwoods, earned a Military Medal to send to his widowed mother Ann Jane, in Lover's Lane:

'During the attack at Bellenglise, this NCO shewed absolute disregard for danger and devotion to duty. On several occasions he went out under heavy shell fire to repair broken cable. During the afternoon he manned a visual station under heavy shell fire when all other communication had failed. His courage, cheerfulness and devotion to duty encouraged the men under him to greater efforts. Although wounded during the action, he remained on duty and refused to give up his work.'

Sergeant Walter H Field, son of draper's assistant Stephen and Louisa in Whitfield Street – who wed Lily Markwell of 21 Harcourt Street in 1915 – also earned a Military Medal at Bellenglise: 'This NCO showed great coolness and resourcefulness when commanding his Platoon. His untiring devotion to duty and personal example, coupled with utter disregard for danger, enabled his Platoon to carry out its task successfully.'

Private John William Starr, twenty-two, brought-up in the Angel Inn in Middlegate, received a Military Medal, to the pride of his widowed mother, Emma. One of the 1/8th Sherwoods who swam the St Quentin Canal, he was in charge of a Lewis Gun Section on 3 October as the attack reached Ramicourt, his citation read:

'Throughout the action this man kept his Section together in a most admirable way, and utilised it most effectively as a fighting unit. By means of accurately directed flanking fire, he was on several occasions mainly instrumental in forcing the enemy from strong positions and enabling the advance to continue. He was always perfectly cool and had the happy knack of always being in the right place with his Section. Whilst reorganising his men after the objective had been reached, this man was wounded. Throughout the action, Private Starr showed conspicuous bravery, devotion to duty and great initiative.'

The 'circus' stars had an inspirational leader. The Reverend Bernard William Vann, thirty-one, earned the Victoria Cross, the highest honour for valour, for his inspirational

Lieutenant Colonel The Reverend Bernard William Vann VC MC & Bar. He was the only ordained clergyman of the Church of England to win the VC in the Great War as a combatant. He was killed 3 October 1918 (aged 31) at Ramicourt, France.

leadership; and was leading their advance when he was killed by a sniper. He had only enlisted in the 28th London Regiment in 1914 because he felt the authorities were slow to offer him a chaplain's post while he was teaching at Wellingborough School. Once commissioned into the 1/8th Sherwoods, his reputation soared as one of the most daring officers to bestride France: neither Germans nor wounds held terrors for him; he bore a regular bracelet of wound stripes.

Over the four years he was wounded thirteen times, awarded two Military Crosses and a Croix de Guerre, promoted to lieutenant colonel and finally earned the VC. Announcing the MC award to Second Lieutenant Vann on 15 September 1915, the *London Gazette* recorded: 'At Kemmel on 24 April 1915 when a small advance trench which he occupied was blown in, and he himself wounded and half buried, he showed the greatest determination in organising the defence and rescuing buried men under heavy fire. Although wounded and severely bruised he refused to leave his post until directly ordered to do so. At Ypres on 31 July 1915, and subsequent days, he ably assisted another officer to hold the left trench of the line, setting a fine example to those around him. On various occasions he has led patrols up to the enemy's trenches and obtained valuable information.'

He was Lieutenant (Temporary Captain) Vann MC by 14 November 1916 when the *Gazette* announced the award of a Bar to his MC:

'for conspicuous gallantry in action. He led a daring raid against the enemy's trenches, himself taking five prisoners and displaying great courage and determination. He has on many previous occasions done fine work.'

His VC citation in the *Gazette* on 14 December 1918 would refer to the wrong waterway – the Canal du Nord – but provide a graphic account of the sheer madness of the assault:

'He led his Battalion with great skill across the Canal du Nord [sic: the St Quentin Canal] through a very thick fog and heavy fire from field and machine guns. On reaching the high ground above Bellenglise, the whole attack was held up by fire of all descriptions from the front and right flank. Realizing that everything depended on the advance going forward with the barrage, Lieutenant Colonel Vann rushed up to the firing line, and with the greatest gallantry led the line forward. By his prompt action and contempt for danger the whole situation was changed, the men were encouraged and the line swept forward. Later he rushed a field gun single-handed, and knocked out three of the detachment. The success of the day was in no small degree due to the splendid gallantry and fine leadership displayed by this officer.'

Bernard Vann was killed four vicious days later, eight miles further north. His widow Doris, a Canadian nursing aide with whom Bernard had ten days' leave in Paris in autumn 1918, gave birth to their son in June 1919 at Battle in Sussex. She christened him Bernard.

Bertha Drabble, twenty-three, was astonished and elated to discover her accident-prone brother Arthur, twenty, had earned a Military Medal. A gardener, he was accepted in the Lincolnshire Regiment in October 1916. After only a month in France, a gun fell on his head, inflicting severe injuries: he lost his sight for a time and was in hospital for eighteen months. Astonishingly, he was returned to the Western Front. During the St Quentin/Cambrai battles he went out of the trenches with one of his pals and bombed a German trench, capturing a machine gun and 'a few prisoners'.

The Reverend Reginald Thomas Newcombe, thirty, well-known in local football circles while studying at Kelham College near Newark pre-war, was awarded the Military Cross while serving as a chaplain:

'During an action he displayed great courage and devotion to duty in bringing in the wounded under heavy fire. Although wounded in the leg and sent out of the Line to rest, he insisted on returning and continuing the work of finding the wounded with the stretcher squads which he had voluntarily organised. He continued to work thus for three days, until he was again wounded by the explosion of a shell. His self-sacrifice and endurance were a fine example to all ranks.'

He recovered to serve the Church and to work as a chaplain in the Second World War; and was eighty-three when he passed away.

Sergeant Roy Leonard Dalton, twenty-four, earned the Distinguished Conduct Medal with the 2nd Battalion, Hampshire Regiment on 3 October,

'For conspicuous gallantry and devotion to duty. When our troops were attempting to establish themselves in a certain position, he went forward alone under heavy machine-gun fire and, taking up a suitable position, covered the advance of the attacking party. The next day, under heavy machine-gun fire and bombs, he went forward and bombed, single-handed, an enemy shell-hole post, capturing the two surviving occupants. His gallantry and resolute devotion to duty were most marked.'

Roy, who also won a Military Medal for 'bravery in the field', had found time to pop home on 4 August 1917 and marry Marguerite (Maggie) Watts, thirty-five Jubilee Street – and, by the spring of 1919, was back toiling in Ransome's workshops.

One of six battling brothers, Corporal Richard Francis, from Beacon Terrace off Friary Road, earned the Distinguished Conduct Medal with the 1/8th Sherwoods. His citation read:

'This NCO showed great daring during an attack on an enemy gun post at Regnicourt on 17 October 1918. He crawled forward with one man, rushed the post, killing the officer in charge and taking about 30 prisoners. Throughout the whole attack he was absolutely regardless of all personal danger and showed great devotion to duty.'

Of the other five soldier sons of William and Mary Francis from Barnbygate, two had been killed and three were in France.

What made the success even more spectacular and unexpected was the fact that the 'circus' – along with the rest of the British Army – had been trounced over pretty much the same ground only a few months earlier.

Defying censorship rules, the Vicar of Christ Church, Newark, the Reverend GH Casson, predicted in his March parochial letter to the men at the Front that there was worse to come:

'We at home imagine that before this magazine reaches you the great German offensive will have begun, and we are anxious about it. You stand between us and our enemies, and you are keeping them away from our homes. We are not anxious as to whether you will stand firm; we trust you fully. But we are anxious as to the price we shall have to pay – I say "we" for we are with you in having to pay the heavy price of victory. You have to pay in hardship, wounds and even death. We at home in dreadful suspense, in sadness and bereavement; and I would remind you that many would choose death as easier to face than bereavement and the lifelong loneliness that it often means. These troubles upon us all alike ought to draw us close to one another; I hope they will.'

His crystal ball was spot-on: Germany launched the *Kaiserschlacht*, the biggest offensive of the war on the Somme front on 21 March, aiming to destroy the over-stretched British Fifth Army, split them from the French Army, and then engulf the British from the south. It almost worked. The British suffered unprecedented losses as the Germans drove deep into the area south of the Somme, though the attack before Arras stalled and was then halted.

One of Newark's first casualties was Lorraine Gabbitas, thirty-two, who could have been at home with his wife Harriett and three-year-old son Lorraine junior and working on the Midland Railway. He had finished his second stint in the Army almost two years earlier but signed on with the Sherwoods again. He served in the Dardanelles, where he contracted enteric fever. Even then, he insisted on fighting on.

Michael Price, twenty-seven, a Newark hero ever since he rescued a drowning woman from the Trent a few years earlier while working at Warwick's brewery, went missing as the 2/5th Lincolnshire Regiment was swept aside. It would be nine months before his death was confirmed to his widowed mother Isabella, sixty-nine, in Victoria Gardens.

Elijah Salmon, twenty-four, from Cawkwell's Yard, off Lombard Street, was 'third time unlucky'. A builder's labourer before he joined the 2/7th Sherwoods, he was wounded early in the war and then wrote home from the Somme in July 1916: 'I have been buried but I am right again. We have been in a warm corner.' He was the ninth of his parents' sixteen children to die; the other eight had succumbed to the diseases that pervaded Newark's slums.

It was 8 May before William Foulds' parents in Harcourt Street learned he had been missing 'since the fighting about Bullecourt' on 21 March. 'He may be a prisoner but that is only a very faint hope,' wrote a Sherwoods' chaplain. Months elapsed before William got word home that he was indeed a PoW.

Private Henry S Bembridge, thirty-four, went missing in the early hours of the attack, leading his wife Lizzie to issue a heartfelt plea for news six weeks later. She still heard nothing – but Henry would return from a PoW camp in Germany in time to spend Christmas 1918 at home in Bradley's Yard, off Chatham Street.

Corporal William Ernest Fisher's heroics in the hellish first few minutes of the onslaught earned him a Military Medal. The youngest son of the fifty-two-year marriage of Richard, seventy-six, and Emily, seventy-nine, in Millgate, he had been a driver in the Army Service Corps since October 1914; and when he was on leave in Newark at Christmas 1917, 'his many friends remarked on his healthy and robust appearance', said the *Advertiser*. He needed all his strength on 21 March. He carried a wounded comrade to a train and got him safely away, then went back for a lorry hit by one of the many shells raining down. Despite already suffering a hand injury, he started the engine, whereupon the lorry burst into flames. He put out the fire and got the lorry away even though shells continued to burst all around him. William, born 1883, survived, wed Kate Stenton in 1921 and lived to the age of sixty-one.

The Hickmans in Lincoln Street feared that they had lost two sons. Harry, twenty-two, a lieutenant signaller with the 1/8th Foresters disappeared on 21 March. Joseph, twenty, a private signaller in the 7th Leicestershire went missing on 22 March. On 26 May, their parents, John, a foreman maltster, and Penelope, received two letters, one from each boy, each with the same message: they were PoWs. Harry was in Restaat, desperate for a change of underclothing and carbolic soap. Joseph was in Limberg and quite well.

It would be 23 September before John Taylor Hardy, fifty-seven, a stoker-fitter, and his wife Jane in Charles Street, received official confirmation of the death of their son Tom, twenty: 'He fell on the battlefield between Quéant and Norcine during March 1918, and the date of death of 306015 Pte T Hardy, 7th Sherwood Foresters, has been assumed to be between 21 and 31 March.'

Private George Price sent to his brother William in Millgate a parchment certificate from his Divisional Commander:

'In the fighting between the River Somme and Cassel from 25 March to 1 April 1918 Private Price did invaluable work, having on three successive occasions delivered rations to the Battalion in the front line under exceedingly difficult conditions and under heavy fire. He also worked under Headquarters [the number is censored] Infantry Brigade delivering SAA [small arms ammunition] to units in the front line. His devotion to duty and the cheerful manner in which he carried out his work during a trying period set a splendid example to all.'

Fruiterer Arthur Simpson, twenty-eight, whose brother John had been killed in 1917, was one of many captured in the early hours of the onslaught. It was 6 July before his widowed mother, Annie, in Barnbygate, heard he was wounded. It was many more months before she was told that Arthur died as a PoW on 28 April.

Retired Colonel Sir Lancelot Rolleston was incandescent that every English Division in France was faced by eight German Divisions. Addressing the Notts Volunteer Regiment on 24 March he asked:

> 'Where are the remainder of the English? They are in England defending the men who ought to be filling the ranks of the Volunteers and learning to defend themselves! There are in this county alone 10,000 men over military age qualified to bear arms and play their part if only they would dare.'

Ex-Mayor Kew's nephew, Gunner Cyril Everard Parlby, twenty-one, was seriously wounded, necessitating the amputation of his right arm – a dreadful setback for a promising young journalist. One of his comrades sent a graphic account of the terror of the first rush of the Germans towards St Quentin, reproduced on 24 April in the *Advertiser*:

> 'Fritz concentrated all his artillery on us, and sent between 4,000 and 5,000 shells. Both my chums were wounded so I risked it and dragged both of them into a trench. I bound Parlby up with a towel as well as I could, but the other chap died in my arms. I then ran through the barrage for help and bandages but only got bandages as none would risk going back with me. I sat with Parlby for five hours under a tremendous bombardment. Help came at last and we got him away. I thank God I am alive. Officers say it was one of the worst bombardments ever witnessed. The gas and smoke blinded me for twenty-four hours but I refused to go into hospital.'

Gunner Parlby was taken to a base hospital, 'very dangerously ill'. He had volunteered for service early in the War and, as he was working on the *Leicester Mercury* newspaper, joined an artillery unit raised by the Mayor of Leicester. He would survive to become editor of the *Advertiser* and ensure it remained in the same family for much more than a century.

Corporal Joseph Ernest Turner, reared in Tenter Buildings, was killed on 22 March. One of his cousins wrote home: 'I saw him fall'. His Company Quartermaster Sergeant in the Leicestershire Regiment described him as 'one of the best – a true British soldier'.

John Foster, twenty-three, from Depot Yard, was also killed on the second day of the battle. His Machine Gun Corps CO described the lance corporal as 'a lad who was always trusted; a quiet, courageous and efficient soldier. He died bravely facing the enemy and firing his gun.'

One of the Reverend Casson's choristers, George Stanley Hydes, twenty-one, paid the ultimate price for his stubborn patriotism on 6 April. Four times the clothes shop assistant attempted to enlist in the Sherwoods during 1914. Four times he was rejected. So he cycled from home in Boundary Road, along the Fosse Way – and was accepted in the Lincolnshire Regiment in October 1915. Despite the doubts of the recruiting officers and the concerns of his parents, the eighteen-year-old settled into the rigours of life in the trenches so well that all of his letters home to mum Mary and dad James were cheery and positive. He fought through the Battle of the Somme. He earned promotion.

He was wounded badly enough to be shipped to a hospital in Bath, but recovered and returned to France. As recently as 27 March, with the Germans' onslaught raging, he wrote that he had had a very rough time but had obtained a new rig-out and was feeling very fit. He died in the village of Gezaincourt.

On Sunday, 7 April Bertha Foster, 30, in Norfolk Buildings, off Parker Street, discovered that she was widowed with a seven year old daughter: Private Walter Foster, thirty-four, had died on 4 April, eight days after being wounded fighting with the Royal Garrison Artillery.

There was no day of rest, either, for the nurses in France. A matron in the 20th General Hospital found a moment to write to George and Ann Hitchcox in Blyton's Yard, Millgate, sympathising in the death of their son, Francis Cecil, nineteen, a private in the Royal Scots Fusiliers: 'The boy suffered severe gunshot wounds in the abdomen on 1 April and, despite everything possible being done for him, he passed away a few hours ago.'

On 8 April, widow Minnie Jane Colton, who had moved from Harcourt Street to South Scarle Hall, discovered a second son had been killed. She was assured that Second Lieutenant Stanley Edmond Colton, nineteen and the proud owner of the Military Cross, died a hero; but that was scant consolation to a lady who lost her other son, Michael Herbert Edmond, a Sherwood Rangers Private, in the futile fighting at Gallipoli in 1915. Stanley's Commanding Officer, Lieutenant Colonel DFdeC Buckle, wrote:

> 'Please accept my sincerest sympathy in your great loss. Ever since your son joined the Battalion, he has shown himself a thorough soldier and a most capable leader. The bombing attack at Bullecourt, which won him the Military Cross, was a fine feat. On the 28th, the day on which he was killed by a sniper, he did splendidly and was the leader in a bombing enterprise which drove off the Germans at a very critical moment. In his death the Regiment has lost a fine officer who would have risen rapidly.'

The afternoon post was dreadful for Kate Annie Empson, living with her two year old son at her mother's in Parliament Street: her husband Arthur, twenty-four, was dead, following a heavy shell barrage on his battalion of the Liverpool Regiment on 28 March. He had recently returned to action after going down with fever after four months in hospital with leg wounds suffered on Good Friday 1917.

The Newark Arms Hotel was sombre on 9 April 1918. Landlord DJ Morgan and his wife were mourning the death of their eldest, James, twenty. He joined up as soon as he was old enough, went to France on Christmas Eve 1916, and was so badly wounded in March 1917 that he spent eight months in hospital. It was 'somewhat surprising' when he was returned to the Front with the 13th Gloucestershire Regiment in January.

There was death in the air, too. After surviving many brushes with the enemy, Captain John Nigel MacRae, twenty-four, fearless younger son of Stuart and Ethel MacRae of Handley House, Newark, and Loch Fyne, Argyllshire, perished in a flying accident in France on 11 April. Colleagues said he did magnificent work. Fear had no part in his composition. He was an intrepid flyer and a determined fighter. Yet he died testing a machine that had been giving trouble: soon after it rose, it crashed, with fatal results.

When hawker Matilda Sharpe met a telegraph messenger at her door in Rowbotham's

Row, off Water Lane, on 11 April, she wondered whether it was news of her husband or their son, both in France. It was their eldest boy, William, who was dead. He had enlisted as soon as he was eighteen and had been in France for seven months with the Northumberland Fusiliers. Her husband William, forty-one, survived his service in the Labour Corps.

The chaos engulfed Violet Tomlinson, running Halford's Cycle Stores at 13 Cartergate since its manager, her husband Charles, twenty-eight, joined the 1/5th Yorks and Lancs Regiment in September 1916. The last she heard from him was a field card dated 9 April saying he was going back into the trenches. The War Office informed her he was wounded 'between 11 and 15 April'. His officer wrote that it happened on the 15th. His chaplain said it was on the 17th. Months later she received official confirmation that he died on 11 April.

Gardener William Watson and his wife Annie Laura in Beacon Hill Road learnt on 16 April that their son, Lance Corporal John Thomas of the Sherwoods, was killed 'between 21 and 23 March' having previously been wounded three times.

Mother of six Ada Leader of Long Row lost her husband Alfred, thirty-five, when a shell burst on the wagon he was taking to the Front Line around Fouquieres-les-Bethune village. 'I trust the great blow to you will be softened by the knowledge that he did his duty,' wrote his 8th Sherwoods officer, Captain C G Tomlinson.

Mabel Booth, at home in Lime Grove with her eighteen month old son John and about to give birth to their second son, Allan, received a letter on 26 April from the former Minister of London Road Congregational Church, the Reverend Joseph Dobson Burns:

> 'I am deeply grieved to hear today that your husband [John, twenty-eight] was killed in action on the 14th. He was in one of the Batteries I [as Chaplain] had to visit from time to time. I have come into contact with him fairly often since the day on which he first spoke to me in camp. His officers always spoke very highly of him, both as a man amongst men and a very capable sergeant. It was a great pleasure for me to meet him and to exchange Newark news with him. He died doing his duty in a very dangerous spot [Locre, near Ypres] and you, in

Flying ace – Nigel MacRae.
[Advertiser cutting]

all your sorrow, have this great consolation, that he has given his life for his country and a great cause, and that his life, like that of so many others, will not have been given in vain.'

John worked in the Local Government Office in Newark before joining the Royal Garrison Artillery in 1916, gaining rapid promotion to Acting Sergeant Major.

Albert John Herrod, eighteen, was killed on 26 April. He had enlisted as a Sherwoods drummer, aged only fourteen and a half. His father Samuel, a widower, reclaimed him and kept him at home in Cross Street, working in the Great Northern Railway goods yards, until he was old enough to join up. An outstanding schoolboy footballer and eager member of the Newark 5th Scout Troop, he was set for a place on the Army Gymnastic Staff until the German onslaught. Rushed out to France on 29 March, he perished within a month while fighting with the King's Own Yorkshire Light Infantry.

Two of the family that ran Robert Smedley's hairdressing salon in Middlegate were killed. Grandson Charles Eustace Morley, twenty-seven, had enlisted in the Northumberland Fusiliers in March 1915, was drafted to France five months later, wounded in July 1916 but was returned to France in March 1917. He died near Béthune. Nephew Robert Henry Smedley, thirty-seven, second son of parents who ran the Golden Fleece pub in Lombard Street, survived being wounded twice and gassed once but was killed by pneumonia at Étaples.

Thomas and Eliza Newbold in Northgate lost their son, Private John Thomas Newbold, twenty-eight, within a month of his entering the fray with the Lincolnshire Regiment (transferred to the 4th Battalion North Staffordshire Regiment) in the struggle to halt the German advance around Albert. Of his brothers, hairdresser William was a Labour Battalion Private; Herbert, twenty-three, a Sherwoods private, had been invalided home; and Walter, thirty, worked as a cutter-out at Mumby's, having twice been rejected for service.

Captain Arthur H Quibell DSO had a leg amputated but remained in 'a very grave' condition. Special wishes were transmitted to him when a large and representative company gathered in the Town Hall to bid God speed to Dr Ernest Ringrose, Officer Commanding the Newark Company of Volunteers, who had been accepted for medical service overseas. Arthur would return home and wed Dorothy Alice Bailey in June 1919. The good doctor would live to be ninety.

Two Newark lads, aged twenty-one, who enlisted together died side by side in the trenches on 2 May. Alfred was the second son lost in this war by Joseph and Ellen Grosse in Northgate. Tom was the only son of Henry and Lily Gabbitas of Parliament Street. 'He died doing his duty,' said the card to each set of parents from their 2nd Royal Scots Commanding Officer. Alfie was rejected for service no fewer than eight times before he managed to enlist with Tom on 16 October 1916. Both are buried only a few graves apart in Sandpits British Cemetery, Fouquereuil, near Béthune. Tom's Uncle Lorraine had died on the opening day of the German onslaught. Alfie's brother Joseph, nineteen, survived to celebrate the Armistice but succumbed to influenza in France on 2 December.

Miss Edith Fox, only twenty-one but officially head of the family home in King Street with her parents dead and her brothers in the war, was informed on 6 May that her brother Arthur, twenty, had died in Rouen of pneumonia. A chaplain wrote: 'I saw him in the afternoon and noticed a grave change for the worse, but he was quite prepared to go.' She would receive much more heartening news on 20 August: her younger sibling, Albert, eighteen, a clothes store assistant before becoming a stretcher bearer with the King's (Liverpool) Regiment, earned the Military Medal for tending to wounded soldiers under heavy fire. He explained:

> 'A party of men were sent over the top to take a crater. The officer and several men were wounded by snipers and machine-gun fire. I went over the top to tend the wounded. There were two young lads badly hit and unable to get back to our trenches so I carried them on my back one at a time while being sniped at. I again made three unsuccessful attempts to get the officer in who was now killed by a sniper. In the fourth attempt I reached him, and under great difficulties as he was lying close to the enemy lines. I could not drag him in on account of myself being exhausted so I did what I could for him and then got back to our lines, being sniped at and also under machine-gun fire. Don't worry about me. I'm only doing my duty.'

Albert was married in 1925 to Mabel Watson and lived to be sixty.

John and Catherine Esam at 53 Jubilee Street discovered that their second son, George, twenty, was killed [near Ypres] on 8 May. A grocery boy before enlisting in the 2/8th Sherwoods just after his seventeenth birthday, he finished up in the Royal Warwickshire Regiment. To add to his parents' anguish, his brother, William, twenty-five, a corporal in the King's Rifle Corps (a factory mechanic pre war), was so badly wounded that he was confined to depot duties.

It was 11 May before Solomon and Annie Freedman in Victoria Street learnt from East Yorks Regiment Company Quartermaster Sergeant S Mitchell that one of their sons, Maurice, twenty, was killed at Bouzincourt about 30 March.

> 'He was always willing to do anything for anybody, and the men of his platoon missed him when the end came. I thought it my duty to let you know as I am a bred and born Newark man.'

The official casualty list issued on the same day stunningly showed how the Sherwoods suffered in the German onslaught: 600 missing and 250 wounded! And counting.

A War Office wire on 13 May told Edward Broughton's parents that he was dead at nineteen – shortly after they had received a hopeful letter from a comrade saying:

> 'The last time I saw him he was going away on a stretcher, and I sincerely hope it is nothing serious. I expect he will get to England. If so, kindly let me have his address as I should very much like to know how he is getting on ... I miss him very much as we have been together for so long now.'

Ted died on 24 April.

Four months of agony began on 13 May for Mrs Eliza Spicer, twenty-eight, living with her widowed mum, Mary Ann Ives, in Spittal Row, off Northgate. A sergeant in the Worcestershire Regiment wrote that her husband, Private Herbert Spicer, twenty-six, was missing. A baker, he had initially joined the Army Service Corps but was transferred to a front line Regiment when manpower ran low. Weeks later, Eliza was elated to hear he was a PoW. As winter set in, she discovered that he had died in a camp at Munster.

Five children aged between seventeen and four were left fatherless by the death of fish and game shop manager Ernest Cross, thirty-nine, who answered Kitchener's call and joined the Sherwoods in December 1914. Second Lieutenant CG Druce told his widow Florence that he was killed in action on 27 April ... 'I, as his Platoon commander, always found him a reliable and good soldier.'

The Gilstrap Free Library's assistant manager, Edward Hosner Asling, thirty-nine, paid the ultimate price for declining a safe role in the Army in England to continue in the 2/8th Sherwoods as Lieutenant Colonel Coape-Oates' servant in France. A letter from the mess cook arrived for his widowed mother, Mary, sixty-nine, in Milner Street on 16 May:

> 'Just a line to let you know of the very sad news of your loving son Ted: he was killed this morning, about 11am, instantaneously. He is very much missed by all the mess staff as he was one of the best pals we have ever had with us.'

The following day a letter from Lieutenant Colonel Coape-Oates added:

> 'Your brave boy was killed quite close to me this morning but never felt anything. A better man or more devoted friend never lived. What I shall do without him I do not know. He was always so unselfish and thoughtful, and our one consolation is, no one was more fit to go than he. He need not have come out [to the Front] but his sense of duty triumphed over all, and he preferred to come. I have lost a devoted friend I can never replace. Believe me, I sympathise very deeply with you. I shall see him reverently buried tonight.'

Sapper Samuel Whitton returned home to Newark, discharged from the Army as 'unfit' – but not before he had earned a Military Medal for bravery in repairing lines under shellfire while attached to the RE Signallers. Prior to enlisting in September 1914 he was a fitter at Simpson's.

Sarah Ann Gurnell, running the Queen's Head Hotel in Newark Market Place with her second husband, Charles, discovered on 27 May that her only son, William Kirkby, had been killed [in the village of Vieille-Chapelle near Béthune], leaving a widow, Florence May, thirty, and children aged nine and five.

On the same day, Old Magnusian John Auchenlosh Gibson, thirty-six, was among sixty men who disappeared at Craonne Wood. A Master of Arts and Bachelor of Science from London University, he was science master at Tiffin's Boys' School, Kingston-on-Thames; attested under the Lord Derby Scheme but was not called-up until Easter 1917, when he joined the Royal Garrison Artillery. He was gazetted second lieutenant and attached to 116th Siege Battery. In his last letter, dated 21 May, to his wife Catherine, he wrote of much fighting and very little sleep. A late night telegram on 10 June to his widowed mother, Mary Gibson, in Magnus Street, revealed he was missing. A letter from his Captain followed:

> 'He was last seen at the forward section of the Battery with about sixty men, the Major and two other officers, holding the Battery position with rifles against the

Germans after the guns were blown-up. This happened about 8am on the 27th and since then we have heard no news of him or the people who were with him. We have made every effort to find out where he and the others are, but have had no news and so have had to conclude that they were all captured.'

It would be 6 December before verbal recollections collated by the Red Cross assured Widow Mary that John was killed on 27 May. The report came through a returned PoW, who stated he was told by Bombardier Brailsford that Lieutenant Gibson had been killed. He explains:

'I saw Brailsford in hospital behind the German lines in June. He said that after he was taken prisoner at Craonne Wood between Reims and Soissons on 27 May he was being taken back by a 'Jerry' when he passed Lieutenant Gibson lying dead. He had been severely wounded in the shoulder.'

Baby-faced Private William Maule Norcott, eighteen, wrote to his mum Sarah Elizabeth in Cherry Holt Lane on 1 June: 'I got hit in the right shoulder with a piece of shrapnel, but I don't think I shall get to England, so don't keep hoping to see me.' He thought the wound too slight for him to be shipped home and added: 'I am going on fine.' A few days later a Chaplain wrote:

'I happened to be a patient in the American hospital at the same time as he. I spoke to him for a short time the day before he died, but I did not know he was so ill. He became serious very rapidly and he was not conscious when I saw him the next day. The doctors and nurses worked their hardest for him, but all was for no avail and he passed away peacefully at 9pm on 4 June.'

Dressmaker Florence Wilkinson, thirty-one, was due to walk down the aisle of Newark Parish Church on 6 June to marry her brave and beloved Royal Marine, Second Lieutenant Harry Lawford Hunt, twenty-nine. Instead, she locked herself away in the grand home she shared with her seventy-eight year old Aunt Mary, Bradford House, Appletongate, striving to come to terms with the news of his death. 'What can I say to comfort you?' wrote a chaplain. 'It seems to me that it is always the women who have to suffer most.' Over the Trent in Kelham Villas, Harry's parents, Frank and Mary Ann, received an envelope containing decorations awarded to him posthumously along with an explanatory letter from Harry's Commanding Officer:

'I am writing to express my very deep sympathy with you in the loss of your son. He is also a loss to the Service as from my own experience, and from what I have heard from others, I know his value. I always liked visiting the Battery where he and Baseby [Basil, a lieutenant who was also awarded the Distinguished Service Order] were stationed as they were both full of pluck and always cheery. His gun was in action when a six-inch shell burst in his position, killing your son instantly and wounding Baseby and eleven others, practically the whole gun detachment. He was buried yesterday afternoon. A large number of French and Belgian officers were present as your son was very popular with them. The Belgian officer placed the Order of Couronne and the Croix de Guerre on the coffin.'

The killing of the Reverend Joseph Dobson Burns hit Newark like a sledgehammer on

Death of a Chaplain ... Joseph Burns.
[Advertiser cutting]

8 June. Chaplains could surely not be legitimate targets? The Pastor of London Road Congregational Church for seven years, he was 'highly gratified' in August 1917 to be accepted by the War Office and attached to the Royal Garrison Artillery. As recently as 23 May he wrote to one of his worshippers about the *Kaiserschlacht*:

'We were in it all the time, and I have seen some war – enough for a few lifetimes. Our batteries did splendid work and I feel proud to be their padre. But I did not like my job a bit when it came to burying men I had known so well. During the last six weeks I have often had a heavy heart. I wonder when I'll have a look at you all again. I was going on leave once, and was four hours on the boat, waiting for it to sail, then turned back: "All leave cancelled!" I am very fit. I can eat anything – even bully and biscuits – out here. I am very happy with the boys – have great times with them.'

The Reverend Burns is buried among 'the boys' in Ebblinghem Military Cemetery between St. Omer and Hazebrouck.

A postcard in the same post ended six weeks of worry for Harry Hurst, forty-three, joiner and builder, of Barnbygate. It revealed that his son Reginald, nineteen, a Middlesex Regiment private posted missing in April, was a PoW in Germany. He would return home and live to the age of fifty-nine.

One of the Newark area's oldest victims, fifty-two-year-old Robert Jarman passed away on 9 June, laid low by tubercular pleurisy contracted while serving with the drainage section of the RE in France. Although well over military age, he had no hesitation in leaving his job with Ransome's and volunteering at the start of the War.

Corporal Henry Percy Carr's last letter to his widowed mum, Rhoda, in Barnbygate rejoiced that he was due leave 'so expect me any day!' On 12 June Mrs Carr received a dreadfully different kind of message: her youngest son died of wounds, aged twenty-two, on 8 June at a Canadian Casualty Clearing Station on the main road from Lillers to St. Pol. An iron moulder's labourer pre war, he joined the 2/8th Sherwoods in 1915 and was among those mentioned in Battalion Orders for gallantry and coolness in the field during the Irish Rebellion.

Intrigue surrounded a Meritorious Service Medal announced on 15 June for Sergeant Charles Edward Dolphin, twenty-seven, of Kelham Villas, 'in recognition of valuable services rendered' with the REs. The citation merely stated he 'has been engaged on a special piece of work in France' for which he was highly commended. A century later, the Government's official criteria for this medal is: 'Award of the Medal requires good, faithful, valuable and meritorious service with conduct judged to be irreproachable throughout. The Service Boards look for evidence of particular achievements, whether in the course of military duty or in extra mural involvement which benefits the service or the public in the field of sport or such things as charitable work. To reinforce the special character of the MSM, limits are placed on the number that may be awarded annually. No more than forty-nine may be awarded in the Royal Navy, three in the Royal

Marines, eighty-nine in the Army and sixty in the Royal Air Force, though historically many fewer than these numbers are actually awarded.' Before the war Charles began work with Notts County Council in Newark as a steam roller driver, and became Oxfordshire Road Surveyor. Post war he married Emma Weselby in Henley in 1919 and lived to the age of eighty-seven.

Flo Griffin, twenty-five, of Spring Gardens, discovered on 18 June that her husband, Harry, a second lieutenant in the South Staffordshire Regiment, was missing. It sparked a repeat of the nightmare endured by her sister, Miss Ethel Young, twenty-nine, whose fiancée was killed in action in 1917. Harry, twenty, a jewellery shop assistant, suffered considerable ill-health during fifteen months in France; and had only been back in action two days when he disappeared on 27 May. By coincidence, his boss, jeweller and silversmith Charles Henry Whitehouse, was under orders from the Tribunal to prepare to join the Services at the age of forty-two.

Fred Porter, eighteen, youngest (and brightest) son of butcher Thomas Minnitt Porter and his wife Elizabeth in Bargate, disappeared in the same action. While at the Magnus, he secured many prizes for languages, scripture and other subjects, worked in Quibell's offices until he reached military age, and in his one month in France 'saw a great deal of heavy fighting' with the Durham Light Infantry before being posted missing on 27 May. Of his brothers, Thomas William Minnitt Porter, twenty-five, was permanently disabled after service as a trooper with the Sherwood Rangers and lived to the age of fifty-six; and Francis Herbert Victor, twenty, a mechanic with the RAF, lived to be sixty-four.

Only a day after arriving in Skegness to convalesce from a painful illness, Newark's Wheatsheaf pub landlady Minnie Gardner received an urgent phone call on 25 June: her son Harry, nineteen, had been killed on only his third day in the trenches. By the time Minnie and her husband William returned home, an officer's letter awaited:

'I regret very much to have to inform you that while on a working party on the night of the 17th inst., your son was struck in the head by a piece of shell and died shortly afterwards.'

An apprentice turner at Ransome's, Harry had wanted to join the Navy but was placed in the RE Inland Water Transport Section and, in France, transferred to the Duke of Cornwall's Light Infantry. Knowing he was on his way into the front line, he wrote to Minnie: 'Don't worry about me. I shall try and be as careful as I can. But it is up to every man to do his bit and if all do so, this war will soon be at an end.'

Private 41451 Gardner, buried in the British Cemetery on the road between the small town of St Venant and the village of Robecq, was not forgotten by his workmates: they saved up for months to present his parents an enlarged portrait of Harry in a neat oak frame. On a silver plate was inscribed: 'A token of respect and sympathy from the members of Newark No.22

**Ferried the wounded ...
Reynolds Nettleship DCM.**
[Advertiser cutting]

Branch United Machine Workers' Association.'

Fate had it that on 26 June, the *London Gazette* announced that Trent boatman Reynolds Nettleship, twenty-eight, of Tolney Lane had been awarded the Distinguished Conduct Medal for heroics as a corporal in the RE Inland Water Transport Section:

> 'While in charge of a motor launch he ran it continuously through heavy shell fire, handling it with the utmost skill. On three separate occasions he volunteered to run his boat through to the advanced dressing station, and on each occasion succeeded in doing so. His courage and resource were most marked.'

Sidney Harston, a super young sportsman, so eager to join the war that he enlisted in the Royal Air Force a month before his 18th birthday, went missing, presumed killed, while flying Sopwith F1 Camel D3361 over enemy lines on 29 June. He had been engaged in hazardous work as a scout for bombers since going to France in April, his widowed mother Margaret discovered at home in Lombard Street, where his late father had run a painting and decorating business. Sidney first showed his sporting mettle aged thirteen, entering a two mile swimming race and defeating all of the men. He went on to captain the Magnus Rugby 1st XV and become a good all-round athlete.

Local football star Harry Edward Smith – the first volunteer when the Duke of Portland appeared at Newark Kinema in August 1914 to plead for more recruits – suffered an 'exceedingly pathetic' death on 10 July. His parents, Harry and Flora May Smith in Stanley Street, were informed by a brutally honest officer:

> 'He was admitted to hospital suffering from severe abdominal symptoms and was operated on, when it was found to be a very bad appendicitis abscess. He did not respond at all to any treatment, was very sick continually, and became gradually weaker, passing away at 9am. He did not mention anyone to me or send any message.'

Only twenty-two, Harry had been in France since August 1915, suffered an eye wound and was so badly gassed during another action that he lost his sight and voice for eight days.

Edith Kent, twenty-seven, in Wheatley's Yard off Chatham Street, received two letters on 11 July confirming the loss of her husband George, twenty-eight, a Ransome's machinist before he rose to be a lance corporal in the East Lancashire Regiment. A chaplain wrote:

> 'I am very sorry to tell you that your husband was killed last night [at Bertrancourt, on the Somme]. He was one of a mining party. Whilst it must be a terrible blow for you, yet it may be some consolation to know that he died in the service of his country.'

A corporal wrote,

> 'On behalf of the men of both your husband's section and my own, we desire to offer you our deepest sympathy in your sad bereavement. Your husband was a very brave soldier and was greatly respected by all of us. His death caused quite a gloom over our little party and we have missed him very much indeed.'

Harry Randall, eighteen, from Lombard Street, a private in the 15th West Yorkshire Regiment, went missing on 19 July. Fully a year elapsed before he was officially presumed to have died that day at Merville between Béthune and Armentières.

Lance-Corporal Harold Norcott from Cherryholt Lane earned the Military Medal during operations with the 2nd Battalion Loyal Lancashire Regiment from 23 July to 1 August 1918 near the River Ourcq:

> 'He gave to his men the example of the most wonderful courage and, more especially, during the action of 29 July, at the time when his Lewis gun section was put out of action, he single-handed worked the only gun left until he had silenced the enemy's fire.'

Harold, who also earned the Croix de Guerre, fought in five different war zones: Dardanelles 1915, German East Africa 1916, Egypt and Palestine 1917, France 1918.

Lance-Corporal 305570 Thomas Whiles, 13th Battalion Tank Corps, who lived in Tenter Buildings, braved exploding tanks to earn a Distinguished Conduct Medal, which would be presented to him by Mayor Knight in the Town Hall on 13 February 1919. The citation told a spine-tingling story:

> 'For conspicuous gallantry and devotion to duty. On 8 August 1918 near Bayonvillers, the tank in which he was Gunner received two direct hits which killed the driver and tank commander, and set the tank on fire. Repeated efforts to extinguish the fire were frustrated by the exploding ammunition. Though the tank was filled with flames and smoke, he continued to try and get the bodies of his Commander and the driver outside until, seeing that life was really extinct and he himself was quite exhausted, he left the tank. Later on he rescued a man from another tank that had been set on fire by a direct hit, and of which the ammunition was exploding in all directions. Throughout the action the conduct of this NCO was a splendid example of resolution and contempt of danger.'

Corporal H Martin of Eldon Street won the Military Medal and Bar – and might have had more – as the advance progressed over the waterways:

> 'On the night of the 8-9 August whilst crossing the Milk Way Road in front of positions just captured by our troops near Clydesdale Camp, Corporal Martin saw a party of men coming towards him who he challenged. These men turned out to be enemy machine gunners, who promptly fired on him. Corporal Martin fired back at them and drove them away; and himself captured the light machine which they were about to fire. Corporal Martin was slightly wounded and refused to go back.'

He was awarded a Bar for:

> 'Gallantry and devotion to duty under fire on several occasions, especially on the night of 18-19 October 1918 whilst engaged on a reconnaissance of the crossing of the Lys at Courtrai. On this occasion he made a careful survey of a floating bridge under enemy machine gun fire, crawling to the end of the bridge within twelve feet of the opposite bank, which was held by the enemy, thereby obtaining valuable information. This NCO also did extremely good work in assisting to build a bridge across the canal at Knocke on the 21-22 October. His courage and sense of duty have been at all times of the highest quality.'

The *London Gazette* announced a Meritorious Service Medal for a member of an old-established Newark family, Company Quartermaster Sergeant B/2671 H Wilkins of the Rifle Brigade, for 'carrying supplies to the Front Line at Passchendaele'. It is believed this is Henry Wilkins, born 1876 to Post Office clerk Thomas and Hannah Wilkins in Barnby Road. He worked as a pawnbroker's assistant until he was old enough to enlist in the Army, fought in South Africa and returned to service in 1914.

Blacksmith's son Jim Stoakes, twenty-two, earned a month's furlough at home in Cross Street by saving a comrade's life while himself in hospital with trench foot. As soon as he heard an appeal for blood for a fellow soldier on the verge of death, Jim volunteered. He gave two pints and the recipient lived. Jim, too, recovered to return to the 5th North Staffordshire Regiment – and wished his younger brother George, twenty-one, had been as fortunate. Both boys played for Newark Schoolboys football XI and won events as athletes. Alas, George was wounded in September 1917 fighting with the Sherwoods and had his left leg amputated.

Septuagenarians Thomas and Margaret Blagg in Cartergate heard on 13 August that their youngest son, Sidney, was dead. They knew from an earlier letter that he had been wounded; and thought he had been cut off by a German attack on 29 July and taken prisoner. But his Royal Sussex Regiment Commanding Officer explained that when the 1st Battalion retook ground that they had lost, they found his body. Sidney had written home only two days before he died saying he had been promised leave at the end of the month. Aged thirty-seven, he was educated at the Magnus, worked for the Union of London and Smith's Bank, spent eight years in the South Notts Hussars; and during the war fought in Salonika and Palestine, was mentioned in despatches by General Allenby for services in Egypt, was gazetted with the Sherwood Foresters in March 1918, went to France at the end of June and was involved in 'some of the most strenuous fighting'.

Four years and seven days after joining the Army aged fifteen, former Newark Parish Church choirboy John Thomas Thorpe of Cromwell Road laid down his life on Sunday, 18 August. His widowed mother Emma heard the news by instalments. First she received a letter from John, bright and cheery as ever:

'Sorry I haven't written sooner but, Mother, it is a case of can't write because of the great advance and the fact that we are following the Germans up, and it has been impossible to get even a card away. You must understand how well we are doing here, with bags of guns and prisoners, and the "old boy" is still falling back. I can stand going after him, but I don't want him running after me again like he did in March.'

John added that he was in good health but in need of 'cigs'. Mrs Thorpe was still smiling at his spirit when another letter arrived, from a Rouen hospital sister: he was seriously ill. A telegram of the same date, 18 August, warned he was dangerously ill from 'gas shell wounds'; his mother could not visit him. The next letter, from the sister next day, was the worst: he died during the night.

Monday 19 August was a red letter day, for a different reason, for the family of one of Newark's home-born sapper: Lieutenant Frederick Charles B Wills, thirty-six, had been awarded the Military Cross. His citation read:

> 'When the enemy had broken through the Front Line trenches, this officer with a small party of Sappers manned a support trench and held on with great determination until both his flanks were turned and he was obliged to withdraw. He fought his way back, inflicting great loss on the enemy and delaying their advance.'

Brought-up in Crown Street, Newark – his father Edmund was a brewer's travelling salesman – Fred was a civil engineer before the war.

More evidence that the fightback was succeeding came from Sergeant James Herbert John Burgess, twenty, of the 9th Sherwoods, youngest son of six children of iron moulder John and Mary Ann Burgess up Beacon Hill. He was awarded the Distinguished Conduct Medal,

> 'for conspicuous gallantry and devotion to duty. On 19 August, together with two officers, he went on a daylight patrol which entered the enemy's line and stayed there for four hours, gaining much valuable information. On 21 August he volunteered to take part in a similar patrol and again succeeded, not only in entering the enemy's line but in exploring a portion of his tunnelling system. His utter disregard of danger is an example to all under him.'

It was a far cry from Hole's Brewery, where he was a clerk. James enlisted in the 8th Sherwoods in November 1914 aged sixteen years and ten months, was wounded at the Hohenzollern Redoubt in October 1915, returned to the Front early in 1916, rose through the ranks, but declined promotion to Quartermaster Sergeant because 'I didn't want to be a shirker'. He continued fighting until he was hit in the knee on 11 October. He returned home, married Winifred Smith in Newark in 1922, and lived until 1982.

Stonemason Samuel Charles, sixty, of Victoria Street was advised by the War Office on 22 August that his son, Signaller Henry Laurence Thrale, twenty-one, had been blinded by a gas shell. Samuel rushed to his boy's bedside in Le Trépont to discover he was much better: his sight had returned after only three days. Henry married Phyllis Shearsmith in 1922 and lived to the age of seven-four.

The Reverend Henry Babb paid tribute at Barnbygate Wesleyan Church on 25 August to Charles Kirk, twenty-six, who followed his brother Herbert in giving his life for his country. Herbert, a private in the Sherwoods, was killed on 6 October 1916 but not declared officially dead for more than a year. And his grieving widowed mother, Sophia Elizabeth, a confectioner in Appletongate, was suffering agonised *déjà vu*: Charles, a North Staffordshire Regiment private, was not officially dead according to the War Office. Yet his mother had received this unequivocal communication from the Red Cross in Geneva:

> 'We are grieved to inform you that the following report appears on the lists despatched from Berlin: "10-7-18 – Charles Kirk, No.235153, NC, was picked up dead on the battlefield, two [kilo]metres [sic] west of Bullecourt, about 300 metres from the road Bullecourt-Crossvelles. Buried 3-4-18." Should we receive further particulars at a later date we shall let you know. We trust you will accept our deep sympathy with you in your great loss.'

As a result, Sophia wrote to the War Office and had a reply from Infantry Records,

Lichfield, which perhaps owed more to red tape than commonsense:

'With reference to your letter in connection with No.235153 Pte C Kirk, North Staffs Regt, whose death has been reported by the Geneva Red Cross Society, I have to inform you that the soldier's death has not yet been officially accepted pending further inquiries by the War Office. On receipt of War Office instructions, the notification of death will be issued to you immediately.'

It was months before the War Office accepted that Charles was killed on 3 April.

William and Sarah Sefton of Mapledene, Lime Grove, discovered on 28 August that they had lost a third son in action. Cecil was killed on 3 July 1916. Charles, thirty-two, died of wounds on 31 March 1918, despite being invalided home from the Dardanelles with enteric. And the latest letter from a fellow officer, Jack Greenhalgh, informed them that their youngest, Percy, twenty-eight, 'received a direct hit from a large shell.' The letter went on:

'I was with him at the time and the day is one I shall never forget. We took over a section of the line on Thursday last and from the first, bad luck attended Percy. Within the first few minutes of taking over, two shells dropped into his post, killing five and wounding three. Like the very fine officer he was, he stuck to his post, dressed the wounded and cheered up the remainder of his Platoon, setting them a fine example of pluck. There is no wonder that his men loved him ... No words of mine can express how much we, his fellow officers, miss him; always cheery, helping one whenever he could, a fine example to officers and men. As I saw him lying there on the battlefield, Shakespeare's grand compliment to Brutus flashed through my mind and I said unconsciously: "This was a man." Percy is dead but his spirit lives with us.'

Old Magnusian Percy enlisted in 1914, received a commission in the East Lancs; and had been married only a year to May T Halph-Smith from Peterborough, who lived with his parents after he went abroad.

Northgate Railway Station's helpful and popular porter, James Peet and his wife Alice lost their youngest son Herbert on 30 August. A fitter at Nicholson's, he had been invalided home from France once and only returned on his twenty-sixth birthday in June. He sent his parents a field postcard on 28 August saying he was well. But by the time it reached them in Cliff Nook Lane, he was dead. A letter from his Sherwoods captain explained: 'He was killed instantly by an enemy machine gun whilst out on patrol preparatory to his Platoon advancing.'

Corporal Charles Matthew Britten, twenty-one, was buried with military honours in Newark Cemetery on 2 September – dead because he defied enemy fire to rescue kit his officer mislaid. The second son of Charles Matthew Britten senior, foundry labourer, and Amelia from Beacon Hill was wounded on 19 July: he and an officer of the Machine Gun Corps had gone over the top to a gun emplacement but were spotted by the enemy, who opened fire. The officer said they had better return. But on doing so, he noticed he had left some kit. Young Charlie returned for it but was wounded. The officer carried him towards safety until he was also wounded, and then sent for help. Eventually Charlie was carried to a first aid post, then hospital, and later shipped to St George's Hospital,

London. There he passed away on 22 August surrounded by his family.

Second Lieutenant Harry Jackson Knight, thirty-four, of the Royal Field Artillery, was severely wounded in a gas attack, but recovered sufficiently to rejoin his widowed mother, Annie Selina Knight, in their Market Place drapery shop. He died, aged fifty, in 1934.

Albert Victor Page, twenty, only left his job as a moulder at Bradley's Foundry on 15 April. He went to France, with fellow townsmen, on 17 August. He was killed on 5 September. His mother Florence – already terrified at home, in 72 Appletongate, because her other son, George, had been missing since 21 March – received a letter from a chaplain in the Cambridgeshire Regiment on Friday, 13 September: 'Your boy was hit in the head and chest. It may be some comfort to you to know that he did not lie out on the battlefield lingering in pain.'

His words of comfort were similar to those offered to Rose Ethel Mary Matthews, thirty-two, in Vernon Street with her daughter Doris, nine. Her husband and Doris's dad, Arthur Robert Matthews, thirty-three, left Ransome's to join the Leicestershire Regiment on 11 April and had been in France only three weeks before he was killed on 6 September. 'He went "over the top" with the Battalion in the early morning,' wrote the chaplain, 'but during the action was hit in the chest by a machine gun bullet, which penetrated his heart. Your poor husband did not lie out in the battlefield lingering in pain.'

On 17 September came news of the battle that took the lives of four Newarkers in the Cambridgeshire Regiment twelve days earlier: Albert Page, Arthur Matthews and two boys called Jarman, both aged twenty, both from Newark, both apprentice turners at Ransome's. Private Harold Jarman's parents, Richard and Mary in Sleaford Road, received a chaplain's letter: 'The news is the more sorrowful because his cousin was

Cousins killed – the inseparable Jarmans – left, Private Harold Jarman and right, Ernest William Jarman. *[Advertiser cutting]*

killed at the same time.' The cousin was Private Ernest William Jarman, whose parents George Thomas and Sarah Elizabeth, lived in Stanley Street beside Ransome's workshops. The chaplain added in letters to both:

> 'I am the more grieved because I cannot find out where they are buried. Those two brave lads were in charge of a machine gun. Being brought under enemy machine gun fire, they were retiring when they were both hit.'

A few days' later the chaplain sent another envelope to Mary Jarman. It contained a photograph found in Harold's breast pocket. On the back of a portrait of his father, Harold had written:

'Good-bye, Mother, if this reaches you.

'I thought of home to the last.

'Ever your loving son, Harold.'

In fact they are now buried side by side in Péronne united in death as in life.

Mother of eleven, Mary Jane Turner, forty-eight, holding the fort at the family home on London Road while most of her menfolk were at war, learnt on 20 September that son George William, twenty, was killed with the 10th Sherwoods on 29 August. She could not share the news with her husband George, forty-seven, a foreman in Mumby's cutting department: he was in France, as was another son, while a third was fighting in Italy. Young George's first wartime job in 1914 was with fellow Boy Scouts guarding the Tubular Bridge that took the Great Northern Railway over the Trent. He was a Patrol Leader in the 5th Newark Troop; and even before leaving Barnby Road School, worked for a butcher. He joined the Colours as soon as he was old enough, was wounded twice, but always retained a bright and cheerful disposition.

Even ignoring the war, Anscombe Stewart Freshney, twenty-three, had a traumatic last few years. He was seventeen when his father Alfred died. His mother, Amy, was remarried in 1915 to Ernest W Bullimore, who died in the autumn of 1918. A few weeks later, on 20 September, Amy was informed that Stewart was wounded and missing from the Tank Corps. His last letter to her in Lombard Street was dated 12 August. Yet the War Office eventually decided he died on 9 August!

Teenage tragedies arrived at the double. Only days after arriving at the Front, nineteen year old Thomas Ball – such a hot-shot that his mates nicknamed him 'The Marksman' – was killed with the Queen's Royal West Surreys at Vendhuile, north of St Quentin, on 23 August. His parents, Willit and Emma in Vernon Street received the news on 27 September in a letter from Private John Thomas Judson, who was with him in the St John's Ambulance Brigade in Newark. What nobody knew until five weeks later was that eighteen year old Johnny Judson himself was also dead by the time his letter arrived. Tommy, eager at all sports from his school days, was an apprentice plate fitter in Ransome's moulding shop, carried his enthusiasm into the SJAB so well that he won the Maltese Cross and passed the VAD examinations; and once in the Army, qualified with flying colours for 'cross-guns' as a marksman, also passed-out on his bombing course and became chief barbed-wirer. Johnny's death was first reported to Lilly Johnson in St Mark's Lane by William Braithwaite, twenty, whose family lived in Tenter Buildings. Johnny worked as a coal carter for ex-Mayor Kew before enlisting. William survived to return home, marry Minnie Pass in 1922 and live to the age of seventy-four.

Lilly's neighbours in St Mark's Lane were less fortunate. Basket maker Harry Poynton and his wife Harriett found out 28 September that their son Harry, twenty, had become the fifth Newark victim of the 1st Cambridgeshire Regiment's action at Péronne on 5 September.

Joseph and Mary Ann Wilson at 3 Boundary Road asked the *Advertiser* readership at the Front on 24 September to help discover what happened to their son Joseph, a private in the 2/7th Sherwoods who went missing on 6 December 1917. The very next post contained a letter from an officer about their other son, John, a sergeant in the Royal Horse Artillery, who had already earned the Military Medal:

> 'By the time you get this you will have heard of the sad loss of your son. [They had not.] I was his section officer and I can very truly say that he was always the very keenest and best soldier whom I have had under me.'

Aged thirty-one, John served in the Royal Horse Artillery from leaving Christ Church School aged fourteen; was in the Mons retreat and many major battles thereafter, unscathed until 2 September 1918, when he fell shortly after informing his parents he was about the return home to accept a commission. He had earned his Military Medal in March 1916 for carrying in wounded comrades at Vimy Ridge and three weeks later was recommended for a Bar for supplying ammunition at a critical time when nearly the whole of the Battery had become casualties, thus saving the situation. Joe was eventually deemed to have been killed on 6 December 1917.

When Mary Ellen Gray, of Scales Row off Farndon Road, received a missive from the War Office on 8 October she wondered if it was about her husband, William, who was called up on 5 July or their son John Henry, who enlisted on 29 May 1917 and had been in France seven months. It was about the boy: Private 52716 Gray of the East Yorks Regiment was killed at Grandcourt, near Albert, on 26 August, aged eighteen.

On the same day, mother of two Emma Parker discovered that her husband Fred, thirty-one, also died on 26 August. One of the original Sherwoods 'circus', he was invalided first in April 1916 and again in March 1918; and died less than a month after he returned to the Front.

Sergeant Horace Powell, thirty-four, past captain of Newark Rowing Club and a clerk at Warwick's brewery before joining the 'circus', received the Military Medal 'for continuous devotion to duty' as artillery clerk throughout the mighty ebb and flow of battle from 21 March to 6 November 1918. His citation reads:

> 'He has repeatedly carried out his arduous duties under hostile bombing and shell fire, and in very trying conditions. During the advance from Albert to Landrecies, when the Brigade HQ moved almost daily – often into very exposed positions in which the performance of his duties was exceptionally difficult – he never failed to execute his duties with the greatest efficiency.'

Newark policeman Harry Brunt, thirty-six, a sergeant-major in the Sherwoods, wrote a racy letter home that attempted perspective:

> 'We have done a bit of chasing up and down the country the last few months, just to get old Jerry thinking and wondering where our Division had gone to, but I fancy he knows where we are now. Big events and big successes are all the sweeter

Part of the old Somme battlefield at Pozières in 1918.

because we are fighting over practically the same ground that our second line got such a cutting-up on in the spring of last year.

'A lot of the 2/8th are buried quite close to where we are at present. But what a scene of desolation everywhere! We crossed over the old Somme battlefield of 1915-16 – nothing but a huge waste of country and stumps of trees; not a building in sight. At different spots we came to a great heap of powdered bricks and masonry with a notice up stating: "This was such-and-such a place". There is one thing about the Boche; he is thorough in everything he does. The news from Bulgaria and Turkey is great, and we are all prepared to hear of further surrenders.

'If given an opportunity of surrendering on this Front, the Boche is not slow to take every advantage of doing so, and to see the long lines of prisoners passing us to our cages is a good omen. A German officer told us yesterday that the morale of all his men had gone, as our artillery fire was hell itself, and when our aircraft were about them they were completely panic-stricken. I can quite believe him.

'The Boche thought he would try a little stunt of his own two nights ago. He came over just after dark with his planes over our headquarters, dropped his parachute lights, which shew up the country for miles and, seeing a great assembly of soldiers just below him, he unshipped his load of bombs and cleared off – no doubt to report he had caught our men en masse ready to attack. If he was elated at his success he would no doubt feel a bit damped if he could have been told that they were his own men (prisoners) who were waiting to be escorted back to the cages. There were over fifty killed and over 100 wounded; not bad to be done by one of their own men! No doubt he would get an Iron Cross for it, but they don't place much pride on that decoration now. One of our men got one a few days ago for a packet of Player's cigarettes! Prisoners don't require any handcuffs to take them now. It is a common sight to see batches of 400 to 500 Germans being taken to the rear with just a lance-corporal and four or five men. They only require someone to guide them and they will go themselves.'

Such incredible success had come at a high price. The stories of death far out numbered the tales of heroism.

A chain of events began on Monday evening, 30 September that led to the death of one of Newark's most forward thinking employers, William Mumby JP, head of the huge clothing manufacturers. He was at home at the splendid 'Belvedere', London Road, with his wife and daughter Gladys Mary Darcy, twenty-six, when word arrived that Gladys's husband of less than three years, Captain Arthur Geoffrey Howitt of the Royal Field Artillery, had been severely wounded and shipped to the Fort Pitt Hospital, Chatham. Daddy immediately rushed with Gladys to the gallant officer's bedside. They discovered Geoffrey, whose family owned a Nottingham printing company, had been leading an advance towards Cambrai when a shell exploded, inflicting a deep wound in the back of his right hip. He recovered and lived to the age of seventy-three. William Mumby, the first Newark employee to give workers shares as co-partners in the business, collapsed a few days later with a cerebral haemorrhage. He comforted his wife Harriett: 'If I do not recover, I die with my mind at peace. I have always tried to lead an upright life. I have done no man any harm that I know of.' He died aged fifty-nine.

Caring employer ... William Mumby JP.
[Advertiser cutting]

On 9 October Charles and Emily Chappell discovered that their youngest son, somewhat appropriately christened Arthur Reckless Chappell, twenty, was killed in the massive 23 September assault having been transferred from the Sherwoods to the 12th ('The Rangers') London Regiment. Two years earlier his brother Harry of the Warwickshire Regiment died from pneumonia in France.

Two days later corset-maker Richard and Susannah Scales in Norfolk House, London Road, learnt that their younger son Edwin Herbert had been killed after less than three weeks at the front line with the 1st Battalion The Buffs (East Kent), having been retrained for the infantry after thirty months in the Army Service Corps.

On 12 October a French hospital matron wrote to George and Mary Eliza Short in Newton Street, about their son Leonard, nineteen, who had been so eager to join the Sherwoods that he enlisted a fortnight before he was legally old enough:

'Your little boy passed away at this hospital this afternoon at 3pm. He was admitted on 30 September with a bad wound in the chest and seemed to be going along all right, but gradually he got weaker and weaker. He often talked about you and his young brother and said how you would worry if you knew he had been wounded, but he had no idea how badly he had been hit.'

Terror literally hit Newark on 15 October. An aeroplane smashed into the town cemetery while making a forced landing and the pilot, Lieutenant Harry Beresford, twenty-three, was killed. Horrified witnesses watched the engine break down and the machine descend steeply. They watched the pilot scramble onto the wing and desperately leap off just before it hit the ground.

On 17 October Lieutenant Colonel Alfred Hacking MC, son of the Archdeacon of Newark, was in a London hospital with wounds to his right arm and thigh. Alfred, who had been transferred from the 1/8th to 1/5th Sherwoods, survived to be awarded a DSO [announced in the *London Gazette*, 2 January 1919], become a Conservative candidate for Parliament in 1921 and settle in Sussex, where he died, aged seventy-eight, in 1963.

A day later Mary Branch, widow of a glass and china dealer in Castlegate, discovered that her son Louis, twenty, was killed on 27 September in Steenwerck, a village held by the Germans since April.

Alex John Mort, twenty-one, who arrived on the front line in August, died on 18 October of severe head wounds, his parents, cutler George Henry and Annie in Church Street, were informed.

It was 24 October before maltster John Tinkler and his wife Emma, at 35 Sleaford Road discovered that their son John Edward, twenty-eight, had been killed crossing the Canal. Captain J B White wrote:

'I am sorry I have not written before, but we have been in action and I really have not had the time. Your son died like a true Englishman on the day when the Division stormed the St Quentin Canal and broke the Hindenburg Line.'

News arrived on Sunday, 3 November that the Tyers twins, of Bridge Cottages, Barnby Road, were both dead; both killed when they were poised to be withdrawn from the front. Arthur, twenty-one, who was awarded the Military Medal and promoted sergeant in the field in September 1916 for enfilading the enemy with a Lewis gun during a counter-attack, was reported missing on 23 July 1917 and was at last presumed to have been killed on or about that date. Fred was killed in action on 24 September. After studying at Christ Church School, Arthur went to work in a china shop in the Arcade, Fred became a gardener. When they were old enough, long before the war, both joined the Army. Though they were in different units, both went to France on 16 September 1914. After the Battle of the Aisne, Fred spent eight months in hospital recovering from appendicitis. Most poignantly, Arthur was about to return home to train as an instructor and Fred was poised to accept a commission. A comrade of Fred's wrote to their mother, Martha:

'He was a good and brave man. I shall never forget the morning when I past [sic] him in the morning before the attack, when he threw his arms around me and wished me the best of luck.'

Twin tragedy – Fred and Arthur Tyers.
[Advertiser cutting]

Inferring that Fred and his men were mown-down as he went 'over the top' the comrade goes on:

'He was found at the head of his Section. All were lying with fixed bayonets, facing the enemy. They were all buried in the same village where they got killed' [Bellicourt, seven miles north of St Quentin, under which runs the canal.]

On the same Sunday, after a period of terrible suspense during which nobody seemed aware of what had happened to Private Thomas Carter Huckerby, twenty-four, his widowed mother Jane Elizabeth in Lime Grove, received notification from the War Office that he was killed with the 1st Battalion Leicestershire Regiment on 15 September. Mrs Huckerby first became concerned about him in mid-September when parcels she had despatched to him were returned.

John R Garfoot, twenty-four, reared in Tolney Lane, earned the Distinguished Conduct Medal during the period 4-6 November:

'This NCO displayed the utmost gallantry and determination. On 4 November near Landrecies, an enemy strongpoint near a farm had been offering a stiff resistance and had held up the advance in the neighbourhood for a considerable time. Sergeant Garfoot went forward with a Lewis gun and two men to try to locate the enemy position. After searching the farm, this party located the enemy in a strong and well-concealed trench position. This NCO skilfully and daringly took his party to a flank, but by this time their movements had been noticed and they were heavily fired on by machine gun and anti-tank gunfire. They engaged the machine gun, knocked it out, and then rushed the post, capturing the garrison, which consisted of one officer, one sergeant-major and twenty men together with a machine gun and anti-tank rifle. By this gallant action, the attack was able to continue. The value of this was inestimable.'

On the opposite bank of the Trent, greengrocers William and Elizabeth Hoe in Millgate discovered on 4 November that their son John Arthur, twenty-four, was another victim of the audacious attack. Having enlisted at the Duke of Portland's recruitment rally in August 1914, he died on 29 September from wounds sustained when the 1/8th Sherwoods broke through the defences.

The enormity of the Sherwoods' contribution to the success was spelt-out by Allied Supremo, Marshal Ferdinand Foch, on a visit to the 46th (North Midland) Division in France:

'Men of the Sherwood Foresters, I am proud indeed to be among you, though my pride is tinged by regret that I am not able to meet face to face some of the heroes of your great Regiment who have died to make it possible for us to celebrate the great victory that has been won over the forces of the Boches. I have watched the work of your Regiment for the whole of the time I have been directing the operations of the Allied Armies, and in that time I have never had occasion to make the slightest complaint of your work. You have been tried as men are seldom tried, but on each occasion you have shown yourselves worthy of the great trust we reposed in you, for you have faced the difficulties in your path with the courage of lions, and you have overcome them as you deserved to overcome.

'I recall one critical stage in the operations of last March, when it was a question of meeting an unexpected attack by the Boches. They had suddenly appeared before a part of the Allied Line with almost a Division of the best troops they had in the

Allied Supremo, Marshal Ferdinand Foch.

field. I was anxious regarding the position because there was only one Battalion of British troops available to hold that part of the Line. The British general to whom I confided my anxiety looked up the data supplied from his headquarters and said to me:

'"It's all right. The Sherwood Foresters are in the Line there, and they are equal to any German Division".

'I know enough of the record of your Regiment to see the force of that remark, and for the first time I was easy in my mind. I gave orders to move troops around that region without fear of consequences, for I knew that I could rely on your Regiment, and I was not disappointed. You met the repeated attacks of great enemy forces, and not only met but vanquished them. For more than nine days you held that part of the Line, and by holding it you enabled us to develop the counter-moves which ultimately brought about the crushing defeat of the enemy.

'France and humanity owe you a debt that can never be paid. I personally feel when I am congratulated on the winning of this war that success could never have been obtained had it not been for the glorious work of Regiments such as yours. Since that dark period, you have been called on to attempt almost impossible tasks, but you have always succeeded.'

Even so, given the horror stories pouring through the post – and the fact that Newark was in the midst of 115 dying of influenza in the final three months of 1918 – it is little wonder that folk found it hard to believe peace had broken out on 11 November.

The *Advertiser* reported Armistice Day thus: Following the sensational news that the German envoy returned to German Supreme HQ with the Armistice terms of the Allies, and that the reply was hourly expected, there was a feeling of supressed but intense excitement in Newark on Monday morning. The area was charged with an electric tension and before 10am rumours were mysteriously circulating that the enemy had signed the terms. At 11am a well-known bank manager visited the Town Hall to inform the Mayor that the news had

Peace arrives … how the news reached Newark.
[Advertiser cutting]

been announced in London. His Worship [re-elected to serve an unprecedented fourth consecutive term only a few days earlier] refrained from sanctioning any public notification by bell ringing or otherwise until fifteen minutes or more later, when he received the news officially. He suspended the sitting of the Police Court and proceeded to the Town Hall balcony. A large number of people had congregated in the Market Place. At 11.20am they come forward in response to signals from the Mayor ... When silence had been obtained, he announced:

> 'I am very pleased to make known to you that the Armistice was signed by Germany at 5 o' clock this morning and the firing ceased at 11am.'

On the call of the Mayor, the crowd fervently sang the National Anthem and cheers were heartily given for the King, our Soldiers, our Sailors and the Mayor. While His Worship was speaking, the bells of the Parish Church broke into a joyous peal and, in response, the buzzers and hooters were sounded at the works. The Mayor led fellow Council members, Corporation officials and such a large public throng into the Parish Church that every pew, every space and every aisle was filled for a spontaneous Thanksgiving Service, led by the Reverend Parkinson, priest-in-charge. In the afternoon, a voluntary service for soldiers was conducted in the Market Place by the RE. A united service was held in the Barnbygate Wesleyan Church in the evening, with practically all the Free

More exhausted than happy – Armistice celebrations in Newark Market Place.
[NEKMS 2172 W656]

Church ministers in the town taking part.

Newark Town Council opened its monthly meeting that night by singing God Save the King. Captain Bevan of the RE attended and a committee was appointed to meet with him and organise celebrations. Even while they were deliberating, the Band of the RE Training Centre played lively and patriotic airs from the Town Hall balcony and children danced joyously in the Market Place, where huge crowds assembled. Soldiers and sailors in uniform paraded the streets with instruments of varied pedigree – tins, whistles, bagpipes, mouth organs – making a joyful noise and hooraying to their heart's delight. An effigy of the Kaiser was burned on one of the several bonfires lit in and around the Market Place. Rockets were fired from the roof of the Town Hall. Verey lights illuminated the heavens. Whizz-bangs made deafening detonations. It was well after 11pm before the ebullient spirits began to quieten. Even then, there were sporadic explosions and sing-songs to be heard in the chill night air.

It was not joyous for the Harrop family in Lover's Lane and the Johnsons on Sleaford Road. They had just heard of the killings of nineteen year olds Ernest Harrop and Albert Johnson. Ernest, a timber worker before becoming a private in the 2nd Worcestershire Regiment, 'was killed in action or died of wounds received in action' with the Warwickshire Regiment on or about 29 September. Richard and Susan Johnson were not told how their boy, Albert, died, either. He worked for Gilstrap's before enlisting in the Foresters on 29 May 1917, was transferred to the Lincolns before going to France on Easter Monday 1918 and was killed on 8 October.

The year of relentless death, destruction and daring had begun with Military Crosses for three local warriors in the New Year's Honours List: commercial traveller's son Captain Geoffrey Owen Lockwood RE, thirty; Old Magnusian Captain Charles James Neal, Royal Field Artillery; and Major Henry Becher Wigginton, for ten years the manager of the drug and perfumery department at Harrods' famous store in London, whose father and grandfather were eminent Newarkers and who said he had escaped lightly throughout the war apart being wounded in the early days of the Battle of the Somme, 'a whiff of gas' and several narrow escapes from big gunfire.

On the first Tuesday of January 1918, Simpson's workers discovered that one of their office clerks, Frederick Goodey, thirty-seven, of Milner Street, had lost a leg fighting with the Sherwoods. On the second Friday, Sapper William Gordon Haggas, twenty-eight, who had sailed from Canada to join the RE, died in the Lombard Street VAD Hospital of internal haemorrhaging sustained by lifting 'a heavy weight' a few weeks after arriving in France. Of his brothers, Walter, a policeman in peacetime, had been killed while

Lighting-up ... Royal Engineers build celebration bonfire on Beacon Hill.
[NEKMS 3555/11]

fighting with the Scots Guards in 1914, while John and Raymond had joined the US Army, which was now playing its part in overwhelming the enemy.

Two more Newarkers, both twenty-one, earned Military Medals in and around Cité St Eloi, Belgium, on 2 January. Apprentice bricklayer William Henry Martin, of 50 Cross Street, earned his by helping to repulse a raid and bringing in prisoners at Hairpin Craters. One of a family of eleven, he enlisted in September 1914 and had never been wounded, though he once had a portion of his rifle shot away. Of his brothers, George, a private in the Foresters, was killed in October 1917; Herbert, an RE sapper, was in hospital in Italy; and Percy, a Private in the RFC, had been in France a year. Corporal John Bryan, a Quibell's labourer before he found himself in the 139th Machine Gun Company, earned his accolade on the night of 2-3 January, to the delight of his parents, brewer's carter Harry and mother of six Annie, at 44 Stodman Street: 'During a hostile raid, this NCO showed great coolness and courage in the manipulation of his gun. On seeing the SOS signal he opened fire with the least possible delay. The hostile shelling round his position was very heavy, and on one occasion he was knocked off the fire step by the force of the explosion close by. He promptly jumped up again, readjusted his gun and carried on with the firing. Throughout the raid he set a fine example to the other members of the team.'

When Newark's Tribunal reconvened after the Christmas break, Military Representative Cherry-Downes announced his reports into the town's baking and boot repairing trades – which unsurprisingly concluded that more men could be spared for military duty – were being adopted as examples of good practice by the Ministry of National Service. Bestowing 'warm approval' on his investigations in its weekly bulletin, it ordered other towns through the UK to follow his methods.

Bombardier John Toynbee of Lover's Lane earned approval, too. He was awarded a Military Medal for carrying in wounded under shell fire throughout the month whilst serving with the Royal Garrison Artillery near St Julien, near Ypres.

Among exchanged military and civilian prisoners arriving at Boston, Lincolnshire, on 7 January was severely disabled Private Benjamin Eddison, brother of Miss Gertrude Eddison, who lived on private means at The Haven, Milner Street, Newark, with their siblings Sidney, thirty-seven, an architect; Ann, thirty-five, principal of a girls' private school; and Charles, thirty, an engineering company cost clerk. It sparked one of the most heart-breaking examples of red tape trouncing common sense in the heat of battle. If Private Benjamin believed his agonies were over, he was mistaken; he would never be able to settle in The Haven again. For he had been in Australia when war broke out, having emigrated from England after serving for nearly four years with the 3rd Hussars. He was so anxious to join the war that he enlisted on 28 December 1914, declined a commission and was sent to Egypt in the 14th Battalion Australian Imperial Force. Among the first to land at Anzac Bay, he fought through the Dardanelles campaign, suffered enteric fever, yet afterwards was sent to France. He was posted missing on 11 April 1917; and was so seriously wounded that he lost an eye, a leg and the use of his left arm. He was a PoW in Stettin until his repatriation. He was taken to a London hospital, and Miss Eddison hoped to welcome her brother to Newark as soon as he was

		"DUN. CASTLE"	A.M. Form D2.
Station	D.A.B. SYDNEY	AUSTRALIAN MILITARY FORCES.	(For use in Australia.) Revised 1.4.19.
Date	18 May 1919		

MEDICAL REPORT ON AN INVALID.

1. Number 1480   2. Rank Pte.   3. Name EDDISON B.
4. Unit 14th Btn.   5. Age 35   6. Trade or Occupation Laborer
7. Place of Enlistment CHILTERN VIC.   7A. Date of Enlistment 28.12.14
8. Disability in respect of which invaliding is proposed

MEDICAL OFFICER'S STATEMENT OF CASE.

9. Date and place of origin of disability
Date of arrival from overseas 18 May 1919
10. Date and place where disability first caused man to become a Casualty
11. Essential facts of Medical History (including causation)

Wounds: Amputation L. Leg, April 1917.

Loss of L. eye. Same date.

L. arm elbow joint (stiff) same date.

Has temporary peg leg.

12. State whether disability was (a) Due to Military Service, (b) Aggravated by Military Service, or (c) Independent of Military Service. (d) Due to, or aggravated by, want of proper care on man's part, intemperance, misconduct, &c.

13. What is his present condition and progress?

Heart clear.   L. Glass eye.
Lungs clear.   L. Peg leg, amputation 8" above ankle
Hearing good in R.   L. elbow stiff joint (slight movement) wound
  nil in L.   L. Hand wd. of 2nd metacarpal 1st. finger
                            limitation of movement.

14. If the disability is an injury, state whether it was caused (a) in action, (b) on field service, (c) on duty, (d) off duty
15. If a Court of Inquiry was held, state place, date, and opinion
16. Was an operation performed? If so, what?
17. Was an operation advised, and declined?
18. In the case of loss or decay of teeth—Was it due to, aggravated by, or independent of, Military Service?
19. Give particulars of any other disabilities existing
20. Do you recommend discharge as permanently unfit for general service?

G. Harper Major
Medical Officer in charge of case.

I, having satisfied myself of the general accuracy of this report, concur therewith, except

D.A.B. SYDNEY 2nd M.D.
Officer in charge of Hospital.

Station   Date

discharged. But officials insisted that Benjamin was Australian. He was shipped back Down Under – and was last heard of appealing for a war pension. Miss Eddison passed away in Newark in the autumn of 1945 aged seventy-four.

Charitable Edith and George Pink in Whitfield Street, who had done most to ensure parcels were sent regularly to Newark's PoWs, received a 'thankyou' letter in mid-January from Corporal George E White, formerly a Great Northern Railway shunter from Vernon Street. Freed to The Hague in Holland, he wrote that he and his comrades would never have reached such a haven of rest and goodness if it had not been for those at home, adding, 'I want you all to do everything you possibly can for my comrades from Newark. Please accept my thanks from the bottom of my heart.' George, of the 2nd Duke of Wellington (West Riding) Regiment, returned home before the year's end.

Albert Parr's despairing suicide on 14 January was the greatest indication yet of what shell-shock would do to a considerate mind. The decapitated body of former postman Albert, forty, a Salvation Army member who resided in Sleaford Road, was found on a railway line near his Nottingham birthplace. He had been acting 'out of character' since his discharge from the East Yorkshire Regiment. Once, he began throwing eggs at a house. When challenged, he claimed, erroneously, that the property was his so he had every right to 'shell it'. His landlord eventually evicted him, his wife and family because he had not paid rent. Friends found them another house; but the wife and family went into the care of the Board of Guardians while Albert drifted away.

At the other end of the class hierarchy, Coldstream Guards Captain Sir Ralph Henry Sacheveral Wilmot, 6th Bart, of Winthorpe Grove, passed away aged forty-two on 14 January after a long illness contracted at the front early in the war: he left £79,517 4s 3d in his will.

Twenty-four hours later Mrs Frances Weightman, in Harcourt Street with children aged thirteen and eight, was stunned to learn that her husband, fish fryer William Henry, had died aged thirty-seven. She heard on 22 December that he was 'seriously ill' in hospital but subsequent messages were optimistic that he was recovering. He died in Abbeville of kidney inflammation. Ransome's labourer George William Lacey, twenty-eight – wounded, buried alive and twice gassed since he became a Sherwoods' private in 1914 – was killed in action on 19 January. A good footballer with Newark United, he won a twenty-six-mile cross country run in France during respite from the trenches in 1917.

A telegram on 14 February informed Richard and Agnes Hindley in Victoria Street that their sailor son Robert, had perished, aged thirty-three. They had the task of relaying the news to his wife of nine years, Jessie Louisa, thirty-five, in Lime Grove with their daughter, six. A clerk in Peacock, Willson's Bank [later taken over by Lloyds] he joined the Royal Navy in 1915 and applied for special service on the boat on which he met his death, HMS *Cullist*, a merchantman equipped with hidden guns designed to trap U-boats: forty-three of the crew of seventy were killed when she was sunk off Drogheda by *U97*. A later communication added poignancy: the Lords Commissioners of the Admiralty approved his promotion to Acting Paymaster, back-dated to 15 November 1917.

Also on Valentine's Day, Charles and Jane Robinson in Warburton Street received a card from the War Office: it presumed that their son Robert, twenty-two, a gardener prior to becoming a private in the 7th Leicestershire Regiment, was killed on 3 May 1917 at Fontaine.

Even more shattering, shortly after John and Sarah Holwell in Barnbygate waved-off to war their third son, William, thirty-six, on 19 February, they discovered that their other two boys were dead. They knew they had lost Walter, thirty-three, on 30 January 1915 after he was wounded at La Bassée. Now the Records Office reported that no further hope could be entertained that James, twenty-seven, survived at Lens on 23 April 1917 after he had taken part in the 1/8th Sherwoods' heroics at the Hohenzollern Redoubt.

County Court officer Archibald Langrish Knight, twenty-two, of Hawton Road was killed on Sunday, 24 February while serving with the RE Signal Service near Arras.

Newark's teacher trapped in the midst of the Russian Revolution, Janet Cubley, penned from Irkutsk a letter to her family on 25 February:

'I am afraid that you have not received any of my letters as I have had no reply. Things are in a terrible state here, but how terrible no one in England can imagine ... and at present there seems no prospect of a better state of affairs. I should be thankful to get away from it all but have no means of doing so, so there is nothing to be done but hang on and take all risks as they come. But do please send me a line immediately if you receive this letter. Fortunately I have plenty of work and now am most comfortably settled in another room. I have also made acquaintance with several more people and am feeling more at home here, but I am so busy that I have very little time to go visiting. One of the worst things is not being able to get news from England. The last paper I had was one a pupil brought to me (8 December) more than two months old; also for November I saw a few that Mr Nash, our consular agent pro tem, brought me one day. I do hope you are all well. It is now nearly a year since I have had a letter from home ... Happily I have been very well this winter, thanks to the glorious climate. Soon we may expect the weather to be a little warmer. Already we have had a thaw, but it was only temporary, and today it is very cold again.'

It took six months for the letter to reach Newark.

Newark Town Hall was full on Wednesday night, 27 February, to see cousins George and George Henry Parr receive Military Medals from Mayor Knight, who introduced them thus:

'They volunteered three years ago to fight for what we believe to be right – the maintenance of the honour of England. They have not only done their duty, but done it to great distinction. They have fought shoulder to shoulder.'

George left Ransome's for the King's Own Yorkshire Light Infantry in August 1914, was wounded in October 1916, returned to action in February 1917, was wounded in July and gassed in September. He won the medal for carrying important messages under heavy enemy fire at Guedecourt. George Henry also worked at Ransome's and enlisted in the KOYLI in 1914. Gassed on 24 September 1918, his medal was awarded for stretcher-bearing under heavy fire at Langemarck on 16 August 1917.

On the same day, builder Cuthbert Lane and his wife Martha had good news in Harcourt Street: a Belgian Croix de Guerre awarded to their son Walter, thirty-four, a fettler at Ransome's before he graduated to sergeant in the 1/8th Sherwoods and moved to the 139th Machine Gun Company.

John Fincham, seventy-nine, a retired groom living in Hospital Cottages with his wife Sarah, seventy-six, learnt on 5 March of the death of one of their five fighting sons, Robert, forty-eight. His wife Elizabeth was informed by his CO:

'Your husband died at 2.30 on the 19th. He was hit by an aeroplane bomb at 10 last night. He was my servant for more than three years, and he was far more than a servant. He saved me when I was on the [Gallipoli] Peninsula, and was the only friend who has kept with me since the beginning of the war. He was a model soldier and had an excellent influence on all the men around him. He looked after me in the most splendid way.'

George Arthur, nineteeen, of Zion Square was killed by a shell on the Somme on 8 March. 'Your son was a very good soldier,' his Sherwoods captain wrote to his parents. 'His name had just gone forward for a stripe.'

Former Magnus head boy Alfie Balmer, nineteen, went missing on 20 March. A bright lad, he had passed his Senior Cambridge examination with first class honours and in 1916 became a Surveyor of Taxes before joining the Civil Service Rifles (1/15th London Regiment). It was months before his parents, Great Northern Railway bookstall manager George Buckle and Emma Taylor Buckle, were assured he was wounded and a PoW at Limberg.

Private George Stafford, twenty, of Cross Street was awarded the Military Medal for bringing in wounded under shell fire while with the Manchester Regiment at Hargicourt throughout March. He worked in Newark iron foundries before enlisting in time for the Irish Rebellion.

On 28 March, Maggie Storey, in Lawrence Place off Lawrence Street, put on her glad rags – fox fur wrap and all – and quietly took an expenses paid, third class train ride to Nottingham. By command of His Majesty the King, she received the Order of the British Empire from the Duke of Portland for saving 500 lives. She did not know which act of bravery earned it! She explained she had 'been in several fires' over the couple of years she worked in a Yorkshire munitions factory. The Duke informed her that the award was for 'courage and high

Newark's greatest heroine … Maggie Storey OBE.
[Nottingham Evening News cutting / Nottingham Central Library]

example in extinguishing a dangerous fire at an explosives factory during exceptionally risky circumstances.' This appeared to narrow it down to either an incident that happened eight months earlier or another tense experience in February. The official citation made the spine tingle even more:

> 'During her temporary absence from a hydro extractor, the valve handle became detached and fell into a pit below. At great personal risk, she hurriedly descended into the pit, recovered the handle and brought the machine under control. Had she not done so, 500 lives would have been endangered.'

Presumably it was the censor who prevented the munitions factory being identified. It is also mysterious that she was called Maggie Storey; the Newark weeklies explained that, since her heroics, she had become Mrs B M Thickett.

Newark's St George's Day Parade on 21 April, concluded with Mayor Knight presenting the Military Medal to labourer's son Lance Corporal George Whiles – and suggesting, rather saucily, that, as he was one of twelve children, it was his mother Agnes who deserved the medal. Of George's siblings, Thomas, twenty-seven, was a corporal in the Tank Corps; John, nineteen, a private in the Machine Gun Corps; and Nottingham-based William, thirty-five, a sergeant in the King's Royal Rifles. Oh, and young William Herbert, nine, was one of the Newark Scouts invited to receive achievement badges at the same ceremony. His badge was for – War Service. There would be another landmark for George in 1919: he married Eliza Wilson.

While the presentation provided a brief respite from bad news, two brothers from the third generation of a respected Newark family lay wounded on two different continents – having travelled from opposite sides of the world to fight. Stanley Manterfield, a private in the Australian Forces, was wounded in the left leg in France and recovering in Kitchener's Hospital, Brighton. John Thomas Manterfield, 40, who served his time in the Lincolnshire Regiment pre war and was fighting as a second lieutenant in the Machine Gun Corps, was in No. 45 Stationary Hospital, El-Arish, Egypt, suffering with a gunshot in the right arm. Stan survived but John would be killed on 21 September between Péronne and St Quentin.

The Middle Eastern Front was largely forgotten, with so much going on across the Channel. The Sherwood Rangers, once more on horseback, were so far away that it was more than two months before Newark received a letter written on 7 February by Corporal Walter Samuel Hunt, twenty-three, in Palestine. He pointed out they were so far 'up country' that their gifts arrived long after Christmas. Moreover, their remoteness meant that a pint of water was valued at five shillings.

Chemist Jonathon Henry Smith learnt on 4 April that the nephew he was training to take over his Bridge Street business had been killed in Palestine. Second Lieutenant Thomas Rowland Smith, twenty-nine, born in Bakewell, had lived with his uncle since he was eight, went to the Magnus, became an eager oarsman with Newark Rowing Club, an intrepid horseman and was studying chemistry at Edinburgh University in 1914. As he was already a trooper in the Sherwood Rangers, he was posted to Egypt and thence to Gallipoli, where he was promoted sergeant as reward of his bravery in the hard fighting. After a home leave about a year previously, he was on a ship that was torpedoed with the loss of the regiment's horses; but all the men survived and reached Egypt. Tommy was then commissioned in the Sherwood Foresters and attached to the Imperial Camel Corps. His last letter to his uncle had been 'in an entirely happy vein'.

The news that he died on 13 March emerged in a letter from his Commanding Officer: '… just a short line to tell you how we feel the loss of your gallant nephew. His Company bore the brunt of the three days' hard fighting on the 28, 29 and 30 March. And they answered in the most gallant fashion to any call that was put on them. There is nothing, I know, that can compensate for the loss of the boy, but the knowledge that he died a most gallant death, and doing his duty most manfully, is something.'

A brother officer added more detail:

'We were at a place called Amman on the Hedjaj Railway, about fifty miles east of the north end of the Dead Sea. The [censored] Battalion Camel Corps were attacking the town whilst a demolition party were engaged in blowing up the railway. On the night of the 28th we attacked the redoubt in front of the town, which we captured and held during the next day. On the morning of the 29th your nephew was running to me to take an order, and was sniped and hit in the chest. He was buried with two brother officers at a place about two miles west of Amman on the main road to Jericho.'

And then the focus returned to Europe in the early morning darkness of St George's Day, 23 April 1918 – to the ever-defiant George hurling himself against the fiery dragon of massed German defences. Royal Marines attacked a great half-moon-shaped Mole

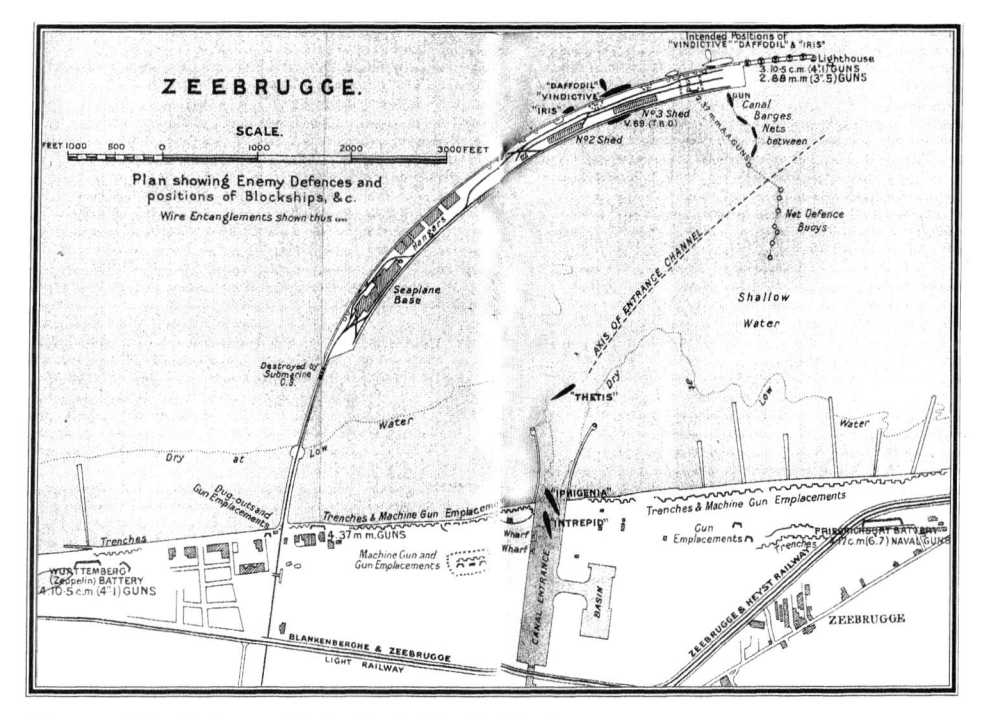

The arc of the Zeebrugge Mole attacked by the Marines.
[http://www.navy.gov.au/history/feature-histories/australian-sailors-zeebrugge-1918]

British cruiser HMS *Vindictive*.

guarding the Zeebrugge Canal in an attempt to neutralise the key Belgian port of Zeebrugge. As they disembarked from an old and dispensable cruiser, the *Vindictive*, the wind changed direction and lifted the smoke screen, exposing them to heavy German fire-power.

'The hidden harbour exploded into light,' the official British Admiralty report stated.

'A star shell soared aloft, then a score of star shells; the wavering beams of the search-lights swung round and settled to a glare; the wildfire of gun flashes leaped against the sky; strings of luminous green beads shot aloft, hung and sank; and the darkness of the night was supplanted by the nightmare daylight of battle fires. Guns and machine guns along the Mole and batteries ashore woke to life, and it was in a gale of shelling that *Vindictive* laid her nose against the 30 foot high concrete side of the Mole. The men were magnificent. The geography of the great Mole, with its railway line and its many buildings, hangars, and store-sheds, was already well known, and the demolition parties moved to their appointed work in perfect order. One after another the buildings burst into flame or split and crumpled as the dynamite went off. A bombing party, working up towards the Mole extension in search of the enemy, destroyed several machine-gun emplacements. The Canal is effectively blocked.'

There were 500 British casualties, including 200 dead.

Sergeant Albert Combes wrote a vivid description of the 'hell' of Zeebrugge to his parents George and Caroline, who had six more children at home in Charles Street:

'The Marine Battalion left Deal for Dover on 6 April and went on board the *Daffodil* and later got on board the *Vindictive*. On the Sunday we were told we were going to land at Zeebrugge, and we had to fall-in in our respective places. We were very well armed with bombs, hammers, lights, plenty of ammunition, etc. We were now steering through the enemy's minefields with several ships following in rear, including *Iris* and *Daffodil*. All the time there were big crashes of gunfire, but we didn't fire a shot to give our position away. The guns were manned by Blue Marines, ready at any moment. The Germans were sending up star shells, which gave a splendid light, but thanks to the smoke screen they couldn't see us.

'Well, the order came for everyone to lie down, and just then we entered hell – there's no other word ... Our pompoms and Lewis guns started, and crash went something against our bows: we had run a German torpedo boat down. The Germans got their searchlights on us, and shot and shell came in and through the ship. Down went our gangways, the ropes that held them being cut in two by a shell, and as we went alongside The Mole they were all smashed except two. The flame-throwers were on the go; it seemed to scorch our faces. I sat on a reel of wire during all of this lot. The only words I spoke as we went alongside were: 'Keep cool, men.' A shell hit a water pipe and burst it, and another put out the flame-thrower and burnt the oil tanks and the oil was all running along the decks. The wounded and dying were heard now and again but we could only remain where we were until we got the order to go over. The gun crews were killed and others took their places, and several of the officers were killed, including the Colonel.

'At last we got the order: "Over you go, Royals." And, my word, we went! Once ashore we had to drop fifteen feet but we took ladders with us. I was hit three times: one on the head, not very bad thanks to my steel helmet; one in the stomach; and one in the right leg. Don't worry. I am quite all right apart from the bruises; and I don't mind that as they got more than bruises.'

Able Seaman Ernest Hall, twenty-three, working quietly in Howitt's ironmonger's shop a year earlier, found himself among flaming metal. He wrote that the *Vindictive* was 400 yards off the Mole when the Germans sent up a star shell and opened on them with eight batteries of guns. When the Marines assembled for landing there was a terrible lot of casualties. With dead and dying all around him, he only received a slight scratch on the arm and got on the Mole all right, but minus his leaders, who had already fallen. With fixed bayonets they charged the gun positions and found them deserted. Having disabled the guns, they proceeded along the Mole.

Ernest was sent with a Bengal rocket to light up the lighthouse so as to give the bearings of the concrete ships. He had only got halfway to his objective when shrapnel struck him in the back, igniting the rocket and 'carrying out its purpose without me lighting it'. His wound was only slight and he 'carried on' with the other gallant lads. Charging across the Mole, they espied a German torpedo boat manned by German officers, the crew having fled. The marines hurled grenades at her and her magazine; and up she went. After the signal to return to the *Vindictive* was given, Ernest had just stepped onto the gangway when he was again hit in the back. The gangway was forced up, pitching the occupants onto the deck. Ernest regained consciousness twenty minutes later with a broken shoulder. Back in England, he was treated at Deal Infirmary.

Far away from this bravado, father of three Harry Squires, 37, quietly lost his battle for life on St George's Day. The son of coachman George and Mary Squires in Baldertongate, he had left a job as a groom in Newark for a coal miner's higher wages in the west of the county, became a pioneer in the RE but never recovered from being wounded and gassed in France and died in a Liverpool hospital, leaving his widow Mary Jane to rear children aged nine to five.

May began with a stirring story of how Sapper 120794 F Wilson RE (Newark) earned a Distinguished Conduct Medal. The *London Gazette* recorded:

'His conspicuous gallantry and devotion to duty during a raid on the enemy's trenches. He went forward and placed explosives in the enemy's wire before our barrage had lifted from the enemy's position. One of the charges failed to explode and he went forward to investigate the misfire under a heavy enemy barrage. As the wire was only partially cut, he set to work with wire cutters though he was knocked over three times by bursting shells. By his courageous and determined efforts he succeeded in making a gap in the wire which was of the greatest assistance to the raiding party.'

There was also much news of prisoners of war. Mrs Nesta Clarke, daughter of one of Newark's maltster families, received a postcard from her husband of eighteen months, Major Alfred C Clarke of the Sherwoods: he was a PoW in Karlsruhe.

As PoWs were released from Germany to Dutch internment camps, the importance of Edith Pink's Comforts Fund became starkly evident. 'It would be no exaggeration to say that Mrs Pink's labour of love has saved many precious lives, which would otherwise have been lost through starvation,' reported the *Advertiser*.

'Some people – not many, but a few here and there – have expressed sympathy with the work but ventured to doubt if the parcels had ever reached their destination. Even the production of postcards signed by Newarkers in Germany expressing grateful thanks for parcels received, have been met with the suggestion that the prisoners may have had to sign the postcards at the point of a bayonet while a greedy Hun guard ate the contents of the parcel. Happily, for more reasons than one, many of our gallant men who have been captured in earlier battles have now been exchanged and are enjoying comparative freedom in Holland. Here they are free to say the truth and it is very gratifying to learn that although it seems to be the deliberate intention of the Hun to keep our men short of food, they allow them to have the food parcels sent from England. This is placed beyond all doubt by letters received recently by Mrs Pink.'

Corporal AE Ross of the 2nd Sherwoods, captured six months earlier, wrote:

'After being knocked and buffeted about and practically eaten alive by vermin in Germany, you may guess what it means to us to be free once more. Before I say any more I wish to thank you and your staff, also the inhabitants of Newark, for your kindness to me while I was in Germany. It is only such kindness which is keeping the prisoners alive. If they ever became dependent on the pig feed the Germans call food, the number of deaths from starvation would be enormous. I can honestly say that it is only through the kindness of you, dear friends, that I am alive today to enjoy my freedom.'

Sergeant George William Robinson, twenty-four, who joined the Sherwoods in 1911, aged 17, said:

'It gives me very great pleasure to write and thank you for your kindness to me while a prisoner of war in Germany. Perhaps you do not quite realise all the parcels meant to us. I can honestly assure you that they were everything to us. I must congratulate you on the contents which, I must say, were very good stuff of a varied nature. I could always place my parcel beside that of another prisoner from another district, and consider the one I had by far the best.'

Sergeant Warriner of the Northumberland Fusiliers, a prisoner since 1915 and who had had a cousin killed in action, wrote:

'Things are very dear here, but we must be thankful to have our freedom. I thought the boys would go mad when they were exchanged, and they are doing extraordinarily well here under the circumstances.'

He added that there was such a severe food shortage that basic necessities were '100 per cent more expensive' in Holland than in Newark.

Then came a reminder from the *Advertiser*: 'It costs £160 a month to keep this work going. Money is urgently needed. Send subscriptions to Mrs Pink, 1 Whitfield Street, Newark.' Major Clarke returned home, along with half a dozen other Newarkers, at the end of November.

Thomas Martin, seventy-one, retired goods agent on the Great North Railway, sadly left home in Spring Gardens, on 29 May and took the train to Manchester to support his daughter Annie, thirty-four, at the funeral of her husband, Alfred Hanley, twenty-nine, a second lieutenant in the 1st/5th Durham Light Infantry. He had been in France for three months as a signalling instructor when he became embroiled in stemming the rush of the German hordes. He suffered a head wound on 1 April and, after three weeks in hospital in Rouen, was transferred to London for more specialist treatment. Meningitis supervened and he passed away on Empire Day.

While inclement weather forced Newark's Empire Day celebrations to be postponed to 30 May, the teacher in the midst of the Russian Revolution, Janet Cubley wrote again to her family:

'I am quite well but very disturbed as I have just been told that the family of my friend, Mrs Campbell Clarke, has had notice from the Bolsheviks to clear out of their house in a week's time. What they will do, I don't know as there is not a flat to be had in the whole town. The house is the only thing the Bolsheviks did not take from them last December, and now that is gone. Everything is in the most dreadful state here, trade completely paralysed, prices dreadfully high, thousands of people out of work, and murder and robbery rampant everywhere. The worst thing to bear is absence of news of the war. The Bolsheviks only allow such news to be printed as pleases them, and all that is known comes from German sources. Very occasionally we manage to get a paper from Japan or China but that is all. One good thing is that Mr Nash has been appointed English Consul here, so that we have someone to appeal to for advice.' It was three months before this missive reached home, with the one she posted on 25 February.

Ex-Mayor Kew became the first Newarker to be made a Member of the Order of the British Empire (MBE) in the King's Birthday Honours on 3 June. The Mayor of Newark 1913-15, his war time roles included chairing the Newark Division Parliamentary Recruiting Committee, Newark Rural Tribunal, Newark Rural War Savings Association, Newark Rural Food Control Committee, North Notts Advisory Committee with special functions on demobilisation, Newark War Emergency Committee, Newark Board of Guardians and Newark Rural District Council – as well as editing the *Newark Advertiser*.

Not surprisingly, recruitment was even more rampant. Newark Borough Tribunal on 12 July warned Royal Navy veteran Frank Mottram, forty-seven, of Hatton Gardens he would have to rejoin the Service on 12 January though he was 'working all hours' as sugar boiler for many of the town's confectioners and spending his spare time in the St John's Ambulance Brigade.

And after Church Parade on Sunday morning, 14 July, when Boer War veteran Brigadier General George Peabody Scholfield RE presented bravery medals to six sappers in Newark Market Place, he surmised many men among the crowd 'had yet to go to the battlefield': no doubt they would be going in future and he hoped they would do their best and win honours for themselves and their Regiment. A Military Medal and Meritorious Service Medal went to Charles John Richard Elms; Military Medals to Second Lieutenant Thomas Oldershaw, Sergeant Robert Thompson and Second Corporal F Padley; Bar to Military Medal to Sergeant W Normanton; Belgian Croix de Guerre to Sergeant A J Heath.

As July ended, there was a reminder that the war was also still raging deeper into Europe. Battery Sergeant Major William Dickenson, thirty-two, whose father Harry was a well-known Newark maltster and whose grandfather, Ralph Whittle, was engineer and manager of the Waterworks on Muskham Bridge, was mentioned in despatches from Salonika.

The fear of Zeppelins returned late on 5 August. Newark's special constables were called to 'take air raid action' at 11.30pm. They were quickly at their posts, which was adjudged 'creditable', as no air attacks of any kind has been made since Whit Sunday'. The 'all-clear' was received at 1.30am. The official explanation: 'Hostile airships approached the East Anglian coast about half-past nine but have not penetrated far inland.'

The far-sighted Borough Surveyor Wilkes, a captain in the RE, wrote in August to a colleague in the Corporation:

> 'Shan't be sorry to say farewell to Egypt with its desert glare and sandstorms and mosquitoes. The summer heat is bad, too – up to 120 degrees in the shade. It is a treat to get back to this town, where the shade temperature is only about 90, and where there are fans and baths. Glad to say I have lost nearly a stone and am still knocking off flesh by cutting out a lot of eating. Only thing that has affected me is rheumatism, brought on by the moist heat and cold dawns … It does not do to trifle: I met a Major a day or two ago who was complaining of headaches. The poor fellow died last night with a malignant form of malaria.

> 'One feels disgusted at being out of France at such a time but "orders is orders" as the Sergeant has it. Johnny Turk is about finished on this Front; he has been a good, clean fighter, brave occasionally, an excellent sprinter often. Poor old Johnny, he knows he backed the wrong horse and is sad about it. One must admire him for being decent to the wounded and not using gas.'

Lieutenant John K Bousfield, twenty-four, whose great grandfather and grandfather were among Newark's engineering pioneers, was able to tell His Majesty the King on 16 September how he and twenty-eight other officers escaped from a German prisoner of war camp at Holzminden, Hanover, in July – the most spectacular break out of the war. His opportunity arose when he finally received the Military Cross awarded to him for dangerous reconnaissance work during the 1916 Somme battle – an auspicious occasion delayed initially by his hectic duties first with the RE and later the RFC, and then by him being captured on 6 April 1917 while he was observer in an aeroplane brought down twenty miles behind German lines. He repeated the escape story to gentlemen of the Press:

> 'When I got to the camp, the work of digging the tunnel had been well started. When we had finished it was fairly deep, running over a length of sixty-five yards, and about 12ft down, with an entrance under a staircase and an outlet into a vegetable garden. We made our escape on the night of 23 July and immediately split into small groups, each of which took a different direction. I and two others formed one party which kept together until we had covered the greater part of 170 miles, which was the distance I travelled before getting clear of Germany. We each had a little store of food to keep us going, and we picked apples, making our way through downpours of rain and sleeping most of the nights in the open air, or wherever we could find shelter of any kind. Altogether I was on my travels for thirteen nights, sometimes going through water, sometimes venturing on the roads, but all the time making sure of clearing any possible surprises or observations by local people or police. Everything went well until near the end of our journey, but one night a sentry, who had seen us from a bridge, or seen something that made him suspicious, fired his rifle in our direction, compelling us to separate. I did not see the other two again. My movements after this were not detected by the enemy and I was able to get across the border without further incident. The Dutch papers subsequently announced that three British officers had escaped across the frontier.'

The adventurous Bousfield went on to marry in Switzerland and settle in Canada.

Private John William Hempsall, thirty-one, a blacksmith's striker, provided light relief in a letter to his wife Annie in Newark about his three and a half years with the Norfolk Regiment in Egypt and Palestine. It was a beautiful land. The orange and lemon groves beyond Gaza were delightful. He felt almost at home seeing engines, ploughs and harrows made by Hornsby's of Grantham and Clayton & Shuttleworth of Lincoln. He was not impressed by the few horses. But the donkeys, of which there were many, were generally big and strong. John had time for this reflective message because he was in the 21st General Hospital recovering from an attack of malaria.

Widow Emily Laura Hough in Jubilee Street discovered on 8 October that her eldest son, David, died in a German prisoner of war camp on 26 June. Worse, she had to pass on the news to his wife Lizzie and their daughter Gladys, three. David, a Home and Colonial Stores assistant before joining the Sherwoods, died 'from exhaustion and internal catarrh'.

Company Quartermaster Sergeant Alfred Ford, third son of a pioneering coach builder and Annie Ford in Appletongate, plus Lieutenant Thomas Walter Harrison, an Old Magnusian serving with the 1/4th Lincolnshire Regiment, were among 501 souls lost when the Irish mail boat, the *Leinster*, was torpedoed sixteen miles out of Kingstown (Dun Laoghaire) on the way to Holyhead on 10 October. They were sailing home on leave when two torpedoes ripped into the defenceless vessel. It was the greatest ever loss of life in the Irish Sea and the highest ever casualty rate on an Irish owned ship.

By coincidence, it was reported at the same time that Gunner Walter R Burn, twenty-five, whose widowed mum, Maria, kept a shop in Kirkgate, had been financially rewarded for sinking a German submarine while on a merchant ship owned by Sutherland & Company in springtime. A letter accompanying his cheque [the amount remained secret] from Sutherland's director said:

> 'We are directed by the Shipping Controller to inform you that, acting on the recommendation of the Merchant Ships Gratuities Committee, he had approved the grant of an award to you for your gallantry and good seamanship on the [censored] occasion.'

By then, Newarkers had been assured in newspapers that they 'have every reason to be proud of the courage and devotion of the local lads in the local regiments' during the Palestine Campaign. The Sherwood Rangers took part in the capture of Nazareth in mid-September and were unfortunate not to capture the German Commander-in-Chief, Liman von Sanders, 'but that astute Hun had packed up his tent and stolen away the night before'. A correspondent reported:

> 'Although our gallant infantry is primarily responsible for the success, it is the cavalry which enabled us to exploit the advantage to the uttermost. General Allenby commands one of the finest forces of cavalry gathered together in this War. As soon as the infantry had opened the way through the Turkish lines, a group of cavalry, which comprised Sherwood Rangers Yeomanry and Indian Imperial Service Cavalry, crossed the marshes south of the Falik Brook at seven o' clock and by evening were established twenty miles further north, having overcome

slight opposition and taken 150 prisoners. Continuing after dusk, they reached Nazareth at six o' clock the following morning. The resistance of the troops in Nazareth was quickly overcome, 2,000 prisoners being taken, including 200 of a German technical corps. Since then they have gone on still further ahead until the Turk has now been bundled bag and baggage out of the Holy Land.'

Inevitably, there was a downside. A telegram arrived in Barnbygate on 23 October, announcing the death from malaria in Egypt of Private Edward Alexander Knight, twenty-six, of the Rangers. The son of a grocer, he gained a scholarship from the Wesleyan School to the Magnus, and became articled to chartered accountants in Nottingham. Despite being in Newark Rowing Club, he was never robust; and after mobilising with the Rangers, was too ill to join them until October 1916. Nevertheless, as he fought with them for two years, his death from illness was a terrible shock to his widowed mother, Emma Eleanor, running the family grocer's business.

Another widow, Ann Keetley in Spittal Row, off Northgate, lost the youngest of her three serving sons, George, 23, on 1 November – in Newark Hospital. An apprentice moulder at Bradley's before he joined the 1/8th Sherwoods on 22 October 1914, he went to France on 19 June 1915, and experienced much fighting before suffering an arm wound in August 1917. After six months in England, he was transferred to the 10th Sherwoods and was gassed in France in April 1918. He was allowed home on fourteen days' convalescent leave – and contracted pneumonia, which proved fatal. He was given a funeral with military honours in Newark Cemetery. Ann, who worked as a cleaner at Warwick's brewery to make ends meet, had plenty more to worry about. Another boy, Harry, thirty, was eventually presumed dead, having been missing since 9 August 1917. Only the oldest, Sam, thirty-nine, returned home. He reached the age of sixty, passing away in 1938. Ann was seventy-one when she died in 1933.

George's unhealthy home was but one more reason why Newark Council spent much of 1918 planning a large estate of new houses for 'artisans' returning from the war to homes that had been barely habitable before they went to fight. Only one councillor, a builder, initially dissented, arguing that private enterprise not public money should build such a venture. The Newark Tradesmen's Association was also unimpressed when details of the 'Beaumondville Estate' were published. The final nail in its coffin was applied by the Local Government Board ordering the Council to find less expensive land. It would be two decades before construction began.

So the Armistice did not herald a better Newark. Neither did it stem the killings. Within a fortnight of becoming magistrates, the town's Labour stalwarts, Samuel Grocock and George Alvey Rouston, discovered even while Newark celebrated peace on 13 November that they had each lost a son.

Private Harry Rouston, thirty-one, who did valuable work as secretary of Newark Old Age Pensions Committee before joining the Sherwoods and being transferred first to the North Staffordshire Regiment and then the 7th South Staffordshire Regiment, died of Spanish Flu. He had been shot through the ankle in September and had returned to the front shortly before he fell fatally ill.

Mrs Kate Grocock in Charles Street received a letter from an officer: her husband, platoon Sergeant George Grocock, thirty-four, Samuel's second son, was buried in 'a pretty little orchard behind the Lines'. George, a decorator, joined the 8th Lincolnshire Regiment in November 1914, suffered twenty-nine shrapnel wounds on 18 April 1917, but recovered sufficiently to go out again at the start of 1918. He left widow Kate to rear Alec, ten, and Nora, eight – and took with him one of the men who worshipped him. Fred Warner, twenty-six, from Sydney Street perished alongside George on Sunday, 3 November 1918. It was 7 April 1919 before William and Ellen Warner received confirmation that their foster son had been killed eight days before the Armistice was announced. They often cared for waifs and strays; and they were so determined that Fred should not be forgotten that Ellen pestered the authorities with letters, finally asking if any of his belongings had come to light. Second Lieutenant J Leonard Woods MC replied:

> 'I am very sorry but fear there is little hope of any effects being forwarded to you. When his body was recovered it was found that all his effects had been removed by the enemy. He was buried, together with others who fell at the same time, just outside the village of Ghissignies near to the more important town of Le Quesnoy. As one who was present at the operation in which he was killed, I should like to pay a tribute to his memory. As one of a small section of men, he went forward bravely, fought magnificently, and died a credit to his country.'

With censorship over, two Newark lads wrote on 19 November about the Sherwood Rangers' Middle East exploits, including a forced march of about 600 miles in six weeks. Sergeant Herbert F Stephenson, twenty-one, of the town's foremost agricultural engineering family, had bullets fly through his cap, tunic sleeve and saddle during service in Egypt, then against the Bulgars and finally against the Turks, yet had not suffered a scratch. He reported with the Rangers about ten miles north of Aleppo, at the junction of railways to Baghdad and Constantinople. They had started from Jaffa and:

> 'Our Division, the 5th Cavalry, was the first to enter Haifa, Acre and Aleppo. We had a bit of a scrap at Haifa and our Regiment captured some guns. Haifa is quite a nice place. We had a great reception there; the inhabitants were very pleased to see us as the Turks had given them a rotten time, stealing everything they could get hold of. The Syrian people were, on the whole, very hospitable towards us, and they look very picturesque in their native clothes. I suppose there would be some grand doings in Blighty when the Armistice news reached you. For ourselves, we let off some Verey lights and had a sing-song.'

Private Edward Glazebrook, whose family ran a nursery in Priory Road, wrote that the Rangers:

> 'Have done some record marching. It has been rather trying at times but I don't regret being in it. I cannot mention all the places I have visited during the last few weeks since we started up the coast from near Jaffa. I think we travelled about 600 miles altogether in less than six weeks. It was wonderful how the horses stood it; they had so much to carry.'

Winifred Baily of Hatton Gardens, was not totally consoled by the news that, when her husband, Corporal John Francis Baily, twenty-nine, died in Beyrout (now Beirut) after four days' illness, his brother, Lance Corporal Hugh Shaw Baily, twenty-seven, a Royal Marine on HMS *Gloucester*, was at his bedside.

Four wives looking forward to welcoming their menfolk home from freshly-peaceful Europe discovered in the last week of November that they were widowed. Young mother Annie Bradley, in Smith's Row off Water Lane, lost her husband, Private Robert William Bradley, thirty-one, of the 9th Sherwoods, on 4 November at Sebourg. Daisy Poole, in Sheppard's Row with son William, two, learnt that Private George Henry Poole, twenty-four, of the Northumberland Fusiliers was killed on 27 October on the somewhat forgotten Italian Front. Jesse Charlesworth, thirty-six, died on 15 November of wounds received in France with the 15th Lancashire Fusiliers, leaving a widow, Mary, daughter Phyllis, ten, and mother Louisa in Bowbridge Road. And Phyllis Fanny Beeston became Newark's youngest war widow: only 18, she was at home in Charles Street with her ten-month-old daughter, Vera, when she was informed her husband of thirteen months, Private Thomas Beeston, twenty-two, died in France – not as the result of any of the fierce battles he had survived, but of pneumonia.

Relatives and friends crowded into Newark Town Hall on 2 December when three soldiers received Military Medals from Mayor Knight. Corporal J Young of Scales Row, one of the Sherwoods 'circus', was rewarded for gallantry with the 11th Sherwoods on 30 March 1917 for which he had already received a medal from an Italian Army general. He had been fighting on the Italian Front and went out with a patrol to find an enemy position that had eluded detection for no less than eighteen months. After five hours' search he found the enemy's stronghold and, as the Mayor put it, 'the necessary steps were taken'. Auctioneers' clerk William Eastgate Alcock, 31, of Bowbridge Road was awarded for gallantry with the 10th Sherwoods between 31 July and 5 August 1917 at Pilkem near Ypres. He carried despatches and maintained communications with the signal line under very heavy shell fire. Rifleman Percy Leonard Reeve earned his medal on 23 March 1918 in fighting around St Quentin during the *Kaiserschlacht*. When two companies were cut-off from the battalion, he went up the line with a message and brought them safely back. There was one awkward moment in the otherwise joyous proceedings: Mayor Knight handed each Newark recipient a £5 cheque but regretted his income would not permit him to extend this beyond the Borough to Rifleman Reeve, domiciled a few miles away at Collingham.

The next ceremony was on 12 December: the Colours of the 8th Foresters, in the care of the Vicar and Wardens of Newark Parish Church since 1915, were ceremonially reclaimed by a Colour Party, including Company Sergeant Major Albert Cobb, twenty-five, one of a family of eight in Paxton's Court off Kirkgate whose Distinguished Conduct Medal was to be gazetted on 12 March 1919, and Sergeant George Martin, one of ten siblings, whose wife and child lived in Cross Street. They had no time to celebrate: the Colour Party left Newark at 3am to return to France. Cobb's DCM citation reads:

> 'During the attack on Regnicourt on 17 October 1918 he showed the greatest gallantry and devotion to duty. Upon his Company gaining its objective he organised a party of thirty men, dug in under intense machine gun fire, patrolled

EMPLOYEES OF
Abbott & Co. (Newark) Ltd.

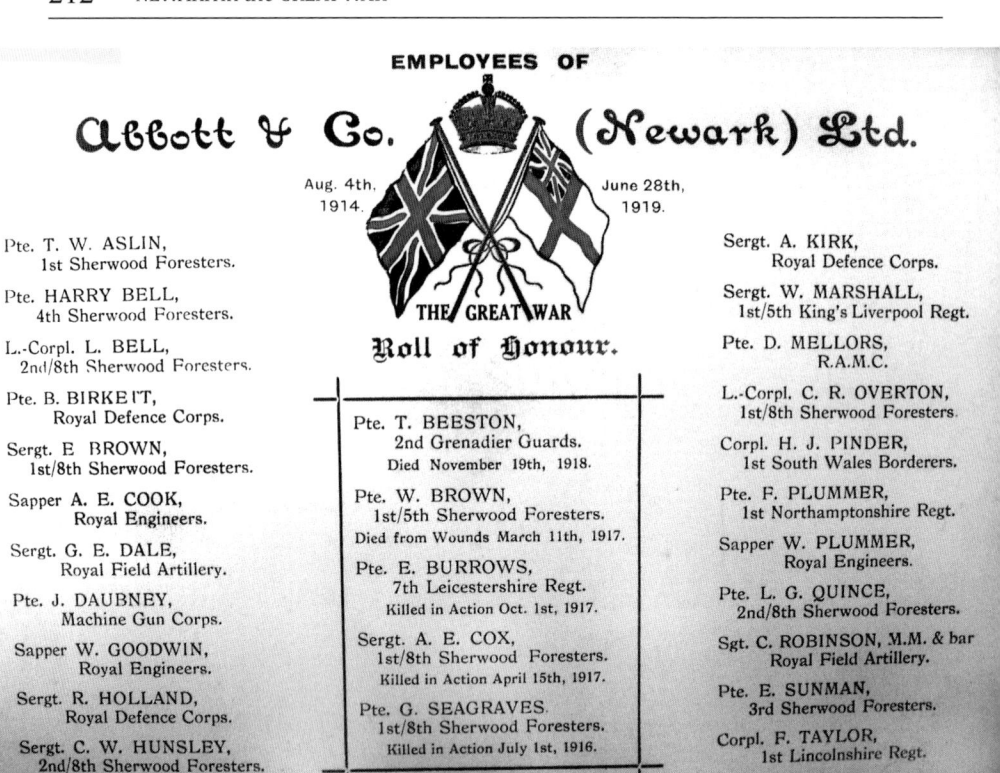

Aug. 4th, 1914. — June 28th, 1919.

THE GREAT WAR
Roll of Honour.

Pte. T. W. ASLIN,
1st Sherwood Foresters.

Pte. HARRY BELL,
4th Sherwood Foresters.

L.-Corpl. L. BELL,
2nd/8th Sherwood Foresters.

Pte. B. BIRKETT,
Royal Defence Corps.

Sergt. E. BROWN,
1st/8th Sherwood Foresters.

Sapper A. E. COOK,
Royal Engineers.

Sergt. G. E. DALE,
Royal Field Artillery.

Pte. J. DAUBNEY,
Machine Gun Corps.

Sapper W. GOODWIN,
Royal Engineers.

Sergt. R. HOLLAND,
Royal Defence Corps.

Sergt. C. W. HUNSLEY,
2nd/8th Sherwood Foresters.

Pte. T. BEESTON,
2nd Grenadier Guards.
Died November 19th, 1918.

Pte. W. BROWN,
1st/5th Sherwood Foresters.
Died from Wounds March 11th, 1917.

Pte. E. BURROWS,
7th Leicestershire Regt.
Killed in Action Oct. 1st, 1917.

Sergt. A. E. COX,
1st/8th Sherwood Foresters.
Killed in Action April 15th, 1917.

Pte. G. SEAGRAVES,
1st/8th Sherwood Foresters.
Killed in Action July 1st, 1916.

Sergt. A. KIRK,
Royal Defence Corps.

Sergt. W. MARSHALL,
1st/5th King's Liverpool Regt.

Pte. D. MELLORS,
R.A.M.C.

L.-Corpl. C. R. OVERTON,
1st/8th Sherwood Foresters.

Corpl. H. J. PINDER,
1st South Wales Borderers.

Pte. F. PLUMMER,
1st Northamptonshire Regt.

Sapper W. PLUMMER,
Royal Engineers.

Pte. L. G. QUINCE,
2nd/8th Sherwood Foresters.

Sgt. C. ROBINSON, M.M. & bar
Royal Field Artillery.

Pte. E. SUNMAN,
3rd Sherwood Foresters.

Corpl. F. TAYLOR,
1st Lincolnshire Regt.

They will remember – Abbott's memorial to their workers who fought, survived or died.
[Mrs G C H Smith / NEKMS 7/72]

forward 2,000 yards in front of his objective in order to find the enemy's positions, and returned with accurate information. He worked for over a mile through a wood with dense undergrowth. Here he came under fire from three enemy machine guns, but still pushed on. Owing to denseness of undergrowth, his task was extremely difficult, but he worked untiringly the whole time.'

By 19 December Borough Surveyor Wilkes was in hospital in Dar-es-Salaam, pronounced unfit for further service. Shortly before being confined, he wrote:

'This is a brute of a country. In the early mornings when there are clouds on the mountains and it is fresh and cool, life seems all right; but then the loneliness, the pests of beast and snakes, the diseases galore, and the rest make one want to be back home above a bit. There is plenty of sport: word has just come in that two lions have crossed the road not far away. A few nights ago I shot a hyena, and this morning we bagged a snake of a deadly type. He came into the door of my tent but fortunately I heard him and gave a yell, when he scooted; then the hunt started. A very sharp boy – picked up locally – threw an assegai right through his neck and pinned him to the ground. I gave the boy a present and made him my own guard. I shall always take him with me.

'Last night I went to find the local Jumbi to see about food, but he thought I wanted a wife and four smart young ladies were on view in no time! I declined with thanks. The only money used is cloth – the brighter the better and more valuable. I am travelling along, prospecting, and have only one white with me. It is strange to sleep all alone in the bush. One gets the wind up at weird sounds and so on but, thank goodness, sleep comes and I wake up cold and happy each dawn. We live on meal, banana pudding and roasted monkey nuts. We can't get milk. Cows, donkeys and horses can't live here because of the tsetse fly. Fancy beating the donkey at the living game! What a strange country!

'I look out of my tent to see big mountains about two miles away. Their tops are conical and shrouded in a haze of blue; up their sides are green-treed ravines with here and there a cave, the home of some wild beast. In the foreground is a forest. Birds sing almost like English thrushes; guinea fowl croak away near the river at the foot of the mountain. About twenty-five yards away are five natives, whom my Blacks call "Shinzie" or "wild men". They have come to have a look at me, and try to get some bright cloth for the hundredweight or so of something which they have brought. They are in full dress – a bit of red bark about their loins. The sky is cloudy – especially dangerous – for the violet rays of the sun pierce my double tent and make my head ache so much that I have to put on helmet and spine pad. Such is life out here…'

Such was life in Newark, as 1919 began with news of more deaths.

Mary Lizzie Tailby, in Stanley Street, learnt on 3 January that her husband, Private John James Tailby, forty-one, a lady's butler before moving to munitions work with Ransome's and later joining the Sherwoods, had been killed at Ghissignies.

On the same day Frederic Arthur Dixon, thirty-two, passed from the 18th Stationary Hospital in Salonika to 'that generous host, that ethereal army of invisible heroes' who had paid the price of our salvation, leaving in Newark a young widow, Gertrude Annie in Spring Gardens and parents Frederick and Mary at their butcher's shop in Middlegate. Twice he had been laid low by malaria; but he survived to take part in a September 'epic' when British, Greek and French troops attacked and broke the 'impregnable' Bulgarian Front and opened the door to another crucial Allied victory. From the inhospitable and barren mountains, the troops undertook a 700 mile march to Deadagatch before the Armistice was signed. Along the way, Fred wrote from Stavros of his delight at the thought of getting home at last, for the first time since 19 June 1916: he longed to hear again the beautiful organ in the Parish Church and reclaim his place in the choir...

Five years to the day after Archduke Franz Ferdinand of Austria and his wife Sophie were killed by a Bosnian Serb nationalist, sparking the Great War, Germany and the Allied Powers signed the Treaty of Versailles on 28 June 1919, officially marking the end of hostilities with Germany.

Two days later, Mayor Knight was still handing out £5 notes and gallantry awards to ordinary men who had become noble heroes in 'the big show' – a Military Medal to Lance-Corporal William Watts, twenty-three, of Grove Cottages, Barnby Road, for his bravery during a Lewis gun action; a Meritorious Service Medal to Sergeant William

Pacey of Castlegate, the historical highway that doubled as both the Great North Road and Fosse Way through town – the focal point of why Newark would have been a coveted jewel for an invader. William Watts, the son of an iron worker, was in reality a grocer's assistant. William Pacey belonged to a family of Trent workers.

As they walked down the steps of the Town Hall into the Market Place from which the Sherwoods 'circus' had marched in August 1914, they knew that their biggest battle lay ahead: to put behind them the 'the show' and settle back into normal life: whatever 'normal' might be after that unforgettable 'circus'.

The Newark Town Memorial to 456 of those who died in the Great War. It is in the Cemetery, London Road.

Postscript

The Daredevil Heroes Return – but the Crowd's Gone Home

Hundreds of well-wishers cheered Newark's territorial 'circus' out of town on Sunday, 10 August 1914. In contrast, one man welcomed a token group of survivors back on Saturday, 21 June 1919. It was as if the audience had thrilled to the fantastic exploits of the daring young men on the flying trapezes and yet drifted away while they were in the very act of somersaulting down into the safety net in anticipation of thunderous acclaim…

The anti-climax began on 17 June 1919 with news that the 1/8th Sherwoods had left mainland Europe. Mayor Knight stood by to sound the air raid 'buzzer' on the Town Hall roof once he received notice of their approach. It was hastily announced they were on a train, lest folk charge off along the Fosse Way or Great North Road in excited attempts to register the first sighting.

The air raid siren shrieked at noon on 21 June. Flags and bunting appeared outside houses and shops. Mayor Knight received a telegram from Dover Station: the cadre (small party of officers and men) and colours of the 8th Sherwoods would arrive in Newark at 20.43. A 'royal welcome' was prepared.

It would be the second grand ceremony on a Newark railway station within two months. On 28 March a large party of Belgian refugees departed. At the farewell ceremony at the Midland Station, Mayor Knight praised the refugees for giving every satisfaction to those who looked after them; their conduct had been honourable in every possible way and the womenfolk wonderful in the management of their children. Ex-Mayor Kew, who had met the first refugees at Northgate, praised their exemplary conduct and fine courage; and hoped they would find great joy in once again being in their own land.

One of the refugees, Louis van den Bruggen, related their journey:

'Our ship carrying more than 500 men, women and children from Dover went straight for the French coast. A ship full of soldiers and bound for Dover went by while much cheering was done on both sides. It came spontaneously and right from the heart. About half past two, we could see Nieuport, De Panne, Mariakerke and Westende, all places well known in the recent fighting. All that we could make out were heaps of ruins. There was not a bit of life to be seen. Not one soul.

'Singing and laughing had stopped on board. Every one of us looked on the destructions with feelings of bitterness, mingled with the ever-increasing joy of seeing the land of their birth. We steamed into Ostend harbour with high tide …

A great mass of people awaited our arrival. When we got near the entrance of the harbour, the cheering, singing and waving started. I saw people crying and laughing at the same time. Some were quite out of their usual behaviour and paced up and down the ship's deck in a nervous manner. Others were calling their friends or acquaintances on the shore loudly, and their faces told you a tale. And all the while the ship kept on whistling its siren. Everyone was much excited and all tried to land first, especially those who had their people awaiting them. After our luggage had been passed by the customs officer and put in the railway van for Ghent, we went towards the town station. It was already dark outside. A few electric lights on the landing quay and around the town station were all I could see.

'The whole town was without light as far as the streets and the majority of houses was concerned for the Germans had destroyed the gasworks. The town station did look miserable and dirty; everything that went to embellish it was gone, such as things in the domain of art: paintings, brass or copper materials all stolen by the Germans. Here and there I could see signs of the bombardment. We had to wait until about half past eight before we could get in the train – a dirty German train with broken windows; and it was freezing outside! And the train was not heated.

'We arrived in Ghent at half past ten. Except for the station at Bruges, all other stations, the houses in the immediate neighbourhood, and the bridges over rivers and canals were all destroyed. Our train stopped in the street at Ghent. There were no cars or cabs.

'Of course we had to live elsewhere for a few days. Things were all upside down in our house. Everything was dirty and there were no windows, and a man was living in it. Although we had to go through a lot, we may call ourselves lucky in every respect; for what these people have suffered here – well, it goes beyond imagination, beyond description. They have been through nothing else but hell. Nay, worse.'

It was a graphic reminder of what invasion would have meant to England; what a debt was owed to men like the Sherwoods who had stood firm at such terrible cost.

The message that a few were on the way home spread around Newark faster than wildfire on 21 June. Demobbed officers, NCOs and men of the Battalion turned out in khaki with arms kindly loaned by the RE. They were joined by the locally raised C Company of the 12th Foresters, the Mayor and Corporation, plus magistrates, all on the north-bound platform of the Northgate Station.

The 20.43 train jolted to a halt. There was an expectant pause as the throng peered through the steam and smoke. followed by a mild sensation. Our heroes were not there. The Mayor contacted Doncaster to establish they had not been on an express that had roared through minutes earlier. He called Grantham Station. No, the heroes had not alighted a stop early. London King's Cross could not help: seeking a specific bunch of soldiers was too akin to seeking the proverbial needle in a haystack.

The Mayor, weary from giving disappointing news, cleared his old throat and advised that 'some hitch has occurred'. The Borough Band silently led the deflated procession back to the Market Place, whence they drifted away.

Only one man decided to maintain a vigil. The new Vicar of Newark, the Reverend Dr James Walker, inducted only six months earlier, reasoned that 'those blokes must be somewhere'. So he met the 9.40pm at Newark Midland Station. Again there were no Sherwoods.

Undeterred, he traipsed back to Northgate and waited. Approaching midnight, another train pulled up. A handful of Terriers stumbled out. A Vicar they had never seen before hustled towards them, legs stiff from sitting so long but face beaming and hands out-stretched in welcome, chuckling: 'Our heroic Sherwoods, I presume?'

Once the manly handshakes were over, they marched through the deserted streets to the Drill Hall on Cherryholt Lane. They were hastily found bunks for the night: not quite home sweet home; but heaven after the horrors.

The following morning, Dr Walker announced the homecoming from the Parish Church pulpit but it was agreed Sunday was not a day for riotous celebrations.

So the official welcome took place two days late, on 23 June. The *Advertiser* cast a positive angle on the delay:

> 'It was fitting that Newark was able to welcome home the Cadre of its own Territorial Battalion just prior to the news arriving that the Germans had accepted the Peace Terms.'

Dr James Walker: patience rewarded.

As the circus ringmaster would sing: 'Always look on the bright side of life, ta-da, ta-da, ta-da-ta-dum'.

Great enthusiasm characterised the homecoming; towns people thronged the Market Place. The bells of the Parish Church rang joyously. The Mayor, Corporation, Magistrates and former officers of the Sherwoods gathered in the Town Hall. The Royal Engineers, with fixed bayonets, formed a hollow square in the Market Place. The United Works Silver Band played music while all awaited the arrival of the Cadre.

Headed by the Newark Borough Band, a procession was formed on Cherryholt Lane of the Regimental Colours, Cadre, demobilised NCOs and men of the Battalion, C Company of the 12th VB Foresters, Boy Scouts and Girl Guides. Townspeople cheered their every step.

Once they were centre-stage in the Market Place, there were speeches by Mayor Knight, MP Starkey, dignitaries from Retford and Mansfield, Brigadier-General Scholfield CMG, RE and Lieutenant Colonel RW Currin DSO, Officer Commanding 1/8th Sherwoods since 1917. The proceedings concluded with the General Salute, singing of the National Anthem, and three cheers for the King. The Cadre was then entertained to supper in the Town Hall.

The euphoria did not last. As if they were stepping out of the big top back into the real world, the remaining 'circus' heroes returned to the same old hovels; and the hoped-for new houses were not built until nigh on twenty years later – by which time a German soldier they had defeated ... a chap by the name of Hitler ... was on the way to proving that they had not fought 'the war to end all wars' after all. The rest is history.

It is only fitting that the final words in this commemoration should be autographs of Newarkers who fought in the Great War – including the heroic Dr Harry Stallard – and who attended a dinner in their honour given by Ransome & Marles on 23 August 1919.
[Nottinghamshire County Archive DD141/11]

Where the bombshells fell on Newark

1914 to 1918

Every notification of the death a serviceman came as a bombshell to family and friends.

What if every bombshell letter and telegram had been a real shell exploding in Newark. The following maps plot where the notifications from the War Office' arrived informing relatives of a dear one's death .

The following information is reproduced from the comprehensive research of Adrian Carter, which covers the villages around Newark as well as the town itself and can be found on the Newark Archaeological and Local History Society website.

1914

1 – Lance Corporal Harry Leach / 1st Royal Warwickshire / 27 King Street / 8 September 1914
2 – Drummer Rowland James Baker / 8th Sherwood Foresters / 49 Albert Street / 28 September 1914
3 – Private Thomas Bowers / 8th Sherwood Foresters / 4 Eldon Street / 9 October 1914
4 – Private Ernest Woolley / 1st Northumberland Fusiliers / 2 Queen Street / 14 October 1914
5 – Corporal William Clarence Slater / 2nd Sherwood Foresters / Christchurch / 20 October 1914
6 – Private Arthur Harold Ellis / 2nd Royal Warwickshire / Castle Terrace / 25 October 1914
7 – Lance Corporal Thomas Walster / 4th Royal Fusiliers / boxing fame / 28 October 1914
8 – Private Archibald Lambert Walsh / 1st Coldstream Guards / 16 Cross Street / 29 October 1914
9 – Lance Corporal Charles William Arnold / 3rd Northamptonshire / Cross Street / 1 November
10 – Private Harry Holberry / 1st Lincolnshire Regiment / 10 Lindum Street / 11 November 1914
11 – Private Septimus George Backhouse / 1st Sherwood Foresters / Barnbygate / 17 November 1914
12 – Private Alfred Squires / 1st Lincolnshire / Mount Pleasant / Millgate / 29 November 1914

1914 'Bombshell' Map

13 - Private Thomas Hall / 1st Sherwood Foresters / Wilson Street // 14 January
14 - Private William Hurst / 1st Sherwood Foresters / Water Lane // 15 January
15 - Private Levi Sibcy / 2nd/8th Sherwood Foresters / Victoria Gardens / Baldertongate // 15 January
16 - Stoker Frank Neal / HMS Victory / Appletongate // 29 January
17 - Private Walter Howell / 1st Lincolnshire / 182 Barnbygate // 31 January
18 - Private William Warriner / 1st Royal Scots Fusiliers / 24 Albert Street // 10 February
19 - Sapper Thomas Eustace Preston / 15th Signal Company Royal Engineers / a Newark postman // 19 February
20 - Private Robert Sanders / 1st Sherwood Foresters / Ward's Row // 11 March
21 - Private Harold Walter Addy / 1st Sherwood Foresters / 22 Long Row / New Town // 12 March
22 - Sergeant Ralph Joseph Inwards / 1st Lincolnshire / 8 Cross Street // 28 March
23 - Private Harry Gregory / 2nd Sherwood Foresters / 1 Victoria Gardens // on 7 April
24 - Private William Richard Copley / 1st 8th Sherwood Foresters / 39 William Street // 13 April
25 - Private Henry Trickett / 1st 8th Sherwood Foresters / 45 Albert Street // 20 April
26 - Sergeant George Thomas Percival Wilmore / 1st 8th Sherwood Foresters / 17 London Road // 21 April
27 - Private Herbert Sketchley / 1st 8th Sherwood Foresters / Alliance Street // 22 April
28 - Private Richard East / 1st 8th Sherwood Foresters / 21 Chatham Street // 24 April
29 - Private William Godfrey / 1st 8th Sherwood Foresters / 41 Bowbridge Road // 24 April
30 - Private Charles Redmile / 1st 8th Sherwood Foresters / 42 Vernon Street // 24 April
31 - Lance Corporal William Markwell / 1st 8th Sherwood Foresters / 24 Albion Street // 30 April
32 - Rifleman Albert Rose / 3rd King's Royal Rifle Corps / 6 Pelham Street // 30 April
33 - Private Alfred Joynes / Chatham Battalion / Royal Marine Light Infantry / 3 King Street // 1 May
34 - Private Robert Revill / 1st Border / 4 Priests Yard / Chatham Street // 8 May
35 - Private Herbert Kirk / 1st 8th Sherwood Foresters / 15 Appletongate // 8 May
36 - Private William Brewster / 1st 8th Sherwood Foresters / 4 Mount Zion Square / Eldon Street // 9 May
37 - Lance Corporal Alfred Priestley / 1st 8th Sherwood Foresters / Eldon Street // 9 May
38 - Sergeant Edwin Cecil Coy / 15th Canadian Infantry (Central Ontario Regiment) / Lincoln Street // 21 May
39 - Private Thomas Hardy / 1st 8th Sherwood Foresters / Stanley Street // 24 May
40 - Private John William H Shaw / 3rd Lincolnshire / Robin Hood Hotel / Lindum Street // 31 May

1915

41 - Private Tom Massey / 1st 8th Sherwood Foresters / Market Place // 6 June
42 - Stoker Samuel Asman / Torpedo Boat No.11 / 4 George Street Row // 10 June
43 - Mrs Florence Smith / Farndon Road / fatally wounded in Zeppelin raid on Southend // 15 June
44 - Private George Richardson / 1st 8th Sherwood Foresters / Wright Street // 16 June
45 - Private William Richardson / 1st 8th Sherwood Foresters / 26 Baldertongate // 16 June
46 - Private George Alfred Benton / 1st 8th Sherwood Foresters / 21 Elgin Place // 20 June
47 - Private John Pond / 1st Sherwood Foresters / Cawkwell's Road // 5 July
48 - Driver William Smith / 106th Field Company Royal Engineers / Spread Eagle / Middlegate // 12 July
49 - Private Christopher William Taylor / 1st 8th Sherwood Foresters / 64 Castlegate // 21 July
50 - Private Robert Huckerby / 1st 8th Sherwood Foresters / 15 Wright Street // 30 July
51 - Private Frederick Parker / 1st 8th Sherwood Foresters / 194 Barnbygate // 30 July
52 - Private Frank Walster / 1st 8th Sherwood Foresters / 5 Depot Yard / Kirkgate // 30 July
53 - Private Charles Crampton / 1st 8th Sherwood Foresters / Barnby Crossing // 5 August
54 - Private Herbert Moore / 1st 8th Sherwood Foresters / Mount Pleasant // 7 August
55 - Private Thomas Frederick Gumsley / 1st 8th Sherwood Foresters / 23 Parliament Street // 8 August
56 - Private Ernest Allison / 6th Lincolnshire / 12 Queen Street // 9 August
57 - Private Richard Gill / 2nd Sherwood Foresters / Blyton's Yard // 9 August
58 - Lieutenant William Hector Mathers Ridley / 2nd Sherwood Foresters / Castlegate // 9 August
59 - Acting Lance Corporal James John Whitelock / 6th Lincolnshire / 3 Vernon Street // 9 August
60 - Pioneer Maurice Henry Dare / 68th Company Royal Engineers / 13 Harcourt Street // 15 August
61 - Private Michael Herbert Edmond Colton / Sherwood Rangers Yeomanry / Harcourt Street // 22 August
62 - Corporal Albert Jollands / South Notts Hussars / Clinton Arms / Market Place / died 24 August

1915

63 - Private Thomas Tournay / 2nd Sherwood Foresters / 45 Barnbygate // 25 August
64 - Private Robert Ronald Richardson / 6th York and Lancaster / 28 Appletongate // 29 August
65 - Private Larendon H Swann / 9th London (Queen Victoria's Rifles) / Northgate // 4 September
66 - Lance Corporal Herbert Leslie Durham / 1st Lancashire Fusiliers / 31 Charles Street // 6 September
67 - Private William Thomas Marshall / 1st 8th Sherwood Foresters / 54 Bowbridge Road // 16 September
68 - Private Alfred Savage / 9th Leicestershire / 6 Newnham Road // 22 September
69 - Corporal Arthur William James George / 8th Queen's (Royal West Surrey) / 29 Charles Street // 25 September
70 - Private William Henry Guy / 12th Sherwood Foresters / 5 Chester Place // 26 September
71 - Sergeant Alfred Charles Dench / 1st Grenadier Guards / 6 Middlegate // 29 September
72 - Private Thomas Marsden / 2nd Cheshire / 46 Bottom Row / Beacon Hill // 3 October
73 - Lance Corporal Charles Edgar Harrison / 1st 8th Sherwood Foresters / Farndon Road // 5 October
74 - Sergeant Charles Lionel Richard Haines / 73rd Field Company Royal Engineers / Newark School of Science and Art, Middlegate // 10 October
75 - Private Arnold Henry Grant / 1st 4th Lincolnshire / 28 Harcourt Street // 13 October
76 - Private Cyril Sydney Harrison / 1st 8th Sherwood Foresters / Cherry Holt Lane // 14 October
77 - Private Horace Wilkinson / 1st 8th Sherwood Foresters / 52 Milner Street // 14 October
78 - Lance Corporal Harold Woodhead / 1st 8th Sherwood Foresters / Winchilsea Avenue // 14 October
79 - Private Sydney Broughton / 1st 8th Sherwood Foresters / Long Row // 15 October
80 - Private Fred Bryan / 1st 8th Sherwood Foresters / 94 Beacon Hill // 15 October
81 - Lance Corporal Frederick J Lowe / 8th Sherwood Foresters / 2Egglestone's Yard // 18 October
82 - Private Edward Smith / 4th Grenadier Guards / 13 Sleaford Road // 21 October
83 - Private Archie Robb / 6th (King's Own) Royal Lancashire / 2 Whitfield Street // 26 October
84 - Sapper Albert Edward Robinson / 171st Tunnel Company Royal Engineers / 55 William Street // 29 October
85 - Private Cecil Henry Cliffe / 1st 8th Sherwood Foresters / Victoria Street // 2 December
86 - Private William E Pykett / 8th Lincolnshire / Christ Church // 8 December
87 - Private Reginald John Wright / 1st 4th Duke of Wellington's (West Riding) / Barnby Crossing // 19 December
88 - Private John Lunn / 1st Northamptonshire / Taylor's Yard, Millgate // 24 December

1915 'Bombshell' Map

1916

89 - Major John Pickard Becher / 1st 8th Sherwood Foresters / Newark County Magistrates' Court // 1 January
90 - Shoesmith Arthur Green / 68th Brigade Royal Field Artillery / Appletongate // 12 January
91 - Major Samuel Boyd Quibell / 4th East Yorkshire / London Road // 5 February
92 - Private James Walter Hammond / 6th Royal Shropshire Light Infantry / Trent Bridge House // 12 February
93 - Private Arthur Day / 3rd Leicestershire / Mount Pleasant // 13 February
94 - Private Adolphus Grant / 1st 8th Sherwood Foresters / 5 Rowbotham's Row, Water Lane // 14 February
95 - Sergeant Thomas Claude Carter / 27th Siege Battery Royal Garrison Artillery / Barnbygate // 6 March
96 - Petty Officer Frederick Birkett Turgoose / Torpedo Boat No.11 / Sleaford Road // 7 March
97 - Private Fred Footitt / 1st 8th Sherwood Foresters / Slaughterhouse Lane // 21 March
98 - Private Harry Footitt / 1st Northumberland Fusiliers / Slaughterhouse Lane // 27 March
99 - Private Charles Ernest Ellis / 1st 8th Sherwood Foresters / Stanley Street // 28 March
100 - Private Ernest Alfred Hill / 1st 8th Sherwood Foresters / Lindum Street // 5 April
101 - Private Edward Harry Mutton / 1st 8th Sherwood Foresters / 5 Eggleston's Yard, Lombard Street // 17 April
102 - Lance Corporal John Footitt / 1st 8th Sherwood Foresters / 12 Boundary Road // 18 April
103 - Company Sergeant Major Henry Charles Dixey / 2nd 8th Sherwood Foresters / 47 South Parade // 27 April
104 - Assistant Paymaster John Stuart Frost / Royal Naval Reserve, HMS Russell / Magnus Grammar School // 27 April
105 - Second Lieutenant Reginald John Carey Leader / 14th Durham Light Infantry / Newark Baptist Church // 28 April
106 - Private Ernest Stanley Sanderson / 4th South Wales Borderers / 16 Sleaford Road // 13 May
107 - Gunner Ernest Kelham / Royal Marine Artillery, HMS Invincible / 5 Nicholson Street // 31 May
108 - Able Seaman George William Price / HMS Queen Mary / 5 Sydney Street // 31 May
109 - Private Harold Tye / 1st East Yorkshire / Cross Street // 4 June
110 - Private George Edmund Harold Coulsey / 14th Highland Light Infantry / 1 St Mark's Place, St Mark's Lane // 14 June
111 - Second Lieutenant Harold Barling / 8th Leicestershire / Lincoln Row // 15 June
112 - Private George Archibald Bingley / 1st 8th Sherwood Foresters / Lenton Terrace, Millgate // 20 June
113 - Private Ernest Priestley / 2nd 8th Sherwood Foresters / 36 Warburton Street // 20 June
114 - Private Alfred Edward Pulford / 1st 8th Sherwood Foresters / Bowbridge Road // 20 June
115 - Private Leslie Tyers / 1st 8th Sherwood Foresters / 36 Harcourt Street // 20 June
116 - Private Thomas Cope / 1st 8th Sherwood Foresters / 39 Wood Street // 24 June

1916

117 - Private Mountna Johnson / 1st 8th Sherwood Foresters / 48 Warburton Street // 26 June
118 - Private Ernest Judson / 1st 8th Sherwood Foresters / 26 Cawkwell's Yard, Stodman Street // 26 June
119 - Corporal Walter Gilbert Moore / 1st 8th Sherwood Foresters / Farndon Road // 26 June
120 - Lance Corporal Alma Adolphus Grant / 1st 8th Sherwood Foresters / 14 Charles Street // 27 June
121 - Private George William Howitt / 11th Sherwood Foresters / Bowbridge Road // 1 July
122 - Private George Seagrave / 1st 5th Sherwood Foresters / 140 Barnbygate // 1 July
123 - Private William Stephenson / 24th Royal Fusiliers / Newark Golf Club // 1 July
124 - Private John W Tye / 1st East Yorkshire / Cromwell Road // 1 July
125 - Lance Corporal Arthur West / 6th Wiltshire / 22 Boundary Road // 2 July
126 - Lance Corporal Alfred Parry / 1st 5th King's Own Yorkshire Light Infantry / 14 Elgin Place // 5 July
127 - Private Cecil Sefton / 20th Royal Fusiliers / Lime Grove // 5 July
128 - Private Ralph Shepperson / 10th Sherwood Foresters / 3 Blyton's Yard, Millgate // 5 July
129 - Private William Henry Theaker / 2nd Lincolnshire / Newark Post Office // 7 July
130 - Private Frederick William Thurman / 1st Sherwood Foresters / London Road // 8 July
131 - Lance Corporal Ernest Pride / 1st 8th Sherwood Foresters / Farndon Fields // 13 July
132 - Lance Corporal Hassell Ernest Robinson / 7th Queen's Own (Royal West Kent) / 78 Harcourt Street // 13 July
133 - Private John William Cavey / 7th Leicestershire / 1 Bullen's Buildings, Boundary Road // 14 July
134 - Private Oliver Farrance / 8th Queen's Own (Royal West Kent) / Dr Barnardo's Home // 15 July
135 - Private John James Gravell / 2nd South African Infantry / Boundary Road // 15 July
136 - Private James H Harper / 8th Leicestershire / 85 Sleaford Road // 15 July
137 - Private George William Collett / 1st 8th Royal Warwickshire / Harcourt Street // 18 July
138 - Private William Derry / 1st Australian Infantry / Stodman Street // 21 July
139 - Company Quartermaster Henry Lawrence Jackson / 9th Northumberland Fusiliers / Market Place // 26 July
140 - Sergeant Charles William Smith / 17th Sherwood Foresters / Newark Police Station // 1 August
141 - Private Ernest Mountney / 19th Sherwood Foresters / 22 Northgate // 3 August
142 - Private George Nicholas Harvey / 1st 7th King's Liverpool / 2 King Street // 10 August
143 - Rifleman George Cobb / 7th King's Royal Rifle Corps / 76 Sleaford Road // 19 August
144 - Private Thomas Newstead / 4th West Yorks (Prince of Wales Own) / Chatham Street // 23 August

145 - Private Ernest Frederic Smith / 2nd Sherwood Foresters / 11 Pelham Street // 26 August
146 - Lance Sergeant Christopher Winn / Machine Gunn Corps (Infantry) / Midland Hotel // 26 August
147 - Private William Henry Davis / 1st Sherwood Foresters / 23 Portland Street // 31 August
148 - Private John Charles Hudson / 16th Sherwood Foresters / Tenter Buildings, Appletongate // 3 September
149 - Lance Corporal George Henry Pilsworth / 17th Sherwood Foresters / 19 Eldon Street // 3 September
150 - Gunner Walter Vacey / Z 30th Trench Mortar Battery Royal Garrison Artillery / 3 Malt Kiln Terrace, Northgate // 6 Septer
151 - Private Robert Welch / 6th Lincolnshire / 13 Tolney Lane // 9 September
152 - Private William T Grocock / 8th Duke of Wellington's (West Riding) / 6 Clinton Street // 14 September
153 - Private Percy White / 26th Royal Fusiliers / Barclay's Bank, Market Place // 18 September
154 - Shoe Smith Corporal Alfred Smith / Royal Field Artillery (23rd Division) / Saracen's Head Yard //20 September
155 - Private Arthur Atkinson / Sherwood Rangers Yeomanry / 37 Jubilee Street // 23 September
156 - Sergeant William Swann / Sherwood Rangers Yeomanry / Boundary Road // 23 September
157 - Lance Corporal Leonard George Simpson / 12th Middlesex / Castlegate // 26 September
158 - Lieutenant Christopher Chowler Gilbert / 8th Duke of Wellington's (West Riding) / Harcourt Street // 29 September
159 - Second Lieutenant Hubert Everard Clifton / 1st Devonshire / Barnbygate // 4 October
160 - Sergeant Charles William Crowder / 2nd Sherwood Foresters / Bowbridge Road // 12 October
161 - Private George Crowder / 2nd Lancashire Fusiliers / 45 Sleaford Road // 12 October
162 - Private Frederick Harry Jepson / 2nd Lancashire Fusiliers / 7 Friary Road // 13 October
163 - Private William Fretwell / 2nd Wiltshire / Charles Street // 18 October
164 - Sergeant James Edward Munton / 18th Machine Gun Corps / 19 Clinton Street // 21 October
165 - Private Thomas Brown / 2nd Lincolnshire / Millgate // 23 October
166 - Private Harry Chappell / 10th Royal Warwickshire / Parliament Street // 29 October
167 - Private Philip Woolfitt / 43rd Canadian Infantry (Manitoba Regiment) / Lime Grove // 1 November
168 - Private Charles Frederick Titchener / 16th West Yorkshire (Prince of Wales Own) / 2 Wellington Road // 13 November
169 - Private Ernest Barton / 1st 7th Northumberland Fusiliers / 20 Lombard Street // 14 November
170 - Rifleman George Martin Henderson / 13th King's Royal Rifle Corps / Barnbygate // 14 November
171 - Driver Roland Hadfield Smith / British Red Cross Society / London Road // 1 December
172 - Sergeant Joseph Naylor / 9th Leicestershire / 10 Albion Street // 12 December
173 - Private George Henry Baines / 1st Grenadier Guards / 6 Spital Row, Northgate // 16 December
174 - Wheeler Sydney Hunt / Royal Horse Artillery / Hatton Gardens // 17 December
175 - Private George Walter Martin / 1st Lincolnshire / 77 Northgate // 25 December

1916 'Bombshell' Map

1917

76 - Private George Footitt Stanley / 21st Manchester / 36 Beacon Hill // 10 January
177 - Private Frederick Norton / 7th North Staffordshire / 45 Baldertongate // 13 January
178 - Private Reginald Knee / 1st 8th Sherwood Foresters / 35 Cross Street // 24 January
179 - Private William Henry Jackson Measham / 7th North Staffordshire / 33 Stanley Street // 25 January
180 - Sapper Walter F Collins / Inland Waterway Transport Royal Engineers / 26 Barnbygate // 6 February
181 - Private John Thomas Day / 16th Sherwood Foresters / 5 Britannia Buildings, Parliament Street // 21 February
182 - Corporal Arthur Linsey / 2nd Leicestershire / Heppenstall's Row, William Street // 22 February
183 - Private Frank Tye / 1st East Yorkshire / 33 Cross Street // 25 February
184 - Private James William Marston Sooley / 2nd Sherwood Foresters / 45 London Road // 10 March
185 - Private William Brown / 1st 5th Sherwood Foresters / 7 Lawrence Place, Lawrence Street // 11 March
186 - Private William Wright Thacker / 2nd Sherwood Foresters / 16 Whitfield Street // 24 March
187 - Major John Maxwell Heron / 5th Essex / Hole's Brewery, Albert Street // 26 March
188 - Lance Corporal Henry Francis / 3rd King's Royal Rifle Corps / 111 Barnbygate // 4 April
189 - Private William Catley / 2nd 8th Sherwood Foresters / 4 Mount Pleasant, Millgate // 7 April
190 - Private Roland Combes / 2nd 8th Sherwood Foresters / 1 Charles Street // 7 April
191 - Lance Corporal James Cope / 2nd 8th Sherwood Foresters / 19 Wright Street // 7 April
192 - Private Percy Charles Pratt / 2nd 8th Sherwood Foresters / William Street // 7 April
193 - Lance Sergeant William Smith / 2nd 8th Sherwood Foresters / New Street // 7 April
194 - Private William Manterfield / 7th 8th King's Own Scottish Borderers / 40a Albert Street // 9 April
195 - Private Harold Revill / 25th Northumberland Fusiliers / 4 Priest's Yard, Chatham Street // 9 April
196 - Private Vincent Oswald R Taylor / 15th Durham Light Infantry / 83 Charles Street // 9 April
197 - Lance Corporal Wilfred Gelsthorpe / 1st Lincolnshire / 3 Vernon Street // 11 April
198 - Private John Thomas Cragg / 1st Sherwood Foresters / Hatton Gardens // 12 April
199 - Private Frank Smith / 8th Leicestershire / 17 Chatham Street // 13 April
200 - Sapper Thomas Asher / Royal Engineers / 15 Eldon Street // 16 April
201 - Private James Holwell / 1st 8th Sherwood Foresters / 182 Barnbygate // 23 April
202 - Lance Corporal Robert Vacey / 1st 8th Sherwood Foresters / 3 Malt Kiln Terrace, Northgate // 23 April
203 - Corporal Arthur Edward Cox / 1st 8th Sherwood Foresters / 126 Northgate // 24 April
204 - Private Albert Henry Wilson / 1st 5th Border / 2 Meyrick Road // 25 April
205 - Private Joseph Henry Nicholson / 1st 8th Sherwood Foresters / 19 Tenter Buildings // 26 April
206 - Private John Cecil Belton / 2nd 8th Sherwood Foresters / 2 Bargate // 27 April
207 - Private Charles Cobb / 8th Lincolnshire / St Leonard's Court, Kirkgate // 28 April
208 - Private Henry Gray / 10th Lincolnshire / 6 Scales Row // 28 April
209 - Private Harry Smith / 11th Suffolk / 73 Barnbygate // 28 April
210 - Private Fred William Wright / 27th Northumberland Fusiliers / 13 Queen Street // 28 April
211 - Private William Henry Kay / 18th (West Yorks) Prince of Wales Own / 4 Massey Street // 29 April
212 - Rifleman Joseph Pamment / 9th Rifle Brigade / 33 Sleaford Road // 3 May
213 - Private Robert Robinson / 7th Leicestershire / 6 Warburton Street // 3 May
214 - Private Tom Turner / 2nd 5th King's Own Yorkshire Light Infantry / Eldon Street // 3 May
215 - Rifleman George Henry Walker / 9th Rifle Brigade / 2 Tolney Lane // 3 May
216 - Sapper Walter Hanson / Z Special Company Royal Engineers / Wood Street // 6 May
217 - Corporal Arthur H Grocock / 17th Sherwood Foresters / 1 Lincoln Street // 12 May
218 - Sapper Frank James Carter / 89th Field Company Royal Engineers / 5 St Leonard's Court // 18 May
219 - Private James Riley / 2nd Duke of Wellington's (West Riding) / 62 Sleaford Road // 19 May
220 - Private George Sanders Edlin / 12th Sherwood Foresters / Whitfield Street // 7 June
221 - Sergeant Albert Edward John Graveney / 2nd 8th Sherwood Foresters / 15 Newton Street // 7 June
222 - Private Edward John Rodwell Rich / 8th North Staffordshire / 88 Beacon Hill Road // 7 June
223 - Private Harry Sanderson / 1st Gordon Highlanders / 6 Sleaford Road // 14 June
224 - Private Ernest Bond / 9th Sherwood Foresters / Sheppard's Row, Northgate // 16 June
225 - Lance Corporal John Henry Ayto / 2nd 8th Sherwood Foresters / 66 Northgate // 19 June
226 - Private Horace Buckler / 1st 8th Sherwood Foresters / Winchilsea Avenue // 23 June
227 - Private Thomas Grosse / 1st 8th Sherwood Foresters / 21 Pelham Street // 23 June
228 - Private Andrew Brown / 2nd 8th Sherwood Foresters / 7 Water Lane // 25 June
229 - Private James Harold Fox / 1st 8th Sherwood Foresters / 34 Charles Street // 26 June

1917

230 - Drummer Somerfield R Willingham / 1st 8th Sherwood Foresters / 13 Wilson Street // 26 June
231 - Second Lieutenant Henry Graham / 74th attached 67th Punjabi / 6 Wellington Road // 28 June
232 - Private John Joseph Hawarden / 1st Queen's (Royal West Surrey) / 13 Lawrence Place // 29 June
233 - Private William Percy Walker / 2nd 10th King's (Liverpool) / 39 Portland Street // 30 June
234 - Private William Edward Ansell / 1st 4th Lincolnshire / 13 Kelham Villas // 1 July
235 - Private Thomas White / 1st 5th Sherwood Foresters / 16 Sheppard's Row // 1 July
236 - Leading Signaller Isaac Overton / HMS Pembroke / 64 Castlegate // 3 July
237 - Rifleman Joseph Maull / 2nd King's Royal Rifle Corps / 10 Currie Road // 10 July
238 - Sergeant Henry Hurst / 15th Sherwood Foresters / 28 Water Lane // 11 July
239 - Private George Lambert / 2nd Lincolnshire / 6 Collingham Row, Queen's Road // 17 July
240 - Sergeant Arthur Tyers / 1st Leicestershire / Bridge Cottages, Barnby Road // 23 July
241 - Private George H Clayton / 19th Welsh / 62 William Street // 28 July
242 - Private Arthur George Musgrove / 18th Manchester / 40 Albert Street // 29 July
243 - Private John Richard Arnold / 4th Middlesex / 27 Lincoln Street // 31 July
244 - Private Percy Doncaster / 1st Coldstream Guards / 21 Appletongate // 31 July
245 - Private John Sentance / 8th Suffolk / 20 Lindum Street // 31 July
246 - Private John Thomas Cree / 1st 8th Sherwood Foresters / Lincoln Road // 1 August
247 - Private Albert George Sherry / 17th Sherwood Foresters / New Street // 1 August
248 - Private Joseph Smith / 17th Sherwood Foresters / 82 Beacon Hill // 4 August
249 - Lance Corporal Herbert Taylor / 1st Sherwood Foresters / 1 Eldon Place // 4 August
250 - Lance Corporal Joseph Henry Harrison / 16th Sherwood Foresters / 39 Vernon Street // 6 August
251 - Sapper Henry Keetley / 87th Field Company Royal Engineers / 11 Spittal Row // 9 August
252 - Corporal Frederick Herbert Northen / 6th Royal Berkshire / Kirkgate // 12 August
253 - Private Evelyn Edgar Golland / 1st 13th London / 34 William Street // 16 August
254 - Corporal Leonard Thomas Wakefield / 15th Sherwood Foresters / 31 Baldertongate // 19 August
255 - Private Arthur Hutchinson / 13th Royal Scots / 3 George Street // 22 August
256 - Private Edward John Probert / 4th South Wales Borderers / 44 Victoria Street // 22 August
257 - Private Arthur Stamper / 2nd 4th Oxford and Bucks Light Infantry / 13 Parliament Street // 22 August
258 - Private George Smith / 8th South Staffordshire / 30 Eldon Street // 16 September
259 - Rifleman Ralph James Boness / 7th King's Royal Rifle Corps / 2 Sheppard's Row // 18 September
260 - Airman Charles Holme Kingston Hogg / 6 Squadron Royal Flying Corps / 7 Lovers Lane // 18 September
261 - Private William Frederick Parker / 16th Sherwood Foresters / 152 Barnbygate // 20 September
262 - Private Charles B Bradley / 8th Field Ambulance Australian Army Medical Corps / 4 Stone Terrace, Victoria Street // 21 September
263 - Private James Willows / 4th Seaforth Highlanders / Farndon Fields // 21 September
264 - Private Frederic Wilson Boulton / 2nd 4th Lincolnshire / 29 Cartergate // 26 September
265 - Company Sergeant Major Thomas Catley / 2nd 8th Sherwood Foresters / 47 Beacon Hill // 26 September
266 - Private William Davison / 2nd 7th Sherwood Foresters / 10 Cherry Holt Lane // 26 September
267 - Private Joseph Edward Hardy / 1st 8th Sherwood Foresters / 5 George Street Row // 26 September
268 - Private Walter Newbound / 1st Royal Scots Fusiliers / 72 Chatham Street // 26 September
269 - Private Aaron Sharp / 1st 8th Sherwood Foresters / 8 Guildhall Street // 26 September
270 - Private George Brown Southerington / 2nd 8th Sherwood Foresters / 9 Northgate // 26 September
271 - Private Charles William Statham / 14th York and Lancaster / 20 Whitfield Street // 26 September
272 - Private Cecil Windey / 1st 8th Sherwood Foresters / 180 Barnbygate // 26 September
273 - Private George Richard Young / 2nd 7th Sherwood Foresters / 5 Mount Square // 26 September
274 - Private Lawrence Alfred Hollis / 2nd 8th Sherwood Foresters / 38 Parliament Street // 27 September
275 - Private Frank Selby / 2nd 8th Sherwood Foresters / 32 Whitfield Street // 29 September
276 - Private Ernest Burrows / 7th Leicestershire / 38 Albert Street // 1 October
277 - Corporal Alfred Cobb / 298th Bde Royal Field Artillery / 74 Sleaford Road // 4 October
278 - Captain James Ernest Ford / 1st King's Own Scottish Borderers / 11 Appletongate // 4 October
279 - Private Joseph Freedman / 9th King's Own Yorkshire Light Infantry / 1 Victoria Street // 4 October
280 - Lance Sergeant John Edward Walker / 1st Lincolnshire / 3 Wood Street // 4 October
281 - Second Lieutenant Grosvenor Garnet / 3rd Lancashire Fusiliers / 6 Wellington Road // 9 October
282 - Private Harry Newman McKears / 2nd 9th Manchester / 11 Wellington Road // 9 October

283 - Private George Martin / 10th Sherwood Foresters / 50 Cross Street // 12 October
284 - Private Alfred Ernest Southerington / 5th 6th Royal Scots / 9 Northgate // 14 October
285 - Gunner Edgar Marshall / 186 Siege Battery Royal Garrison Artillery / 109 Bowbridge Road // 15 October
286 - Lance Corporal Frank William Shaw / 194th Company Machine Gun Corps / 12 Crown Street // 17 October
287 - Corporal Albert Stevenson / 2nd Sherwood Foresters / 13 Lincoln Row, Northgate // 17 October
288 - Sergeant Albert Bernard Andrew / 16th Sherwood Foresters / 19 Lincoln Street // 19 October
289 - Private George Morley / 16th Sherwood Foresters / 4 Lincoln Street // 19 October
290 - Private Ernest Birkett / Army Service Corps / Cross Street // 21 October
291 - Sergeant Frank Handley Smith / 17th Sherwood Foresters / 57 Hatton Gardens // 23 October
292 - Private John William Turner / 15th Sherwood Foresters / 14 Cross Street // 23 October
293 - Lance Corporal William Gumsley / 1st 5th Northumberland Fusiliers / 23 Parliament Street // 26 October
294 - Corporal Charles Young / 2nd 8th Sherwood Foresters / 28 Lombard Street // 31 October
295 - Private Ernest Bryan / 2nd 6th Sherwood Foresters / 45 Bottom Row, Beacon Hill // 2 November
296 - Acting Bombardier George Lunn / 63 Siege Battery Royal Garrison Artillery / Collingham Row, Queen's Road // 2 November
297 - Private Edgar Sharp / 1st 8th Sherwood Foresters / Farndon Fields // 2 November
298 - Second Lieutenant James Allan Christie / 6th Queen's (Royal West Surrey) / Castlegate // 6 November
299 - Private George W Hill / 14th Field Ambulance Royal Army Medical Corps / 50 Sleaford Road // 6 November
300 - Private Herbert Wiggins / 2nd Sherwood Foresters / 3 Railway Terrace, London Road // 20 November
301 - Corporal Ernest William Frisby / Sherwood Rangers Yeomanry / 3 Northern Buildings, Lovers Lane // 28 November
302 - Private George Henry Johnson / 1st 6th Sherwood Foresters / 20 George Street // 28 November
303 - Private John George Haywood / 18th King's (Liverpool) / 47 Milner Street // 4 December
304 - Private Joseph Arthur Wilson / 2nd 7th Sherwood Foresters / 3 Boundary Road // 3 December
305 - Private John Henry Simpson / 11th Royal Scots / 102 Barnbygate // 7 December
306 - Private Percy William Drabble / 13th King's (Liverpool) / 53 Alliance Street // 12 December
307 - Private Harry Gumsley / 1st Lincolnshire / 23 Parliament Street // 18 December
308 - Third Officer Cyril David Slater // SS Waverley / Millgate // 20 December

1917 'Bombshell' Map

1918

309 - Acting Bombardier William Henry Weightman / 133 Siege Battery Royal Garrison Artillery / 22 Harcourt Street // 13 Janu
310 - Private Charles Marriott / 5th Sherwood Foresters / 2 George Square // 18 January
311 - Private George William Lacey / 2nd Sherwood Foresters / Beacon Hill // 19 January
312 - Private George Arthur Keeley / 15th Sherwood Foresters / 8 Zion Square, Eldon Street // 8 February
313 - Paymaster Robert Muir Hindley / Royal Naval Reserve HMS Cullist / 55 Lime Grove // 11 February
314 - Private Robert Fincham / 33rd Machine Gun Corps / 6 Hospital Cottages // 19 February
315 - Private Archibald Langrish Knight / 2/6th Sherwood Foresters / 98 Hawton Road // 24 February
316 - Second Lieutenant Thomas Rowland Smith / Sherwood Foresters attached Imperial Camel Corps / Bridge Street // 13 M
317 - Private Herbert Frederick Jenkins Tinsley / Royal Army Medical Corps / 33 Castlegate // 19 March
318 - Private William Quinningborough Ash / 16th Sherwood Foresters / Portland Street // 21 March
319 - Rifleman Arthur Hill / 9th King's Royal Rifles Corps / 50 Sleaford Road // 21 March
320 - Private George Herbert Page / 2/7th Sherwood Foresters / 72 Appletongate // 21 March
321 - Private Michael Price / 5th Lincolnshire / 10 Victoria Gardens // 21 March
322 - Private Elijah Salmon / 2/7th Sherwood Foresters / 6 Cawkwell's Yard, Lombard Street // 21 March
323 - Private Herbert Towlson / 2/7th Sherwood Foresters / Farndon Fields // 21 March
324 - Private George Hayes / 1st Leicestershire / 9 Top Row, Beacon Hill // 22 March
325 - Private Ernest Mabbott / 1st Leicestershire / 17 Lindum Street // 22 March
326 - Corporal Joseph Ernest Turner / 11th Leicestershire / Tenter Buildings // 22 March
327 - Private Frank Cook / 7th Queen's (Royal West Surrey) / 31 Cross Street // 23 March
328 - Regimental Sergeant Major Lorraine Gabbitas / 10th Sherwood Foresters / 21 King Street // 23 March
329 - Private Sidney Holland / 12th Sherwood Foresters / 70 Victoria Street // 27 March
330 - Second Lieutenant Stanley Edmond Colton / 1st Northumberland Fusiliers / Harcourt Street // 28 March
331 - Lance Corporal Arthur Empson / 13th King's (Liverpool) / Parliament Street // 28 March
332 - Private William Sharpe / 12th 15th Northumberland Fusiliers / 4 Rowbotham's Row, Water Lane // 28 March
333 - Private Maurice Freedman / 7th East Yorkshire / 1 Victoria Street // 31 March
334 - Private Tom Hardy / 7th Sherwood Foresters / 2 Charles Street // 31 March
335 - Corporal Charles C Sefton / 2/5th Sherwood Foresters / Spring Gardens, Victoria Street // 31 March
336 - Private Charles Kirk / 2/5th North Staffordshire / Bowbridge Road // 3 Apil
337 - Private Walter Foster / 15th Sherwood Foresters / 1 Norfolk Buildings, Parker Street // 4 April
338 - Private John Lewis Morgan / 13th Gloucestershire / Newark Arms Hotel // 4 April
339 - Lance Corporal George Stanley Hydes / 8th Lincolnshire / 13 Boundary Road // 6 April
340 - Private Francis Cecil Hitchcox / 1st Royal Scots Fusiliers / 5 Blyton's Yard, Millgate // 7 April
341 - Private Charles Eustace Morley / 1st Northumberland Fusiliers / Millgate // 9 April
342 - Private Arthur Lacey / 1st 6th Northumberland Fusiliers / 1 Stanley Terrace, Beacon Hill // 10 April
343 - Captain John Nigel MacRae / 83rd Squadron Royal Air Force / Handley House // 11 April
344 - Private Charles Thomas Tomlinson / 1/5th York and Lancaster / 13 Cartergate // 11 April
345 - Private Charley Seagraves / 4th Grenadier Guards / 3 Stanley Terrace // 13 April
346 - Sergeant John Booth / 164th Siege Battery, Royal Garrison Artillery / 21 Lombard Street // 14 April
347 - Private John Thomas Newbold / 4th North Staffordshire / 178 Northgate // 15 April
348 - Private Thomas Archibald Taylor / 2/6th North Staffordshire / 34 Baldertongate // 15 April
349 - Private Charles Dent / 1st Lincolnshire / 3 Almshouses, Bedlam Lane // 16 April
350 - Private George Ernest Bryan / 2nd Lincolnshire / 9 Albert Street // 18 April
351 - Private Alfred Leader / 8th Sherwood Foresters / 14 Long Row, New Town // 18 April
352 - Pioneer Harry Squires / G Depot Company Royal Engineers / Baldertongate // 23 April
353 - Private Edward Broughton / 2nd Devon / 21 Tenter Buildings // 24 April
354 - Private Fred Hickman / 15th Durham Light Infantry / 37 Wood Street // 24 April
355 - Private John Harry Gibson / 2nd Yorkshire / 18 Tomlinson's Yard, Castlegate // 25 April
356 - Lance Corporal Albert John Herrod / King's Own Yorkshire Light Infantry / 15 Cross Street // 26 April
357 - Corporal Ernest Cross / 1/8th Sherwood Foresters / 56 William Street // 28 April
358 - Private Arthur Simpson / 9th Princess Victoria's (Royal Irish Fusiliers) / 104 Barnbygate // 28 April
359 - Private Arthur Fox / 15th Sherwood Foresters / 27 King Street // 2 May
360 - Private Alfred Grosse / 2nd Royal Scots / Northgate // 2 May
361 - Private Tom Gabbitas / 2nd Royal Scots / 54 Parliament Street // 4 May
362 - Private George Esam / 10th Royal Warwickshire / 53 Jubilee Street // 8 May

1918

363 - Private Edward Hosner Asling / 2/8th Sherwood Foresters attached 2/4th Royal Berkshire / 70 Milner Street // 9 May
364 - Private Robert Henry Smedley / 1st 10th King's (Liverpool) / Golden Fleece, Lombard Street // 9 May
365 - Gunner William Kirkby / 307 Bde Royal Field Artillery / Queen's Head, Market Place // 10 May
366 - Corporal Herbert William Gross Paine / 2nd Wellington Regiment, New Zealand Exp. Force / Beaumond Street // 16 May
367 - Private Rich Alfred Beardmore / Royal Defence Corps / 5 Pacey's Court // 22 May
368 - Second Lieutenant John Auchenlosh Gibson / 116 Siege Battery Royal Garrison Artillery / 2 Magnus Street // 27 May
369 - Private Frederick David Porter / 15th Durham Light Infantry / 10 Bargate // 27 May
370 - Second Lieutenant Harry Lawford Hunt / Royal Marine Artillery / 15 Kelham Road // 29 May
371 - Private Arthur White / 1st 6th South Staffordshire / 32 Portland Street // 31 May
372 - Private Robert Scraton / 47th Machine Gun Corps / General Post Office // 3 June
373 - Private William Maule Norcott / 1st 4th Northumberland Fusiliers / 4 Cherry Holt Lane // 4 June
374 - Reverend Joseph Dobson Burns / Royal Garrison Artillery / London Road Congregational Church // 7 June
375 - Corporal Harry Percy Carr / 1/5th Sherwood Foresters / 81 Barnbygate // 8 June
376 - Private Joseph Kelly / 1st Lincolnshire / 48 Millgate // 14 June
377 - Private Harry Gardner / 1/5th Duke of Cornwall's Light Infantry / Wheatsheaf Inn, Slaughterhouse Lane // 17 June
378 - Private George Kent / 1/5th Lincolnshire / 1 Wheatley's Yard, Chatham Street // 22 June
379 - Private David Hough / 61st Machine Gun Corps / 5 Jubilee Street // 26 June
380 - Lieutenant Sidney Harston / 204 Squadron Royal Air Force / 23 Lombard Street // 29 June
381 - Lance Corporal Harry Edward Smith / 1/8th Sherwood Foresters / 21 Stanley Street // 10 July
382 - Private Harry Charles Lawton Randall / 15th West Yorkshire (Prince of Wales Own) / 21 Lombard Street // 19 July
383 - Private Bertie Jenkinson / 2nd 4th King's Own Yorkshire Light Infantry / Alliance Street // 28 July
384 - Second Lieutenant Sydney Blagg / Sherwood Foresters attached 1st 4th Royal Berkshire / 25 Cartergate // 29 July
385 - Sapper Jesse Tatem Shelbourn / 92nd Field Company Royal Engineers / 91a Baldertongate // 6 August
386 - Private Anscombe Stewart Freshney / 15th Tank Corps / 45 Baldertongate // 9 August
387 - Private Frederic William James Kelsall / 1st Sherwood Foresters / 98 Victoria Street // 17 August
388 - Corporal John Thomas Thorpe / 10th Sherwood Foresters / 13 Cromwell Road // 18 August
389 - Corporal Charles Matthew Britten / Machine Gun Corps / 112 Beacon Hill // 22 August
390 - Second Lieutenant Percy Sefton / 13th East Lancashire / Lime Grove // 22 August
391 - Private Thomas Ball / 7th Queen's (Royal West Surrey) / 15 Vernon Street // 23 August
392 - Private John Henry Gray / 1st East Yorkshire / Scales' Row // 26 August
393 - Private Fred Parker / 10th Sherwood Foresters / 2 James Row, Millgate // 26 August
394 - Lance Corporal George William Turner / 10th Sherwood Foresters / 43 London Road // 29 August
395 - Private Herbert Peet / 1/5th Sherwood Foresters / Cliff Nook Lane // 30 August
396 - Sergeant John Wilson / A Battery, Royal Horse Artillery / 3 Boundary Road // 2 September
397 - Private Ernest William Jarman / 1/1st Cambridgeshire / 31 Stanley Street // 5 September
398 - Private Harold Jarman / 1/1st Cambridgeshire / 52 Sleaford Road // 5 September
399 - Private Arthur Robert Matthews / 1/1st Cambridgeshire / 42 Vernon Street // 5 September
400 - Private Albert Victor Page / 1/1st Cambridgeshire / 72 Appletongate // 5 September
401 - Private Harry Poynton / 1/1st Cambridgeshire / 10 St Mark's Lane // 5 September
402 - Private Herbert Spicer / 2nd Worcestershire / 9 Spittal Row, Northgate // 9 September
403 - Lance Corporal Ira William Turner / 2nd King's Royal Rifles Corps / 1 Nicholson Street // 10 September
404 - Private Thomas Carter Huckerby / 1st Leicestershire / 21 Lime Grove // 19 September
405 - Private John Thomas Judson / 7th Queen's (Royal West Surrey) / St Mark's Lane // 21 September
406 - Rifleman Arthur Reckless Chappell / 1st 12th London (The Rangers) / 2 Britannia Buildings, Parliament Street // 23 September
407 - Corporal Frederick Tyers / 1/5th Leicestershire / Bridge Cottages, Barnby Road // 24 September
408 - Private Louis Branch / 23rd Lancashire Fusiliers / Castlegate // 27 September
409 -Private Ernest E Harrop / 2nd Worcestershire / 15 Lover's Lane // 29 September
410-Lance Corporal John Arthur Hoe / 1/8th Sherwood Foresters / 55 Millgate // 29 September
411- Private John Edward Tinkler / 1/8th Sherwood Foresters / 35 Sleaford Road // 29 September
412 - Company Sergeant Major John Francis Rawding / 1/8th Sherwood Foresters / Union Row, King Street // 30 September
413 - Midshipman Robert Graham / Royal Naval Reserve HMS Vivid / 6 Wellington Road // 2 October
414 - Private Hezekiah Mendham / 11th Sherwood Foresters / 12 Elgin Place // 5 October
415 - Private John Robert Bell / 1st East Yorkshire / 4 Philadelphia Place, Albert Street // 6 October
416 – Private James Evison / 10th Royal Warwickshire / 1 Sheppard's Row, Northgate // 8 October

1918

417 - Private Albert Johnson / 8th Lincolnshire / 73 Sleaford Road // 8 October
418 - Company Quartermaster Sergeant Alfred Ford / 866 HT Company Army Service Corps / 34b Appletongate // 10 October
419 - Lieutenant Thomas Walter Harrison / 1st 4th Lincolnshire / Magnus Grammar School // 10 October
420 - Lieutenant Edwin Herbert Scales / Army Service Corps attached 1st East Kent / Norfolk House, London Road // 11 Octo
421 - Private Leonard Short / 1st Norfolk / 22 Newton Street // 12 October
422 - Private Thomas Smith / 2nd King's Own Yorkshire Light Infantry / 3 Regent Street // 15 October
423 - Lance Corporal Alexander John Mort / 10th West Yorkshire (Prince of Wales Own) / Church Street // 17 October
424 - Private Harry Alexander Knight / 1st 1st Sherwood Rangers Yeomanry / 1 Barnbygate // 18 October
425 - Sergeant Arthur Fox / 15th Sherwood Foresters / Newton Street // 20 October
426 - Harry Lawson / invalided out of Royal Field Artillery / Elgin Place, Appletongate // 23 October
427 - Private George Henry Poole / 11th Northumberland Fusiliers / 15 Tenter Buildings // 27 October
428 - Private Joseph Asman / 2nd 8th Sherwood Foresters / 7 Lincoln Street // 30 October
429 - Lance Corporal George Keetley / 10th Sherwood Foresters / 8 Spittal Row, Northgate // 1 November
430 - Sergeant George Grocock / 6th Lincolnshire / 46 Charles Street // 3 November
431 - Private Fred Warner / 8th Lincolnshire / 12 Sydney Street // 3 November
432 - Private Robert William Bradley / 9th Sherwood Foresters / 5 Smith's Row, Water Lane // 4 November
433 - Private John James Tailby / 10th Sherwood Foresters / 15 Stanley Street // 4 November
434 - Captain Edward Lionel Scales / 4th Middlesex attached King's African Rifles / 62 London Road // 11 November
435 - Private Harry L Rouston / 7th South Staffordshire / 37 Milner Street // 13 November
436 - Driver Harry Booth / 666 HT Company Army Service Corps / Spring House, Millgate // 14 November
437 - Private Jesse Charlesworth / 15th Lancashire Fusiliers / Bowbridge Lane // 15 November
438 - Private Thomas Beeston / 2nd Grenadier Guards / 32 Charles Street // 19 November
439 - Corporal John Francis Baily / 54th Division Signal Company Royal Engineers / 76 Hatton Gardens // 20 November
440 - Private Joseph Grosse / 14th Northumberland Fusiliers / 58 Northgate // 2 December
441 - Private Percy Walter Toder / 2nd 5th Sherwood Foresters / 75 Beacon Hill // 10 December
442 - Private Arthur James Duke / Sherwood Foresters / 1 Smith's Row // 14 December

1918 'Bombshell' Map

INDEX

PEOPLE
Abbott JT 105, 145.
Abbott's 68, 71, 79, 90, 93, 114, 124, 151, 212.
Addis E 156.
Addison W 149.
Addy HW 222.
Alcock A 140; **W** 140; **WE** 140, 211.
Alexander F 109.
Allen G 90, 136; **J** 90; **L** 136; **S** 90, 136; **T** 90; **WH** 90.
Allenby G 180, 208.
Allison E 89, 223.
Andrew A 31; **AB** 150-1, 232; **E** 150; **M** 174; **P** 93; **R** 93; **SE** 93.
Ansell AE 134; **F** 134; **WE** 134, 231.
Appleby FH 28, 151.
Arnold CB 15, 220; **E** 15; **G** 135; **J** 135; **JR** 135, 231.
Arthur G 199.
Ash WQ 234.
Asher E 128; **J** 128; **T** 128, 230.
Aslin C 103.
Asling EH 174, 235.
Asman J 64, 236; **S** 64, 223.
Asquith R 101.
Atkinson A 78, 228; **JH** 100; **M** 78.
Ayto JH 131, 230.

Backhouse SG 220.
Bailey AE 121; **DA** 172; **E** 153.
Baily HS 211; **JF** 211, 236; **W** 210-11.
Baines GH 228.
Baker JH 99; **RJ** 9, 220.
Ball E 184; **T** 184, 235; **W** 184.
Balmer A 199; **ETB** 199; **GB** 199.
Barker L 135.
Barks GW 83.
Barling H 87, 226.

Bartlett A 46.
Barton E 106, 228; **K** 106.
Baseby B 175.
Bates P 135.
Battle Rev AG 71.
Beardmore RA 235.
Bebb Rev H 181.
Becher A 59; **JP** 50-3, 57, 59, 226; **V** 53, 59.
Beckett E 89; **J** 90; **T** 90.
Beeston PF 211; **T** 211, 236; **V** 211.
Bell JR 235; **JV** 19.
Belper Lord 153.
Belton JCB 114, **JC** 83, 114, 230; **MJ** 114.
Bembridge HS 168; **L** 168.
Benjamin Q 64-5.
Bennett EG 149.
Benson 80.
Bentley E 133; **H** 133-4; **F** 98; **T** 102, 133.
Benton GA 223.
Beresford H 188.
Beswick R 154.
Bevan 193.
Billyard R 90.
Bingley GA 226.
Inney E 154.
Binnington H 121.
Bird H 75.
Birkett E 150, 232.
Bishop Rev AS 32.
Bisseker Rev TW 77.
Blackburn E 24.
Blake 145.
Blagg M 180; **S** 180, 235; **T** 186.
Blount Sir W 99.
Blythe J 37.
Bond E 134, 230; **H** 20, 134; **M** 20.
Boness RJ 231.
Booth A 171; **H** 236; **J** 171, 234; **M** 171.
Boothwright E 84; **T** 84.
Boulton E 146; **FW** 146, 231.
Bousfield JK 207-8.
Boville 154.

Bowers S 59-60; **T** 220.
Bowen 154.
Bradley A 211; **C** 148; **CB** 231; **GA** 148; **K** 148; **RW** 211, 236.
Bradley's 39, 58, 68, 90, 183, 209.
Brailsford 175.
Braithwaite W 184.
Branch L 188, 235; **M** 188.
Branston JG 66.
Brewster A 34; **E** 34; **H** 34; **J** 34; **W** 34, 222.
Britten A 182; **CM** 182, 235.
Brockton G 77.
Broughton E 173, 234; **S** 224.
Brown A 134, 230; **E** 104, 134; **H** 78, 104; **J** 126; **T** 104, 228; **TH** 44; **W** 126, 230.
Brownlow C 129; **H** 129; **T** 129.
Brunner FW 48.
Brunt A 141; **J** 94; **G** 141; **M** 94, 141; **W** 93-4.
Bryan A 106, 195; **D** 150; **E** 150, 232; **F** 106, 150, 224; **GE** 234; **H** 195; **J** 195.
Buckle DFdeC 170.
Buckler H 131, 230.
Bullard E 40.
Bullimore E 184.
Burbridge F 159.
Burgess J 181; **JHJ** 181; **MA** 181.
Burn M 208; **WR** 208.
Burns Rev JD 171, 175-6, 235.
Burrows E 151, 231; **M** 151.
Bussell D 37; **Rev JG** 36.
Butler A 140; **J** 140; **T** 140.

Cafferata B 86; **CC** 86; **E** 71; **RB** 74, 85-86.
Cafferata's 30, 35, 37, 83, 86, 87, 92, 126, 140.
Campbell Rev EP 30.
Campbell-Clarke 206.
Carlin S 70.
Carr HP 176, 235; **R** 176.
Carter F 116; **FJ** 116, 230; **J**

77; **M** 77; **TC** 77, 226.
Casson Rev GH 167, 169.
Catley F 113; **T** 147, 231; **W** 113, 230.
Caunt H 105.
Cavey H 95; **JW** 95, 227.
Cavill WV 116.
Chapman EA 132; **H** 132; **J** 132.
Chappell AR 187, 235; **C** 187; **CW** 35; **E** 187; **H** 187, 228; **WE** 28.
Charles HLT 181; **S** 181.
Charlesworth J 211, 236; **L** 211; **M** 211; **P** 211.
Chart W 30.
Cheetham ME 124.
Cherry-Downe HD 75, 76, 195.
Christie JA 153, 232.
Churchill W 20.
Churchward T 121.
Clarke AC 204-5; **G** 98; **N** 204.
Clayton GH 137, 231; **L** 137.
Cliffe CH 71, 224; **F** 71; **W** 71.
Clifton HE 103, 228.
Coape-Oates Lt-Col 174.
Coaten 88.
Cobb A 149, 211, 231; **C** 115, 230; **F** 149; **G** 98, 227.
Cole W 91.
Colefax HA 86.
Collett GW 73, 95, 227; **J** 73.
Collins L 122; **WF** 122, 230.
Colton J 170; **MHE** 170; **SE** 170; 234.
Combes A 114, 203; **C** 31, 113, 114, 203; **CW** 31; **G** 31, 113, 203; **R** 113-4, 230.
Cook F 234; **H** 131.
Cooke B 89; **MJ** 159.
Cookson K 109.
Cooper RM 125; **Sir R** 118.
Cope A 88, 114; **GH** 114; **H** 88; **PC** 114, 230; **S** 88; **T** 88, 114, 226.
Copley A 29; **CB** 58; **WR** 29, 104, 222.
Cordy CE 159.

Coulsey GEH 87, 226.
Coupe JR 79.
Couper V 79.
Cox AE 115, 230; **E** 115; **F** 62; **JW** 115.
Coy EC 34, 222.
Coyne EC 119; **FE** 119; **GW** 119; **O** 119.
Cragg A 113; **JT** 113, 230.
Crampton C 223; **J** 15; **RHE** 47, 223.
Crane J 154.
Crawford RL 121.
Crawhall 48.
Cree F 135-6; **H** 136; **JT** 135-6, 231; **R** 136.
Crooks E 115.
Cross E 87, 174, 234; **F** 174; **G** 87.
Crowder G 103, 228.
Crowther PT 116.
Cubley B 118-9, 142; **E** 85; **H** 85, 118; **J** 142, 198, 205-6.
Cumming Sir M 86; **T** 125.
Currin RW 217.
Cursham FG 148.
Cutts J 106.

Dady CH 27, 28, 38-39; **H** 27; **W** 27.
Dalton RL 166.
Dare MH 48, 223.
d'Ascanio L 86.
Daubney E 98.
Davenport C 37, 68.
Davies Rev AA 94.
Davis J 14; **L** 99; **WH** 99, 228.
Davison W 231.
Davy HC 60.
Day A 123, 226; **JT** 122-3, 230; **R** 122.
De Robeck J M 43.
Delfosse J 119.
Dench AC 42, 224; **EJ** 118; **K** 42, 163; **JR** 42, 163.
Dent C 234.
Derby Lord 67, 74, 86, 174.
Derry W 97, 227.

Dickenson H 206; **W** 206.
Dickinson C 117.
Ditcham C 48.
Dixey HC 82, 226.
Dixon AE 119; **F** 213; **FA** 213; **GA** 213; **M** 213.
Dobbs CR 12; **M** 12; **W** 12.
Dodman ER 62.
Dolphin CE 176.
Doncaster A 56, 135; **E** 137; **F** 137; **P** 137, 231.
Dooley R 79.
Drabble A 166; **B** 166; **PW** 232.
Dring E 46; **H** 46.
Druce CG 174.
Duckworth A 37; **F** 37; **G** 37.
Duke AJ 236.
Duffin WH 154.
Dunn AE 43.
Durham HL 224.

Eason A 54; **E** 54; **S** 54.
East FL 33; **R** 32-3, 222.
Easterfield WB 140-1.
Eddison A 195; **B** 195-7; **C** 195; **G** 195; **JR** 41; **S** 195.
Edlin F 117; **GS** 117, 230.
Edwards M 124.
Ellis AE 220; **CE** 226; **S** 128; **W** 89.
Elms CJR 206.
Elvidge EA 41.
Empson A 170, 234; **KA** 170.
Esam C 173; **G** 171, 234; **J** 173; **W** 173.
Evans D 138.
Evison EM 155; **J** 155.
Ewin A 10, 48; **H** 48.

Farrance O 97, 227.
Farrar's 68, 90, 137.
Fell A 92; **E** 92-3.
Fenton A 129.
Ferdinand Archduke 213.
Ferguson Sir C 40.
Ferranti 48.
Fields L 164; **S** 164; **W** 71, 164.

Finch CW 124.
Fincham E 199; J 30, 199; R 199, 234; S 30, 199.
Fisher E 168; R 168; WE 168.
Fitchett B 61, M 61.
Fitzpatrick J 84; N 84.
Flower H 86-7; JE 87.
Flynn G 118.
Foch F 190.
Footitt Coroner 124; F 78, 226; H 78, 226; J 226.
Ford A 208, 236; AG 97; E 74; GH 79; JE 148, 231; JHW 148; S 148.
Foster B 170; C 63; J 169; W 170; 234; WT 80.
Foulds W 168.
Fowler GH 52-3, 58.
Fox A 143, 234; 173, 236; E 172-3; JH 132, 230; JL 132; SA 132.
Francis H 35, 126, 230; M 126, 166; R 166; W 126, 166.
Frank TP 139-140.
Freedman A 156, 173; J 156, 231; M 173, 234; S 156, 173.
French Viscount 59, 76, 121, 141.
Freshney A 184; AS 184, 235.
Fretwell W 228.
Frisby EW 159, 234; J 159.
Frost JS 226.

Gabbitas F 48; H 167, 172; L 167, 172, 234; T 172, 234.
Galbraith Dr 128.
Gale E 99.
Gammage F 128; M 128.
Gardener WW 63.
Gardner H 177, 235; M 177; T 100; W 177.
Garfoot J 189.
Garnet G 149, 231; J 149-50; LK 150.
Gelsthorpe W 58, 103, 130, 230.
George AWJ 58, 224; M 18.

Gerard JW 40.
Gibbs Rev A 42.
Gibson C 174; GH 98; JW 14; JA 174-5, 235; JH 234; M 174.
Gilbert CC 228.
Gill ME 31; R 32, 223.
Gilstrap J 36.
Gilstrap's 98, 114, 119, 134, 193.
Gladstone W 41.
Glasby 147-8.
Glazebrook E 210.
Godfrey W 32-3, 222.
Golland E 138; EE 138, 231; F 138; W 138.
Goodey F 193.
Graham H 149, 158, 231; R 235.
Grant AD 88-9, 227; AH 224; C 89; E 154; J 88; M 88; R 89.
Gravell JJ 97, 227; OM 71.
Graveney AEJ 131, 230; H 131.
Gray F 117; H 117, 230; J 125; JH 185, 235; ME 185; W 185.
Green A 226.
Greenhalgh J 182.
Gregg ME 59.
Gregory G 146-7; H 32, 222.
Gresham FB 18.
Griffin F 177; H 177.
Grocock AH 116, 230; AG 116, 210, 236; E 99, 134; H 172; K 209-10; L 172; M 116; S 116, 209; W 99, 228.
Gross-Paine HW 235.
Grosse A 172, 234; E 172; G 16; I 134; J 16, 134, 172, 236; P 134; R 16; T 130, 134, 230.
Groves H 64.
Gumsley G 146; H 39, 232; N 146; TF 39, 223; W 232.
Gurnell C 174; SA 174.
Guy SA 42; WH 42, 224.

Hacking A 188.
Hadican Fr 76.
Haggas J 195; R 195; W 193-5; WG 193.
Hagues C 131.
Haines CLR 224.
Hales JP 29, 57, 113.
Hall E 203; JS 154; T 222.
Halph-Smith M 182.
Hammond F 77; JW 77, 226.
Handford EFS 52-3; HBS 52-3.
Handley A 205.
Hannah T 121.
Hanson F 130; H 130; W 130, 230.
Hardy A 106, 226; EA 157; J 168; JE 157, 231; JT 169; T 168, 222, 234. Harper EJ 94; J 94; JH 94, 227.
Harrison CE 42, 224; CS 120, 224; E 120, 136; EA 42; J 42; JG 151; JH 136, 231; T 68, 74, 120; TE 120; TW 208, 236.
Harrop EE 193, 235.
Harston M 178; S 178, 235.
Hart Brig 158; Rev TW 103.
Harvey C 98; GN 98, 227; VD 80.
Hawarden JJ 231.
Hayes B 65; C 65; G 65, 234.
Haywood E 114, 157; J 114; JG 157, 232.
Heath AJ 206; GW 121; R 46.
Helliwell B 19; F 19; TH 19.
Hempsall A 208; JW 208.
Henderson GM 228; J 79.
Hense EM 121.
Heron JM 230.
Herrod AJ 172, 234; S 172.
Hickman F 234; H 168; J 86; 168; P 168.
Higgs H 79.
Hill A 234; EA 78, 226; GC GW 157, 232; H 78; J 125; J 154; MA 78.
Hildage SA 33.

Hind J 66, 90; V 90.
Hindley A 197; JL 197; R 197; RM 197, 234; Canon WP 9, 56.
Hines F 73.
Hitchcox A 170; FC 170, 234; G 170.
Hitler 218.
Hodgkinson RFB 19-20, 32.
Hoe E 190; J 132; JA 190, 235; W 190.
Hogg CHK 145, 231.
Holberry A 14; H 14-5, 220.
Holland S 234.
Hollis LA 147, 231; P 147.
Holmes W 106.
Holt J 121.
Holwell J 198, 230; S 198; W 198.
Hopesmith M 146.
Hopkinson G 80; J 80.
Hoskyns Dr E 50.
Hough D 208, 235; EL 208; G 208; L 208; RF 16.
Howard G 154.
Howell W 222.
Howitt A 93, 134-5; AG 187; C 134; E 93; GW 93, 227; H 135; J 93.
Huckerby J 125; JE 189; R 39, 223; TC 189, 235.
Hudson JC 228.
Hunt E 150; HL 175, 235; J 150; S 59, 228; W 33; WS 200.
Hunter BH 148.
Hurst H 134, 176, 231; R 176; W 222.
Hurt W 33.
Huskinson A 19.
Hutchinson A 146, 231; C 148; H 148; T 148.
Hydes GS 169, 234; J 132, 169; M 169.

Iliffe AW 31.
Inwards F 30; J 30; KM 30; RJ 30, 222.

Ives MA 173.
Jackson HL 227.
James A 146; BT 48; R 121.
Jarman EW 183-4, 235; GT 184; H 183-4, 235; M 183; Richd 183; Robt 176; SE 184.
Jeeps C 138.
Jellicoe Sir J 87.
Jenkinson B 235.
Jepson FH 104, 228.
Jex GW 41-2; N 41.
Johnson A 193, 235; FH 69-70. GH 59, 156, 232; H 156; M 88, 227. L 184; R 193; S 193.
Jollands A 41, 223.
Jones F 75.
Joynes A 222; H 132.
Judson E 88, 98, 227; J 98; JC 98; JT 184, 235; MJ 88.

Kay EA 116; L 116; W 116; WH 116, 230.
Keeley GA 234.
Keetley A 209; G 209, 236; H 209, 231; S 209.
Kelham AR 86; E 86, 227; H 86.
Kelly J 96-7, 235; M 96.
Kelsall F 26; FWJ 235.
Kent E 178; G 178, 235.
Kettle AS 53.
Kew A 10, 68, 70; JC 9, 11, 18, 36-37, 66, 71, 126, 141, 142, 169, 184, 206, 215.
Killingley E 42; H 42-3.
King EG 130; MWH 125.
Kirk A 21, 25; C 91, 181, 234; H 21, 34, 91, 181, 222; SE 34, 91, 181.
Kirkby F 54; GH 54; SE 54; W 174, 235.
Kirkland E 136; F 136.
Kitchen AJ 83.
Kitchener Lord 9, 148, 174.
Knee R 121, 230; W 121.
Knight AL 198, 234; AS 183; HA 209, 236; HJ 183; HW 69, 109, 124; WE 68-9,

74-78, 89, 99, 118, 120, 146, 151, 164, 179, 191-2, 198, 200, 211, 213, 215-7.
Lacey A 234; E 82; GW 197, 234; J 82, 121, 125.
Lacy GA 75.
Lamb JH 78.
Lambert G 135, 231; J 135.
Lane C 199; M 199; W 199.
Lawrence C 56, 116; CS 56; E 56, 116.
Lawson H 236.
Layhe C 64.
Leach H 220.
Leader A 171, 234; J 78; Rev GC 78; RJC 226.
Lees E 138; I 47.
Linsey A 230.
Lloyd A 114; FJ 11.
Lockwood GO 193.
Lomas SH 125.
Lowe C 53-4; FJ 53, 224; Private 150.
Lunn G 155, 232; J 224; LA 155.

Mabbott E 234.
MacRae D 145; E 170; JN 170, 234; S 170.
Maltby W 12.
Manterfield JT 200; S 200; W 230.
Markham Sir A 75.
Markwell L 164; M 33; W 33, 222.
Marriott C 234; HW 159.
Marsden T 224.
Marsh A 30; M 30.
Marshall AH 68; E 88, 153, 232; WT 42, 224.
Martin E 120; JH 58; G 58, 156, 211, 232; GW 58, 195, 228; H 179, 195; P 195; RE 156; T 205; WH 195.
Mason J 146.
Massey T 35, 223.
Mathers J 15.
Matthews AR 183, 235; D

183; **REM** 183.
Maull J 116, 231.
May F 95; **W** 154.
Mayfield A 128; **J** 128; **R** 94.
McCraith Sir J 60.
McKears C 151; **HN** 151, 231; **W** 146, 151.
McLeod SA 16; **W** 16.
McPheeley A 154.
McQuiston C 133; **W** 133.
Meade E 154.
Measham WHJ 230.
Meehan FE 84.
Mendham H 235.
Mellish H 84.
Merry M 62; **N** 62.
Milbank Sir JP 20, 46.
Miller BA 154.
Mills H 66, 146; **M** 66; **TAR** 148.
Mitchell S 173.
Moens F 87.
Moore Cpl 154; **E** 88; **H** 39, 223; **W** 88; **WG** 56, 88, 227.
Moran HS 64.
Morgan DJ 17; **J** 170; **JL** 234.
Morley CE 172, 234; **G** 153, 232; **J** 153.
Mort A 188; **AJ** 188, 236; **GH** 188.
Mottram F 206.
Mountney E 94, 227.
Mumby GND 187; **H** 187; **W** 187.
Mumby's 17, 30, 132, 149, 172, 184, 187.
Munro-Kyles J 134-5.
Munton JE 56, 104, 228; **R** 104.
Musgrove A 137; **AG** 137, 231; **D** 117; **I** 137.
Mutton EH 60, 226; **MA** 60.

Naylor J 106, 228; **M** 106; **R** 106.
Neal CJ 193; **F** 222.
Need W 71.
Nettleship R 177-8.
Newbold E 172; **H** 172; **JT** 172, 234; **W** 172.
Newbound F 154; **W** 154-5, 231.
Newcombe Rev RT 166.
Newman TA 154.
Newstead T 227.
Newton JW 41.
Nicholson E 34, 114. **EH** 66, 119, 131; **FE** 159; **JH** 34, 114-5, 230; **W** 34.
Nicholson's 33, 34, 39, 60, 70, 113, 182.
Noakes CES 129.
Noland A 10.
Norcott H 179; **SE** 175; **WM** 175, 235.
Normanton W 206.
North J 164.
Northen FH 137, 231.
Norton F 119, 230.
Norval B 87; **P** 87.

Oates JS 34; **WC** 34.
Ogston Sir A 109.
Oldershaw T 206.
Oldrini B 82; **E** 82; **GA** 81-2.
Orlopp A 139.
Osborn S 145.
Overton I 44, 231.

Pacey W 213-4.
Padley F 206.
Page AV 183, 235; **F** 183; **G** 183; **GH** 234; **M** 167, 234.
Pamment J 230.
Parkinson Rev Parlby CE 169.
Parnham H 75; **JT** 75, 109.
Parisotti O 109.
Parker F 39-40, 185, 223, 235; **WF** 153, 231.
Parkin C 66.
Parr A 197; **G** 198; **GH** 140, 198.
Parry A 94, 227; **E** 94.
Pass M 184.
Pateet L 37.
Patterson J 131.
Pauncefote Baron J 78.

Payne H 154.
Peet A 97, 182; **H** 182, 235; **DG** 70; **DJ** 70; **J** 182.
Perry AS 121.
Pilsworthy GH 98, 228.
Pink E 41, 197, 204-5; **G** 197.
Pole-Carew Sir R 60.
Pond J 37, 223; **MM** 37; **W** 37.
Poole D 211; **GH** 211, 236; **Sgt** 98; **W** 211.
Porter E 177; **FD** 77, 235; **FHV** 177; **G** 126; **R** 93; **TM** 177; **TWM** 177.
Portland Duke of 84, 163, 178, 190, 199.
Powell H 185.
Poynton H 184-5, 235.
Pratt PC 114, 230; **W** 145.
Preston TE 222.
Price AE 122; **G** 168; **GW** 226; **W** 168.
Pride A 95; **E** 95, 228.
Priestley A 33, 222; **E** 33, 89, 226.
Probert EJ 139, 231; **JH** 139.
Proctor D 97.
Pulford AE 87, 226.
Pykett A 83; **G** 83; **TA** 83; **WE** 224.

Quibell AH 82, 172; **E** 19, 77, 82, 125; **O** 19, 77, 82; **SB** 77, 121, 125, 226.
Quiningborough F 48; **H** 48; **SA** 48.

Randall HCL 178-9, 235.
Ransome's 16, 19, 28, 33, 35, 36, 49, 53, 54, 64, 68, 76, 87-90, 94, 97, 101, 103, 120, 121-4, 131, 146, 150, 156, 166, 176, 177, 178, 183-4, 197, 198-9, 213, 214.
Rawding JF 163, 235.
Rawling B 132; **M** 132; **WE** 130.
Rawlinson HS 162. **Rawson S** 94.
Ray D 35.

Rayner F 82, 121.
Redmile C 32, 222.
Rees-Mogg L 48.
Reeve PL 211.
Revill H 114, 230; R 114, 222.
Rich EJR 130, 230.
Richardson A 35; AE 130; G 35, 223; J 35, 130; RR 224; W 35, 223.
Richmond F 108-9.
Ridley E 40; WHM 15, 40, 223.
Riley J 129, 230.
Ringrose E 62, 172.
Ritchie A 153.
Robb A 50, 224; H 137; WB 41, 137.
Robinson A 56; AE 56, 224; C 79, 198; EH 151; F 47, 95; GW 205; HE 95, 227; J 56, 198; R 198, 230.
Robson A 93.
Rodgers AC 153.
Rolleston Sir L 169.
Rose A 33, 222; AE 34, 135; E 135; T 34, 135; TC 33, 135.
Ross AE 205.
Rouston GA 209; HL 209, 236.
Rumes M 18.
Russell A 71; B 71.
Rutland (Duke of) 121.

Salman C 105; E 167, 234; M 105; W 165.
Sandbach Maj-Gen 121.
Sanders R 222.
Sanderson E 131; ES 131, 226; H 131, 230; J 131; JA 131; T 131.
Savage A 42-3, 224; W 42; WC 111.
Scales EH 187, 236; EL 31, 236; R 187; S 187.
Scarborough 95.
Scholfield GP 206, 217.
Scott S 64.
Scraton R 235.
Scullion M 136.

Seager HP 125-6.
Seagrave G 93, 227.
Seagraves C 234.
Seaton W 132.
Sefton C 94, 182, 227, 234; P 182, 235; S 182; W 182.
Selby F 146, 231; J 146.
Sentence E 137; F 137; G 137; H 137; J 137, 231.
Setchfield A 26; W 26.
Seymour F 100.
Sharman S 75.
Sharp A 155, 231; E 153, 155, 232.
Sharpe M 170; W 170, 234.
Shaw EH 153; FW 153, 232; JWH 66, 222; L 66; Rev W 153.
Shearsmith P 181.
Shelbourn JT 235.
Shepherd G 32; J 124; M 124.
Sheppard A 50.
Shepperson H 95; R 95, 227; W 95.
Sherry AG 135, 231; S 135; W 135.
Short G 187; L 187, 236; ME 187.
Shrimpton H 154.
Sibcy L 60, 222.
Simpson A 168-9, 234; CB 157; JH 157-8, 168, 232; LG 100, 228.
Simpson's 20, 33, 71, 76, 83, 87, 90, 100, 106, 133, 153, 155, 158, 159, 174, 193.
Sketchley C 33; H 33, 222.
Skinner AS 154.
Slater CD 232; Lt-Col 120; WC 220.
Sleights A 145.
Smedley R 172; RH 172, 235.
Smith A 99, 228; AL 99; C 113, 153, 159; CE 158; CW 97, 227; E 99, 113, 150, 224; EF 228; F 66, 114, 146, 230, 223; FH 150, 232; FM 178; G 13-4, 149; 231; GH 138;

H 71, 115-6, 178 230; HDD 71; HE 178, 235; J 13-4, 114, 138, 231; JH 44, 126, 131, 140, 200; M 66; MC 37; RH 108-9, 228; SA 114, 138; T 236; TR 44, 200, 234; W 37, 113, 153, 181, 223, 230.
Snodin F 125.
Sooley JWM 124, 230.
Southerington AE 149, 232; GB 149, 231; MH 149; S 149; W 149.
Southern H 41.
Spanton Rev EF 25-6.
Speight H 18.
Spencer J 125.
Spicer E 173; H 173-4, 235.
Spick JW 158
Spray T 72, 109.
Squires A 19, 200; G 10; H 10, 204, 234; M 10; MJ 204.
Stafford G 79, 199; GL 79; H 79.
Stamper A 158, 231; E 158; F 158.
Stanfield J 126.
Stanger SW 11; W 12.
Stanley GF 119, 230.
Starr E 164; JW 164.
Statham CW 117-8, 231; N 117-8; W 154.
Stallard H 28, 29-30, 94, 129, 151, 218.
Starkey JR 67, 86, 217.
Stennett J 75.
Stenton K 168.
Stephenson HF 210; M 93; W 93, 227.
Steptoe I 78.
Stevenette B 89.
Stevenson A 153, 232; EA 153; R 153.
Stewart A 115; JAF 153.
Stibbard HJ 130; S 130.
Stoakes G 138, 180; J 180.
Storey M 199-200.
Stroud AE 126.
Stuart-Wortley E 56, 88.
Summerfield H 20.

Swann F 100; LH 224; W 100, 228.

Tacey F 25, 43; H 25; MA 25.
Taddy G 42.
Tailby JJ 213, 236; ML 213.
Tailliez J 70.
Talbot E 145; L 145; M 145.
Tallents G 131; H 100, 131.
Taylor CW 37, 223; E 37; H 135, 231; TA 234; W 37.
Tennant H 84.
Thacker WW 227.
Thompson E 138; F 156; J 139; ME 156; MJ 136; R 206; W 136.
Thorpe A 124; E 180; H 47, 100, 130; JT 180, 235; R 124.
Thurman FW 94-5, 227.
Tinkler E 188; J 188; JE 188, 235.
Tinsley HFJ 234.
Toder PW 236.
Tolworthy A 61-2.
Tomlinson C 171; CT 171, 234; JH 104; V 171.
Tote AAM 37; AG 37; MF 37.
Tournay T 41, 224.
Toulson HJ 125.
Towlson H 234.
Townsend Gen 136.
Toynbee J 195.
Trickett BM 200; H 32, 222; K 32.
Trout J 26.
Turgoose A 78; FB 78, 226; J 78; T 54-5.
Turner F 150; G 117, 150, 184; GW 117; JE 169, 234; JW 88, 150, 232; MJ 117, 184; GW 184, 235.
Tustin JS 75.
Twells H 101.
Twidale LF 126.
Twigg C 146; WE 146.

Tye E 87; F 87, 130, 230; H 87, 226.
Tyers A 188-9, 231; F 188-9, 235; L 37, 87, 226; M 188.
Tyne H 50
.
Unsworth S 159-60.
Upton J 38-9, 87.

Vacey J 98; L 98; W 98-9, 228.
Van Den Bruggen L 215.
Vann Rev BW 164-6. D 166.
Vanns D 88.
Vick B 53.
Vickers RH 159.
Volkaert E 37.
Von Sanders L 208
.
Wade W 22, 136.
Wakefield E 138; LT 137-8, 231; T 138.
Walker AE 125; B 133; E 117; GH 117, 230; Rev J 217; JE 155, 231; QMS 146; S 120; W 133; WP 133, 231.
Walsh AL 220.
Walster F 39, 223; RH 140; T 24, 220.
Ward J 118; Sir E 124.
Warner E 210; F 210, 236; W 210.
Warriner J 87; Sgt 205; W 62, 222.
Warwick HB 71.
Watford PA 141-2.
Watson AL 171; JT 171; M 173; W 171.
Watts M 166; W 140, 213-4.
Wedgwood Benn W 46.
Weightman WH 197, 234.
Welch JW 99; L 99; R 99, 228.
Wells B 25.
Weselby E 177.
West A 49, 94, 227; F 49; J 49.

Wheatley M 16.
Whiles A 200; G 200; J 200; T 179, 200; W 200; WH 200.
White A 235; CSM 154; E 134; GE 40, 197; JB 188; P 99, 228; T 134, 231.
Whitehouse CH 177.
Whitelock JJ 223.
Whittaker AE 20.
Whitten EL 58, 125; S 58, 125.
Whittle R 206.
Whitton S 174.
Wiggins H 156, 232.
Wigginton HB 193.
Wilkes JE 110, 114, 207, 212-3.
Wilkins H 159, 180; T 180.
Wilkinson F 175; HS 120, 224; M 175.
Wills E 181; FCB 1801.
Willows E 149; G 149; J 149, 231.
Willingham M 132; SR 132, 231.
Wilmore GTP 32, 222.
Wilmot Sir RHS 197.
Wilson AH 230; AW 33; J 32, 185, 235; E 100, 200; F 100, 204; H 125; HF 109-10; JA 185, 232; MA 185; W 100-1; 155. Windey C 231.
Winn C 98, 228.
Winter E 146.
Wolfitt Sir D 104; E 105; P 104-5, 228; WP 105.
Woodforth A 106.
Woodhead H 224.
Woods JL 210.
Woolley E 220.
Wregg B 118.
Wright A 17, 24, 41, 62, 66, 76, 109; FW 115, 230; G 106; H 115; J 115, 126; P 126; RJ 224; W 146.

Young C 232; E 177; GR 231; H 42, J 211.

PLACES
Abbassia 45.
Abbeville 59, 197.
Acre 210.
Agulhas 118.
Airon-Karabissar 145.
Aisne 14, 15, 105, 113, 169, 188.
Aix-Noulette 134.
Albert 97, 99, 106, 172, 185.
Aldershot 37.
Aleppo 145, 210.
Alexandria 50, 72, 100, 109, 130.
Amman 201.
Antwerp 11, 15, 18.
Anzac Cove 72.
Arabia 114.
Argyllshire 170.
Armentieres 12, 97.
Arras 88, 99, 100, 111-7, 130, 134, 198.
Asia Minor 145.
Athens 86.
Authuille 99.

Baghdad 145, 210.
Bailleul 37.
Bakewell 200.
Bancourt 104.
Barrow-in-Furness 50.
Bath 170.
Batley 10.
Bayonvillers 179.
Beaulencourt 130.
Beaumont Hamel 95.
Beirut 211.
Bellenglise 162, 163-5.
Bellicourt 189.
Bernafay Wood 100.
Berne 86.
Bertrancourt 176.
Bethune 172, 174.
Boezinge 137.
Bois Grenier 34.
Bouzincourt 173.
Brighton 200.
Bruges 216.

Bullecourt 168, 170, 181.
Bulgaria 100, 186, 213.
Bury St Edmunds 42.

Cairo 44-5.
Cambridge 95.
Cambrai 158, 162, 187.
Cambrin 87.
Carniers 54.
Carso 108.
Cassel 168.
Castleford 94.
Chatham 187.
Chelers 133.
Chilwell 104.
Chocolate Hill 47.
Cite Elois 195.
Colchester 94.
Colincamps 106.
Collingham 211.
Combies 105.
Constantinople 210.
Courtrai 179.
Craonne Wood 174-5.

Dar-es-Salaam 212.
Dardanelles 43-4, 83, 90, 92, 97, 100, 106, 114, 131, 167, 179, 182, 195.
De Panne 215.
Deadagatch 213.
Deal 204.
Deliabour 145.
Delville Wood 97-8, 101.
Derby 8, 9, 26, 68, 108, 123, 128, 138, 155, 163.
Doeberitz 40.
Douvrain 53.
Dover 65, 215.
Drogheda 197.
Dublin 82-4, 97, 114, 125, 131, 134.
Dunkirk 129.
Durban 130.

East Africa 139, 179.
East Stoke 78.
Ebblinghem 176.

Edinburgh 200.
Egypt 44, 80-1, 100, 114, 130, 160, 179, 200, 207, 208, 210.
El Arish 200.
Estmires 133.
Etaples 135, 172.

Falik Brook 208.
Foncquevillers 88, 89, 121.
Fontaine 198.
Fouquereuil 172.
Fouquieres-les-Bethune 171.
Fricourt 96.

Gainsborough 68.
Gallipoli 27, 43, 72, 170, 199, 200.
Gaza 208.
Gezaincourt 170.
Ghent 37, 216.
Ghissignies 210, 213.
Givenchy 97.
Gommecourt 131.
Gorre 98.
Gouzeaucourt 158.
Grandcourt 185.
Grantham 208.
Gravelines 119.
Great Yarmouth 61.
Greece 100.
Guidecourt 100, 198.
Guildford 106.
Gustrow 25.

Hague 197.
Haifa 210.
Hainault 37.
Haisnes 53.
Halifax 129.
Hampstead 70.
Hanover 90.
Hargicourt 199.
Harpenden 9, 19.
Hartarovsk 144.
Hazebrouck 176.
Henley-on-Thames 177.
Hesdigneul 57.

Hindenburg Line 152, 161-2, 188.
Hohenzollern 27, 50-4, 57, 59, 69-70, 78, 97, 120, 181, 198.
Holland 100.
Holyhead 208.
Holzminden 207.
Hooge 36.
Hull 62.
Hulluch 52, 54, 97.

Irkutsk 144, 198.

Jaffa 210.
Jericho 201.
Jerusalem 159.
Jutland 86.
Kelham 166.

Karlsruhe 204.
Kemmel 29, 32, 41, 50, 165.
Kenya 70.
Khartoum 78.
Kimberley 97.
King's Lynn 61.
Kingston-on-Thames 174.
Kingstown 208.
Klug 145.
Knocke 179.
Kroningen 12.
Kuala Lumpur 63.
Kut 136.
La Bassee 53, 198.
Landrecies 185, 189.
Langemarck 140, 198.
Laventie 59.
Le Haucourt 163.
Le Havre 14.
Le Trepont 181.
Leeds 94, 98, 155.
Leicester 169.
Lens 132, 198.
Lichfield 54.
Lille 12, 14, 15.
Lijssenthoek 116.
Lillers 176.
Limberg 168, 199.

Lincoln 38, 208.
Liverpool 76, 204.
L'Ourcq 179.
Locre 36, 171.
London 76.
Longueville 101.
Loos 50-3, 59, 71, 97, 114, 129, 131-2, 159.
Loughborough 76.

Malines 37.
Mailly-Maillet 59.
Manchester 75, 205.
Margate 65.
Mariakerke 215.
Marne 105, 169.
Marsh Chapel 89.
Martinpuich 93.
Meaulte 103-4.
Merville 179.
Mesopotamia 81-2, 119, 131, 136, 144, 149.
Metz-en-Couture 131.
Millencourt 99.
Milky Way Road 179.
Mons 14, 25, 40, 105, 139, 156, 185.
Montbrehane 163.
Moscow 145.
Mosul 145.
Mrogoro 26.
Msalabani 26.
Mudros 43.
Munster 174.
Nazareth 208-9.
Neuve Chapelle 27-8, 32.
New York 62, 65.
Nieuport 215.
Norcine 168.

Ontario 105.
Ostend 37, 129, 215.
Ouchak 145.

Palestine 159, 179, 180, 200, 208.
Passchendaele 152, 159, 180.
Peronne 200.

Persia 114.
Peterborough 89, 182.
Petrograd 71, 142-3.
Philosophe 124, 126.
Pilkem 211.
Pontarlier 86.
Portsmouth 16.
Potijze 41.
Pozieres 97, 186.
Pretoria 130.
Priches 163.

Queant 168.
Queenstown, Ireland 65.

Ramicourt 164-5.
Ramsgate 65.
Regnicourt 167, 211.
Reims 175.
Restaat 168.
Retford 41, 62, 68.
Richmond 130.
Robecq 177.
Roeux 116.
Rome 109.
Rouen 14, 56, 77, 97, 106, 173, 180, 205.
Rougesbanc 38.

Salonika 78, 124, 128, 154, 180, 206, 213.
Scimitar Hill 27.
Sebourg 211.
Serbia 78.
Sheffield 76, 98.
Siberia 144.
Sittingbourne 100.
Smyrna 43-4.
Somaliland 114.
Somme 73, 87, 88, 91, 95, 100-1, 106-7, 125-6, 129, 135, 138, 167-9, 193, 199, 207.
Soissons 175.
Southampton 106.
Southend 66, 223.
St Julien 195.
St Omer 176.

St Paul 96, 176.
St Quentin 161-5, 169, 184, 188, 200, 211.
St Venant 177.
Steenwerck 188.
Stavros 213.
Stettin 195.
Suvla Bay 44, 72, 89, 100, 195.

Tel Aviv 159.
Thiepval 73, 95, 100, 106, 137.
Tirah 158.
Tooting 130.
Trones Wood 95, 100.

Uti de Risement 131.

Vendhuile 184.
Versailles 213.
Victoria, Canada 104.
Vielle-Chapelle 174.
Vimy Ridge 111, 130, 185.

Wakefield 68.
Wellingborough 165.
Westende 215.
Wharncliffe 98, 99.
Wimereux 42.
Wimille 155.
Winnipeg 130.
Wittering 70.
Wroxton Abbey 153.

Ypres 36-7, 41, 70, 77-78, 96-97, 125, 130, 134-7, 140, 146, 149, 151, 157, 159, 165, 173.
Ypres (Menin Gate) 15, 50.

Zeebrugge 201-5.
Zig-a-Zag 100.

MILITARY UNITS
Army Service Corps 86, 150, 168, 174, 187, 232, 236.
Army Veterinary Corps 18, 72.
Australian Imperial Forces 97, 148, 195, 200, 227, 231.

Border 114, 222, 230.

Cambridgeshire 183-5, 235.
Canadian Light Infantry 104, 149.
Cavalry 11.
Central Ontario 222.
Cheshire 46, 224.
Coldstream 137, 197, 220, 231.
Cyclists' Corps 74.

Devonshire 103, 228, 234.
Dorset 158.
Duke of Connaught 86.
Duke of Cornwall's Light Infantry 177, 235.
Duke of Wellington's (West Riding) 99, 129, 197, 224, 228, 230.
Durham Light Infantry 71, 78, 101, 177, 205, 226, 234-5, 230.

East Kent 187, 236.
East Lancs 178, 182, 235.
East Yorks 77, 87, 173, 185, 197, 220, 226, 227, 230, 234, 235.
Essex 230.

Gordon Highlanders 230.
Gloucestershire 170, 234.
Grenadier Guards 42, 101, 122, 135, 153, 228, 224, 234, 236.
Guards 52.

Hampshire 166,
Highland Light Infantry 148, 226.
Hussars 10, 16.

Imperial Camel Corps 201, 234.
Indian Imperial Services Cavalry 208.
Irish 155.
Irish Guards 158.

King's (Liverpool) 98, 133, 157, 173, 227, 231, 232, 234, 235.
King's Own African Rifles 236.
King's Own Yorkshire Light Infantry 10, 101, 103, 116, 125, 135, 156, 172, 198, 227, 230, 231, 234, 235, 236.
King's Own Royal Lancashire 50, 224.
King's Own Scottish Borderers 93, 148, 230, 231.
King's Royal Rifles 98, 128, 134, 156, 173, 200, 222, 227, 228, 230, 231, 234, 235.
King's Shropshire Light Infantry 77, 151.

Labour Corps 135, 171, 172.
Lancashire Fusiliers 103, 104, 131, 149, 179, 211, 224, 228, 231, 235, 236.
Leicestershire 16, 42, 43, 52, 87, 94, 97, 106, 114, 123, 133, 135, 151, 159, 168, 169, 183, 189, 198, 224, 226, 227, 228, 230, 231, 234, 235.
Life Guards 19.
Lincolnshire 14, 52, 58, 89, 90, 92, 96, 99, 100, 104-5, 115, 117, 120, 128, 134, 138, 146,151, 155, 166-7, 169, 172, 193, 200, 208, 210, 220, 222, 223, 224, 227, 228, 230, 231, 232, 234, 235, 236.
Lincolnshire Territorials 116.
Liverpool 106, 170.
London 138, 147, 165, 187, 199, 224, 231, 235.

London (County of) Yeomanry 46.
Loyal North Lancs 140.

Machine Gun Corps 58, 98, 126, 130, 134, 154, 156, 169, 182, 195, 199, 200, 228, 232, 234, 235.
Manchester 119, 137, 153, 199, 230, 231.
Manitoba 130, 228.
Middlesex 32, 58, 60, 100, 118-9, 135, 140, 176, 228, 231, 236.
Military Police 119.

Norfolk 208, 220, 236.
North Staffordshire 13, 103, 104, 119, 130, 172, 180, 181, 209, 230, 234.
Northamptonshire 15, 100, 220, 224.
Northumberland Fusiliers 71, 106, 114, 115, 128, 171, 172, 205, 211, 227, 228, 230, 232, 234, 236.
Notts & Derbys – see Sherwood Foresters.
Nottinghamshire Royal Horse Artillery 74.

Oxford and Blues 159, 231.

Princess Victoria's (Royal Irish Fusiliers) 234.
Prussian Guard 131.
Punjabi 149, 231.

Queen's (Royal West Surrey) 153, 184, 224, 231, 232, 234, 235.
Queen's Own (Royal West Kent) 97, 227.

Rifle 89, 117, 159, 180, 230.
Royal Air Force 70, 177, 178, 207, 234, 235.
Royal Army Medical Corps 53, 103, 105, 136, 157, 232, 234.
Royal Berkshire 231, 235.
Royal Defence Corps 235.
Royal Engineers 30-1, 52, 59, 61-2, 68-71, 75, 79, 80, 88, 90, 97, 101, 116, 121-2, 126-8, 130-1, 133-4, 139, 154, 158-9, 174, 176, 177-8, 180-1, 193, 195, 198, 204, 206, 207, 216, 217, 222, 223, 224, 230, 231, 234, 235, 236.
Royal Field Artillery 59, 79, 99, 132, 136, 149, 154, 183, 187, 193, 226, 228, 231, 235, 236.
Royal Flying Corps 70, 71, 145, 188, 195, 231.
Royal Fusiliers 94, 99, 100, 135, 220, 227, 228.
Royal Garrison Artillery 113, 140, 145, 153, 170, 172, 174, 175-6, 195, 228, 232, 234, 235, 236.
Royal Horse Artillery 59, 185, 228, 235.
Royal Marines 87, 114, 129, 175, 177, 201-4, 211, 222, 226, 235.
Royal Navy 20, 21-24, 34, 44, 64, 78, 86, 153, 176, 197, 206, 222, 223, 226, 231, 232.
Royal Navy Reserve 43, 226, 234, 235.
Royal Scots Fusiliers 14, 25, 62, 146, 149, 155, 157, 170, 172, 222, 231, 232, 234.
Royal Shropshire Light Infantry 77, 151, 226.
Royal Suusex 37, 180.
Royal Warwickshire 26, 58, 73, 155, 173, 187,193, 220, 227, 228, 234.
Royal West Kent 95, 125.

Scots Guards 195.
Scottish Rifles 19.
Seaforth Highlanders 149, 231.

Sherwood Foresters 12, 15, 16, 19, 26, 27, 41, 42, 47-8, 50-54, 59, 60, 63, 69, 71, 74, 78, 79, 82-4,87, 88, 91, 93, 94, 95, 97, 98, 99, 100, 104, 106, 111, 113-7, 120-2, 124-6, 128, 129, 131-8, 140-1, 146-151, 153, 155-7, 161-9, 171-6, 180-1, 184-8, 190, 193, 195, 197, 199, 201, 204-5, 208-9, 211, 213, 215-7, 220, 222, 223, 224, 226, 227, 228, 230, 231, 232, 234, 235, 236.
Sherwood Rangers 20, 27, 44, 50, 69, 74, 78, 97, 100, 106, 131, 148, 159, 170, 177, 200, 208-9, 210-1, 223, 228, 232, 236.
Singapore Rifles 63.
South African Infantry 130, 227.
South Notts Hussars 41, 82, 180, 223.
South Staffordshire 94, 120, 149, 177, 209, 231, 235, 236.
South Wales Borderers 131, 139, 226, 231.
Suffolk 116, 128, 230, 231.

Tank Corps 179, 184, 200, 235.

Veterinary Corps 109.

Wellington 235.
West Yorkshire (Prince of Wales' Own) 12, 37, 94, 106, 116, 128, 178, 227, 228, 230, 235, 236.
Welsh 231.
Wiltshire 94, 227, 228.
Worcestershire 44, 173, 193, 235.

York and Lancaster 60, 117, 146, 171, 224, 231, 234.